Evangelicals
and Nicene Faith

Beeson Divinity Studies
Timothy George, Editor

Beeson Divinity Studies is a series of volumes dedicated to the pastoral and theological renewal of the Church of Jesus Christ. The series is sponsored by the faculty of Beeson Divinity School of Samford University, an evangelical, interdenominational theological school in Birmingham, Alabama.

Evangelicals and Nicene Faith

RECLAIMING THE APOSTOLIC WITNESS

Edited by Timothy George

B
Baker Academic
a division of Baker Publishing Group
Grand Rapids, Michigan

© 2011 by Timothy George

Published by Baker Academic
a division of Baker Publishing Group
P.O. Box 6287, Grand Rapids, MI 49516-6287
www.bakeracademic.com

Printed in the United States of America

Library of Congress Cataloging-in-Publication Data
   Evangelicals and Nicene faith : reclaiming the Apostolic witness / edited by Timothy George.
      p.   cm. — (Beeson Divinity studies)
     Proceedings of a conference held Sept. 28–30, 2009 at Beeson Divinity School.
     Includes bibliographical references (p.   ) and index.
     ISBN 978-0-8010-3926-3 (pbk.)
     1. Nicene Creed—Congresses. 2. Evangelicalism—Congresses. I. George, Timothy.
BT999.E93 2011
238′.142—dc23   2011021708

11   12   13   14   15   16   17   7   6   5   4   3   2   1

Sacred to the memory of
Jaroslav Pelikan
1923–2006

Contents

Preface

Timothy George

Most of the essays in this volume were originally delivered as papers at a theological conference held September 28–30, 2009, at Beeson Divinity School of Samford University in Birmingham, Alabama. The theme of that conference and of this volume was inspired by a talk delivered by the late Jaroslav Pelikan on December 5, 2003, at the Beinecke Rare Book and Manuscript Library at Yale University in connection with the celebration of his eightieth birthday. Professor Pelikan's remarks on that occasion were later published as an essay, "The Will to Believe and the Need for Creed," in *Orthodoxy and Western Culture: A Collection of Essays Honoring Jaroslav Pelikan on His Eightieth Birthday* by St. Vladimir's Seminary Press.[1] In that essay, Pelikan stressed both the confessional and unifying purposes of the creeds as expressions of Christian belief and identity. This was also the basic aim of the Beeson conference and of this volume, which came out of it. This book is dedicated to the memory of Jaroslav Pelikan and concludes with a brief tribute to him.

The fourth-century Creed of Nicea, also known as the Niceno-Constantinopolitan Creed, is the most widely recognized confession of the early church, embraced by Orthodox, Catholic, and Protestant Christians alike. In recent years, the evangelical heirs of the Reformation have come to appreciate and to identify with the early church, not in an effort to "return to Rome" (much less to Constantinople or Moscow!), but rather as a reclamation of the apostolic witness that is the heritage of the entire Christian family. The essays in this volume explore the tensions and possibilities inherent in evangelical engagement with Nicene Christianity. The contributors address a variety of topics, including the significance of the Nicene faith for pastoral work, evangelical worship, the emerging churches, biblical exegesis, and vital expressions of orthodox Christian faith around the globe.

Following the introduction, Tom Oden presents the recovery of ancient Christian teaching as a form of confession, a reclaiming of the apostolic faith by evangelicals no less than by other orthodox believers. This process has resulted in a new ecumenism, in which evangelicals are full participants. As contemporary evangelicals mature in their awareness of ancient ecumenical history, exegesis, and doctrine, both the old denominational barriers and old-line ecumenical structures are breaking down. The next two chapters, by Mark Gignilliat and Frank Thielman, discuss the theological framing of biblical faith in the Old and New Testaments. Most of the chapters in this volume use the Nicene Creed as the benchmark for gauging a full-orbed trinitarian confession in the life of the church. Gerald Bray, however, provides a helpful analysis and stout defense of a later confessional document, the so-called Athanasian Creed. This confession of faith emerged in the West around one hundred years after the received form of the Nicene Creed was promulgated at the First Council of Constantinople in 381.

Two Lutheran scholars and three Baptist theologians present aspects of the Nicene faith within the history of the church. Carl Beckwith gives an account of the Reformation appropriation of the Nicene Creed as a form of "assumed catholicity." Steve Harmon tackles one of the most persistently difficult ecumenical issues—the problem of magisterium. Carl Braaten, who has been a leading ecumenical theologian since the 1960s, examines the classic four marks of the church—one, holy, catholic, and apostolic—and shows how each of these traits is rightly understood in the light of Scripture and the Great Tradition. Matthew Pinson and Curtis Freeman, representing different wings of the Baptist movement, aim to dispel misunderstandings of the Nicene faith within a denomination popularly known for its rhetoric of "No creed but the Bible."

Many of the essays in this volume deal with the historical and theological basis for reclaiming a robust confessional faith today, but a number of papers presented at the Beeson conference had a decidedly practical focus. Elizabeth Newman's essay, "Practicing the Nicene Faith," shows how *deeds* and *creeds* are inextricably linked together in the economy of divine grace. David Nelson pursues this theme into the contested arena of worship studies, whereas Kathleen Nielson brings the perspective of a literature scholar, bridging the kenotic hymn of St. Paul in Philippians 2 and Gerard Manley Hopkins's great poem "The Windhover." Bishop John Rucyahana is a world Christian statesman whose heroic struggles during the genocide in Rwanda lend great credibility to his call for a renewal of credal orthodoxy. Bishop John's presence at the Beeson conference and his essay in this volume remind us that the Nicene faith is thriving, despite great obstacles, throughout Africa and other areas of the

Global South. Within the evangelical culture of North America, the emerging church has garnered much attention over the past decade. Mark DeVine is not entirely dismissive of this phenomenon, but he argues that it will have lasting impact only to the extent that it finds an anchor in the kind of orthodox Christian faith expressed in the Nicene Creed. Ralph Wood offers a moving meditation on the final phrase of the Nicene Creed: "We look for . . . the life of the world to come." Wood shows that the great eschatological breaking-in of Jesus Christ has already inaugurated "the life of the world to come," while its final fulfillment awaits the consummation of all things for which believers in Christ yearn with "a hope that does not make one ashamed."

The closing tribute to the late Jaroslav Pelikan is entitled "Delighted by Doctrine." Cotton Mather once referred to church historians as "the Lord's remembrancers." Jaroslav Pelikan was perhaps the greatest such remembrancer the church has known in modern times. His life's work was to trace the development of Christian doctrine, which he defined as "what the church of Jesus Christ believes, teaches, and confesses on the basis of the Word of God."[2] But Pelikan was also known for his ability to capture profound truths in short, unforgettable statements. One of his best-known statements captures well the theme of this book: "Tradition is the living faith of the dead; traditionalism is the dead faith of the living."[3]

This book appears as volume four in the Beeson Divinity Studies series from Baker Academic, and I am grateful for the encouragement and support provided by the publisher for this project. I have also been greatly blessed by the support of my administrative secretary, Mrs. Le-Ann S. Little; my research associate, Dr. B. Coyne; and our research assistant, Mr. Sam Noone. I am also grateful to the faculty of Beeson Divinity School and to my colleagues and friends (several of whom are contributors to this volume), along with the administration of Samford University, which for the past twenty-three years has supported my efforts to bring together ministry and scholarship in the service of the church.

Contributors

Timothy George is the founding dean of Beeson Divinity School of Samford University. He holds degrees from the University of Tennessee at Chattanooga (BA), Harvard Divinity School (MDiv), and Harvard University (ThD). George is an author of the Manhattan Declaration and has written or edited more than twenty books, including *Amazing Grace: God's Pursuit, Our Response* (Crossway, 2011), *Our Sufficiency Is of God: Essays on Preaching in Honor of Gardner C. Taylor* (Mercer University Press, 2010), *J. I. Packer and the Evangelical Future: The Impact of His Life and Thought* (Baker Academic, 2009), *God the Holy Trinity* (Baker Academic, 2006), *Pilgrims on the Sawdust Trail* (Baker Academic, 2004), *Is the Father of Jesus the God of Muhammad?* (Zondervan, 2002), *Theology of the Reformers* (Broadman & Holman, 1988), and *John Calvin and the Church* (Westminster John Knox, 1988). George serves as general editor of the Reformation Commentary on Scripture, a series of twenty-eight volumes of sixteenth-century biblical exegesis. An ordained minister in the Southern Baptist Convention, George has participated in numerous ecumenical initiatives, including Evangelicals and Catholics Together and the international dialogue between the Roman Catholic Church and the Baptist World Alliance.

Thomas C. Oden is the Henry Anson Buttz professor of theology and ethics emeritus at Drew University. He currently serves as director of the Center for Early African Christianity. Oden has degrees from the University of Oklahoma (BA), Southern Methodist University (BD), and Yale University (MA and PhD). He is an ordained United Methodist elder known for his call for a return to "classical Christianity" as exemplified in his books *After Modernity . . . What?* (Zondervan, 1992) and *The Rebirth of Orthodoxy: Signs of New Life in Christianity* (HarperOne, 2002). He is general editor for the twenty-nine-volume series Ancient Christian Commentary on Scripture (InterVarsity), and the five-volume series Ancient Christian Doctrine (InterVarsity). He has participated in numerous ecumenical initiatives, including Evangelicals and Catholics Together.

Mark S. Gignilliat, associate professor of divinity at Beeson Divinity School, holds degrees from Bob Jones University (BA), Reformed Theological Seminary (MDiv), and the University of St. Andrews, Scotland (PhD). He teaches Hebrew, Old Testament exegesis, and biblical theology. Gignilliat's book publications include *Karl Barth and the Fifth Gospel: Barth's Theological Exegesis of Isaiah* (Ashgate, 2009) and *Paul and Isaiah's Servants* (T&T Clark, 2007).

Frank Thielman is a professor of divinity at Beeson Divinity School of Samford University, where he has taught New Testament since 1989. He was educated at Wheaton College (BA), the University of Cambridge (BA and MA), and Duke University (PhD) and holds memberships in the Evangelical Theological Society, the Institute for Biblical Research, the Catholic Biblical Association, the Society of Biblical Literature, and Studiorum Novi Testamenti Societas. His books include *Ephesians*, Baker Exegetical Commentary on the New Testament (Baker Academic, 2010), *Theology of the New Testament: A Canonical and Synthetic Approach* (Zondervan, 2005), *The Law and the New Testament: The Question of Continuity* (Herder & Herder, 1999), *Philippians*, NIV Application Commentary (Zondervan, 1995), *Paul and the Law: A Contextual Approach* (InterVarsity, 1994), and *From Plight to Solution: A Jewish Framework for Understanding Paul's View of the Law in Galatians and Romans* (Brill, 1989).

Gerald R. Bray holds degrees from McGill University (BA) and the University of Paris-Sorbonne (MLitt and DLitt). He taught full-time at Beeson Divinity School in the areas of church history, historical theology, and Latin from 1993 to 2006, when he was named research professor. Bray's books include *We Believe in One God* (ed.) in the Ancient Christian Doctrine Series (IVP Academic), *Ambrosiaster's Commentaries on Romans and 1–2 Corinthians* (trans. and ed.) (InterVarsity, 2009), *Tudor Church Reform* (Boydell Press, 2005), which contains the Henrician Canons of 1535 and the Reformatio Legum Ecclesiasticarum, *Biblical Interpretation: Past and Present* (InterVarsity, 2000), *The Anglican Canons 1529–1947* (Boydell Press, 1998), and *The Doctrine of God* in the Contours of Christian Theology series (gen. ed.) (InterVarsity, 1993). Bray also edited three volumes in the Ancient Christian Commentary Series and is a minister in the Church of England.

Carl L. Beckwith is associate professor of history and doctrine at Beeson Divinity School. Beckwith has degrees from St. Olaf College (BA), Trinity College in Dublin, Ireland (MPhil), Yale Divinity School (MA), and the University of

Notre Dame (PhD). His publications include a translation of Johann Gerhard's *Handbook of Consolations* (Wipf & Stock, 2009), *Hilary of Poitiers on the Trinity* (Oxford University Press, 2008), and articles in the *Journal of Early Christian Studies*, *Journal of Ecclesiastical History*, *Scottish Journal of Theology*, and *Concordia Theological Quarterly*.

Steven R. Harmon is adjunct professor of Christian history at Gardner-Webb University School of Divinity in Boiling Springs, North Carolina. Until recently, Harmon was associate professor of divinity at Beeson Divinity School. He holds degrees from Howard Payne University (BA) and Southwestern Baptist Theological Seminary (MDiv and PhD). Harmon received a dissertation fellowship for study at Westfälischen-Wilhelms Universität, Münster, Germany. He also studied at Catholic University of America, the University of Dallas, and Duke Divinity School (sabbatical research). A specialist in patristics and ecumenical theology, he has taught Christian ethics as well as church history and doctrine. His writings include *Ecumenism Means You, Too* (Cascade Books, 2010), *Towards Baptist Catholicity: Essays on Tradition and the Baptist Vision* (Paternoster, 2006), and *Every Knee Should Bow: Biblical Rationales for Universal Salvation in Early Christian Thought* (University Press of America, 2003). He publishes articles in several journals and serves on the Commission on Doctrine and Christian Unity of the Baptist World Alliance and is a member of the Faith and Order Commission of the World Council of Churches. He is also the book review editor for *Perspectives in Religious Studies*.

Carl E. Braaten is emeritus professor of systematic theology at the Lutheran School of Theology at Chicago, where he taught from 1961 to 1991. Together with Robert Jenson he founded the Center for Catholic and Evangelical Theology. He is an ordained minister of the Evangelical Lutheran Church in America, and he served as pastor of Lutheran Church of the Messiah in Minneapolis (1958–61). He holds degrees from St. Olaf College (BA), Luther Seminary (MDiv), and Harvard University (ThD). He has studied at the University of Paris, the University of Heidelberg, and the University of Oxford. He was the founding editor of two journals, *Dialog: A Journal of Theology* and *Pro Ecclesia: A Journal of Catholic and Evangelical Theology*, where he continues to serve as senior editor. He has written eighteen books, edited twenty-five books, and written more than two hundred articles and chapters. His most recent books are *Because of Christ: Memoirs of a Lutheran Theologian* (Eerdmans, 2010), *That All May Believe: A Theology of the Gospel and the Mission of the Church* (Eerdmans, 2008), *Principles of Lutheran Theology* (Fortress, 2007), and *Mother Church: Ecclesiology and Ecumenism* (Fortress, 1998).

J. Matthew Pinson is the president of Free Will Baptist Bible College. He received degrees from the University of West Florida (BA and MA), Yale University (MAR), and Vanderbilt University (EdD). Pinson also did graduate studies at Regent College, Vancouver, and doctoral studies at Florida State University. He has authored several books and pamphlets, including contributing to *Perspectives on Christian Worship: 5 Views* (B&H Academic, 2009), *Free Will Baptists & Church Government* (Randall House Publications, 2008), *The Washing of the Saints' Feet* (Randall House Publications, 2006), and *Four Views on Eternal Security* (Zondervan, 2002).

Curtis W. Freeman is research professor of theology and director of the Baptist House of Studies at Duke University Divinity School. He holds degrees from Baylor University (BA and PhD) and Southwestern Baptist Theological Seminary (MDiv). He has edited two books—*Baptist Roots: A Reader in the Theology of a Christian People* (Judson Press, 1999) and *Ties That Bind: Life Together in the Baptist Vision* (Smyth & Helwys, 1994). Freeman writes articles that seek to describe the development of a distinctly Baptist theological tradition as well as articles relating to Baptist and free church theology. He is a series editor of *Studies in Baptist History and Thought* (Paternoster Press) and serves on the Commission on Doctrine and Christian Unity of the Baptist World Alliance.

Elizabeth Newman is professor of theology and ethics at Baptist Theological Seminary in Richmond, Virginia. She holds degrees from Wake Forest University (BA), Southern Baptist Theological Seminary (MDiv), and Duke University (PhD). Newman is the author of *Untamed Hospitality: Welcoming God and Other Strangers* (Brazos Press, 2007). She also serves on the steering committee for Young Scholars in the Baptist Academy and the editorial board of *Studies in Baptist History and Thought*.

David P. Nelson is provost/chief academic officer at the University of North Carolina School of Arts. He holds degrees from Hardin-Simmons University (BM and MM) and Southeastern Baptist Theological Seminary (PhD). He was editor of *The Bible and the Mission of God* (B&H Academic, 2010) in The Mission of God series and *A Theology of the Church* (B&H Academic, 2007) and was a contributor to *Calvinism: A Southern Baptist Dialogue* (B&H Academic, 2008) and *Authentic Worship* (Kregel Publications, 2002). He received a Faith as a Way of Life grant from Yale Divinity School for work focused on the study of faith and culture.

Kathleen B. Nielson holds degrees in literature from Wheaton College (BA) and Vanderbilt University (MA and PhD). She has taught in the English departments at Vanderbilt University, Bethel College, and Wheaton College.

Nielson directs and teaches women's Bible studies at several churches, speaks extensively at conferences and retreats, and serves on the board of directors of Focus on the Family. She has authored numerous Bible studies, including *Ecclesiastes and Song of Songs: Wisdom's Searching and Finding* (P&R, 2009), *Psalms: Songs along the Way* (P&R, 2009), and *Proverbs: The Ways of Wisdom* (P&R, 2007), as well as various articles and poems.

John Rucyahana served as bishop of the Shyira diocese within the Episcopal Church of Rwanda. He holds degrees from Inyemeramihigo College (BA) and Trinity Episcopal School for Ministry in Pennsylvania (MAR). In 1993, Bishop Rucyahana was instrumental in establishing the Blessed Mustard Seed Babies Home in Hoima, Uganda, a home for abandoned children and those who had lost both parents to HIV/AIDS. In 1997, the genocide and subsequent violence decimated Rwanda's infrastructure and destroyed local services, schools, churches, health-care systems, and the economic base. This left Rwanda an impoverished and broken nation desperately in need of reconciliation, with over four hundred thousand orphans, one hundred thousand of whom were located in the Shyira Diocese. Bishop Rucyahana began an orphanage to help these children. He is the chair of Prison Fellowship Rwanda and serves on the global board of directors of Prison Fellowship International. Recently retired as bishop, John Rucyahana was appointed president of the National Unity and Reconciliation Commission.

Mark DeVine is associate professor of divinity at Beeson Divinity School. He teaches church history and doctrine. He holds degrees from Clemson University (BS) and Southern Baptist Theological Seminary (MDiv and PhD). DeVine is the author of *Bonhoeffer Speaks Today: Following Jesus at All Costs* (B&H Academic, 2005). He served as a missionary in Thailand and contributed to *Evangelicals Engaging Emergent: A Discussion of the Emergent Church Movement* (B&H Academic, 2009) and to *The Disciple's Study Bible* (Cornerstone Bible Publishers, 2003).

Ralph C. Wood, professor of theology and literature at Baylor University in Waco, Texas, holds degrees from Texas A&M University-Commerce (BA and MA) and the University of Chicago (MA and PhD). Wood serves as editor-at-large for the *Christian Century* and as a member of the editorial board of the *Flannery O'Connor Review*. His books include *The Gospel According to Tolkien: Visions of the Kingdom in Middle-earth* (Westminster John Knox, 2004), *Flannery O'Connor and the Christ-Haunted South* (Eerdmans, 2004), *Contending for the Faith: The Church's Engagement with Culture* (Baylor, 2003), and *The Comedy of Redemption: Christian Faith and Comic Vision in Four American Novelists* (University of Notre Dame Press, 1988).

Introduction

The Faith We Confess

TIMOTHY GEORGE

One of the signs of getting older is that one's friends and contemporaries begin to die. Not long ago Dr. Frank Forrester Church, one of my best friends from my student days at Harvard Divinity School, passed away. Forrest Church and I arrived at Harvard in the same year, he from the West Coast and I from the Deep South. We bonded almost immediately. We both loved classics and church history, and we both studied under the same professor, George Huntston Williams, who taught all of his students to appreciate what another great Harvard professor, Georges Florovsky, once called "the ecumenism of time as well as space." Forrest majored on the early church, and I on the Reformation. At the time, my goal was to be a pastor; he wanted to become an academic. Somehow the wires got crossed, however; I became the academic, he the pastor. Forrest served just one church during his entire ministry: the Unitarian Church of All Souls in New York City. When he went there, there were some one hundred people, more or less (usually less), rambling around that great cathedral-like sanctuary. His obituary in the *New York Times* reported an average attendance of over one thousand in recent years. Who said Unitarians couldn't have church growth!

Over the years Forrest Church and I had many discussions about orthodoxy and heresy, about doctrine and faith, about what it means to be a Christian in today's world, about the will to believe, and about the need for creed. Within the context of his denomination, Forrest was a flaming traditionalist, which means he believed in God! We each took our bearings from a different part of Harvard's past. For Forrest, it was the Harvard of Ralph Waldo Emerson, William Ellery Channing, and the Unitarian pioneers of the early nineteenth century. For me, it was the Harvard of the Puritan founders whose motto was included on one of the early seals of the college: *Veritas Christo et Ecclesiae,* or "Truth for Christ and the Church."

So now we, as pastors and professors, students and committed persons of the church from many different denominations and locations, are still struggling with the same issues Forrest and I debated on the banks of the Charles those many years ago. It is a long conversation stretching back across the centuries to Arius and Athanasius, including Abelard and Bernard of Clairvaux, Erasmus and Luther, Jonathan Edwards and Charles Chauncy, and, although they were separated by nearly a century, Friedrich Schleiermacher and Karl Barth.

I have been told that the theme of this book will generate a lot of conversation and raise eyebrows in some quarters. What are they trying to do down at Beeson—with Methodists and Baptists and Presbyterians and Lutherans and Anglicans, with moderates and conservatives and Calvinists and Arminians, all mixed up on the same program? We may be mixed together, but I hope we're not mixed-up! Can I say that we have come together because, while the distinctives I have just mentioned (and many others that could be added) are important to each of us—the last thing we want to do is to concoct a homogenized, ecclesiastical pea soup—we want to declare our unity in *unum Deum,* as the Latin text of the Nicene Creed says: in *unum Dominum Iesum Christum,* the Son of God, and in *unam, sanctam, catholicam et apostolicam ecclesiam,* and we confess *baptisma in remissionum peccatorum.*

"The Will to Believe and the Need for Creed" is the title of an essay by the late Jaroslav Pelikan, based on a talk he originally presented at Yale University in 2003 at an event celebrating his eightieth birthday. Pelikan reminds us that "the will to believe" part of his title was not original with him. It was originally the title of an article and later a book by William James. James was a famous Harvard philosopher, the founder of the philosophy of pragmatism and psychology of religion in this country. James was perhaps best known for another book he wrote, *The Varieties of Religious Experience.* Buffeted by what Dostoevsky called "the whirlwinds of doubt," James had little use for what he called "our positive dogmas about God"[1]—credal formulas or confessions of faith.

When I was a student at Harvard, I would often walk across Harvard Yard, as we called the central quadrangle. On those walks I would pass Emerson Hall, which was built to house the department of philosophy during the tenure of William James. James was appointed the chair of the committee charged with recommending a legend to be carved in stone on the portals of Emerson Hall. James and his committee proposed the ancient Greek saying "Man is the measure of all things." But he was overruled by President Charles W. Eliot, who suggested instead Psalm 8:4, "What is man that you are mindful of him?"[2]—which undoubtedly irritated James until the day he died. It was William James who defined religion as "the feelings, acts, and experiences of individual men in their solitude,"[3] which is not so far from Arius's definition of the preexistent Logos as "the Alone with the Alone."[4] James was a great promoter of "the will to believe," but he saw little use for "the need for creed."

To assert boldly, as we have done in this volume, something so robust, so premodern, so outré as a statement of theological belief formulated nearly 1,700 years ago, is certainly to fly in the face of countervailing headwinds in our culture today. We have chosen to approach this classic confession through the prism of the Nicene faith and evangelical life. For the purposes of this project, evangelicalism may be defined as a worldwide renewal movement within the one, holy, catholic, and apostolic church, embracing—but not limited to—puritanism, pietism, and pentecostalism. Evangelicals are increasingly coming to understand themselves not as a newly generated byproduct of the post-Enlightenment modern church, but rather as legitimate heirs of the apostolic faith expressed for all orthodox Christians in the Creed of Nicea. This claim cannot be made in a straightforward way, however, without acknowledging several significant obstacles and objections. I want to signal three of these at the outset.

The Evanescence of Meaning

One cannot understand the best-selling appeal of the new atheism today without taking into account what T. S. Eliot called "The Wasteland," the title of his masterpiece written in the ashes of World War I. Postmodernism did not begin, as is often claimed, with French literary criticism, much less with the later musings of Richard Rorty and Stanley Fish. It was born in the trenches of the Somme, Ypres, and Verdun. All of this means that any appeal to a tradition is suspect; any appeal that we make to traditional formulas of faith is automatically suspect. Even a theology as sophisticated and as attuned to modern scientific questions as that of Wolfhart Pannenberg is utterly without respect in a secularized academic culture that has learned to live "without God, without creed," to quote the title of James Turner's superb book on the history of unbelief in America.[5]

The evanescence of meaning affects every field of endeavor, not just theology. Look back to an artistic movement such as Dadaism. Now, do not rush over to the library and try to find an artist named Dada in the dictionary. You will not find him there. You will find Derrida but not Dada! Dada is a nonsense word. It does not mean anything and was not meant to mean anything. It was chosen at random to express the inherent meaninglessness of the human project.

Listen to how the Dada Manifesto, published at Zurich in 1918, described this artistic movement: "We are a furious wind, tearing the dirty linen of clouds and prayers, preparing the great spectacle of disaster, fire, and decomposition." One could not find a better description of 9/11 than that. In this kind of world, to make so robust a confession as the Nicene Creed is to fly in the face of the cultural assumptions and prevailing worldviews that mark the times in which we live.

Consider another field of human creativity: architecture. In the run up to World War II, Mussolini in Italy and Hitler in Germany were both attracted to buildings designed in neoclassical form. In their efforts to build a new Rome and a new Reich, they turned to classical models from the past, even though the results were often garish and utilitarian. After World War II, with the defeat of the Nazis and the Fascists, classical architecture fell into disrepute, for no one wanted to use a style of building associated with the horrible tyranny of the middle part of the twentieth century. This, I think, makes all the more impressive the fact that in the early 1950s, when the campus of Samford University was being designed on the hillside on which it now sits, Major Harwell Davis, the university president, and those who helped him plan this campus made a deliberate decision to use Georgian colonial architecture. In the decades since, this architectural paradigm has been maintained with consistency under the presidencies of Leslie Wright, Thomas Corts, and Andy Westmoreland, with consequences one can still see when visiting one of the best-planned and most beautiful campuses in our country. All of this is the result of that post–World War II decision to swim against the tide, to construct a special space "for learning and for God" (Samford's motto) that harks back to the harmony and beauty of the Great Tradition, even though the classical model of architecture had been discredited by the leaders of empires then in ruins.

Thus, Reid Chapel on the other side of this campus was built very much in the style of the First Baptist Church of Rhode Island, a great colonial church building with a spire reaching to the heavens. And later, even though we have a very different form of architecture at Beeson Divinity School, when we designed Hodges Chapel, we still wanted continuity, harmony, and beauty to be conveyed in the very space in which we meet to worship God. We deliberately and intentionally did this, over against all other models that were considered and promoted. Of course, this does not mean that one must be in a cruciform-shape building like Hodges Chapel, with the Apostles' Creed etched in stone in the back and *Soli Deo Gloria* painted in gold over the organ, in order to worship God. No! We may surely worship God in a sawdust revival tent, or a crystal cathedral, or a country church, or a basketball arena, for "God is spirit, and those who worship him must worship in spirit and truth" (John 4:24). But if the purpose of a divinity school in a Christian university setting is to nurture, sustain, and transmit the deepest textures of meaning that form the ultimate reasons for the existence of such an institution, then how we shape the buildings in which we work and worship says a lot about what we believe and how we want to live.

Creeds and Credalism

John Stott has said that evangelicals are gospel people and Bible people. This is a shorthand way of saying that evangelicals affirm both the material and the formal principles of the Reformation: justification by faith alone and *sola scriptura*. In the early years of the Reformation, the question of scriptural authority came to a boiling point. In 1519, Luther and Johannes Eck met in a public debate at Leipzig. In the heat of that exchange, Luther declared that popes could err and had erred, that church councils could be wrong and had been wrong, and that he would henceforth stand forthrightly on the holy written Word of God alone. The radicality of Luther's insight cannot be denied. He declared that Scripture alone was the true lord and master of all writings and doctrine on earth. He said that a simple layperson armed with Scripture should be believed above a pope or a council without it. All of Luther's reforming work proceeded from this basic assumption.

Yet calling Luther a champion of private interpretation and the heroic forerunner of modern individualism will not bear close scrutiny. For how else can we understand his concluding remark in the "Disputation against Scholastic Theology" repeated in other settings: "In all I wanted to say, we believe we have said nothing that is not in agreement with the Catholic Church and the teachers of the church."[6] Luther argued *against* tradition, but *from* tradition and *for* tradition. To put it differently, he was arguing from a shallower tradition to a more profound one.

The retrieval of tradition, even for the sake of the gospel, seems to run counter to that strain of evangelical piety expressed by the slogan "No creed but the Bible." Bible-church Christians, restorationists, and some Baptists, among others, have elevated this expression to a fundamental article of faith. "We have no creed but the Bible," they say—thus making a creed out of their commitment to creedless Christianity! Sometimes such rhetoric becomes a cover for the discounting or denial of the doctrinal content of historic Christianity. "No creed but the Bible" can easily devolve into neither creed nor the Bible. Despite its abuse and popular misuse, however, this expression reminds evangelicals of the real dangers of *credalism*, as opposed to the valid and helpful use of creeds in the life of the church. Evangelicals are among the most ardent champions of religious freedom and have often opposed, at great personal cost, state-imposed religious conformity and its attendant civil sanctions. Also, in keeping with the Scripture principle of the Reformation, evangelicals refuse to elevate any humanly constructed doctrinal statement above Holy Scripture. The Bible alone remains the *norma normans* for all teaching and instruction, the supreme standard by which all human conduct, creeds, and religious opinion should be tried.

Despite this aversion to credalism, evangelicals today are finding that the historic creeds of the church are a resource for faith and spiritual life. Evangelicals are engaged in a process of retrieval for the sake of renewal. In this way, they are coming to stand side by side with Orthodox and Catholic believers in affirming the Nicene faith of the early church. Jaroslav Pelikan has defined Christian doctrine as "what the church of Jesus Christ believes, teaches, and confesses on the basis of the Word of God."[7] John Webster has described how the act of confession is the means by which the church binds itself to the gospel; in so doing, it makes known its commitment to Christ and the Bible.

> Confession is the act of astonished, fearful, and grateful acknowledgment that the gospel is the one word by which to live and die; in making its confession, the church lifts up its voice to do what it must do—speak with amazement of the goodness and truth of the gospel and the gospel's God. Creeds and confessional formulas exist to promote that act of confession: to goad the church toward it, to shape it, to tie it to the truth, and so to perpetuate the confessional life and activity of the Christian community. In this way, creeds and confessional formulas are the servants of the gospel in the church.[8]

Applied Christianity

We encounter a further objection in arguing for "the need for creed" among evangelicals today. The objection is simply put: emphasizing the creeds reduces the Christian faith to dead orthodoxy and an intellectualism devoid of faith and life. We have heard it said, "Why does it really matter what we *say*? It is how we *live* that matters."

Such a protest was at the heart of the pietist reaction against Lutheran and Reformed orthodoxy in the seventeenth and eighteenth centuries. Pietists like Philip Jacob Spener have argued that appeals to the classic texts from the past, whether the ancient creeds or the writings of the Reformers, are not enough. They wanted to emphasize *Wiedergeburt*, the new birth: a living, vital, personal relationship with Jesus Christ. Although pietism has problems of its own—not least in providing the seedbed for theological liberalism, as in Schleiermacher, who became "a Moravian of a higher order"[9] but a Christian of a lower one—we must recognize the truth at the heart of its concern. There are more than two hundred confessions of faith included in Jaroslav Pelikan's great anthology *Creeds and Confessions of Faith in the Christian Tradition*, including the Creed of Nicea. But we must not forget an even earlier confession of faith, the one from the man who was born blind in John 9. He confessed, "Though I was blind, now I see" (John 9:25). That is a personal confession of faith, and it speaks about the personal, transforming work of God in the life of a sinner saved by grace.

The traditions of pietism and revivalism, for all their downsides, remind us of this basic reality: the Nicene faith is a matter of heart religion, of life religion, and not just head religion. So we attend not only to believing the Nicene faith but also to practicing it. Practice means to perform something habitually, to make a habit of it. A habit is not just a custom; it is also a form of clothing worn by certain members of religious orders. To practice is to make a habit of; it is to be clothed with; it is to exercise or perform repeatedly, regularly, in order to acquire a proficiency or skill of some kind.

But what does it mean to practice the Nicene faith? Well, it means we have to keep practicing it—in our worship, our liturgy, our deeds of mercy, our love for others, our life of prayer—because we have not yet gotten it right. We have not yet gotten ourselves right. This is why we are called to church week after week: to sing the same old songs, to hear the same old sermons, to receive the collection in the same old way. This is a part of what it means to practice the Nicene faith. It is about life. It is about worship. It is about the disciplines that shape our discipleship. We remember that we are called to do this because Jesus Christ has transformed our lives. He has changed our destiny, and he has called us to serve, love, and obey him in life and in death.

The words of the Niceno-Constantinopolitan Creed have come down to us in two variant texts. One is a first-person singular form, and the other is a first-person plural one. Both of these versions of the creed are attested in the fourth century. Some scholars think that the first-person singular text was a result of the fact that the Nicene Creed was used as an early baptismal confession of faith: "I believe in one God, the Father Almighty. I believe. . . ." The creed was also used corporately, however, to express the common faith that we share together. There is a place for both "I believe" and "We believe" in our expression of the Nicene faith today. As we affirm our solidarity with Orthodox, Catholic, and evangelical believers around the world and through the ages, and as we pray, "*Our* Father, who art in heaven . . . forgive *us*," so too we confess the faith of the church in words that place us among that company of forgiven sinners, which is the body of Christ extended throughout time as well as space.

> We believe in one God,
> the Father, the Almighty,
> maker of heaven and earth,
> of all that is, seen and unseen.
>
> We believe in one Lord, Jesus Christ,
> the only son of God,
> eternally begotten of the Father,
> God from God, Light from Light,

true God from true God,
begotten, not made,
of one being with the Father.
Through him all things were made.
For us and for our salvation
he came down from heaven:
by the power of the Holy Spirit
he became incarnate from the Virgin Mary,
and was made man.
For our sake he was crucified under Pontius Pilate;
he suffered death and was buried.
On the third day he rose again
in accordance with the Scriptures;
he ascended into heaven
and is seated at the right hand of the Father.
He will come again in glory
to judge the living and the dead,
and his kingdom will have no end.

We believe in the Holy Spirit, the Lord, the giver of life,
who proceeds from the Father [and the Son].
With the Father and the Son
he is worshiped and glorified.
He has spoken through the Prophets.
We believe in one holy catholic and apostolic Church.
We acknowledge one baptism for the forgiveness of sins.
We look for the resurrection of the dead,
and the life of the world to come.

AMEN.

PART 1

Identity

1

The Faith Once Delivered

Nicea and Evangelical Confession

THOMAS C. ODEN

Beloved, although I was very eager to write to you about our common salvation, I found it necessary to write appealing to you to contend for the faith which was once for all delivered to the saints.

Jude 3

Introduction

In this essay I am asking *how*. My dialogue hopes for visible evidences of the concrete implementation of *how*. *How* to do what?—Present the faith! Bring life to faith! Bring faith to life! Not just any generalized faith, but the faith once delivered to the saints. The apostolic faith. The faith of the original eyewitnesses to God's own coming to give humanity a new start.

The apostles were chosen and sent by the risen Lord into all the world—to every culture in every language—to embody this faith. Does this faith change with changing times? Trust the apostolic witness on this: "Jesus Christ is the same yesterday and today and forever. Do not be led away by diverse and strange teachings" (Heb. 13:8–9). This goes against the grain of our modern pretensions to improve on the apostles. The gospel does not change with each new cultural situation. The style of language may vary, since the history of language changes. But the content of the witness, the gospel, remains the same. The deposit is rock-hard, like Peter (*petros*, "the rock"), who was called to guard the apostolic teaching: to "feed my sheep."

This faith is not first delivered to one audience as truth and then later to another audience as a modified truth or an altered view corrected by time. The faith is only once delivered to specific apostles sent to proclaim the changeless truth of God's coming, once, for all, in every language and culture. Count them: twelve, symbolic of a newly covenanted Israel.

Their deposit was delivered to whom? The saints—the gathered community of worship whenever and wherever they meet to celebrate the truth made known in the incarnate Lord. All these varied forms of Christian community in history have in common their shared life in Christ, who is just as alive with each of them as he was in his Last Supper with his closest disciples.

Why is this testimony needed today? Because it is life-giving and culture-transforming? Yes, but wait—there is more. This testimony is needed today because it is true. Ours is an age of increasing syncretism and radical pluralism. We imagine that we have at last become inoculated against the fantasy of the truth. Postmodernity, which lacks orthodoxy, has only minimal interests in truth claims. Truths, it says, are just competing finite powers with winners and losers. The winner is the truth socially recognized, but only for a time. Just wait till the next alleged truth comes along. Postmodern orthodoxy is wholly focused on one pivotal truth claim: Jesus Christ is Lord.

So how do we present the apostolic testimony, the faith once delivered to the saints, one by one to persons who are living in a culture spinning out into fragmentation? That is the question that brings us together for this essay. Let us look more closely.

"Our Common Salvation": Ancient Creed and Modern Confession

Upholding the Original Apostolic Tradition

Timothy was instructed: "Follow the pattern of the sound words that you have heard from me, in the faith and love that are in Christ Jesus. By the Holy Spirit who dwells within us, guard the good deposit entrusted to you" (2 Tim. 1:13–14). The first task of the Christian teacher is to "hold fast" to the sound teaching passed on from the apostles. Timothy was not at liberty to teach his own private opinions or prejudices. Paul had provided a living model for the Christian leader to follow (Tertullian, *Praescr.* 25).

Jesus taught his disciples that the Spirit is being given to "guide you into all the truth" (John 16:13). Paul faithfully passed on the tradition he had received, which he regarded as unalterable: "For I delivered to you as of first importance what I also received." What is the core of it? That "Christ died for our sins in accordance with the Scriptures" (1 Cor. 15:3).

Paul regarded those in public ministry as "stewards of the mysteries of God" who are required to "be found trustworthy" in passing along the tradition (1 Cor. 4:1–2). Timothy was implored to "guard the deposit entrusted to you. Avoid the irreverent babble and contradictions of what is falsely called 'knowledge,' for by professing it some have swerved from the faith" (1 Tim. 6:20–21). Along with objective accuracy, there remains a personal element in the transmission of tradition: "Continue in what you have learned and have firmly believed, knowing from whom you learned it and how from childhood you have been acquainted with the sacred writings, which are able to make you wise for salvation through faith in Christ Jesus" (2 Tim. 3:14–15; cf. Gal. 1:8–9; Jerome, *Letters* 52.7).

The Creed

The apostolic faith is concisely summarized in the creed. The purpose of preparation for baptism is to learn the core teachings that come directly from the apostles, in order to know what your baptism means and to avoid false advertising. Get this apostolic faith wrong, and everything else about Christianity will be misdirected. Nicea was called to define that core ecumenically—east and west, north and south, on the broadest possible scale—and to defend it against distortions. Nicea was a milestone not because it presented something new, but because it held to that same faith that had been received directly from the apostles through the Spirit and with minimal perversion. The Creed of Caesarea of 325 ended: "We have thought all this in heart and soul ever since we knew ourselves, and we now so think and speak in truth, being able to show by evidence and to convince you that we in past times so believed and preached accordingly" (Eusebius, in Socrates of Constantinople, *CH* 1.8, *COC* 2:30). By 431 AD, it was consensually defined that no one within classic Christian teaching has acquired the right "to declare or at any rate to compose or devise a faith other than [Greek, *heteran*] that defined by the holy fathers who with the Holy Spirit came together at Nicea" (Third Ecumenical Council, Ephesus, *SCD* 125).

But don't we need a different foundation for our modern audience? Paul answers: "For no one can lay a foundation other than that which is laid, which is Jesus Christ" (1 Cor. 3:11). Those who pretend to lay a new foundation other than the apostolic testimony do so in vain; such an attempt is like building out of straw. They have already decided to do something else, to build up something quite different from the foundation, "which is Jesus Christ." The foundation is all about a person, and a personal relation with this person. Our relation to this person is what brings us together.

Revitalizing Ancient Ecumenical Teaching: A New Ecumenism

Today, evangelicals are already embodying what is now being called the *new ecumenism*. This does not mean a new organization, but rather a rediscovery of our unity with ancient and contemporary Christian believers. Until recently, evangelicals have not had an adequate or viable ecumenical presence. That is partly due to the false but prevailing definition of ecumenism. Some have not yet recognized that this older, modern ecumenism has lost vital contact with the oldest, ancient ecumenism. That primitive experience of unity in personal trust in Jesus Christ is the emerging work of the Spirit. Those who define the ecumenical movement by church officials negotiating their institutional relations with each other—rather than by celebrating the unity of their personal relation with the incomparable Person, the incarnate risen Lord—will here become hard of hearing. But the day of ecumenism being defined by politics is over. That has not been blessed by the Spirit. The rapid demise of the twentieth-century ecumenical movement is due to its detachment from the ancient ecumenical movement. But the Spirit is doing something new, as the Spirit is always prone to do.

I hesitate to even bring up the term *ecumenism*, because it has been so long distorted. Its closest cognates are *catholic* and *orthodox*, both of which have been battered in modernity. So I will write only of ecumenism in an ancient, orthodox, and catholic sense. Confessing evangelicals are uniting to call for the vital recovery of ancient ecumenical teaching today. They constitute living evidence that God the Spirit is calling into being a renewed awareness of our unity in Christ—a new ecumenism. Confessing Christians are seeking the recovery of doctrinal integrity throughout the whole range of world Christianity. This healing is not a mere fantasy but already a palpable reality.

Evangelicals are no longer thinking of the renewing body of Christ simply within the context of recently created denominational walls. Walls that have been erected between Christian institutions have often been bound within the narrow limits of modern assumptions, hence without reference to the communion of saints. Contrary to a popular stereotype, evangelicals are no longer prone to venting spleen, but rather showing their unity in the body of Christ and its plausibility through faith active in love.

This Spirit-filled, personally grounded form of unity in Christ is most alive among young people, many of whom live in Asia and Africa. I have seen their faces. They are weary of accommodating to modernity. They are seeking grounding in ancient ecumenical teaching. Modern ecumenism rightly began in worldwide evangelical mission movements. I speak of the earliest expressions in the World Evangelical Alliance of 1846, and extending to the Edinburgh Conference of 1910. But sadly, by 1966 this modernizing movement had lapsed into a merger mentality represented by defensive bureaucracies, and it finally deteriorated into divisive advocacy and extreme politicization.

Postliberal ecumenism is actively returning to the wellsprings of unity in apostolic truth and classic Christian teaching. Wise Catholic leadership has recognized the weaknesses of the bureaucratic and liberal Protestant ecumenical elites and is now engaging actively in an ongoing conversation with worldwide evangelicals. Wherever lives are hidden in the risen Christ, we have much to consider.

Nicea and Evangelical Confession

A modest expression of this unity and vitality is the Ancient Christian Commentary on Scripture (ACCS), a project once located in Drew University but now is at Eastern University in Philadelphia. A lengthy project begun in 1993, the last of its twenty-nine volumes was recently completed. These early exegetes are supplying Catholics, Orthodox, and Protestants—both evangelical and liberal—with new roots in patristic teaching and exegesis.

Beeson Divinity School in 2009 was the proper place and time for announcing and celebrating the launch of the newest extension of the ACCS effort: the Ancient Christian Doctrine Series. It is a successor series—a five-volume patristic compendium of classic doctrinal definitions, organized around the familiar key phrases of the Nicene Creed. Each volume unpacks the most widely received classic definitions, often called articles, of the Niceno-Constantinopolitan Creed of 325 (with clarifications in 381).

Here the richest doctrinal treasures of the patristic period are being mined and ordered as a commentary on this most authoritative and widely received doctrinal confession of the early church. The Nicene Creed remains the most commonly confessed affirmation of worldwide Christians concerning the heart of the biblical revelation.

These classic texts from the first eight centuries illumine those key decisive phrases of that summative creed. Nicea was written under heretical challenges that defined, for subsequent Christian preaching, liturgy, and catechetics, the boundaries of the faith received from the apostles. The Spirit-blessed efforts of the consensus-bearing exegetes of Scripture are again proving to be the most reliable basis for holding together the core of early Christian teaching, the gist of the gospel.

Relearning the Meaning of Our Baptism

The orderly teaching of Christian doctrine arose out of prebaptismal teaching based on consensually received scriptural exegesis. Drawing the whole course of Christian teaching into a single, cohesive statement was the motive of every early Christian teacher commissioned to prepare persons for baptism.

The creed was a convenient way of drawing together the entire diverse narrative meaning of the Old and New Testament Scriptures into a simple, memorizable affirmation of baptismal faith. This is why Christians all over the world still appeal to this most widely received of all ancient confessions.

Christians have a right to know the meaning of their baptism. Clergy have a sacred duty to teach it. Those rightly prepared for baptism understand what it means to believe in God the Father Almighty and in God the Son, illumined through God the Spirit.

This ancient confession still serves as the most fitting and durable framework for the postmodern rediscovery of classic Christian teaching. Like all ancient baptismal confessions, it is set forth in a triune sequence. The three articles of the creed summarize the being and work of the one God who reveals himself in history as Father, Son, and Spirit. This is the one God to which all of Scripture attests.

The core of this sequence for summary teaching appeared in short form in Matthew 28:19–20 in the formula for baptism, in which the resurrected Lord concluded his earthly teaching with this charge: "Go therefore and make disciples of all nations, baptizing them in the name of the Father and of the Son and of the Holy Spirit, teaching them to observe all that I have commanded you. And behold, I am with you always, to the end of the age." In this way, the Lord Jesus himself forever linked two crucial acts: baptizing and teaching. In all subsequent periods of Christian history, they have remained intimately interwoven.

The room for private opinion is vast among Christians of very different languages and cultures and historical times, provided those opinions are not repugnant to the core of biblical faith (John Chrysostom, *Hom. 2 Tim.* 2–3). Nothing is required of any believer other than that which is revealed by God the Spirit to conscience through Scripture, as necessary for salvation and as affirmed consensually by the Christian community.

Baptism is intrinsically voluntary. No one can be rightly forced to believe. It is a free response to a free gift. The task of Christian teaching is to clarify, illuminate, cohesively interpret, and defend the convictions distinctive to Christianity that empower and enable life in Christ (Mark 7:4–9; 1 John 2:12–14).

The most influential teaching summaries of the creed were written as catechetical lectures on the creed by Cyril of Jerusalem (*Catechetical Lectures*), Gregory of Nyssa (*The Great Catechism*), John Chrysostom (*Baptismal Instructions*), and Augustine (*Catechizing the Uninstructed* and *Faith and the Creed*). From these came systematic theology.

Teachers as varied as Augustine, Thomas Aquinas, and Luther have held that the Nicene Creed is the best of the condensed statements of Christian faith and the most reliable way to learn the heart of faith. In professing the form of the creed received in Jerusalem, Cyril explains that the believer is helped to keep close to the center of the faith once delivered by the apostles,

> which has been built up strongly out of all the Scriptures. For since all cannot read the Scriptures, some being hindered from the knowledge of them by lack of learning, and others because they lack leisure to study, in order that the soul should not be starved in ignorance, the church has condensed the whole teaching of the Faith in a few lines. This summary I wish you both to commit to

memory when I recite it, and to rehearse it with all diligence among yourselves, not writing it out on paper, but engraving it by the memory upon your heart, taking care while you rehearse it that no catechumen may happen to overhear the things which have been delivered to you. I wish you also to keep this as a provision through the whole course of your life, and beside this to receive no alternative teaching, even if we ourselves should change and contradict our present teaching.[1]

The creed, says Rufinus, serves as a "short word" summarizing the whole of biblical faith, providing "standard teaching to converts," and offering "a badge for distinguishing" those who preach Christ according to apostolic rule. It is constructed "out of living stones and pearls supplied by the Lord" (*Symb.*).[2] Rufinus was among the earliest (345–410) of many classic commentators on the rule of faith. He thought that the Holy Spirit had superintended its transmission in order that it "contain nothing ambiguous, obscure, or inconsistent." Poignantly, he explained: "The reason why the creed is not written down on paper or parchment, but is retained in the believers' hearts, is to ensure that it has been learned from the tradition handed down from the Apostles, and not from written texts, which occasionally fall into the hands of unbelievers." Rufinus based his commentary on the personally remembered "text to which I pledged myself when I was baptized in the church of Aquileia."

"Contend for the One Faith": Conciliar Tradition in Evangelical Protestantism

The Primitive Rule of Faith

By the end of the first century, the baptismal formula (Matt. 28:19) was taken to be an established summary of the essence of faith (Ignatius, *Phld.* 7–9; Irenaeus, *Adv. Haer.* 3.17). It drew together common points of consent in a brief way that any believer could memorize and confess from the heart. By this simple confession the mass of material in sacred Scripture was, by common assent, tightened, unified, organized, and reliably transmitted.

The rule of faith (*regula fidei*) defines in summary what is to be believed as necessary for salvation. The Bible contains all that is necessary to be believed, and the church is commissioned to teach nothing less than that faith revealed in Scripture (Second Helvetic Confession).[3] The creed is derived closely from the whole course and gist of Scripture (Luther, *Brief Explanation*, WML 2). The rule of faith is summarized in baptismal confession.

An article of faith must be based upon revelation of the truth declared in Scripture, and ecclesiastically defined with ecumenical consent (Gallican Confession, CC 3; Vincent of Lérins, *Comm.* 2, 20–24). Alleged consensual teachings that lack these features may remain matters of opinion and left open for continued debate and speculation, but not taught as apostolic truth fit for the salvation of souls.

Newly devised human traditions that claim to be divine revelation but disavow the apostolic witness must be gently and charitably resisted. They must not be confused with the divinely revealed good news received from the apostles. "See to it that no one takes you captive by philosophy and empty deceit, according to human tradition, according to the elemental spirits of the world, and not according to Christ" (Col. 2:8; see also 1 Tim. 1:4). Jesus rebuked the Pharisees because they neglected the commandment of God "in order to maintain the tradition of men" (Mark 7:8; Tertullian, *Praescr.* 7). The godly transmission of the memory of Jesus Christ must be maintained accurately and faithfully, since it is the living memory of God's own coming to humanity (John Chrysostom, *Comm. Gal.* 1.6).

Irenaeus conversed personally with Polycarp, who himself had talked with the eyewitness John about the events surrounding the life of Jesus (to Florinus, in Eusebius, *Hist. eccl.* 5.20). Thus through only one intermediary, Irenaeus understood himself to be personally and accurately in touch with a reliable eyewitness to the original events of Christian revelation.

The Apostles' Creed is the Western form of the received text of the consensual memory of the earliest baptismal confession, which developed as a summary exposition of the baptismal formula of Matthew 28:19 (*Didache* 7.1; Justin Martyr, *1 Apol.* 61). Irenaeus regarded the rule of faith as the "canon of truth which he received in his baptism" (Irenaeus, *Adv. Haer.* 1.9.4; 1.10.1; see also Tertullian, *Bapt.* 11; Clement of Alexandia, *Strom.* 8.15; Cyprian, *Epistles* 69.7; 70.2). As early as in Paul and Matthew, there is a fixed formula for baptismal confession (see also Ignatius, *Magn.* 11; *Eph.* 7; *Trall.* 9; and Justin, *1 Apol.* 13, 31, 46; *Dial.* 85). The twelve spare phrases of the Old Roman Symbol are direct descendants of the easily memorizable and earliest baptismal confessions that derived from the Pauline and Petrine decades. The *Didache* called believers to guard what they had received without adding or subtracting. Irenaeus (*Adv. Haer.* 3.4.3) and Tertullian (*Praescr.* 29–35) thought that all heresies would be easily recognizable by their self-deceptive habit of tacking on innovations to the received apostolic tradition as if essential. Clement of Alexandria appealed to the antiquity of the apostolic witness as prior to all subsequent distortions of it (*Strom.* 7.17).

By searching the Scriptures, any believer can compare later proposals for Christian understanding with the apostolic witness. In *On First Principles*, Origen accepted as orthodox teaching only that which had been taught by the apostles and accurately mediated through consensual tradition (*OFP*, Preface).[4] Antiquity of teaching—meaning the ancient teaching of the apostles—was one of the three criteria constituting the Vincentian rule, the other two being catholicity of reception and universality of consent (Vincent of Lérins, *Comm.* 2–3).

Even the heretics tried to appeal to the apostolic tradition for support, only to find their views in due time rejected by the church itself on behalf of the apostolic written testimony. The Holy Spirit was promised to the apostolic successors not in order that they might make known new doctrine, but that by the Spirit's assistance they might "inviolably keep and faithfully expound the revelation or deposit of faith delivered through the apostles" (Vatican Council I, *Constitution* 1.4).[5]

When divergent teachings arose, the churches spread across the ancient empires appealed to the joint consensus of the most ancient churches of Jerusalem, Rome, Antioch, and Alexandria to maintain apostolic teaching accurately. They sought to guard those documents that most accurately presented the original tradition. The position of Rome as capital of the empire made it an obvious center for Christian guardianship; yet churches there were always seeking to be in concert with Alexandria, representing the African continent, and with Jerusalem and Antioch, representing the Eastern churches.

General Consent to the Core Narrative of Scripture

Any ancient Christian exegete had authority only by correspondence with the general consent that accurately represented the mind of the whole church—by reasoning, by analogy of faith—upon the whole scriptural narrative.

No single voice taken alone can claim to carry every nuance of the full consent of the whole church in all things. Even the church's greatest theologians may err, wrote Vincent of Lérins, but these errors are in time corrected by the lack of consent (*Comm.* 10–11, 17, 28).

The surest medium of consensual Christian teaching is liturgy, through the language of common prayer. The practices of baptism, Eucharist, Lord's Day services, and many elements of the Christian year are powerful safeguards for the retention of the teachings of the apostles. Even if preachers were known to be phony and heretical, as long as they celebrated Holy Communion and baptism in due order, the liturgy had not been invalidated. Indeed, the liturgy itself performs the ironic task of contradicting what has been badly taught (Augustine, *C. litt. Petil.* 45, 82).

By this means, the Holy Spirit again and again turns human pride and distortion into the praise of God. The church has been guided by God's Spirit through many historical crises. New languages, concepts, and symbol systems have arisen repeatedly in the history of Christian teaching. For a time, a disproportionate emphasis may have been given to one or another concept, but eventually all these concepts must stand the test of time and either be confirmed or rejected by the living ecumenical church under the guidance of the Spirit. The result is that by Scripture, creeds, transgenerational institutions, liturgy, and catechetical teaching, the Spirit continues to illuminate the mind of the church and to make the apostolic teaching recognizable.

The Spirit calls us to test all things in relation to divine inspiration: "Do not quench the Spirit. Do not despise prophecies, but test everything; hold fast what is good" (1 Thess. 5:19–21).

The Creed

The creed points not to itself but to the revelation it attests. It is not significant in itself except as a gathering up of the whole gist of scriptural teaching. The creed is, at heart, a confession of the cumulative meaning of the prayers, liturgy, and common acts of the whole Christian community of all times and places. The creed expresses the common sense of the faithful about what the revelation of God in Scripture narrates and proclaims. It does so in a short form that seekers and youthful initiates may grasp and understand, and that all believers everywhere may confidently confirm as reliable biblical teaching. When new ideas were tested, they were tested by this rule of baptismal faith. Arguments from Scripture were proposed by both heretics and orthodox to decide upon the consensus of the faithful that had been received from the apostolic testimony and believed always. That is what the Nicene Creed represents prototypically for the whole of ecumenical Christianity.

This consensus sets the boundaries for the shared confession of the worldwide worshiping community. Many ideas were able to be freely examined within these boundaries, but some were out of bounds. When advocates of these nonconsensual views turned up purported texts by alleged apostles, they were judged and rejected in relation to the consensus that had emerged from and been fairly tested by the earliest communities of faith as expressed in their baptismal confessions. These became the rule of faith (*regula fidei*) for the worshiping community—the trustworthy rule by which the boundaries of scriptural teaching could be marked out.

Today we live amid a flurry of well-publicized and desperate efforts to revive these heresies, which are attempts to give even the weirdest ideas the faint aroma of legitimacy. Speculating scholars have gained doting press attention by focusing on long-rejected ideas, claims, and their documents. It has become a profitable media game to defend the poor heretics against the oppressive winners and elitists who wrote the rules of orthodoxy.

The truth is the opposite: the most elitist of all false claimants to Christian truth were the gnostics, who were contemptuous of the naïve consensus of uninformed believers and were never even interested in gaining the hearts of ordinary believers. Yet these ordinary believers could easily see that these later speculations did not match the authenticity and beauty and clarity of the original apostolic witnesses.

The creed is a window into the earliest Christian reflection on the most decisive points of saving faith. The Triune God, the saving work of Christ, and the power of the Holy Spirit in church and ministry are not optional but required points of classic teaching commonly assumed among these living communities of Christian worship in vastly different cultures and centuries.

The Patrimony of the One Body

This tradition is the rightful patrimony of all global Christians today, whether Protestant, Orthodox, Catholic, or charismatic. It rings true because it radiates the light of the Spirit and the warmth of divine grace.

How are such varied Christians able to find common dogmatic inspiration in the ancient rule of faith? Why are these texts and extracts so intrinsically ecumenical, so broadly catholic in their cultural range? Because all modern ecclesial traditions have an equal right to the truth borne by the earliest apostolic teaching. All of these traditions can, without a sacrifice of intellect, draw modestly together to ponder the texts most common to them all. These classic texts have decisively shaped the wider subsequent history of doctrine in global Christianity in all centuries.

Hence, Protestants are recognizing the scriptural faithfulness of the pre-Lutheran fathers, while charismatics are being reawakened by the Spirit of the ancients. Catholics are owning their premodern sources once again, and Orthodox are rejoicing with the glory of these belated recognitions. Cyril is not owned by Alexandria, nor Gregory by Rome. All believers have a right to all the most faithful consensual teachers of God's revelation. These influential minds are the common possession of the whole church: African, Asian, European, and elsewhere.

The Core Patristic Conciliar Tradition Welcomed within the Classic Reformation

This tradition of general lay consent continued and was received in the Reformation by the repeated acceptance of the three creeds: Apostles', Nicene, and Athanasian (*Quicunque vult*) as evidenced in the Augsburg Apology, the Smalcald Articles, Melanchthon's Thesis of 1551 (The Three Chief Symbols, *BOC*:17–23), and the Thirty-Nine Articles. "The three creeds, Nicene Creed, Athanasian Creed, and that which is commonly called the Apostles' Creed, ought thoroughly to be received and believed; for they may be proved by most certain warrants of holy Scripture" (Thirty-Nine Articles, 8).

Melanchthon followed the earlier Reformers in arguing that Protestant teaching was grounded in a genuinely "Catholic association, which embraces the common consensus of prophetic and apostolic doctrine, together with the belief of the true church. Thus in our Confession we profess to embrace the whole doctrine of the word of God, to which the church bears testimony, and that in the sense which the symbols show" (*CR* 24.398). He condemned as novel whatever might clash with the most ancient consensual symbols of the church (*symbola accepta*; *Loci Communes* 19.19–20).

Defining Evangelical Confession of the One Faith

Five years ago, J. I. Packer and I compiled a topically arranged volume of extracts selected from the most widely quoted evangelical statements of faith produced internationally since 1950.[6] I remain indebted to the incomparable J. I. Packer and to the wisdom and gentleness he brought to defining the evangelical consensus.

Theologically, the roots of modern evangelicalism go back much further than its nineteenth-century identity name would suggest. Evangelicals build upon the same foundation as the apostles and fathers. This received tradition embraces: (1) the trinitarian, incarnational, and socially transforming consensus realized in the classical Christian patristic period; and (2) the consensus of the Magisterial Reformation on biblical authority and justification by faith only, through grace only, in the work of Christ alone.

As denominations wilt and inventive theology grows ever more wildly eccentric, the unifying force of the core apostolic tradition is gradually increasing. Put simply: those united by their personal relation to Jesus Christ are discovering each other.

"Once for All Delivered": Binding the Generations

The Ecumenical Council's Authority Grounded in General Lay Consent

The authority of the ecumenical councils is grounded in general lay consent under the guidance of the Spirit based on the canonical written Word. What makes the general councils reliable is the presence of the Holy Spirit assisting in the interpretation of the apostolic witness at the depths of conscience and common sense.

The ecumenical council that gathered at Chalcedon declared its intention to "make no new exposition" but merely to take away all haziness by defining clearly the consent of the whole church in a "united exposition and doctrine"— "further than this we can say nothing. . . . This is the orthodox faith; this we all believe; into this we were baptized, into this we baptize" (Ecumenical Council, Chalcedon, Session 2, *NPNF*[2] 14:248–49).

The councils were pledged to "not move the ancient landmark that your fathers have set" (Prov. 22:28). For it was not merely human ingenuity that spoke in the councils but "the Spirit himself of God" confirmed by general lay consent (Third Ecumenical Council, Ephesus, *Letter of Cyril to John of Antioch, NPNF*[2] 14:253). Since Gregory the Great, this formula has been widely received: those are orthodox (i.e., consensually acknowledged ecumenically) who gratefully receive what the ecumenical councils received and reject what they rejected (Gregory I, *Letters* 1.25; 5.51–54; 6.66).

Since the ancient ecumenical councils were "constituted by universal consent, one who rejects them does not overthrow them but himself" (Gregory I,

Letters 1.25, *NPNF*[2] 12:82). At the time of Gregory's writing, there had been only four synods of general lay consent, which he summarized so concisely that it has become a standard formula: "The Nicene, in which Arius, the Constantinopolitan, in which Macedonius, the First Ephesian, in which Nestorius, and the Chalcedonian, in which Eutyches and Dioscorus, were condemned" (Gregory I, *Letters* 4.38, *NPNF*[2] 12:159). Boundaries are necessary if faith is to be valued over against its counterfeit currencies.

The Transgenerational Community and the New Ecumenism

The unity of believers is not limited to contemporary voices. In this *consensus fidelium* are voices from all cultural histories, all continents, and all languages—not just modern westerners north of the equator. The confessing and renewing and charismatic movements are being drawn back toward this classic consensus of faith. This consensus is enabling an emerging new configuration of the one body of Christ. These movements are being given life not for boasting or dialogue but for repentance and witness.

The new ecumenism is not an organization but an emerging spirit. It is not a new institution but a burgeoning convergence of consciousness that echoes the unifying work of the Spirit.

Modern evangelicals are maturing in their awareness of ancient ecumenical history, exegesis, and doctrine. Worldwide believers are becoming more familiar with evangelical commitments, vocabulary, and values. The orthodox are reviving, while the revivalists are becoming more orthodox. The Catholics are becoming more Spirit-led, while the charismatics are becoming more catholic. It may appear to be nothing more than a cloud the size of a person's hand (to use a biblical metaphor), but it is gathering steadily to burst out in the latter rain.

Many of those who once looked unavailingly to the modern ecumenical movement for an expression of unity in the body of Christ have become disillusioned. Out of the pain of these illusions, they are now looking toward ancient ecumenism for contemporary wisdom. They see noble figures of the Reformation tradition such as Luther, Calvin, Cranmer, and Wesley as expressions of the Great Tradition stemming from the apostolic witness of the early church.

The Unity of Apostolic Consensus in the First Generation

The apostles themselves had a fully formed and sufficient vision of the Lord's teaching. But that did not prevent Peter and Paul from earnest debate on Jewish legal practices, which led directly to a further-refined consensus. Tensions of culture and language between the proclamations of Mark and John and between James and Paul have required all subsequent adherents of apostolic teaching to search for their common ground. Their personal styles did not mark fundamental doctrinal differences. The apostles were firmly convinced that the Spirit was uniting them in a common faith, not divergent doctrines as so often interpreted (John 17:20–26; Cyprian, *Dom. or.* 30).

It was not the unique or peculiar features of any one apostle's teaching that defined the consensus; rather, the consensus emerged out of the Spirit-led recollections of eyewitnesses as their faith was embraced in a convergence. Apostolic consensus did not develop out of a democratic groupthink process that groped after the most imaginative solutions to human problems. Instead, it lived out of the worshiping community that wholeheartedly consented to the Lord's teaching under the guidance of the Spirit.

Lay Consent a Protestant Principle

The ancient principle of general lay consent is firmly embedded in the confessions of the Protestant Reformation. Augsburg cautioned against ecclesial burdens "introduced contrary to the custom of the universal Christian church" (Augsburg, *BOC* 105).

The objection of the Reformers to medieval Catholicism was not that it had grown too old, but that it was much too new and mistakenly innovative. It had invented "an unprecedented novelty" in relation to apostolic testimony. Sadly, the novelty was introduced precisely through leaders appointed to guard the tradition, who, "under pretext of the power given them by Christ, have not only introduced new forms of worship and burdened consciences with reserved cases and violent use of the ban, but have also presumed to set up and depose kings" (Augsburg, *CC* 98).

The congregational tradition more directly assumed a due process of lay consent that is entered into "not only expressly by word of mouth, but by sacrifice," with or without taking the written form of confessions (Cambridge Platform, *CC* 391). The Baptist consensual statement of 1925 argued that Baptist statements of faith "constitute a consensus of opinion of some Baptist body, large or small, for the general instruction and guidance of our own people and others concerning those articles of the Christian faith which are most surely held among us. They are not intended to add anything to the simple conditions of salvation revealed in the New Testament" and are "not to be used to hamper freedom of thought or investigation" (*CC* 345).

The Whole Laity through Time Is the Consenting Community: Multigenerational Consent

General consent is transmitted through many generations. Hence, it is intrinsically multigenerational. That differs from modern notions of experiential consent epitomized by Schleiermacher, in which consent depends primarily upon contemporary feelings of individuals now. This tends to demean reasoned voices of the past generations.

When a consensual council or regional synod seeks to clarify or better articulate the faith once for all delivered to the saints, in effect it is proposing an interpretation to the remembering church and humbly asking the church of subsequent generations for steady confirmation of that interpretation, not as if it were new, but on the assumption that it is apostolic. A local or regional body may contribute to the attempt to define the larger consensual ecumenical teaching, but not without the subsequent intergenerational consent of the whole church.

Yet no one should assume that absolute unanimity is required for ecumenical consent; otherwise, no question would ever be closed, and a single heretic or tiny cadre of objectors would be an absolute obstacle to ecumenical teaching and unity in Christ.

Durable Consensus Is Recognized Only within Longer Time Frames

The deposit of apostolic teaching does not change with time. Since reporting on a once-for-all event, it is not subject to revision. No one adds or subtracts from it (Rev. 22:18–19). The risen Lord, who is always the same, meets us within our changing times. It is not he whom time changes, but he who changes time. Thus, the one message—always one and the same truth and way and life in every age—is capable of responsive hearing amid the ever-changing flow of human language.

The laity is stretched out over twenty centuries and is still growing. It seems at first glance that this longevity encompasses too many cultures to pretend that any viable consensus exists among believers. But this is the unmistakable miracle: there is a consensus. It can be seen only through large portions of time. So those who see only small hunks of time, like the present, are likely to miss it altogether. It is a picture that can be seen only through a historical lens.

Meanwhile, general consensus is often misunderstood as absolute unanimity. Whatever occurs in history is imperfect. The church occurs in history, so its consent is always imperfect. Perfectionistic views of absolute consensus always fail to grasp the need for daily repentance. Exaggerated hopes prevent the recognition of rough-hewn, durable forms of working consensus that have been articulated repeatedly and lived out culturally.

These consensual achievements are known because they have a conspicuous textual history of authority in the worshiping community. Consensus is already a fact. What we have not adequately explained is why that fact is so persistent and yet so ignored by historians. It is a datum hard to see if you have blinders on or glasses that filter out the brilliance of its radiance.

Self-assertive human beings are always going to be tempted to use an alleged consensus as a ploy for power rather than as a servant of the truth. So the history of Christianity exposes many attempts to use a true consensus falsely, to use it instrumentally for special interests or class privilege. Yet even these attempts must stand the test of general lay consent over long stretches of time.

Many Mansions

Within the vast historic archive of orthodox teaching, there are many colors of permissible interpretation. There is plenty of room for these and more, provided the *regula fidei* is not neglected. Consensus clarification is not looking for a single interpretation that would bind up the written Word and make the Spirit strictly subservient to a passing culture or economic class or political bias. It is interested in offering life.

No statement of the unity of Christian teaching is unchallengeable. But every challenge to date has failed to erase the core of Christian confession.

It is a fact that people keep on being baptized, even when they only partially grasp the full meaning of their baptism. The Spirit is giving them time to learn. Yet whenever the faithful lift up their Spirit-led unity in praise, someone is always there to try to shoot it down. Some detractors appear to have a holy calling to expose all the weaknesses and limitations of the emerging classic Christian consensus. Others want to make some political use of it that is not consistent or confirmable within the consensual texts themselves.

Is the laity to conclude that because we do not see a fully formed consensus on every disputed question (e.g., omniscience or millennialism), we must be silent about it? My view is that we can and must say something, even though we need not try to say everything. The modest effort of this compendium runs many risks in the attempt to speak for the historic worshiping community. But the greater risk is to make no attempt at all.

Paul instructed Timothy to guard what had been committed to him (1 Tim. 6:20). Vincent commented that Christian teaching consists in "what you have received, not what you have thought up; a matter not of ingenuity, but of doctrine; not of private acquisition, but of public Tradition; a matter brought to you, not put forth by you, in which you must be not the author but the guardian, not the founder but the sharer, not the leader, but the follower." The *ekklesia* is not seeking to discover a new word for each culture but to proclaim the truth of the most primitive gospel ever anew, so that "by your expounding it, may that now be understood more clearly which formerly was believed even in its obscurity" (Vincent of Lérins, *Comm.* 22.27, *LTCF* 27). It is tampering with evidence to pretend to improve upon apostolic testimony itself, although our perceptions of the apostolic witness may improve or worsen.

This does not imply that there can be no progress in church teaching. Vincent argued that there is progress, but true progress is not change. True progress is an advance in understanding of that which has been given fully in the deposit of faith (Vincent of Lérins, *Comm.* 23.28). The inner cohesion of the witness of the Spirit does not wait or depend on our analysis. Our analysis can only confirm it, not create it. You know what you have seen, beheld, heard, and been addressed by. No one can take that from you.

Lowercase-c *catholic* as a description of Christian faith means "according to the whole" (Greek, *holos*), and the biblically proper reason for applying the

term to the church, or any part of it, is that the wholeness and fullness of the
biblical revelation of God's truth are faithfully held within it. The witness of
the Holy Spirit is integral to catholic faith; hence, the perception of evangelical
consensus—that is, of the integrated message of the Bible—is basic to catholic
identity. The evangelical consensus claims catholicity as being essentially an
integrated, organic grasp of the biblical vision of God and godly living.

Evangelical Christians are those who read the Bible as God's own Word,
addressed personally to each of us here and now. To embrace the evangelical
life is to live out of a personal trust in, and love for, Jesus Christ as Lord and
Savior. The evangelical confidence is that anyone who engages seriously with
the Bible, humbly asking God for light, will duly share the sight of what mil-
lions of Christians from the beginning have been privileged to see.

Let us pray with Jerome:

> Lord you have promised
> that in your kingdom all are equal
> from least to greatest
> but how can there be a lesser or greater if all are equal?
> we give you thanks because the blessed secret is disclosed
> by One who incarnated it:
> whoever shall do and teach shall be great
> whoever shall teach and not do shall be least
> we rejoice that all shall know you, as written,
> from the least of them to the greatest.
> We come to know ourselves
> by knowing ourselves in you
> as you bind all together
> by yielding to share our weakness.
> Amen.
>
> Adapted from Jerome, *Jov.* 2.27[7]

2

The Gospel Promised by the Prophets

The Trinity and the Old Testament

MARK S. GIGNILLIAT

Introduction

The Old Testament has been a—if not *the*—major battleground for Christian theology since the church's inception. Every first-year church history student is introduced to the name Marcion as the first major heretic in the early church. What is of note with Marcion is the kind of heretical aberrancy we find him espousing. Marcion saw radical discontinuity between the God of the New Testament, identified with the person Jesus Christ, and the Old Testament's lowercase-g *god*. In fact, Marcion's major work, *Antithesis*, is a series of exegetical arguments in which he places New Testament texts alongside Old Testament texts in order to show the striking difference between the two in their portrayal of God.[1] How could the god of the Old Testament, whose involvement in the messiness and physicality of Israel's history, have anything to do with Jesus Christ, whose spiritual pureness and otherness seems so markedly contrasted with the former? One is left with Paul, who alone understands the gospel, and an edited Luke.

Such theological sentiments, rooted philosophically in a form of gnostic dualism, drew fire from some of the early church's most well-known theologians.[2] Tertullian's response to Marcion is entitled *Contra Marcion*. Marcion uses the knife to exegete Scripture, complains Tertullian. Marcion receives his lashes from Irenaeus in his *Adversus Haereses*. Irenaeus describes Marcion's editorial exegesis as "the most daring blasphemy against Him who is proclaimed as God by the law and the prophets." Marcion, again according to Irenaeus, "mutilates the gospel." He "dares to mutilate the Scriptures." He is an instrument of Satan, and because he is so, "I purpose specially to refute him."[3] How is it that Irenaeus will seek to refute Marcion? On the basis of Marcion's own claims and Irenaeus's exegesis of Scripture. Despite Harnack's overreaching claim that the early church's theological discourse fell prey to alien forms of Greek metaphysical categories and, in turn, destroyed the purity of the apostolic age, one observes that these ante-Nicene fathers' struggle for trinitarian grammar takes place in the context of the exegesis of Scripture (and by Scripture, I mean primarily the Old Testament). To put the matter simply, theology for the early church (and for us too!) *is* exegesis.

Marcion's ghost continues to haunt the church; despite being dead, he unfortunately still speaks. Schleiermacher, of course, denigrated the role of the Old Testament and suggested its excision from the Christian canon. Harnack, in his famous work on Marcion, applauds the early church's efforts to silence Marcion, while in the same breath says that it is merely a weakness of knee that keeps modern Protestant Christians—those of us come of age—from removing the Old Testament's canonical status. Even those Christians who identify themselves as evangelicals today fall prey to neo-Marcionite tendencies. This does not happen in the confessional line of our thought; we would all affirm the inspiration of both the Old and New Testaments. It happens de facto as one looks at our preaching practices. Why preach the Old Testament when the New Testament is so much easier to handle? In light of the preceding, maybe Gunneweg's claim is not an overstatement: "Indeed, it would be no exaggeration to understand the hermeneutical problem of the Old Testament as the problem of Christian theology, and not just one problem among others, seeing that all the other questions of theology are affected in one way or another by its resolution."[4] In other words, the struggle to identify the God we worship and name is a struggle to understand what the fathers called the "mind" (*dianoia*) of Scripture. Trinitarian theology is first and foremost exegetical theology.

The early church's struggle for trinitarian grammar is, in large measure, the early church's struggle to come to grips with two confessional beliefs. First, the apostles and their early progeny assumed the canonical givenness of the Old Testament as their Scriptures. As Hans von Campenhausen so helpfully articulates, "Christ is certainly vindicated to unbelievers out of the Scriptures; but the converse necessity, to justify the Scriptures on the authority of Christ, is as yet nowhere even envisaged."[5] For the apostles and figures such as Ignatius, Clement of Rome, Justin Martyr, and Irenaeus, the Old Testament's canonical status is never called into question. It is assumed. And this is despite the complexities of the canonical formation of the Old Testament in its pre-Masoretic form and the role of the Septuagint as translation.[6] The Scriptures of Israel are received in the form delivered to the church, even if in translation, and are not redacted to suit the church's theological purposes.[7] There are no Septuagint recensions of Isaiah 52:13 that say, "Behold my servant, Jesus Christ." They receive the Old Testament and allow its own wording, in light of the rule of faith (more on this later), to function straightforwardly as Christian Scripture. There is no impulse in the early church to justify the canonical status of Israel's Scripture—which brings us to the second confessional position.

The church also confesses that the God of Israel's identity is bound up with the person and work of Jesus Christ and the Holy Spirit who attests to his work. An eschatological or apocalyptic element to the early church's exegesis of Scripture works in dialectical and mutually informing relationship with the Old Testament's given status. In other words, there is a revelatory dimension at work for the apostles in their understanding of Jesus's identity as Son of God and partaker in YHWH's identity. Paul says in Romans 1 that Jesus Christ is authenticated as Son of God in the resurrection. I take this to be an eschatological or apocalyptic claim from Paul. Jesus's identity as Son of God receives its justification, not its actualization, in the resurrection from the dead. We now, by the illumination of the Spirit, see more clearly. Or to paraphrase Hebrews 1:1: he spoke in various ways in the Old Testament economy, but now his definitive Word is Jesus Christ. Because of this, a fuller understanding of God's identity is more readily available, and this understanding does not supersede YHWH in the Old Testament. Rather, it demands that the identity of YHWH be understood in essential relationship to Jesus Christ—Abraham and the prophets yearned to see this day.

Essential for our understanding of the matter is differentiating noetic reception of revelation in a given moment in the divine economy from the ontology or identity of the divine being that precedes that given moment. The revelation that God's identity—that which is unique to God that allows us to characterize him in the plot of Scripture as *this* God as opposed to something else—and Jesus's identity coinhere has noetic implications in the divine economy. Something new is being revealed. But the newness of the revelation that has to do with Jesus Christ is revelatory of something antecedent or prior to that economic moment. As the older Reformed theologians understood the matter, the Logos is either on the way to "incarnation" (*incarnandus*) or "is incarnate" (*incarnatus*).[8] In either case, the identity of the second person of the Trinity is bound to the concrete expression of the incarnation in the man, Jesus of Nazareth. The triune identity of Israel's God, YHWH, ontologically precedes the full noetic reception of this revelation in the concrete moment of Jesus of Nazareth's history (and the written, apostolic testimony that witnesses sufficiently and authoritatively to his history). Suffice it to say that at this moment, this ontological confession—the Logos precedes the Old Testament—provided the warrant for the early church to do a trinitarian or christological reading of the Old Testament in ways that strike modern readers of Scripture as naïve.[9]

The Rule of Faith and the Mind of Scripture

This particular aspect of the early church's confession is exemplified in its appeal to a *regula fidei*, or "rule of faith." Precisely here one begins to see the dialectical relationship between the assumed canonical character of Israel's Scripture and the church's confession that Jesus Christ is part of the divine identity of Israel's God. In the exegetical arguments of the early church, it was not enough to have one's proof texts here or there. Every heretic had a bit of raw exegesis on his side—for example, Arius's claim that Proverbs 8:22 provides scriptural warrant for the creation of the Son. What one needs in order to put together properly the various canonical voices is a rulebook, a guide to help one understand the mind of Scripture.[10] Irenaeus uses the image of a guide given to those who purchase a mosaic from a foreign land. It is not enough to have the various colored tiles at one's disposal; one also needs a guidebook on how to put the tiles together so that the resulting picture is of a fish and not of an elephant.[11] In short, when interpreting particular passages, one must be sensitive to the overarching mind of the Scripture's total witness, and the rule of faith (or canon of truth) provides the correct context (*hypothesis*) for reading Scripture.[12]

The rule of faith was exactly this guide in the ante-Nicene period before the final stabilization of the New Testament in the canonical shape in which we have received it. After the recognition of the Scriptures as a two-testament canon composed of both an Old and a New Testament, which respectively share a common subject matter, the two-testament canon itself becomes this rule of faith, along with other ecclesial commitments that understand the Bible's particular place inside the church and the necessary reading virtues that come from this ecclesial placement. "Those who are situated outside the church are not able to acquire any understanding of the divine discourse," says Hilary of Poitiers.[13]

For our purposes, it is important to see how the rule of faith, an early trinitarian formulation that might look something like the Apostles' Creed, functions hermeneutically when it came to intratextual matters. Again, it provides the correct hypothesis for understanding the mind of Scripture.[14] Even this formulation is a bit too sloppy, for it does not take into account the nature of the rule as something itself born out of the mind of Scripture.[15]

In David Yeago's terminology, the rule of faith is a concept that receives its "pressure" from an intratextual judgment.[16] Terms such as *Trinity* or *homoousias* may not be found in the Bible, but their substance surely is. Or, as in Georges Florovsky's sentiment, "Tradition [for the early church] is Scripture properly understood."[17]

Frances Young demonstrates that the impulse to use language other than the Bible's to express theological content has its root in ancient rhetorical theory and pedagogy. These acts of *hermeneia* assumed that the same thing could be expressed in a multitude of ways.[18] Moreover, is this not what theology is: a wrestling with Scripture, in the context of the church's tradition, with language and grammar other than a mere repetition of what the Bible says? Theology is an act of application. Theology is a struggle to understand Scripture and speak in our own idiom. Or in Barth's terminology, Christian dogmatics is not saying what the apostles and the prophets said. Rather, it is saying what we should say on the basis of what the apostles and prophets said.[19]

Here is the interplay between a norming canon, confession, and the rules that help govern how we understand the canon's continuing "over against" status. In other words, there is a bit of circularity going on here. How does one read the Old Testament in a trinitarian fashion? Answer: via the governing constraint of the rule of faith. Well, then where does one get the rule of faith? Answer: the rule of faith comes from the Scriptures of Israel, in conjunction with the apostolic faith delivered unto the church. This circularity is necessary, because it takes into account both the givenness of the Old Testament as the church's Scripture and the significance of God's revelation of himself in Jesus Christ handed down in the apostolic faith.

But let it be stated that for someone like Irenaeus, this is not just a hermeneutical shell game in which meaning is found only in the mind of the reader. If so, the triune character of God's identity in the Old Testament is an alien imposition onto the text. Rather, for Irenaeus, this confessional posture has ontological significance—so much so, in fact, that now, in light of the revelation given to the apostles, one cannot read the Old Testament as anything other than the voice of anticipation preparing the way for Jesus Christ. Or as Gerhard Sauter states, "Faith does not work like a pair of glasses, however, that allows us to decode the text; glasses can be taken on and off. Faith, on the other hand, is constitutive, like the retina, which makes sight possible in the first place but can only cast an image of what is real!"[20] God's revelation of himself in Jesus Christ provides sight in an otherwise opaque landscape.

For Irenaeus, the Logos precedes the Old Testament. Even more than this, one sees the second person of the Trinity, the Logos who in time will be known by the name Jesus Christ, as fully operative, though in veiled form, in the Old Testament economy as well.[21] In this sense Childs is correct to state, "The church's struggle with the Trinity was not a battle *against* the Old Testament, but rather a battle *for* the Old Testament, for the one eternal covenant of God in both unity and diversity."[22] With the resurrection of Jesus as vindication for his powerful claim in John 11:25 ("I am the resurrection and the life"), we understand more fully the profoundness of Jesus's life, his *ego eimi*, as that which flows from his own participation in the eternal being of God himself.[23] The Son precedes the Old Testament, and the plurality of persons within the Christian's monotheistic claim is no *novum* in the eternal identity of God. In the language of Colossians 1:17, καὶ αὐτός ἐστιν πρὸ πάντων (He is before all things).[24]

Revelation and the Historical-Critical Instinct

Such theologically driven hermeneutical instincts began to unravel in the period we refer to as the Enlightenment, or modernity. There were exegetical debates before this period, to be sure; one thinks of the difference between Luther and Calvin regarding the *proto-euangelion* (Gen. 3.15, the first Gospel). But these exegetical debates all took place within a theological framework that assumed the Old Testament and the New Testament shared a common subject matter—namely, God's triune revelation of himself in the person and work of Jesus Christ. Indeed, the execution of these instincts on the ground may differ markedly, but the framework, or "family resemblance," as Childs calls it, does not.

With figures like Spinoza in the seventeenth century, this hermeneutical framework gave way to an overly historicist sensibility that locked the meaning of Scripture into the original situation out of which it arose. Now the literal sense of Scripture becomes conflated with the historical sense, whereas before this period, again allowing for differences in exegetical execution, the Old and New Testaments were understood to be within the one divine economy of God. Appeals to the literal sense of Scripture assumed this theological starting point. Therefore, appeals to "contextual exegesis" within a Christian framework of reading demand that the divine economy itself be a constitutive aspect of the text's context.[25] Again, it is the rule of faith that gives shape and scope to the nature of this divine economy as a redemptive *ad extra* move toward humanity by the Father, Son, and Holy Spirit.

With the historical-critical instincts that one finds in figures like Spinoza and that is worked out more fully in people like De Wette, Vatke, Wellhausen, and Gunkel, the Scriptures now morph into a *source* for critical retrieval—*historie* as subsumed under the canons of positivism or religious-historical experientalism—rather than a *witness* to the Triune God. The Bible is something to be worked through in order to arrive at the original situation, dismissing the ongoing revelatory status of the text. It is nearly impossible to overemphasize the negative effect that the reduction of the "literal sense of Scripture" to the "historical sense" (*historia Scripturae* or *sensus historicus*) has had on Christian exegesis. Or, maybe to rephrase a bit more clearly, the reduction of the Bible's historical character to that of immediacy or proximity to the events themselves, with no recourse to the eschatological ordering of history within God's divine and redemptive economy, is problematic.[26] Again, with the Reformers, I think Christian readers of the Bible should assume the veracity of the historical events to which the Bible refers.[27] But the reduction of the text's meaning to the eventfulness of the historical event, or to the proximity to that event stripped of its substance, is a hermeneutical instinct that awaits a figure like Spinoza when the canonical function of the Scriptures is neutered.[28]

Spinoza is especially important here, but not because he is the first to raise critical issues regarding the Bible. One sees historical-critical sensibilities already at work in Thomas Hobbes's *Leviathan* and the writings of French Catholic La Preyère, both of whom precede Spinoza.[29] What makes Spinoza so fascinating is his bold and bald application of a Cartesian philosophical framework to theology and especially to biblical studies. Even Descartes did not do such a thing—or at least did not think he was doing so. Now with Spinoza, the natural light of reason, located in the philosophical disciplines, is where *truth* is to be found. But truth has nothing to do with the meaning of the text. The meaning of the text is what the prophets, with all their imaginative and intellectually suspect rhetoric at work, said to the original hearers. Biblical meaning and truth are divorced from one another in such a way that theology and philosophy must be kept as distinct disciplines.

For example, in the biblical study of the prophets, we find an emphasis on the moral virtues of charity and justice. That is it for Spinoza. The miracles recounted there, an accommodation to simple minds, and all the claims about God and the law are understood to be specific to that situation and have no binding metaphysical or theological relevance. These elements can be dismissed on certain assumptions about natural law and a deistically governed universe. The prophets are about justice and charity: that is all we can take from them. Any metaphysical claims about reality, providence, and how God orders our knowing is off-limits to biblical studies. Truth is now a philosophical matter, as the mind becomes the final arbiter on philosophical matters.

The major point here—and I believe this is the fundamental difference between the critical and precritical world—is that revelation plays the constitutive and necessarily basic role in our understanding of the Bible, both in its witnessing capacity and historical ordering. As Karl Barth famously stated, "Revelation is not a predicate of history, but history is a predicate of revelation." Revelation governs our understanding of history; history does not govern our understanding of revelation. It is the Christian confession that God speaks, and that his spoken revealed word, orders and shapes our understanding of history via a christological or trinitarian lens.

If one affirms Barth's formulation, then our hermeneutical approach to identifying Israel's God, witnessed to in the Old Testament, cannot be governed by a general hermeneutic adopted across the humanities. By that hermeneutic, in the words of Benjamin Jowett, we would "read the Bible like any other book."[30] If theological hermeneutics—as we see on the ground in the New Testament's own reading of the Old Testament and in figures as diverse as Irenaeus, Aquinas, Luther, Calvin, and Barth across large swaths of the church's history—is to be substantially Christian, then it must take an approach to the subject matter that is consonant with it. Those familiar with the theological science of T. F. Torrance will be familiar with such language. For theology to be scientific requires that the approach to the subject matter be taken in light of that subject, namely, the Logos.[31] Again, we are immediately back into the world of confession, or confession governed by our belief that God has spoken and is speaking in the words of the prophets and the apostles, with the concreteness of this Word being Jesus Christ (John 1:18). This is our confession regarding the ontology of the Bible as divine Word, which governs our understanding of the identity of God.

The Material Form of the Canon and Our Triune God

When we move to biblical theological reflection, which is something other than the way the New Testament reads the Old Testament or various forms of *Heilsgeschichte* (the history of salvation), we now have to wrestle with the way the material form of the canon governs our understanding of the identity of the one God with whom we have to do. How do the Old Testament and New Testament, in their discrete yet mutually informing voices, witness to the one God Christians name as Father, Son, and Holy Spirit? What do we learn about God in the discrete witness of the Old Testament and in the discrete voice of the New Testament? Our task in this essay is to seek answers in relation to the Old Testament itself, although assumptions about the New Testament's construal of the matter will obviously be present.

YHWH Demands Total Allegiance

Many things could and should be said here, but I will limit my discussion to three matters with the Old Testament. First of all, we learn that Israel's God, whose name is YHWH, is to be worshiped alone. He does not share his glory with another. We all know the Shema[32] well: "Hear, O Israel: The LORD our God, the LORD is One" (Deut. 6:4). This does not lead us into the debate over whether or not monotheism meant that early Israel did not believe there were any other gods or deities—that is a different matter.[33] What we do know is that YHWH did not share his glory with any other and demanded total allegiance. In fact, one could read the entirety of Israel's history as a loggerhead encounter with this claim from its God. We read in Isaiah 45:5, "I am the LORD [YHWH], and there is no other."

YHWH Carries a Salvific Identity

Secondly, we understand from the canonical shape of the Old Testament that the revelation of the divine name so closely tied to Moses's burning-bush encounter demands that we understand the divine name in the context of God's salvific movement toward his people and ultimately the nations. This is where I will part company with Karl Barth. For Barth, the revelation of the divine name in Exodus 3 is, in effect, an attempt at divine veiledness. "I am who I am" is a no-name. It is an intentional veiling of the divine identity that may unfortunately be wrapped up in a Hegelian move toward the New Testament that nullifies the significance that the God we worship as Christians is YHWH. Here I part with Barth because I think, with Childs and others, the proper reading of the Hebrew אהיה אשר אהיה is "I am who I will be" or "I will be who I will be."[34]

The claim made by the divine voice speaking to Moses is not an appeal to the abstract category of being—as is the case with the rendering of the Septuagint (LXX) Ἐγώ εἰμι ὁ ὤν (Greek meaning "I am")—but is an appeal to the revelation of the divine identity within the narrative trajectory of Israel's history with God. Moreover, this plot in the divine economy is represented faithfully in the narratives of the Old Testament.[35]

I am who I will be. My nature is not a static being but is revealed in my acts of redemption. I am who you will see me to be when I raise you, Israel, from the dead; when I move past you, in the language of Ezekiel, and tell you as you gasp in your own afterbirth under the grueling regime of Pharoah to live. And not only do I make you live, I make you my wife (see Ezek. 16). *I am who I will be. I am the Creator, whose unique act of creation is organically linked with redemption in the Old Testament's idiom* (see Isa. 43:1). *As I created the world out of nothing, so too, will I create you, Israel, out of nothing. In the language of the prophets, I am the one who will re-create you despite the reign of sin in your midst. I am, which assumes being and anteriority and otherness, and my being is narratively identified. You will know me because I am your God, and I redeem my people as I move toward them in loving acts of judgment and loving acts of salvation.*

In Neil MacDonald's helpful formulation, YHWH's narrative identity in the Old Testament is a judging yet desisting and forbearing self.[36] The identity of YHWH in the Old Testament is a salvific identity. At once one recognizes that the Bible's formulation of the identity of God does not allow us to separate God's being from his acts. His being and his acts mutually inform one another as we seek to identify who God is. In other words, *who* questions, regarding the identity of God, should feed into *what* questions, having to do with God's nature. By natural extension to the New Testament, it should not surprise us when God reveals himself in the person and work of Jesus Christ to see a similar dynamic at play. For example, in John 1, Jesus is described as the λόγος (Word), who was with God in the beginning and actually is God. Within the same chapter, the λόγος is described by John the Baptist as the Lamb of God who takes away the sins of the world. It is within the nature of God to identify himself in his redemption movement toward his people. He did so with Israel; he did so with Jesus.

YHWH Holds a Trinitarian Plurality

Finally, what we learn from the Old Testament regarding the divine identity is that within the oneness of God, a plurality of otherness is already seen. Or YHWH demonstrates his presence often by something other that can still be identified as YHWH. Here mention must be made of Richard Bauckham's very important work on this subject, *Jesus and the God of Israel*. Bauckham has carefully shown that the philosophical world of the Greeks did not have a conceptual apparatus ready-made for trinitarian logic (à la Harnack). In fact, the dynamic of the oneness of God within a plurality of otherness is something that the Old Testament itself anticipates. Again, the language of "pressure" should be applied to the central role the Old Testament plays in our trinitarian formulations. A few examples should suffice.

The angel of YHWH (*mal'akh YHWH*) is understood in different ways within the Old Testament economy. To quote von Rad, "Again, the stories differ in the way in which they conceive of the relationship of the angel to Jahweh himself."[37] In certain cases, the angel of YHWH may be an ordinary angel sent with a divine mission; that is, the identity of the (angel) is distinct from YHWH himself (2 Sam. 24:16–18). In other instances, the angel of YHWH is more closely identified with the character of YHWH. To quote von Rad again, "The most interesting are those which are not really able to distinguish between Jahweh and his angel, and which therefore do not take the angel as only a messenger, but as a form of manifestation of Jahweh himself. The angel of Jahweh is Jahweh himself, appearing to human beings in human form."[38] Although von Rad does not use the language of narrative identity, one observes from the substance of von Rad's claim that the narrative descriptors and speaking voice of the angel of YHWH and YHWH *in se* (himself) bleed into one another.

For example, the angel of his presence in Isaiah 63:9 mediates the salvation of God to his people. Here the actual presence of the Lord is mediated to the people of God via this angelic figure.[39] Or one notes in the poetic structure of Genesis 18 a *locus classicus* (classic text) for Old Testament trinitarian reflection, that the direct speech of YHWH and the speech of the angelic mediator (the one addressed as *Adonai*) overlap in such a way that at times it is difficult to tell who is directly speaking to Abraham. When Abraham raises his sacrificial knife over his son in Genesis 22, the angel of YHWH stops Abraham. Then he speaks a second time and says, "By myself I have sworn, declares the LORD" (Gen. 22:16). The identity of YHWH and the identity of the messenger are entangled in such a way that they cannot be separated. One sees a similar dynamic in Judges 6:17–40 with God's encountering of Gideon. And Jacob's blessing in Genesis 48:15–16 uses the term angel (מלאך) in synonymous parallelism with God (אלהים). The angel is the particular means of God's redemption of Jacob and his sons. To quote von Rad once more, "The little hymn reaches the climax of its attempt to identify Jahweh in descriptive terms in the third title. Any idea that the 'angel' means a being subordinate to Jahweh is of course ruled out."[40]

Again, this is not an attempt to find Jesus under rocks and trees, nor is it a claim that the Old Testament authors had a fully developed trinitarian theology. One recalls the previous claim of the importance of making a proper distinction between God's being and noetic reception of God's triune identity within a given moment within the divine economy. God's triune identity precedes the full understanding of this dynamic. This is an attempt to see that the robustly monotheistic claims about the uniqueness of Israel's God, and the diversity within this unified monotheistic Creator/ Redeemer, are up and running in the Old Testament. Bavinck helpfully states, "So much is clear: that in the *Mal'akh Yahweh* who is preeminently worthy of that name, God (esp. his Word) is present in a very special sense. This is very evident from the fact that though distinct from Jehovah this Angel of Jehovah bears the same name, has the same power, effects the same deliverance, dispenses the same blessings, and is the object of the same adoration."[41] Though Bavinck does not use the language, what he is in effect appealing to is the overlap of narrative identity between the angel of YHWH and YHWH. Descriptors and actions unique to the one are being performed by the other.

Space does not allow a fuller exposition of this, but one could trace the unique roles the Word of the Lord (Ps. 33) and the Wisdom of the Lord (Prov. 3:19; 8:15; Ps. 104:14–15) play as agents and mediators of divine actions unique to YHWH himself. Similarly, arguments could be made about Ezekiel's vision of the one with the likeness of a man who inhabits the space unique to YHWH himself: his throne room. About this text, Robert Jenson asks the question, "Why does the second person of the Trinity, appearing above the throne in Ezekiel's vision, look like a man? Christian theology must answer: because the second person of the Trinity *is* a man—Jesus of Nazareth."[42] What other man, asks Jenson, can actually have the *kabod* (glory) of God? For the glory of the Lord is itself the manifestation of YHWH's presence that is identified with God himself even while the glory of the Lord performs a mediator role. Or what is the significance of the fact that Isaiah's servant in 52:13 is described as raised and exalted (ירום ונשא), which, as we see elsewhere in Isaiah (2:10–22; 6:1), are descriptors unique to YHWH himself? The servant and YHWH overlap in narrative identities. All of these texts witness to differentiation in unity within the divine identity.

Other aspects of the divine identity could be discussed here, and probably should be. What I think we observe, however, is the indispensable character of the Old Testament for trinitarian grammar. We would not have certain aspects of trinitarian thought without the Old Testament's constraining voice. And what these three issues in particular reveal is that trinitarian grammar, as it is born out of the Old Testament, does not have its source only in various proof texts here or there that might find Jesus hiding in nooks and crannies. It allows the Old Testament's own shape and discrete voice to play a governing role in our understanding of who God is; by necessity, the rule of faith located in the apostolic testimony demands that our understanding of Jesus be in accord with the Old Testament. Perhaps Brevard Childs says it best:

> The message of the Old Testament is not the same as that of the New. Prophecy is different from fulfillment. Yet in the light of God's full revelation in Jesus Christ, these ancient writings of Israel can now be understood, not only according to their original historical contexts, but also as the living Word of God testifying to the eternality of God as Father, Son, and Spirit. Thus, the church prays, as did Israel, with the words of the Psalter, but instinctively understands that the Lord, who is our shepherd (Ps. 23:1), is also the good shepherd of John 10:11. Like faithful Israel who awaited the salvation of its covenant God, we Christians also live in hopeful expectation of our redemption and that of "all Israel" with whom we will be finally united in God's time.[43]

How else are we to understand the character and identity of the self-same God who raised Israel from the dead and Jesus from the dead?[44]

Conclusion

In light of the preceding, let me make a few synthesizing comments regarding the theological exegesis of the Old Testament as Christian Scripture.

(1) We recognize that the Old Testament is not the New Testament; rather, its primary voice is that of anticipation. In Karl Barth's terms, the Old Testament is *die Zeit der Erwartung*. One must be careful not to confuse promise and fulfillment. The Old Testament's plain sense, however, now following the apocalyptic unveiling of Christ within the apostolic witness, can be extended figurally in light of the trinitarian identity of Israel's God. Here is the necessary retrospective reading of the prophets in light of the fullness of revelation. Again, one must distinguish between noetic reception within the divine economy and ontological identity before that moment of reception; "He is before all things" (Col. 1:17).

(2) Our confession, which is rooted in an Anselmian epistemology (belief precedes knowledge), allows for a dialectical and mutually informing relationship between the Old Testament's literal sense and the apostolic testimony

preserved in an ecclesial confession like the Nicene Creed. Or, more to the point of the material form of the canon as we now have it, the Old Testament and the New Testament mutually inform one another in dialectical relationship. Again, one recalls Augustine's very helpful formulation: the New is latent in the Old, and the Old is revealed in the New.

(3) The Nicene Creed is a witness to the fact that Christian dogmatics and preaching are ongoing necessities in the life of the church. In other words, there is no periscope within the New Testament that succinctly frames the issue like the Nicene Creed does. The language of Nicea is analogically related to the logic of the Scriptures, even though language not found in the Bible is found within Nicea.[45] In other words, the Scriptures do not deal with the specificity of every heretical or ethical aberration that threatens the church. Still, the Scriptures are the *norma normans* (Latin for "the ruling rule") in such struggles and demand careful attention and application to the church's current strife. In short, Christian dogmatics must be "in accord with the Scriptures." In this sense, historical theology is the history of the church's struggle to hear the Scriptures well. One begins to see the theological deficiency of hermeneutical formulations that make a distinction between meaning and significance, or between interpretation and application, or that limit authorial intentionality to the human *persona* (person) of the Scriptures with no dogmatic ordering of the Holy Spirit as *auctor primus* (primary author). The Nicene Creed in fact witnesses to the continuing demand for Christian dogmatics and preaching in the church as it seeks to order its life and thought under the authority of Scripture. As Karl Barth states, "To say that Jesus Christ rules the Church is equivalent to saying that Holy Scripture rules the Church. The one explains the other; the one can be understood only through the other."[46] Dogmatics and preaching governed by the authority of Scripture are organically related to the continued lordship of Christ over his church via his spoken and life-giving word.

(4) One final thought: what we learn from the apostolic era—and from the ante-Nicene period especially—is that the divine economy, or God's gracious revelation of himself in time and space culminating in the person and work of Jesus Christ, is in fact a constitutive aspect of the Old Testament's "context." Context, context, context are the three unbreakable rules of exegesis. I would concur—as long as within a confessional posture we allow the divine economy itself to be the governing contextual sphere for the Old Testament texts we read. In other words, it is not merely a move of application or an add-on at the end of Old Testament exegesis to ask how this text relates to the apocalyptic unveiling of Christ that in the fullness of time will make its mark on the anticipatory voice of the Old Testament. The gospel is the contextual sphere for a Christian reading of the Old Testament.

Question 25 of the Heidelberg Catechism asks: "'Since there is but one divine Being, why namest thou three, Father, Son and Holy Ghost?' *Answer:*

'Because that God hath thus revealed Himself in His Word, that these three distinct persons are the one true eternal God.'" In short, the struggle to name our God as Father, Son, and Holy Spirit, substantially correlated to one another in indivisible unity, is a struggle with the exegesis of Holy Scripture: our two-testament canon composed of both Old and New Testaments whose discrete voices share a common subject matter. May faithful readers of Scripture ever continue this struggle.

3

The Road to Nicea

The New Testament

⸌━⊹━⸍

Frank Thielman

In his highly regarded study of Arius, Rowan Williams makes the case that the disagreement between Arius and his opponents was not an argument about whether the god of the philosophers or the god of Abraham, Isaac, and Jacob was the Christian god. Everyone agreed that God was unchanging, unembodied, and self-sufficient. His nature was "unique and immaterial." The question Arius apparently tried to answer was how all this could be true, as he certainly believed it was, and yet his bishop, Alexander, could speak of the Son as "coming out of God" and sharing God's substance.[1]

Plato's Demiurge

The story of how the discussion of the relationship of Jesus to the one eternal God, Creator of the universe, reached this point, and the question of whether the Nicene Creed was and is really necessary, has to begin with Plato. The god of the philosophers that Williams says everyone on all sides took for granted was, to a large extent, Plato's god. There were critical differences between Plato's theology and the theology of the fourth-century church fathers, but the similarities are vital for understanding why the issues that led to the formulation of the Nicene Creed were thought to be problems. Plato's *Timaeus*, which describes the creation of the universe, exercised enormous influence in antiquity,[2] and in it Plato describes the demiurge—the God who crafted the universe—in the following terms:

- He is largely unknowable. Finding the maker of the universe is very difficult, and describing him to people is impossible (28c), so Timaeus can only come up with an account of God that is highly tentative, and can judge its merits only on the basis of whether it is not less likely than any other account of him (29c).
- God is everlasting, and when he gave birth to the universe, he gave it a nature that was as close to his own everlasting nature as possible. The universe, therefore, is eternal, but its eternity differs from God's own eternity. "It isn't possible," says Timaeus, "to bestow eternity fully upon anything that is begotten" (37d).[3]
- The universe God begat is itself "a blessed god" (34b), but a god with a body, intelligence, and a soul (30c–39e).
- The uncreated God also created other gods whom he instructed to imitate his creative work and produce human beings. Human beings were to be made so that they could feel sensations such as love, pleasure, pain, fear, and anger, and the purpose of these feelings was to test them to see whether they were just or unjust (42a–b). Sensation, then, was the province of humans, not of the uncreated God, and as Plato explicitly says in another dialogue, "It is not to be supposed that the gods feel either pleasure or its opposite" (*Phileb.* 33b).

To summarize, Plato understood the God who created the universe to be unknowable, eternal, and untouched by pleasure or pain. He created other gods, the most important of whom is the living universe. He did not directly create human beings, but created the gods who created human beings. He is, therefore, distant from their world of love, pleasure, pain, fear, and anger.

The Jewish Scriptures and the Conundrum of Christ and God

Although the writers of the New Testament lived in a world in which ideas like these were common, their understanding of God came from the very different world of the Jewish Scriptures. Two differences are particularly important for understanding how the New Testament writers thought about the relationship between the God of Israel and Jesus Christ.

First, Richard Bauckham has persuasively argued that whereas Greek philosophy was concerned with the nature of God, the Jewish Scriptures are far more interested in the identity of God.[4] The God of the Jewish Scriptures is a person. He has both a name and a personality. He is Yahweh, and he is "merciful and gracious, slow to anger, and abounding in steadfast love and faithfulness" (Exod. 34:6). He feels jealousy when his people worship other gods (Exod. 34:14) and anger when they disobey him (Exod. 32:10). The Israelites are alternately his children and his wife, and God has a relationship with them not unlike that of a good father or husband with a wayward brood of children or an unfaithful spouse (Deut. 1:31–32; 8:5; Isa. 1:2; Ezek. 16; Hosea 1–3). The Jewish Scriptures certainly portray God as "other" than his human creation, and make clear that their anthropomorphic descriptions of God are used metaphorically, but God is far from an impassible and nameless demiurge whose primary characteristic is rationality.

Second, the God of the Jewish Scriptures is knowable to a far greater extent than Plato's cosmic craftsman. Plato's creator has not revealed anything about himself to humanity, and so describing him is a matter of clever deduction and guesswork. Timaeus can only use his reasoning powers, limited by his mortality, to speculate about the nature of God and God's creation. "So we should accept the likely tale on these matters," he tells Socrates. "It behooves us not to look for anything beyond this" (*Tim.* 29d). By comparison, the God of the Jewish Scriptures reveals his character, his purposes, his actions, and his commands on a massive scale to his people. He is the God, says Daniel, who "reveals deep and hidden things" (Dan. 2:22). The psalmist prays, "The unfolding of your words gives light; it imparts understanding to the simple" (Ps. 119:130).

The New Testament Approach to Jesus and God

When the New Testament writers approach the question of the relationship between Jesus and God, they do so within the conceptual boundaries laid down by the Jewish Scriptures. What is unimaginable in Platonic terms—the identification of the Creator of the universe with a human being who suffers and dies—is clearly articulated in the New Testament. Although a number of New Testament texts could illustrate this, four are particularly important.

Mark's Gospel as Witness to the Relationship between Jesus and God

First, the narrative structure of Mark's Gospel seems designed to answer the question of the relationship of Jesus Christ to the God of Israel. Mark announces itself in its first line as "the gospel of Jesus Christ, the Son of God" (Mark 1:1), and within a few paragraphs, Mark presses the issue of whether this means that Jesus is the God of Israel. Jesus forgives the sins of the paralytic, and this prompts the scribes to ask, "Why does this man speak like that? He is blaspheming! Who can forgive sins but God alone?" (2:7). Mark wants us to see in this question the way in which he has defined the / title, "the Son of God," in 1:1. In Jesus's case, to be t⌐ God: only God can forgive sins, and this is exactly w' message is the same in Mark's account of the quieting ⌐ the fear of the disciples, at first directed to the storm, is then dⁿ⌐ who awoke from sleep on a cushion in the boat to issue a simple ⌐ the wind and to say to the sea, "Peace! Be still!" (4:39). When the discip⌐ ask, "Who then is this, that even the wind and the sea obey him?" (4:41), the attentive reader is in little doubt. Mark is claiming that Jesus, who calmed the wind and sea with a word, is the God of Israel who created the wind and the sea with a word and who, according to Psalm 107, rescues those who are in distress on the sea. "Then they cried to the LORD in their trouble," says the psalmist, "and he delivered them from their distress. He made the storm be still, and the waves of the sea were hushed" (Ps. 107:28–29).

But what about Jesus's words to the man who addressed him as "Good Teacher" and asked, "What must I do to inherit eternal life?" (Mark 10:17). Followers of Arius liked to point to Jesus's answer as proof that he did not identify himself with the "true God" who was alone good.[5] "Why do you call me good?" Jesus asks, "No one is good except God alone" (10:18). Jesus does not say here, however, that he is not good. To the contrary, Mark has already affirmed that Jesus is good, in the words of the people of the Decapolis who were astonished that Jesus could heal a deaf man with a speech impediment. "He has done all things well," they comment (7:37). If no one is good but God alone, and Jesus does all things well, then the implication is reasonably clear that Jesus is the one God.

By the time Mark reaches the end of his narrative and the centurion at the cross identifies Jesus as the Son of God (Mark 15:39), Mark has redefined that traditional term to identify Jesus with the God of Israel, the Creator of all things. This is a climactic confession in which, for the first time in the narrative, a human being correctly identifies Jesus.[6] Jesus is the Son of God in the sense that he is God, and he is all this precisely at the moment of his death on the cross.

John's Explicit Connection of Jesus and the Creator

John's Gospel also identifies Jesus as the Son of God who is God and who suffers and dies, and it does so even more explicitly. John explicitly calls Jesus the Creator of all things: "All things were made through him, and without him was not any thing made that was made" (John 1:3), something that could be said only of God himself in the Old Testament. As Richard Bauckham comments, "However diverse Judaism may have been in many other respects, this was common: only the God of Israel is worthy of worship because he is sole Creator of all things and sole Ruler of all things."[7] The role given to sonified Wisdom or to the Word in ancient Jewish descriptions of creation, argues Bauckham, is not an exception to this. Wisdom and Word in these texts are, without exception, understood as aspects of God's identity—they are God's Wisdom and God's Word, not independent agents who aid him in his creative work.[8] John's description of Jesus's role in creation, however, is different. Jesus is not described as the Word of God but simply as the Word who was with God from the beginning; who was God, without whom nothing was made; and who, perhaps most importantly, was the source from which life sprang (John 1:4).

John goes on to say that Jesus makes the unseen God visible: "No one has ever seen God; the only Son, who is in the bosom of the Father, he has made him known" (John 1:18 RSV). The meaning of this becomes clear as Jesus identifies himself with God throughout the narrative in various ways. One of the most important of these is Jesus's use of the phrase "I am" of himself in a way that recalls God's revelation of his personal name to Moses in Exodus 3:14 ("God said to Moses, 'I AM WHO I AM.' And he said, 'Say this to the people of Israel, "I AM has sent me to you"'"). So when the woman at the well hints that Jesus might be the Messiah, Jesus affirms her suspicions with an unusual phrase that, translated literally, reads, "I am—the one who is speaking to you" (John 4:26).[9] He comforts his terror-stricken disciples who see him walking across the lake in the same unusual grammar: "I am—do not be afraid" (6:20). And he identifies himself to a skeptical audience of Scripture scholars with the astonishing statement, "Before Abraham was, I am" (8:58; cf. 8:24, 28). Jesus is trying to lead people—and John is trying to lead his readers—to the conviction that Jesus is the "I am." "Unless you believe that 'I am,' you will die in your sins," he says to the scholars from Judea (8:24; cf. 8:28), and he prophesies his own betrayal at the hands of Judas so that "when it happens," his disciples "might believe that 'I am'" (13:19). When the band of soldiers approaches Jesus to arrest him in the garden, he identifies himself to them with the two words: "I am." John tells us that when Jesus said this, they "drew back and fell to the ground" (18:5–6). Why did John find the stumbling of the soldiers at precisely this point so significant that he put it in his narrative? Because when some of them tripped and fell, they were taking a posture appropriate for people in the presence of God.

The reader is prepared, then, for the climactic confession of Jesus's identity in John's Gospel when Thomas, confronted with irrefutable proof that the crucified Jesus has risen from the dead, exclaims, "My Lord and my God!" (John 20:28). For Jewish monotheists like Thomas and John, this could mean only that Jesus is the God who created all things and who alone deserves their worship.[10] In a way not unlike what happens in Mark's Gospel, Thomas recognizes that Jesus is God when he sees clear evidence of his suffering. "Put your finger here, and see my hands," Jesus tells him, "and put out your hand, and place it in my side. Do not disbelieve, but believe" (20:27).

Paul on the Suffering and Exaltation of Christ as God

The same pattern is present in the Pauline corpus. Jesus is identified with the God of Israel, and his suffering is a critical part of this identification. Nowhere is this clearer than in the famous description of the incarnation in Philippians 2:6–11. The Philippian Christian community was divided and needed the admonition to "do nothing from rivalry or conceit, but in humility count others more significant than yourselves" (Phil. 2:3). To show that this approach to others should be the characteristic posture of those who are "in Christ" (2:5), Paul describes how Christ himself thought and acted in this way. He existed in the form of God, Paul says, and was equal to God, but he did not consider this exalted and powerful mode of existence something to be used for his own advantage. Instead, he emptied himself by taking the form of a slave and becoming like a human being. He was so thoroughly human that he experienced death, and not just any death, but death on a cross. As a result of this, God exalted him to the highest place and gave him the name above every name so that all might give him the worship that is his due.[11]

If this reading is correct, then by the early sixties AD, Christians were already identifying Jesus with the "name above all names," which in the monotheistic context of first-century Judaism can only be Yahweh, the personal name of God.[12] They were also affirming that Jesus's conduct revealed something about Yahweh's character. His character led him not to use his lofty status as God for his own advantage, but to the contrary, to consider the needs of others.[13] This aspect of his character led, in turn, to his suffering and death, and to a form of death reserved for the Roman Empire's lowest social classes. Just as in John and Mark, once this aspect of his character is revealed, his exalted status as God also becomes clear; and just as in John, this leads to worship, something reserved for God alone in the context of Judaism.

Revelation's Connection of the Lamb and God

Finally, the same pattern appears in the Revelation of John, a text so profoundly steeped in the language and imagery of the Jewish Scriptures that it cannot be understood without a detailed knowledge of them.[14] Here too, Jesus, portrayed as a slaughtered Lamb, is identified with God himself and receives the worship that in the Jewish Scriptures and in first-century Judaism belongs to God alone. In the book's first heavenly vision (Rev. 4–5), John describes the throne room of God. Twenty-four elders, themselves crowned and enthroned, encircle the throne of God. God's throne is further surrounded by four living creatures, one on each of the throne's four sides. The living creatures and the twenty-four elders all give glory, honor, and thanks to God, who is seated on the throne. Then, in Revelation 5:6, a new figure is introduced suddenly into the vision: a slaughtered Lamb who is nevertheless alive. The translations and the commentaries are divided about the location of this Lamb. He is either "between" the throne and the four living creatures, as the New Revised Standard Version has it, or he is "in the middle of the throne with its four living creatures," as the New Jerusalem Bible puts it. If the New Jerusalem Bible is correct, then the Lamb is being identified with God who is on the throne. The Greek can be taken either way, and since the Lamb takes the scroll from the right hand of the one who sits on the throne, some commentators have reasonably concluded that the Lamb cannot be sitting on the throne.[15]

The trouble with this view, however, is that at the end of the passage "every creature in heaven and on earth and under the earth and in the sea, and all that is in them," ascribe eternal blessing, honor, glory, and might "to him who sits on the throne and to the Lamb" (Rev. 5:13). In other words, they direct worship both to the one on the throne and to the Lamb. In a monotheistic context, this must mean that the Lamb is somehow to be identified with the one on the throne. This is confirmed in chapter 7, where once again worship goes to the one on the throne and to the Lamb (7:9–10), but then the Lamb is said to be "in the midst of the throne" (7:17). Here there is no ambiguity: the Lamb occupies the middle of the throne.

John was not worried about how the Lamb could both be in the middle of the throne and receive the sealed scroll from the one who is on the throne, nor was he concerned to explain how worship could both go to the one on the throne and to the Lamb, and yet how the Lamb could be the one on the throne. The Lamb and the one on the throne are in some way identical to each other, and yet separate from each other. John's vision is like a hologram. Turned one way we see the one whose appearance is "like jasper and carnelian" (4:3), and turned another way we see a fatally wounded Lamb who is nevertheless alive and able to lead his suffering followers to springs of living water (7:17).

Early Attempts to Envision the Character of God

It is difficult to imagine what Plato might have said about the vision of the character of God that emerges from these four New Testament texts. Perhaps he would have said first that this vision is impossible, because God simply does not make himself known in the way that the Jewish Scriptures claim for him. "Now to find the maker and father of this universe is hard enough, and even if I succeeded, to declare him to everyone is impossible" (*Tim.* 28c, PCW). We are reduced to reasoned speculation about God: it is all we can do as mere mortals (29d). Plato would perhaps then comment on how God could not even create mortal human beings since he is immortal, much less become like them to the point of experiencing death. "It is at any rate not likely that the gods experience either pleasure or the opposite" (*Phileb.* 33b, PCW 421). If this is true of the gods, how much more true Plato must have thought it was of the cosmic craftsman who made the gods. The biblical understanding of God and the Platonic understanding seem utterly incompatible.

At least Celsus, the great second-century opponent of Christians, thought so. After parodying the biblical portrait of God as a person, he complained that Christians had not read their Plato. In the *Republic*, Celsus says, God "does not even participate in being. . . . This God of the philosophers is himself the underivable, the unnameable; he cannot be reached by reason. Such attributes as we may postulate of him are not the attributes of human nature, and all such attributes are quite distinct from his nature. He cannot be comprehended in terms of attributes or human experience, contrary to what the Christians teach; moreover, he is outside any emotional experience."[16] When it comes to the suffering of Jesus, Celsus is practically beside himself. He mentions it over and over, amazed that Christians would worship a god so weak that he could be crucified. "God does not suffer," he says in one of his outbursts, "and God cannot be humiliated."

Since the religious atmosphere of the Greco-Roman world was thoroughly infused with Platonism, and since the early Christians were ridiculed for their lack of philosophical sophistication, it is not surprising to find apparent attempts to make them compatible. Already in the New Testament itself, the apostle John had to warn those under his apostolic care about "progressives" who, he says, have moved beyond apostolic teaching about Jesus and refuse to "confess the coming of Jesus Christ in the flesh" (2 John 7; cf. 1 John 4:2). The first-century teacher Cerinthus believed that the world was created by a god inferior to the highest god and that Christ, who came from the highest god, occupied the flesh of a certain Jesus from the time of his baptism until prior to his crucifixion. It was apparently important to Cerinthus that only "Jesus suffered and rose again, while Christ remained impassible, inasmuch as he was a spiritual being" (Irenaeus, *Adv. Haer.* 1.26.1, ANF 1:352).[17]

Not many years later, Ignatius reminded the Ephesian Christians that "there is only one physician, who is both flesh from Mary and from God, first subject to suffering and then beyond it, Jesus Christ our Lord. Therefore," he continues, "let no one deceive you. . . ." (*Eph.* 7.2–8.1, Holmes 98).[18] He similarly warns the Magnesians "not to get snagged on the hooks of worthless opinions but instead to be fully convinced about the birth and the suffering and the resurrection that took place during the time of the governorship of Pontius Pilate" (*Magn.* 11, Holmes 106). He tells the Trallians to be deaf to those who teach something other than that Jesus was really born, both ate and drank, was persecuted, crucified, and died (*Trall.* 9.1). The Lord Jesus Christ did not, he tells the Smyrnaeans, suffer "in appearance only" (Trail. 10, Holmes 121; cf. *Smyrn.* 2). Very probably the false teaching Ignatius describes attempted to distance Jesus from human flesh and suffering as a way of preserving his deity within contexts in which some form of Plato's view of God, however attenuated, provided the conceptual framework for understanding God.

Plato's Influence on Justin Martyr

The same struggle to make sense of Jesus within a broadly Platonic understanding of God appears in Justin Martyr. For Justin, Plato provided a common language by which to interpret Christianity to the hostile environment
that surrounded it. Although "they are not in all respects similar" (*1 Apol.*
13.3, *ANF* 1:193), he says, the teachings of Plato approach those of Christianity. This should not be surprising, since God sowed the seeds of his Word
within the world, and Plato, like other philosophers who occasionally spoke
the truth, was able to benefit from them (*1 Apol.* 44.10; *2 Apol.* 13.3). Justin
thought that he could even detect evidence in Plato's *Timaeus* that Plato had
read Moses (*1 Apol.* 59–60). This idea was important to Justin, because he
wanted to argue that where the philosophers said something true, they were
anticipating the truth as it is more clearly expressed in the Scriptures.

Sometimes, however, the influence seems to have run from Plato to Justin rather
than from Moses to Plato. This is especially true of several statements about the
relationship between God and Jesus. Justin distinguishes rather sharply between
God, who is good, unbegotten (*1 Apol.* 14.2), and impassible (*1 Apol.* 25.2), and
has no name except Father and Lord of the universe (*1 Apol.* 61.10–11), and
his Son Jesus, who is begotten (*1 Apol.* 23.1; cf. 12.7), is the firstborn of God
(*1 Apol.* 21.1; 23.2; 46.2, 63.15), and, as the incarnate Word of God, is the teacher
of Christians (*1 Apol.* 6.2; 13.3; 21.1; 23.2). Jesus is divine, according to Justin
(*1 Apol.* 63.15), and Christians worship him, but they also worship "the host
of other good angels who follow and are made like to him" (*1 Apol.* 6.2, *ANF*
1:164). Christians hold "him in second place" (*1 Apol.* 13.3, *ANF* 1:167)—the
place, Justin argues later, that Plato gave to the human-shaped Logos when he
described God's creation of the universe (*1 Apol.* 60; cf. Plato, *Tim.* 36b–c). The
clear implication of his comparison between the account of creation in Plato's
Timaeus and the nature of the Christian Trinity, however, is that God the Father
created God the Son, just as Plato's demiurge created the living, human universe.

Justin was trying to explain Christianity to hostile unbelievers who thought
of Christians as atheists because they did not share the accepted notions
about the divine. The cultured unbeliever of the second century was willing
to debate the idea that Jesus was an angel.[19] He could remain civil as he explained that God could not come down to earth, for that would violate the
obvious principle that God cannot change.[20] But the notion that God could
suffer crucifixion was summarily heckled off the stage. It was simply beyond
the pale. "You will be a laughingstock," Celsus tells the Christians, "so long
as you repeat the blasphemy that the gods of other men are idols, while you
brazenly worship as God a man whose life was wretched, who is known to
have died (in disgraceful circumstances), and who, so you teach, is the very
model of the God we should look to as our Father."[21] Although Justin wrote
his *First Apology* about two decades before Celsus's *On the True Doctrine*,
he knew the sort of criticisms that Celsus later made of Christianity and felt

their sting. It is precisely here, he reports, that opponents of Christians think that Christian madness is most clearly on display: Christians put a crucified human being in second place after the God who has always existed and who gave birth to all things (*1 Apol* 13.4).

It is understandable that, in such a climate, Justin would try to emphasize the aspects of Christianity that pagans might appreciate. In doing so, however, he seems to have fallen prey to an over-Platonized understanding both of God and of Jesus. To put the crucified man Jesus even in second place to the ineffable, impassible God of Plato's *Timaeus* brought ridicule. To assert his full ontological unity with the Creator may have seemed to Justin a doctrine that his readers would simply not be able to swallow.

Arianism and the Character of God

In his massive study of the Arian controversy, Richard Hanson argues that "the heart of Arianism" lay in the need to take account of two critical convictions. First, Arians believed that Christ was God, that he had taken on human flesh, and that he had really suffered. Second, they also believed that the eternal God could not suffer.[22] Their answer to this dilemma was to affirm that the Son was God but not in the same sense as the Father. They were separate in substance and in eternality. The Father was uncreated and the Son created. Their unity was a unity of wills.[23]

The first of these two convictions stood in full continuity with the apostolic witness to Jesus as it is found in the New Testament. As we have seen, the New Testament affirms in many places that Jesus is God and that his suffering does nothing to diminish this aspect of who he is. The second conviction, however, is Platonic. Rather than distancing the suffering of Jesus from the character of the God of Israel, the New Testament affirms that the suffering of Jesus on behalf of his people is a revelation of the one God of Israel and a critical element of his identity.[24] Arius claimed that his teaching was not an innovation but that he was simply carrying on the traditions he had learned from the church of North Africa. He told his bishop Alexander that he and his followers taught only what "we have learnt from you . . . when you were preaching in the midst of the church."[25] Perhaps the intense pressure to imagine the suffering of Jesus in terms that were acceptable within the broadly Platonic framework of the time helps explain why Arius could make this claim. By the time of Arius, the cross had for centuries presented a profound theological scandal to the cultured elite, whose understanding of God had been influenced by their study of Greek philosophy.[26]

The Nicene Fathers and the Question of Unity between Father and Son

The Nicene fathers were certainly part of the cultured elite of their day, but they apparently realized that on the question of the unity between the

Father and the Son, they could not let a Platonic understanding of the nature of God overrule what a commonsense reading of the Scriptures implied. The Son, they said, was begotten from the Father's very being, and in precisely this full-bodied sense was "God from God, Light from Light, true God from true God." As the Son he must be born, but his birth was not his creation; the fundamental nature of his existence was unified with the fundamental nature of the Father's existence.

Williams is certainly correct when he says that this description of God would not be possible apart from asking the sort of questions about God that the Greek philosophers asked. But no Platonist would have described God in the words of the Nicene Creed. The Nicene Creed reaffirmed the biblical picture of God as a personal being with certain clearly defined characteristics. It also made clear that those characteristics could not be understood apart from the revelation of them in God's Son, the Lord Jesus Christ, who from all eternity shared God's existence.

4

Whosoever Will Be Saved

The Athanasian Creed and the Modern Church

GERALD R. BRAY

Historical Background

Article 8 of the Thirty-Nine Articles of Religion states: "The three creeds, Nicene Creed, Athanasius' Creed, and that which is commonly called the Apostles' Creed, ought thoroughly to be received and believed, for they may be proved by most certain warrants of Holy Scripture." The words go back to Archbishop Thomas Cranmer's Forty-Two Articles of 1553, apart from the addition of the words "and believed," which were inserted into the revised version ten years later. At the time, they represented the view of creedal origins and authority that was generally held in the Western church, and the article was not intended either to provoke controversy or to respond to any contemporary objections to the creeds. A couple of decades later, the Lutheran Formula of Concord made a similar affirmation, and the acceptance of the "three creeds" was a commonplace of both Roman and Reformed doctrinal statements—common ground in an age of religious dissent.

If Article 8 stands out in any way, it is because Cranmer's language was always very carefully chosen. For example, we can see from what he says that

45

in his day the authenticity of the Apostles' Creed was no longer as widely accepted as it had once been. Nobody doubted that what it said was true, but the medieval belief that it had been composed by the apostles themselves, supposedly at a single sitting when they were each inspired by the Holy Spirit to contribute one of its clauses, had been almost universally rejected in scholarly circles. The Nicene Creed, however, was still attributed to the fathers of the first Council of Nicea (325), and it is only in modern times that historians have recognized that it is somewhat later in origin, dating most likely from the first Council of Constantinople (381) or shortly afterward. Cranmer's wording also shows that it was still generally accepted that the third creed was the work of Athanasius, bishop of Alexandria from 328 to 373 and the most renowned opponent of Arianism, the arch-heresy of the fourth century. Its supposed authorship may be the reason that it was retained without question by the first generation of Reformers.

As a statement of theological orthodoxy, the Athanasian Creed is much fuller than the other two creeds, and its claim of connection to one of the most important fathers of the church gave its usefulness a particular authority. Two-thirds of it is devoted to a detailed exposition of the doctrine of the Trinity, which is implied but not specifically stated in either the Apostles' or the Nicene Creed, and much of the rest is taken up with an explanation of Chalcedonian Christology, which is not found in either of them. For theological students in particular, the Athanasian Creed was a compendium of systematic theology that served them well in an age in which such things had to be memorized. The presentation, which can seem boring and repetitive to a modern reader, was ideal for learning by heart, and the logical structure of the creed made retention of its contents that much easier.

Unfortunately for those who rested their acceptance of the creed on the traditional view of its authorship, the very sophistication of its contents was a prime argument against the view that Athanasius wrote it. For a start, the christological language that it uses did not circulate until after the Council of Chalcedon (451), by which time Athanasius had been dead for two generations. If that were not enough, the trinitarian section includes an affirmation of the doctrine of the double procession of the Holy Spirit, which forms an integral part of the text and is not a later interpolation as it was in the Nicene Creed. This confirms that Athanasius cannot have been the author, and further investigation merely reinforces that conclusion. The creed is a carefully crafted literary composition, and its cadences indicate that the Latin text is the original. The earliest Greek version we know of did not appear until the fourteenth century, when it was used by Byzantine theologians who had been attracted to Western theology and wanted their church to enter into union with Rome. Since it lacks the literary grace of the Latin, it is most likely that they translated it themselves and were insensitive to the literary qualities of the original. That no one else in the Eastern church accepted it as a genuinely Athanasian text is therefore only to be expected—they were right!

In the sixteenth century, however, scholarship in the West had not developed to that extent, and the authenticity of the Athanasian Creed was still taken for granted by both Roman Catholics and Protestants. Doubts surfaced only in the seventeenth century, when contact with the Greek East raised the issue. By the time of the Enlightenment it was generally rejected, both on historical and on theological grounds. It has never really recovered from that assault and is now by far the least known of the creedal statements produced by the ancient church. Even before that happened, though, the Athanasian Creed was infrequently heard by most congregations. Roman Catholics confined it to Trinity Sunday, a practice that seems to have been followed by most Lutherans and continental Reformed churches. It failed to get into the Westminster Confession, perhaps because of the doubts then circulating about its authorship, with the result that it is virtually unknown in the non-Anglican churches of the English-speaking world. Only in the Church of England was its use enjoined on a regular basis: it was to be recited thirteen times in the year, the dates apparently chosen at roughly monthly intervals, with Trinity Sunday being the thirteenth date. We do not know how often it was actually used, but after the American Revolution there was a move to have it taken out of the revised *Book of Common Prayer*. Despite some strong opposition from Bishop Samuel Seabury, that move was successful. When the Americans revised the Articles in 1801, the Athanasian Creed was one of the few things they struck out, with the result that it is now practically unknown in the United States. Elsewhere, the creed has been retained in theory but largely ignored in practice. It is safe to say that today almost nowhere will it be heard in public worship.

But are the attacks on the Athanasian Creed that led to its subsequent disappearance from view justified? That it was not composed by Athanasius is now universally admitted, but the assumption that it must have been a medieval forgery has now been discounted. Modern scholarship has demonstrated that it goes back to the late fifth or early sixth century and is closely associated with the monasteries of southern Gaul, which had a special interest in defining and disseminating the "Catholic faith"—that is, the sum total of the doctrinal decisions that had been taken by the great ecumenical councils held from 325 to 451. The creed has close connections with Vincent of Lérins (d. c. 450) and Caesarius of Arles (d. 542), though Vincent died too soon to have written it and Caesarius seems to have been its great promoter rather than its author. As far as we can tell, it was probably written by one of Vincent's disciples in time for it to have been circulated by Caesarius when he became bishop of Arles in 502. The author may have even been Caesarius's tutor, but that cannot now be known and is no more than a plausible conjecture. What is certain is that it was composed as a memory device and circulated mainly among those who were being specially trained in the orthodoxy of the first four ecumenical councils. Caesarius and others tried to popularize its use in worship, but it never really caught on.

How the name of Athanasius came to be attached to it is unknown, but it may go back to Caesarius, who was fond of circulating theological statements and attributing them to some author more famous than himself. Athanasius was a particularly good candidate for this role, because as the acknowledged defender of orthodoxy and foe of Arianism (one of the main targets of the creed), his theological authority was unchallenged. Caesarius no doubt thought about this in the way that some modern Calvinists think about the canons of the Synod of Dort, which were composed two generations after Calvin's death. As Caesarius would have seen it, the text represents what Athanasius would have thought and said had he been alive at the time, and so it made perfect sense to attribute it to him. The attribution was a theological statement, and it must be judged as that, not as historical fact. Certainly its disappearance from the modern church is due more to theological objections than to its unsuitability for use in public worship, a fact even its most loyal defenders are prepared to admit.

When the first General Convention of the Protestant Episcopal Church met in 1785, theological disquiet about the contents of the Athanasian Creed had become strong enough to persuade the majority that it would be better not to retain it among the doctrinal standards of the church. There were some who were unhappy about the creed's extensive treatment of the Trinity, an unfashionable doctrine at that time, but the real sticking point was the so-called damnatory clauses, which are inserted at the beginning, middle, and end of the creed and which constitute its fundamental framework. Eighteenth-century Enlightenment thinkers did not like systematic theology at the best of times, but the idea that someone who did not dot every "i" or cross every "t" of the Athanasian Creed would perish in the eternal fires of hell was too much for them to stomach. They had little difficulty persuading most of their contemporaries that the unreasonableness of such an assertion made keeping it indefensible. Even those who argued for the creed's retention were prepared to drop the offending clauses, despite the fact that they form an integral part of the text and were probably the main reason that it was composed in the first place.

In the early twentieth century, liturgical renewal and a certain reaction to classical liberalism sparked a new interest in the Athanasian Creed as something more than a purely historical document. In some parts of the Anglican Communion, provision for its use continued to be made, sometimes more generously than at the time of the Reformation. A high point in this revival came in 1963, when the late J. N. D. Kelly was invited to give the prestigious Paddock Lectures at the General Theological Seminary in New York. As Kelly recalls in his preface to the printed version of the lectures:

It should perhaps be placed on record, as a measure of the interest the subject aroused but also for its own sake, that, at the conclusion of the last lecture, the whole company present in the Chapel rose to their feet and (there was, I suspect, some prior collusion with the organist and choir) sang the Athanasian Creed. This must have been almost a unique event since the reorganization of the American church after the War of Independence.[1]

It need hardly be said that Kelly's picture of the Episcopal Church is scarcely recognizable today, when the Athanasian Creed, along with most of the doctrine it contains, has been put back into the closet with the key thrown away. The most that can be said about it is that it returned to the stage for the briefest of academic moments and then disappeared again, perhaps for good. The other churches that retain it no longer use it, and those that never had it show no desire to find out what they may be missing. It is the purpose of this chapter to speak to this dire situation by challenging the wider church to take another look at this long-forgotten text and to consider again whether it really deserves the fate that it has suffered in the past three hundred years.

The Theological Framework

The motive behind the composition of the Athanasian Creed was undoubtedly the need felt at the time to hold and preserve the Catholic faith. The church had just gone through two centuries of theological warfare, and the battles were by no means over. In the Eastern church, the struggle to impose Chalcedonian Christology was still on, and in fact it would never be accepted by the majority in Egypt or Syria, though for very different reasons. The Egyptians rejected Chalcedon for its supposed Nestorianism, and the Syrians rejected it for exactly the opposite reason—it was not Nestorian enough![2] In the West, where the Athanasian Creed was composed, most of the Roman Empire had fallen into the hands of barbarian tribes who had accepted an Arian form of Christianity, even if they had little understanding of what Arianism really was. Not until 589 did the last Arian kingdom convert to Catholicism, and the danger that the heresy might return in some other form (as it did) was ever present. The church needed a clear statement not just of what it believed but of why its beliefs mattered. This comes across clearly in the opening lines of the Athanasian Creed, which later generations were to find so offensive:

> Whosoever will be saved, before all things it is necessary that he hold the Catholic faith. Which faith, except everyone do keep whole and undefiled, without doubt he shall perish everlastingly.

The first thing to notice here is that the creed says nothing about believing the doctrines it contains—at least not in so many words. Instead, the terms used are "hold" and "keep," which is significant. The author of the creed understood that the Catholic faith is not just something we confess, but something that we have received. It has been handed down to us from our forebearers, and we have the duty to accept it, preserve it, and pass it on to the next generation "whole and undefiled." This particular emphasis, coming as it does from a time when it was far from certain that the theological battles of the church were over, reminds us of something fundamental about our faith—it comes as a complete package and has done so from the very beginning. The synods that composed particular statements of belief were doing no more than preserving what had been handed down to them by clarifying what they really meant. Certain aspects of the faith had come under fire and had to be defined and defended, but the substance had been there all along.

The minds of the church fathers can be better understood if we compare their sense of orthodoxy to a human body. When a body comes out of the womb, it is meant to be "whole and undefiled," as the creed puts it. Over time it will grow and develop to maturity, but some parts of it may turn out to be weaker than others, and limbs may be amputated. It may become flabby in places if it is not exercised, and susceptible to various diseases if it is not properly fed and looked after. Total fitness is rare, and particular problems may arise that will require healing and restoration of the body. Yet for all that, the body is still a coherent organism, and if parts of it weaken or fall off, the defects are noticed and regarded as handicaps that diminish its ability to function properly. So it is with the Catholic faith. Individuals may confess it only in part and not understand how some aspects of it fit into the whole. They may notice weaknesses here and there and be confused by them because they cannot relate them to the organic whole. They may even keep some parts of it covered up because they are afraid that full exposure may have a negative effect on those who are less mature in their faith. Some parts of it may go missing without causing fatal damage. It is noticeable that the creed says nothing about important subjects like the government of the church, the composition of the ministry, and the place of the sacraments. These things can be disputed and produce various kinds of distortion, but they do not entail death. On the core issues, however, there can be no wavering, because if the core is harmed, the body will cease to function. Thus, someone who denies the Trinity, who does not understand or accept the incarnation of the Son of God, or who has no expectation of a future life or judgment will not inherit eternal salvation. For them, the future is spiritual death—not because they will be executed on the last day, but because they are spiritually dead already.

The Athanasian Creed is not an examination paper on which the candidate must achieve 100 percent in order to be admitted into the kingdom of heaven. Instead, it is an explanation and celebration of the gift that every believer has received and been entrusted to hold on to. Today we live in a world that prizes originality, rejects tradition, and lets people think that they can make up their own version of the truth. The Athanasian Creed is diametrically opposed to such notions and warns us of the dire consequences that will flow from that attitude. We must take what we have been given, believe it, and bequeath it to those who come after us, so that they will not have to fight the old battles all over again and run the risk of losing the treasure so thoughtlessly discarded by their predecessors.

> And the Catholic faith is this, that we worship one God in Trinity, and Trinity in Unity, neither confounding the persons nor dividing the substance.

Here in a sentence is the sum of our theological inheritance. Again, notice how the author avoids using the word "believe," putting the verb "worship" in its place. True orthodoxy is "right worship," belief worked out in relationship. It is all very well to make the right noises about God, but if we believe what we are saying, then we shall be worshiping him "in spirit and in truth" because that is what God expects of us (John 4:24). As the creed reminds us, our faith follows a particular pattern. First of all, we are called to worship the one God. This is the universal witness of the Old Testament and was the basic belief of those Jesus called to follow him. It was only as they came to know him that he revealed the inner life of God to them: the reality of a Trinity of divine Persons, of which he was one. Once they understood that, they had to go further and see that the three Persons were one in the unity of the divine being; they were not just different names for the same thing. Nor were the Son and the Holy Spirit to be cut off from the Father's divine nature and turned into beings who were, by definition, inferior to him.

The first of these errors is what we call *modalism* or *Sabellianism*, named after an otherwise unknown second-century heretic called Sabellius. Modalism was long thought by the Eastern church to be the "typical heresy" of the West, because Western theology tends to start with the unity of God and move on from there to discover the Trinity inside the divine being. Westerners have always denied this accusation, of course, but it is noticeable how many of our great theologians have been uncomfortable with the term *person* and have even been prepared (as Karl Barth was) to use the term *mode of being* instead. Today, it is not unusual to find definitions of the Trinity that speak of the Creator, Redeemer, and Sanctifier, terms that reduce the personal distinctions in God to the functions that all three of them perform. "Confounding the persons" may sound archaic, but it is more common than we realize.

"Dividing the substance," on the other hand, is Arianism, sometimes regarded as the "typical heresy" of the Eastern church because it emphasizes the Father as the unique source of divinity within the Godhead. Arianism starts from the premise that God is one and that therefore only the Father is truly God in the full sense of the term. The Son and the Holy Spirit may be divine in some sense, but because they derive from the Father they must be inferior to him. Once again, this misconception is more widespread nowadays than we might imagine. Just ask an ordinary Christian whether Jesus was God or not. It is quite likely that he will be puzzled for a minute and then reply that Jesus was the *Son* of God, thereby implying that there is a fundamental difference between him and his Father, which probably makes him inferior in some way. This is not intentional of course, but it shows how naïve reflection on divine revelation can so easily lead to error. It also helps to explain why so many people saw nothing wrong with Arianism when it was first propounded.

The Trinity

The next section of the creed gives an elaborate definition of the Trinity, balancing the uniqueness of each of the Persons with the generic unity of their substance (or "Godhead," as the ET puts it). The first thing to notice is that the author of the creed distinguishes between the inherent status and the external function of each of the divine Persons. In status, or being, their *glory* is equal; in action and sovereignty, their *majesty* is coeternal. This is a fundamentally anti-Arian statement, because Arius believed that the Son was a creature born in time and space, and thus not equal or coeternal with the Father. But neither the Son nor the Holy Spirit can be truly God without being fully God and therefore totally distinct from the creation that God has made out of nothing. This is expressed in the creed by confessing that each of the Persons shares a common divine nature, which is uncreated. The author of the creed employs a triadic formula, which is a standard literary device. The fact of being uncreated implies that they are all equally "incomprehensible" and "eternal," which means that they are not bound by space or time.

The term *incomprehensible* sounds strange to us (the Latin is *immensus*), because we now use it in a purely mental sense. It might be better to translate it as *ungraspable*, because *grasp* retains both the physical and the metaphorical meaning of the Latin word. God cannot be grasped, which is to say that he cannot be pinned down and defined, either by human hands (as in idolatry) or by human minds (as in philosophy). God is above and beyond all of that. As sovereign Lord of the universe, God's being defies all human attempts to understand it.

Having established that, the creed moves on to the divine names, which are also given as three—Almighty, God, and Lord. True to the triadic pattern, it is the first of these that determines how the others are to be understood. In the ancient world there were many gods and many lords, but there was only one Almighty: *El-Shaddai* (Hebrew) or *Pantocrator* (Greek). "Almighty" is not a divine attribute but a name that reveals the uniqueness and absolute sovereignty of the God of the Bible over every other claimant to divinity. "God" reflects his status, and "Lord" his power—once again, we see the balance between who he is and what he does reflected in the language of the creed. God can be God in himself, but he can be Lord only if there is something for him to be Lord of! Having thus sketched out the relationship between the Persons and substance of God, the creed pauses to explain why we believe this:

> For like as we are compelled by the Christian verity to acknowledge every Person by himself to be God and Lord, so are we forbidden by the Catholic religion to say there be three gods or three lords.

The basic structure here is plain enough. The "Christian verity" forces us to believe in a Trinity, but the "Catholic religion" prevents us from abandoning monotheism. What are these things? Great ingenuity has been used to find an adequate definition for "Christian verity" and for "Catholic religion," but knowledge of ancient terminology will tell us immediately what they mean. For the fathers of the church there were two "verities," one Hebrew and the other Christian—in other words, what we would now call the Old and New Testaments. The Catholic religion, on the other hand, was what had been believed by God's people in all ages and at all times, going right back to Abraham. For our purposes, it might be called "the whole Bible," making the sentence read as follows: "For like as we are compelled by the New Testament to acknowledge every Person by himself to be God and Lord, so we are forbidden by the whole Bible to say there be three gods or three lords." In other words, there is one covenant between God and humanity, revealed to us in two dispensations, in the second of which God opens himself up to reveal his inner life as a triune being.

Once that is settled, the creed moves on to explain what makes the Persons distinct. Once again, there are three different ways in which their identity can be expressed—as creation, generation, or procession. The first of these applies to none of them, because they are all part of the eternal divine being and totally different from any creature. The second applies to the Son, who is the "only begotten" of the Father (John 1:14 KJV), but this generation is not a temporal event. It describes not a process but a relationship, because the Son is the heir of all things and coruler with his Father of the entire universe. The third applies to the Holy Spirit (John 15:26), making his relationship to the Father different from that of the Son, so that he is not to be regarded as a second Son or as the Son's twin brother. To say that might imply that there is an alternative route to God the Father that does not involve such messy things as incarnation and crucifixion, which is not the case. The only way we have access to the Father is through the Son, and the only way we can know the Son is in the Spirit.

This raises the question of how the Spirit and the Son are related to each other. Here the Athanasian Creed gives us an answer that is not found in either of the other ancient creeds and that remains controversial to this day. It says that the Holy Spirit proceeds from both the Father and the Son, a doctrine that was taught by Augustine (354–430) and accepted as orthodox in the Western church. This doctrine was accepted not least because it provided an answer to the Arians, who claimed that if the Holy Spirit proceeds from the Father alone, and not from the Son, then the Father has something the Son does not have. If that is so, the Father must be God in a way that the Son is not, and it is to avoid that conclusion that the double procession imposes itself on the Christian mind. In response to this, the Eastern church developed the view that the Spirit cannot proceed from the Son in the same way that he proceeds from the Father, because if he did so, there would be two sources of divinity and the unity of the Godhead would be destroyed. That was obviously not the intention of the anti-Arian westerners, but finding a way to reconcile these different perceptions has so far proved to be impossible. The two halves of ancient Christendom remain divided over the question.

The most successful attempt at finding a solution to this has been to say that the Holy Spirit proceeds from each of the other Persons according to the identity of that Person—in other words, from the Father primarily because he is the source of divinity, but also from (or through) the Son, whose generation takes logical precedence over the Spirit's procession. However this is understood, all three Persons are coequal and coeternal, with none being greater or less than the others. On this, all parties in the dispute about the double procession of the Holy Spirit are fully agreed.

The Christological Question

Having expounded the doctrine of the Trinity, the Athanasian Creed moves on to a detailed examination of the person and natures of Jesus Christ. This had been the immediate cause of the theological disputes of the fourth and fifth centuries, which were far from having been fully resolved when the Nicene Creed was composed and which were still causing problems when this text first appeared. Indeed, it is from what the Athanasian Creed does *not* say about the two natures of Christ that we can venture to date it to the first half of the sixth century. If it had been written after 553 (the date of the second council of Constantinople), it would probably have been even more detailed in its definition of the person and natures of Christ than it is.

The christological section of the creed begins with an extended exposition of the Chalcedonian definition, which confirms that it must have been written sometime after 451. The basic premise is that the incarnate Son of God is both divine and human, having received his divinity from his Father and his humanity from his mother (who, incidentally, is not named in this creed as she is in the others). The most important point it makes is that he was "perfect man, of a reasonable soul and human flesh subsisting." This had been debated at the First Council of Constantinople in 381, when Apollinarius—a disciple of Athanasius who had taken his master's Christology to its logical (but unfortunately also heretical) conclusion—denied that Christ had a human soul. Without a soul, he would not have been a genuine human being, nor could he have become sin for us, since sin resides in the soul (that is to say, in the mind and the will of a human) and not in human flesh.

The Athanasian Creed also explains why Jesus said that his Father was greater than he was (John 14:28) by pointing out that the incarnate Christ was "equal to his Father as touching his Godhead, and inferior to his Father as touching his manhood." In other words, the essential inferiority of the Son to the Father is to be understood in reference to his human nature and not to his personal relationship with the Father as his Son. This is important, because what the divine Son did in response to the Father's will he did voluntarily. The Son was not a slave who had no choice but to obey his master. Rather, as Paul puts it in Philippians 2:6–7: "Who, though he was in the form of God, did not count equality with God a thing to be grasped, but made himself nothing, taking the form of a servant, being born in the likeness of men." The incarnation was therefore the working out of a servanthood that the Son had already assumed by virtue of his divinity. Everything that followed on from that was done in the context of willing obedience to his Father's will.

Interestingly, from the standpoint of the controversy that led to Chalcedon, the author of the Athanasian Creed seems to go out of his way to reach out to both sides of the argument. His description of the incarnate Christ includes the following definition:

> Who although he be God and man, yet he is not two but one Christ; one, not by conversion of the Godhead into flesh, but by taking of the manhood into God.

It had been the contention of the Nestorian party, rooted in the theology of Antioch, that in the womb of the Virgin Mary, the Son of God had joined himself to a human embryo that would have been capable of independent life. The resulting conjunction was perceived as one Christ, but the Nestorians could never really explain who or what had brought that unity about. Had the Son of God simply usurped the identity of the embryo? Or was there some sort of cooperation between him and the man Jesus of Nazareth, so that they spoke with one voice even though they were two distinct (and theoretically separable) beings? The language of the first part of this sentence is fully compatible with Nestorianism and would have been embraced by any Antiochene theologian of the period.

That it is not a Nestorian statement is made clear by the second part of the sentence, which speaks about taking the manhood into God. This was music to the ears of the Alexandrian school, which had always maintained that the incarnate Christ was a single divine Person who had absorbed a human nature into his being. That humanity continued to function as such, but it was not a second nature that could have existed without divine intervention. In Mary's womb, the Son did not unite himself to a human embryo; a human embryo was created for him by the Holy Spirit, who thus took part in the Son's incarnation just as much as the Father did but in a different way. The problem with this was that it was never entirely clear where Christ's divine nature left off and his human nature began. The Alexandrians were rigorously orthodox in their understanding of his divinity, but this made it hard for them to explain how the incarnate Son could really have been tempted, and how he could have suffered and died in any genuinely human sense. When they were forced to pronounce on such matters, they invariably preferred the divine over the human, thus causing the Antiochenes and others to doubt whether they believed that Jesus was a real human being.

The Council of Chalcedon cut through all this by saying that Christ was one, "not by confusion of substance but by unity of person." His divinity and his humanity remained what they were, and although in themselves they were incompatible with each other, they were united by the action of the person of the Son. The Athanasian Creed does not say it expressly, but in stating this, the Chalcedonian definition turned classical Christology on its head. Until then, it had always been thought that a person was the outward and visible manifestation of an underlying nature or substance, which meant that the nature of the substance determined what the person could and could not do. But by proclaiming the unity of person in Christ, Chalcedon was saying in effect that the person of the Son possesses (and can therefore control) a divine nature, to which he added a second nature when he became incarnate. This understanding is then reinforced by the creed when it states: "For as the reasonable soul and flesh is one man, so God and man is one Christ." The "reasonable soul" is not the equal of the flesh but its governing principle. In the same way, the divine person of the Son governs and directs the humanity that he has assumed.

From there the christological section goes on to use terminology familiar to us from the other two creeds' descriptions of the death, resurrection, ascension, and heavenly session of Christ. There are, however, some subtle differences. For instance, the Athanasian Creed makes no mention of the crucifixion or of Pontius Pilate; all that it says is that "he suffered for our salvation." There is also no mention of his burial, although it does say that he descended into hell and rose again on the third day "from the dead," which may be taken to imply that. There is no reason to suppose that the Athanasian Creed differs from the other two on any point of theological significance, but the phrasing indicates that its author was working independently of them, even though he was obviously drawing on a common tradition.

The Last Judgment

Having completed the christological section, the Athanasian Creed finishes with a brief but interesting statement about the last judgment, which is much fuller than anything found in the other creeds. Note, however, that it says nothing about anything else—there is no section on the Holy Spirit, as there is in the Nicene Creed, nor do we find the so-called miscellaneous provisions that are tacked on at the end of the other creeds. There is no mention of the church, of the communion of the saints, or of the forgiveness of sins. Our attention is focused on the resurrection of the body and eternal life, although both of these are set in the context of the judgment that will take place when the Son of God returns in his glory at the end of time.

The scriptural basis for the creed's eschatology can be found in 1 Corinthians 3:11–15. At the return of Christ, everyone—not just the righteous—will be raised from the dead and will be subject to a judgment based on the account they will have to give of their own works. Those who have done good will go to heaven, and those who have not will be consigned to everlasting fire. It is not a pleasant picture, but it at least seems fair, because the deserving will get their reward and the undeserving will be rejected. From a modern perspective, the real question is whether or not the Athanasian Creed teaches salvation by works. It would be surprising if it did, because so much of it reflects the teaching of Augustine, who battled for years against both that idea and its great propagator, Caesarius of Arles, and was also largely responsible for the condemnation of that teaching at the Synod of Orange in 529. But there can be no doubt that the wording is disconcerting to Protestants who have been brought up on Luther's doctrine of justification by faith alone. Perhaps the key to understanding what it means lies in the little phrase "shall give account." What are we supposed to say when God asks us what we have done with our lives? The answer is that, after having done everything, we are still expected to confess that we are unprofitable servants (Luke 17:10). The Christian knows that and attributes all the glory to God, who by his grace works in those who are less than the least of all the saints (cf. Eph. 3:8). Those who try to justify themselves before God will be rejected, but those who give the glory to him alone—as those who have done what is right—will be received into the heavenly kingdom prepared for them from before the foundation of the world.

Here the Athanasian Creed comes to an end. Having taken us through the mystery of the Holy Trinity and explained for us how the Son of God became a man in Jesus Christ, it concludes with a brief reminder of what this means for us. It was for our salvation that the Son came into the world, and for our salvation that God created us in the first place. Thus, it is peculiarly fitting that the creed, which opens with the words "whosoever will be saved," should conclude on essentially the same note: "This is the Catholic faith, which except a man believe faithfully, he cannot be saved." Salvation is what the Athanasian Creed is all about. It is as a proclamation of that gospel that it should be understood and received today.

Part 2

History

5

The Reformers and the Nicene Faith

An Assumed Catholicity

CARL L. BECKWITH

Hermann Sasse, one of the most important confessional Lutheran theologians of the twentieth century, said that "a church without patristics becomes a sect."[1] If you identify yourself with the theological labors of the Magisterial Reformers and hold very dearly the confession of *sola scriptura*, you may be somewhat surprised to hear Sasse insist that a church without an awareness of its catholic history and tradition threatens to become sectarian. After all, we might ask, are not the Scriptures sufficient to teach us all things about Jesus Christ as our Lord and Savior? Do we not as reformational Christians confess in doctrine and practice only that which agrees with Scripture?

The answer to both of those questions is certainly yes. That is the theological import of the exclusive "sola" in *sola scriptura*. At the same time, Hermann Sasse's point remains: we read and learn in community. As Christians, our reading community is comprised of all believers, past and present. Our community is the body of Christ, which is to say, as the Nicene Creed puts it, the one, holy, catholic, and apostolic church. To separate ourselves from such a community is to proceed with arrogance, to privilege particularity, and to undermine the catholicity of Christ's church. Moreover, it is to concede that the Reformation advanced novelty and stood in discontinuity with the long history of the church, its theologians, and its creedal affirmations.

In this chapter we will consider how the Reformers understood the relationship between their theological efforts and the broader history of the church catholic. We will start with a theological consideration of how the Reformers' articulation of the gospel (soteriology), the very heart of the Reformation, dictated their understanding of the church (ecclesiology). This will lay the proper groundwork for us to consider their approach to the theological labors of the church fathers and the early Christian creeds. I will offer two examples of how the Reformers articulated their assumed catholicity. The first example will be a survey of the *Book of Concord*. Here we will learn how Lutherans understood the relationship between Scripture and tradition and how they responded to the ecclesiological challenge of their opponents regarding continuity or discontinuity with the broader history of the church. The second example will come from John Calvin and his prefatory address to King Francis, which stands at the front of his *Institutes on the Christian Religion*. Here too we will see how Calvin understood his theological and ecclesiological relationship to the church fathers and the place of the Nicene faith in his understanding of Reformation theology.

The Gospel and the Church

In the early decades of the Reformation, two significant and certainly related theological issues were addressed by the various reforming parties. The first—what we think of as classic Reformation theology—focused on an evangelical reading of Scripture that taught a proper understanding of the gospel and the sacraments. The Reformers spent a considerable amount of time in their commentaries, dogmatic works, sermons, and catechisms demonstrating the biblical teaching that by grace alone, through faith alone, our sins are freely forgiven and we are imputed with Christ's righteousness. Moreover, the Reformers labored to articulate an evangelical understanding of the sacraments: baptism, absolution, and the Lord's Supper. The mainline Reformers (Lutherans, Reformed, and Anglicans) understood these sacraments to be the visible gospel, communicating the benefits of God's grace and the forgiveness of sins to all believers.

Although discussions about the gospel and especially the sacraments continued throughout the sixteenth century, a second important issue emerged in the 1520s and occupied center stage during the 1530s. This issue was ecclesiology, and a number of practical and theological concerns needed to be addressed. For starters, if our salvation is in Christ alone, and God's grace, the forgiveness of our sins, and salvation itself are preached and administered through the gospel and the sacraments, it is necessary to reflect on how this happens and, especially, where this happens. The Reformers, therefore, directed their attention to a scriptural understanding of what the church is and how the church has been called by God to convey the benefits of Christ's saving work to all people. For the most part, the Reformers agreed that the church is the body of Christ—those brought to faith by the Holy Spirit through the Word, confessing Jesus as Lord and clinging to him alone for salvation.

It should come as no surprise, then, that Luther, Calvin, and Cranmer understood the church as "the assembly of believers among whom the Gospel is preached in its purity and the holy sacraments are administered according to the Gospel."[2] Here we see that the Reformers understood the church not first as an institution—much less a hierarchy of bishops—but rather as a community of believers gathered by the Holy Spirit. Just as the Reformers labored to return priority to Christ in our salvation, so too, when the question turned to ecclesiology, they sought to return priority to the Holy Spirit. Put simply, the church is not something we create but is gathered from above by the Holy Spirit through the means of grace. Therefore, without any doubt, where two or three *are gathered by the Holy Spirit* in Christ's name, there our Lord is present and there is his church.

The Reformers' construal of their theological efforts on the means of grace (Word and sacrament) with their understanding of the church allowed them to emphasize the objective character and power of God's Word in establishing the unity of his people. It also made them susceptible to charges of novelty from their Roman opponents. On the one hand, this construal allowed the Reformers to emphasize the unity of the church that transcends all times and all places and even prevails amid our ecclesial divisions. Although deeply held scriptural convictions and theological disagreements prevent visible unity, they knew that by faith we are one in Christ and that that oneness is a gift from God brought about by his grace. Therefore, wherever the Word of God is present, and specifically wherever the free forgiveness of our sins is declared—as it is throughout the historic liturgy, in holy baptism, in the words of institution, and in the creed, among other places—there the gospel is proclaimed and the Holy Spirit is at work arousing, nourishing, and sustaining faith.

Despite his serious theological disagreement with Rome and his conviction that the pope was the antichrist, Martin Luther could still insist during the 1530s that the Church of Rome is holy and to be regarded as the church because of the work of the Holy Spirit in it. Luther writes:

> So today we still call the Church of Rome holy and all its sees holy, even though they have been undermined and their ministers are ungodly. . . . It is still the church. Although the city of Rome is worse than Sodom and Gomorrah, nevertheless there remain in it Baptism, the Sacrament, the voice and text of the Gospel, the Sacred Scriptures, the ministries, the name of Christ, and the name of God. Whoever has these, has them; whoever does not have them, has no excuse, for

the treasure is still there. Therefore the Church of Rome is holy, because it has the holy name of God, the Gospel, Baptism, etc. If these are present among a people, that people is called holy. Thus this Wittenberg of ours is a holy village, and we are truly holy, because we have been baptized, communed, taught, and called by God; we have the works of God among us, that is, the Word and the sacraments, and these make us holy.[3]

Here we see Luther's great confidence in the objective character of the Word of God and the persistence of the Holy Spirit, who is no respecter of denominational boundaries or human traditions. Where the Word of God is proclaimed and where the sacraments are administered according to that Word, there the Spirit is at work bringing people to faith in Christ Jesus alone, clothing them in Christ's righteousness, and declaring them holy.

On the other hand, because the Reformers construed their understanding of the church with their understanding of the gospel, and because that proclamation was itself contested by Rome as novel, they made themselves susceptible to charges of disunity or discontinuity with the broader history of the church catholic. Examples of this abound during the early history of the Reformation. For example, on the basis of numerous quotations from the early church fathers, Johann Eck repeatedly accused Martin Luther of being an enemy of the church.[4] Cardinal Sadoleto, in a polemical letter to the Protestants in Geneva during Calvin's exile to Strasbourg, writes the following:

> The point in dispute is whether it is more expedient for your salvation, and whether you think you will do what is more pleasing to God, by believing and following what the Catholic Church throughout the whole world, now for more than fifteen hundred years, or (if we require clear and certain recorded notice of the facts) for more than thirteen hundred years approves with general consent; or innovations introduced within these twenty-five years, by crafty, or, as they think themselves, acute men; but men certainly who are not themselves the Catholic Church.[5]

Immediately we see that Sadoleto is working with a different understanding of the church.[6] He identifies it institutionally—which, he argues, can be traced back through the centuries to the early church. Needless to say, the Reformers never conceded the simple argument advanced by Sadoleto that the Roman Catholic Church had some privilege in claiming the fifteen centuries of church history as its own history. We recall here Luther's own narration of his discovery of the gospel. As soon as he came to a proper, biblical understanding of the righteousness of God and justification by faith alone, he turned to the fathers and found his own insights in St. Augustine.[7] With all this said, we also see Sadoleto conflate ecclesiology and soteriology. For him, to be located within the right visible church is to be assured of salvation.[8] For Sadoleto, the question a person must first ask is if he belongs to the true Catholic church. If he says yes, then he can be certain of his salvation. For the Reformers, as we have seen, the questions are turned around. If a person confesses that Jesus Christ alone is his Lord and Savior, then he can be assured that he belongs to the body of Christ and is a member of the one, true, catholic church. The point to be observed here is that all parties, Roman Catholic and Protestant, assumed an intimate relationship between soteriology and ecclesiology, even if they understand these issues differently.

Out of this theological context and amid these charges of novelty, the Reformers were forced to consider closely their relationship to the broader tradition of the church, and particularly to the theological labors of the early church fathers and the decisions of the ecumenical councils from Nicea to Chalcedon. The mainline Reformers never hesitated in accepting the decrees of the ecumenical councils on the doctrine of the Trinity and Christ or the great creeds from the early church. There was no dispute on these matters. The need for creed was simply assumed. Indeed, the Lutherans placed the Apostles', Nicene, and Athanasian creeds before their own confessional documents in the *Book of Concord*. A similar move is made in the Thirty-Nine Articles.[9] Even though Calvin never promoted the Nicene Creed in the same official manner, he most certainly embraced its content and significance.

Although discussion was not needed on the normative character of the early Christian creeds, questions did remain regarding the tradition of the church, its place in theological reflection, and its authority in establishing articles of faith. After all (to use the example of the Lutherans), is it not somewhat inconsistent for them to claim *sola scriptura* and at the same time to embrace the authority of the early Christian creeds? If you accept the creeds as authoritative, why not the rest of the tradition? Why not argue, as the Council of Trent does in the middle of the sixteenth century, that Scripture and tradition (both unwritten and written traditions) are equal authorities in establishing articles of faith?[10] These sorts of questions forced the Reformers to articulate an evangelical understanding of the church's tradition, explaining the relationship between their own sixteenth-century theological commitments and the theological endeavors of the early church fathers and ecumenical councils. Questions dealing with continuity and discontinuity between the fathers and the Reformers, the relationship between Scripture and tradition, and the role of the church in securing the faith handed down by the apostles amid changing historical circumstances compelled these individuals to offer some theological assessment of the relevance and place of patristic exegesis and theology in their own sixteenth-century confessional efforts.

The Reformers and the Church Catholic

Some in our day (whether Roman Catholic, evangelical, or non-Christian) have the impression that the Reformation was about *discontinuity* with the previous tradition of the church. The story goes something like this: the Reformers rejected the corruption of the church and its superstitious practices, which can be traced back to the emergence of Christendom in the fourth century during the reign of Emperor Constantine. During this dark period of history, church and state were confused, and philosophical assumptions foreign to the Scriptures were embraced. Given this historical reality, good evangelicals need not trouble themselves with a study of the early and medieval church—after all, that's Roman Catholicism—but need only read their Bibles. The Bible is their creed; they have no need for anything else. The murky and obscure period—considerable as it may have been and encompassing, among other things, the great creeds of the Christian faith—need not be studied, since it involved only the distortion of the gospel and the so-called hellenization of the Christian faith.

There are many problems with evangelicals embracing this understanding of the history of Christianity. For starters, it stems from a nineteenth-century reading of church history that is defined by Enlightenment assumptions and a rejection of the universal theological claims made by orthodox Christianity. This nineteenth-century historical view sought to liberate itself from the dogmatic captivity of historic Christianity and therefore rejected such things as the biblical teaching on the Trinity, the virgin birth of Christ, substitutionary atonement, imputed righteousness, and the Bible as the verbally inspired and inerrant Word of God. The advocates of this view promoted a liberal theology shaped by a particular understanding of history that wanted little to do with normative Christianity and its creedal affirmations. For those indebted to the theological arguments and conclusions of the Reformers, this view of history—which asserts that the doctrinal claims of early Christianity stand in discontinuity with the witness of Scripture and that we, as reformational Christians, need not engage the patristic and medieval witnesses—must be wholeheartedly rejected. Indeed, when we look at the writings of the Reformers, we find them assuming that they stand in continuity with the broader tradition of the church.

Two examples from the sixteenth century, encompassing the Lutheran and Reformed traditions, follow. These examples show how they understood themselves to be in theological continuity with the great tradition of the church, especially the early church fathers and ecumenical creeds.

A Lutheran Example

The *Book of Concord*, published in 1580 at the end of a long half-century of intense debate, is generally described as a collection of official church documents that define the exegetical and theological understanding of the Lutherans on the disputed issues of the Reformation. While that is true, the *Book of Concord* makes a much grander claim than this. These Lutheran confessions give witness not to occasional and incidental exegetical insights on disputed theological questions; rather, they offer a complete exposition of the Scriptures by establishing with clarity the article on which the church stands or falls: justification by faith alone. This article of faith is at the theological center of the *Book of Concord* because it is at the center of Holy Scripture. Moreover, to properly confess this article of faith is to properly confess the gospel—which, in turn, serves as an evangelical *regula fidei* and hermeneutical key to the inspired and inerrant Word of God. To read the Scriptures in this way is to read them christologically and to rightly divide them as Law and Gospel. To do otherwise, from the perspective of the *Book of Concord*, threatens the purity of the gospel, and, as indicated above, any rightful claim to the name Christian—one brought to faith by the Holy Spirit through the means of grace, clinging to Christ alone for the free forgiveness of sins and the gift of eternal life.

The exposition of Scripture offered in the *Book of Concord* is the norm according to which the confessing and teaching of all believers is to be tested and judged. The believers in question are not only the members of what are designated as Lutheran churches but all believers and all churches of all times. As such, it is not the Lutheran church but the "one holy catholic and apostolic church" that has spoken in the *Book of Concord*.[11] The normative claim that Lutheran confessions are for all times and all peoples—an adamantly catholic position—is the reason that Lutherans never issued confessional statements beyond the sixteenth century. Since Lutheranism, according to the *Book of Concord*, is firmly and faithfully anchored in the unchanging Word of God, it does not conceive of theological evolution or doctrinal development. Any such development is more properly seen as departure from the normative exposition of Scripture in the *Book of Concord* and therefore departure from the one, holy, catholic, and apostolic church. This position does not preclude Lutherans from offering theological opinions on questions or issues not addressed in the *Book of Concord*. On the contrary, this posture of the Lutheran confessions, firmly rooted in the Scriptures alone and justification by faith as the foundation upon which all other articles of faith stand, provides the dogmatic tools necessary to answer any and all questions brought to the Christian.

The catholicity of the Lutheran confession is seen not only in its general theological posture but also in the particularity of its confessional documents. The *Book of Concord* opens not with sixteenth-century confessional works but with the three chief trinitarian symbols or creeds from the early church: the Apostles' Creed, the Nicene Creed, and the Athanasian Creed. The Augsburg Confession, the defining confessional document of Lutheranism and certainly the most influential Protestant confession of the sixteenth century, concludes with a remarkable and bold claim to theological continuity with the catholic tradition of the church. It states in unequivocal terms: "Nothing has been received among us, in doctrine or ceremony, that is contrary to scripture or to the church catholic."[12] The Lutherans are not just denying theological novelty in this statement. Nor are they simply asserting theological continuity with the church catholic. They are boldly claiming to be the *true* catholic church. They, and not their Roman opponents, have received and proclaimed only Scripture and its articles of faith as articulated and defended by the community of all believers gathered by the Spirit through the Word in the church throughout the centuries.

When appeal is made to the catholic church or the Great Tradition of the church, the *Book of Concord* privileges the patristic period. Not only does the *Book of Concord* cite specific church fathers (including the lengthy Catalog of Testimonies unofficially appended to the end of the Confessions, demonstrating the continuity between the church fathers and the Lutheran understanding of Christ's two natures), but it also uses theological definitions from the early church. For example, the first article of the Augsburg Confession confesses the Trinity and appeals specifically to the theological grammar employed by the fathers in discussing the word *person*. Similarly, the second article of the Apology of the Augsburg Confession confesses original sin and appeals specifically to "the patristic definition of original sin" against the false view advocated by the medieval scholastics. After a lengthy discussion of Christ as propitiator and justifier, the Apology ends by saying that this is what the prophetic and apostolic Scriptures teach, the holy fathers confess, and the whole church of Christ (which is to say, the one, holy, catholic, and apostolic church) receives.[13] At the end of the first part of the Augsburg Confession, following the summary of doctrine (*summa doctrinae*) that is preached and taught by Lutherans, we again find a strong assertion of theological continuity with the church fathers and an unequivocal claim to being the true catholic church. We read:

> Since this teaching is grounded clearly on the Holy Scriptures and is not contrary or opposed to that of the church catholic, or even the Roman church (in so far as the latter's teaching is reflected in the writings of the Fathers), we think that our opponents cannot disagree with us in the articles set forth above.[14]

The claim is clear: Lutherans teach only what is firmly grounded in the Scriptures, confessed by the early church fathers, and received by the universal Christian church. Their self-understanding, therefore, is that they are the rightful heirs and claimants of the one, holy, catholic, and apostolic church.

Despite this claim as the true catholic church, the Lutherans knew well that their Roman opponents could cite as much, if not more, tradition in support of their theological opinions. Although the Lutherans may seem at first glance to be making an arbitrary distinction between what constitutes the genuine tradition of the church and what should be regarded as novelty—assigning, no doubt, novelty to positions of disagreement—their distinction has more to do with an understanding of authority. The Lutherans were never interested in indiscriminately accepting the teachings of the early church fathers that stood in obvious tension and contradiction with Scripture. Martin Luther warns in the Smalcald Articles, "It will not do to make articles of faith out of the holy Fathers' words or works."[15] In the Apology of the Augsburg Confession, the rather obvious observation is made that the church fathers were sinful men who could make mistakes.[16] Therefore, we should not be surprised to discover that occasionally they built "stubble" on the sure foundation of Scripture.[17]

A fuller explanation of Scripture and the church fathers is found in the Epitome of the Formula of Concord. Here the Lutherans offer a subtle theological distinction between the authority of Scripture and tradition.

> We believe, teach, and confess that the prophetic and apostolic writings of the Old and New Testaments are the only rule and norm according to which all doctrines and teachers alike must be appraised and judged. . . . Other writings of ancient and modern teachers, whatever their names, should not be put on par with the Holy Scripture. Every single one of them should be subordinated to the Scriptures and should be received in no other way and no further than as witnesses to the fashion in which the doctrine of the prophets and apostles was preserved in post-apostolic times.[18]

The Epitome continues by emphasizing the distinction between Scripture and all other writings. Scripture is the only rule and norm according to which all doctrines must be understood and judged as right or wrong. To use the language of the theologian, Scripture is the *norma normans*. Scripture alone possesses the authority to judge, a point emphasized throughout this section of the Epitome. On the other hand, the symbols of our faith that accurately and appropriately summarize the chief teachings of Scripture are not judges of Scripture but are always judged by Scripture. Again, to use the language of the theologian, these symbols, whether the Nicene Creed or Luther's Small Catechism (which is daringly referred to as "the Layman's Bible" in the *Book of Concord*), are considered *norma normata*. They are witnesses or expositions of the faith that do not judge Scripture but are rather judged by it. Because they stand under the Scriptures and offer faithful expositions of it, they serve as norms for our thinking and speaking as fellow members of the one, holy, catholic, and apostolic church.

For the Lutherans, to confess *sola scriptura* means that Scripture alone determines all articles of faith and that it alone serves as the authoritative voice in the Christian community on matters of doctrine and practice. When we gather together as the body of Christ to hear the Word of God, we do so in a churchly context that includes the whole community of faith, past and present. This, for the Lutherans, is what it means to gather around Word and sacrament as the one, holy, catholic, and apostolic church. Included in that gathering are the saints of old, those heavenly witnesses who have gone before us, from the church catholic.

A Reformed Example

In his dedicatory epistle to King Francis I of France at the beginning of the 1536 *Institutes of the Christian Religion*, John Calvin discusses the charges of Protestant novelty and whether they or their Roman opponents stand in continuity with the early church fathers.[19] Calvin begins with a plea on behalf of the persecuted Protestants in France who teach nothing contrary to the Scriptures. According to St. Paul, notes Calvin, all prophecy, all teaching, must be made in accord with the "analogy of faith" (ἀναλογία τῆς πίστης; Rom. 12:6). Therefore, continues Calvin,

> if our interpretation be measured by this rule of faith, victory is in our hands. For what is more consonant with faith than to recognize that we are naked of all virtue, in order to be clothed by God? That we are empty of all good, to be filled by him? That we are slaves of sin, to be freed by him? Blind, to be illumined by him? Lame, to be made straight by him? Weak, to be sustained by him? To take away from us all occasion for glorying, that he alone may stand forth gloriously and we glory in him (cf. 1 Cor. 1:31; 2 Cor. 10:17).[20]

Calvin ends this beautiful section of the letter wondering why the evangelicals, who set their hope on Christ alone for their eternal salvation, are the ones persecuted, despised, hated, and charged with all sorts of novelty and false teaching. He then specifically turns to the charges of novelty. He writes, "They [his Roman opponents] do not cease to assail our doctrine and to reproach and defame it with names that render it hated or suspect. They call it 'new' and 'of recent birth.' They reproach it as 'doubtful and uncertain.'"[21] Calvin responds with sharp rhetoric. To the charge of novelty or newness, he agrees; it is likely new to his opponents, since to them both Christ and the gospel are new. He who knows the unchanging Word of God, however, knows this teaching to be anything but new. It is firmly rooted in the Scriptures and most fully accords with that ancient preaching of St. Paul, who declared that Jesus Christ was "delivered up for our trespasses and raised for our justification" (Rom. 4:25). Calvin's opponents think the evangelical teaching on the gospel is doubtful and uncertain. Again, that the gospel is doubtful and uncertain for them, Calvin agrees. After all, asks Calvin, is this not what our Lord complained about through the prophet Isaiah: "The ox knows its owner, and the donkey its master's crib, but Israel does not know, my people do not understand" (Isa. 1:3)?[22]

Although Calvin's rhetoric is polemical, his point is clear: the Protestant teaching on Christ and the gospel is not new, doubtful, or uncertain. Rather, it is rooted in the eternal Word of God. Such a claim, however, requires some support beyond the Scriptures, lest Calvin be put in the awkward position of affirming a reading of Scripture unknown from St. Paul to the sixteenth century. This is, of course, the charge of Calvin's opponents. They insist that the church fathers knew nothing of these teachings. Calvin rejects such an argument and responds: "If the contest were to be determined by patristic authority, the tide of victory—to put it very modestly—would turn to our side."[23] Indeed, Calvin continues, "I could with no trouble at all prove that the greater part of what we are saying today meets their [the fathers'] approval."[24] The most important thing we learn from the fathers is that we all belong to the one Christ (1 Cor. 3:23) and that we must obey him in all things without exception (Col. 3:20). If we fail to recognize this hierarchy of authority or distinction between the Word of God and the words of those who throughout the centuries confess Christ, we will have no certainty in anything we believe, teach, and confess. The fathers, though holy men, were, concludes Calvin, "ignorant of many things, often disagreed among themselves, and sometimes even contradicted themselves."[25]

Although Calvin suggests that he can demonstrate the continuity between the Protestants and the church fathers—what would arguably be an exercise in constructive theology—he does not do this. Instead, he proceeds polemically by demonstrating the false claims of his opponents and underscoring their departure from the "good statements" of the fathers. They claim to follow the fathers, argues Calvin, but in fact teach many things that the fathers have rejected. At this point, Calvin strings together a number of patristic citations that reject such things as excess ornamentation and ostentation in Christian worship, Rome's ban on eating meat during Lent, monks who do not work with their hands, the teaching of transubstantiation, the open communion practiced by Rome, communion in one kind, any teaching without clear and evident witness in the Scriptures, and, finally, clerical celibacy.[26] Calvin insists that he could list numerous other departures by the Roman church from the fathers but will let this list suffice to demonstrate the discontinuity between sixteenth-century Rome and the early church fathers.

Calvin ends by turning to the issue of ecclesiology proper. Not only do his opponents charge Protestantism with novelty and discontinuity with the fathers; they charge Protestantism with an abandonment and rejection of the church itself. The problem has to do with the definition of the church. Rome, argues Calvin, looks only to the external, the visible, the walls themselves, and the continuity of bishops. Are they not familiar with the words of St. Hilary of Poitiers, he asks? It was Hilary, continues Calvin, who wrote: "One thing I admonish you, beware of Antichrist. It is wrong that a love of walls has seized you; wrong that beneath these you introduce the name of peace. Is there any doubt that Antichrist will have his seat in them? To my mind, mountains, woods, lakes, prisons, and chasms are safer. For, either abiding in or cast into them, the prophets prophesied."[27] The mark of the church is not outward magnificence or continuity of bishops. According to Calvin, who here echoes the Augsburg Confession, the marks of the church are "the pure teaching of God's Word and the lawful administration of the sacraments."[28] When the Word is preached and the sacraments are administered according to the Scriptures, the Holy Spirit is at work arousing, nourishing, and sustaining faith. This is the church, no matter how small, no matter how desperate, no matter if it be in the flames of a fiery furnace (Dan. 3): Christ is there protecting and defending his church as he has promised to do unto the end of the age (Matt. 28:20).

Conclusion

What I hope we begin to see is that the Reformers' commitment to the gospel and indeed the great *solas* of the Reformation bear on their understanding of the church's catholicity and should, then, bear on our own understanding of church. That is to say, if we assert *sola gratia* and *sola scriptura*, then we must also, as the Reformers show us, assert that the church is created by the Holy Spirit who calls people to faith through the Word. As Martin Luther expresses it in his Large Catechism, the church is "the mother that begets and bears every Christian through the Word of God."[29]

The church, then, is the assembly of all believers, past and present, and continuity and unity exists because of the work of the Holy Spirit. The *una ecclesia* confessed in the Nicene Creed is the body of Christ, the assembly of all believers of all times and places. It is holy, catholic, and apostolic not because of human traditions or definitions of what constitutes the church, but rather because of the work of the Holy Spirit through the means of grace, which are, as the Reformers adamantly insist, the marks of the church. What this means, then, is that where the marks are present—namely, Word and sacrament ministry—the Holy Spirit is, as promised, at work, faith is confessed, and Jesus is present, reconciling believers to the Father. This way of thinking is what leads the Reformers to insist that they are the true catholic church. This is what stands behind Hermann Sasse's insistence that a church that forgets its history and its catholicity is a church that tends toward sectarianism, privileging individuality and particularity.

By reminding ourselves of how the Reformers contextualized their scriptural understanding of soteriology with ecclesiology, we should be encouraged to deepen our own understanding of God's eternal Word by surrounding ourselves with a community of fellow believers who will assist us in our reading and studying of the Scriptures. What better community could we have than one filled with the voices of the early and medieval fathers, the Reformers, and the great Christian voices of our own day? We have that community when we gather together and listen to the words of those faithful Christians who have gone before us. If their goal was to expound only the Scriptures, seeking the truth of God's Word and confessing Christ as Lord and Savior, and if our goal is the same, there could be no better company to keep than Irenaeus, Athanasius, Hilary of Poitiers, Augustine, Bernard of Clairvaux, Thomas Aquinas, Martin Luther, and those many other saints of the church catholic. They are living witnesses because of their faith in Christ and, as members of the body of Christ, as brothers and sisters in Christ, they are our eternal contemporaries.

6

The Nicene Faith and the Catholicity of the Church

Evangelical Retrieval and the Problem of Magisterium

Steven R. Harmon

The year 2009 marked two not-unrelated anniversaries. Ten years earlier, evangelical patristics scholar D. H. Williams, then teaching at Loyola University of Chicago, published *Retrieving the Tradition and Renewing Evangelicalism: A Primer for Suspicious Protestants*.[1] In that book and several subsequent publications, Williams pleads passionately for evangelicals to embrace as their own heritage the patristic tradition, with the fourth-century Nicene configuration of faith and practice as its canonical core.[2] Many evangelicals who long for their churches to manifest a more conscious catholicity have enthusiastically applauded Williams's project, but others have raised hard questions about its viability that are not easily answered. In the Spring 2009 issue of the journal *Pro Ecclesia*, Dennis Martin reviewed Williams's more recent book *Evangelicals and Tradition: The Formative Influence of the Early Church*. I quote here some extended excerpts from Martin's review:

> Following up on several earlier books devoted to a similar thematic, Dan Williams, my former Loyola Chicago colleague, challenges evangelical Protestants

to undertake a ressourcement [a French word for "retrieval"] in the writings of the church fathers of the first five centuries, a specifically evangelical Protestant ressourcement that steps around most of the ecclesial issues. . . . Even for its intended readership, *Evangelicals and Tradition* suffers from another nearly insurmountable problem: even if this or that evangelical reader would seek to enter deeply into the patristic world, not by way of guidance from either an Orthodox or Catholic magisterium but as an individual Baptist, Pentecostal, evangelical Lutheran, or independent Bible church leader, would not those persons or groups who thus answer Williams' call end up with widely different, idiosyncratic portraits of the *catholica* [i.e., the things that belong to the catholicity] of the "patristic tradition"? Why should D. H. Williams' portrait be authoritative for any of his readers? . . . Who gets to define, delimit, describe, and characterize the content and characteristics of [the traditional] memory [of the church]? . . . Given the absence of an articulated theology of authority and the absence of a magisterium among evangelicals, could evangelicals who might take up Williams' challenge get very far? Would they do so as amateur historians or as theologians? Such a question is a roundabout way of suggesting that, unless something like a supernaturally guided, indefectible organic ecclesial magisterium exists and is part of Christ's plan for the church, do not all renewers and reformers function essentially as private historians, at most continually reasserting on their own behalf (against rival private historian claimants) that the Holy Spirit has blessed their particular version of ressourcement?[3]

One does not have to affirm that "a supernaturally guided, indefectible organic ecclesial magisterium exists and is part of Christ's plan for the church" to grant that Martin is right on target in naming the elephant in the room whenever evangelicals talk about retrieving the tradition. What is the tradition that ought to be retrieved? Who decides what the tradition is and to what degree it is authoritative for us? To ask these questions is to inquire about the location of the authority by which the church may teach something regarding Christian belief, worship, or practice as the teaching of the church on these matters. The teaching authority of the church is its magisterium, and anytime some expression of the church proposes something as Christian teaching, magisterium is at work, even if unacknowledged. But since many evangelicals are under the impression that to be Catholic is to have a magisterium and to be Protestant is to reject magisterium, it would doubtless be utterly alien to them to contemplate how they might go about the magisterial implementation of Williams's proposals.

Baptists and the Retrieval of the Catholic Tradition

Though Williams addressed these calls for the retrieval of tradition to a broadly evangelical readership, he is a Baptist by denominational tradition, has served as a Baptist pastor, and since 2002 has taught at Baptist-related

Baylor University. The year 2009 marked the quadricentennial celebration of the Baptist tradition: in 1609 in Amsterdam, a group of English expatriates formed the earliest Baptist congregation. In the years since Williams published *Retrieving the Tradition and Renewing Evangelicalism*, a small but growing number of Baptist theologians have contended that Baptists too must reclaim the Nicene faith and other expressions of ancient catholicity for the sake of their future, arguing that such retrieval is not alien to Baptist identity but very much in continuity with the surprisingly catholic ecclesial outlook of the earliest Baptists.

My own contribution to this recent catholic consciousness in Baptist theology was a book titled *Towards Baptist Catholicity: Essays on Tradition and the Baptist Vision*.[4] In it I defined the catholicity toward which Baptists should move in a way that includes and builds upon historic Baptist affirmations of the church as catholic. Though of course there are many exceptions whenever one generalizes about Baptists, most Baptists should have no quibble with what we might call a *quantitative* understanding of the catholicity of the church, according to which there is a universal church to which all believers belong and that transcends visible local congregations. It is explicitly affirmed in the two most significant Baptist confessions from the seventeenth century. According to the Particular Baptist Second London Confession published in 1689, "The Catholick or universal Church, which (with respect to internal work of the Spirit, and truth of grace) may be called invisible, consists of the whole number of the Elect, that have been, are, or shall be gathered into one, under Christ the head thereof." Likewise, the 1678 General Baptist confession called the Orthodox Creed appropriated three of the four classic "marks of the church" from the Nicene Creed, confessing in Article 29 that "there is one holy catholick church, consisting of, or made up of the whole number of the elect, that have been, are, or shall be gathered, in one body under Christ, the only head thereof," and in Article 30, "We believe the visible church of Christ on earth, is made up of several distinct congregations, which make up that one catholick church, or mystical body of Christ."[5]

But beyond this quantitative recognition that Baptists belong to the whole church and the whole church belongs to Baptists, I argued that catholicity also entails a "pattern of faith and practice that distinguished early catholic Christianity from Gnosticism, Arianism, Donatism, and all manner of other heresies and schisms"; it is therefore "a *qualitative* fullness of faith and order that is visibly expressed in one Eucharistic fellowship."[6]

The Nature of Nicene Catholicity

This chapter will return to my case for a more qualitatively catholic vision of Baptist identity. First, however, some explanation of the ancient Christian usage of the term *catholic* that informed my proposals is in order.[7] The Apostles' Creed professes belief in the "holy *catholic* church." In the Nicene Creed (our convenient designation for the Niceno-Constantinopolitan Creed issued not by the Council of Nicea but by the Second Ecumenical Council, the Council of Constantinople in 381), we confess that we believe in "one holy *catholic* and apostolic Church." In the latter creedal affirmation, unless the Greek καθολικήν (*katholikēn*) is merely a redundant echo of μίαν (*mian*, "one"), it must mean something beyond an affirmation of the oneness of the universal church—although what else "catholicity" might mean is notoriously difficult to define. Historic understandings of "catholic" as a mark of the church range from the (invisible) oneness of the (invisible) universal church all the way to an ecclesial status of communion with Rome.[8]

The earliest Christian use of καθολικόν is in Ignatius of Antioch's letter to the Smyrneans, where in section 8.2 he writes, "Wherever Jesus Christ is, there is the catholic church." It seems clear that a quantitative catholicity is one dimension of what Ignatius means by "catholic" in *Smyrneans* 8, for he emphasizes the christological basis of the church's universality: Wherever Jesus Christ is, there is the "whole" or "universal" church. Yet the quantitative catholicity communicated in this text does not exclude from Ignatius's usage a much more narrow meaning that increasingly became associated with the later patristic use of the Greek καθολικόν and the Latin *catholicus* in reference to the pattern of faith and practice that distinguished early catholic Christianity from heresy and schism.[9] One paragraph prior to the description of the church as "catholic" in *Smyrneans* 8, Ignatius warns the church at Smyrna regarding the doctrine and practice of the Docetists: "They abstain from the eucharist and prayer, since they do not confess that the eucharist is the flesh of our savior Jesus Christ, which suffered on behalf of our sins and which the Father raised in his kindness." Then Ignatius exhorts them to "flee divisions as the beginning of evils."[10]

It is significant that immediately prior to this section, Ignatius links the doctrinal errors of the Docetists, who lacked a truly embodied Christology, with their failures to embody the Christian way of life: "But take note of those who [are heterodox with reference to] the gracious gift of Jesus Christ that has come to us, and see how they are opposed to the mind of God. They have no interest in love, in the widow, the orphan, the oppressed, the one who is in chains or the one set free, the one who is hungry or the one who thirsts."[11] For Ignatius, then, a qualitative catholicity is robustly incarnational. Because it is incarnational, it is also sacramental, and because it is incarnational and sacramental, it is also socially embodied and therefore concerned with social justice.[12] Besides an incarnational Christology and sacramental realism, this qualitative catholicity for Ignatius included the visible unity of the church. For example, Ignatius warns the Smyreans to "flee divisions as the beginning of evils" (*Smyrn.* 7.2). It also included an embodied safeguard of the unity of the church in the ministry of episcopal oversight. In *Smyrneans* 8 Ignatius urges,

> All of you should follow the bishop as Jesus Christ follows the Father; and follow the presbytery [i.e., the elders] as you would the apostles. Respect the deacons as the commandment of God. Let no one do anything involving the church without the bishop. Let that eucharist be considered valid that occurs under the bishop or the one to whom he entrusts it. Let the congregation be wherever the bishop is; just as wherever Jesus Christ is, there also is the [catholic] church. It is not permitted either to baptize or to hold a love feast without the bishop. But whatever he approves is acceptable to God, so that everything you do should be secure and valid.[13]

The precise nature of the office of bishop, as portrayed in the Ignatian correspondence, is much disputed. On the one hand, there are indications of something approaching a monepiscopate; on the other hand, the bishop and the elders collegially share a ministry of oversight—thus the exhortation to follow the elders as well as the bishop. Regardless of how one reads the role of the bishop in these letters, it is indisputable that we have here a threefold ministry—bishop, elder, deacon—in which the office of bishop is distinguished from the office of elder and in which the episcopate serves to guard the church against various threats to catholic unity.

These four marks of qualitative catholicity—incarnational Christology, sacramental realism, visible unity, and the ministry of oversight—are by no means restricted to *Smyrneans* 6–8 in the Ignatian correspondence, for they are interwoven with the anti-Docetic polemic that is a central theological concern of the letters. Whatever else may have been involved in Ignatius's concept of the church as catholic, his understanding of catholicity in qualitative as well as quantitative terms coheres with later patristic uses of καθολικόν. By the fourth century, Eusebius of Caesarea, Athanasius, and Epiphanius were employing the adjective to denote the orthodoxy of the church's faith,[14] and in his catechetical lectures, Cyril of Jerusalem offered an expanded definition of catholicity that is both quantitative and qualitative:

> The Church is called Catholic because it is spread throughout the world, from end to end of the earth; also because it teaches universally and completely all the doctrines which [one] should know concerning things visible and invisible, heavenly and earthly; and also because it subjects to right worship all [hu]mankind, rulers and ruled, lettered and unlettered; further because it treats and heals universally every sort of sin committed by soul and body, and it possesses in itself every conceivable virtue, whether in deeds, words or in spiritual gifts of every kind.[15]

Lest one suppose that the Reformers left this perspective on the catholicity of the church on the Roman side of the sixteenth-century division of the church in the West, one should note Philipp Melanchthon's definition of catholicity:

Why is this epithet added in the article of the creed, so that the Church is called Catholic? Because it is an assembly dispersed throughout the whole earth and because its members, wherever they are, and however separated in place, embrace and externally profess one and the same utterance of true doctrine in all ages from the beginning until the very end. . . . Those are truly called Catholic who embrace the doctrine of the truly Catholic Church . . . that which is supported by the witness of all time, of all ages, which believes what the prophets and apostles taught, and which does not tolerate factions, heresies, and heretical assemblies. We must all be Catholic, i.e., embrace this word which the rightly-thinking Church holds, separate from, and unentangled with, sects warring against that Word.[16]

Melanchthon exemplifies the catholic commitments of the first generation of the Reformers, which frequently seem counterintuitive to their more recent heirs. The "catholicity of the Reformation" stood in continuity with the patristic conviction—expressed inchoately by Ignatius of Antioch and with greater specificity by Cyril of Jerusalem and other fourth-century Christian writers—that the quantitative inclusion of all Christians in the catholicity of the church is inseparable from a qualitatively catholic pattern of faith and practice that characterizes this church and its members.[17]

But is this configuration of the catholic faith biblical? One can argue that the catholic faith we encounter more explicitly in Ignatius of Antioch was already embedded in the New Testament. In the case of Ignatius, we are not only dealing with an early Christian author in close chronological proximity to the Christianity reflected in the New Testament. We are also reading literature that has textual links with various layers of the formation of the New Testament documents.[18] In light of those connections, it is much more likely that we will encounter continuity than discontinuity between the New Testament and the Christianity of Ignatius of Antioch.

By way of illustration, consider the sacramental realism so emphasized by Ignatius. Some Bible-based theologies of the Lord's Supper might suppose that the early doctrine of real presence we find in Ignatius is a discontinuous development beyond the New Testament. But consider the Gospel of John, so closely connected chronologically and conceptually with the letters of Ignatius. John lacks an institution narrative, but its role is fulfilled by the sayings of the Johannine Jesus that have eucharistic functions. John 6:48–60 has the theological function of the Synoptic institution narratives, for John's community has remembered Jesus's declaration that he is the Bread of Life in light of their postresurrection celebration of the Eucharist. They cannot have received these words about eating the flesh and drinking the blood of Christ without relating them to the experience of their own eucharistic fellowship. If Ignatius belongs to a qualitatively catholic trajectory that includes sacramental realism, then so does the Gospel of John.

Catholicity and the Unavoidable Problem of Magisterium

Back to what this has to do with Baptists and other evangelicals. Baptists and other evangelicals need this sort of qualitative catholicity first and foremost because it will help their churches form more faithful disciples of Jesus Christ. To the degree that churches identify themselves as other than catholic in this qualitative sense that includes especially the incarnational and sacramental dimensions of catholicity, there is a good chance that they are forming their members in a quasi-gnostic pattern of faith and practice that is perilously close to being sub-Christian. Thus I tried to argue in *Towards Baptist Catholicity*.

In the foreword to that book, Anglican theologian Paul Avis raised questions similar to those voiced in Martin's review of Williams. Avis wondered "whether authority is an underdeveloped and therefore unresolved issue" in the book, in particular with reference to the episcopal office.[19] I embraced certain ancient marks of catholicity but ignored the historical role of the bishops as the ecclesial location of teaching authority that authorizes the other marks of catholicity. In retrospect, I grant that I largely dodged that difficulty. I attempted to convince my fellow Baptists that we need the lowercase-c *catholic* tradition, but I did not offer a fully developed proposal as to how we might appropriate and configure a fuller catholicity. What, or who, would authorize a catholic pattern of Baptist faith and practice? By failing to clearly locate ecclesial authority, I grant that the argument of my book lacks adequate safeguards against the very thing it seeks to remedy: self-chosen patterns of faith and practice by independent individuals and autonomous congregations in the configuration of a "selective catholicity."[20] I skirted these issues partly because my rhetorical goal was to convince theologically educated Baptists that their communities need a fuller catholicity and that there are precedents within the Baptist tradition itself for a more catholic vision of Baptist identity than currently prevails, and partly because I was not yet satisfied with my own provisional solution.

I am told that some non-Baptists who have taken note of the small but growing number of publications by Baptist theologians who advocate a more catholic identity for Baptists[21] are concerned about the dangers of eclecticism inherent in such an enterprise. I share these concerns. Many Baptist readers of *Towards Baptist Catholicity* have told me that they especially appreciated chapter 8, in which I urged the Baptist retrieval of catholic practices of corporate worship that include celebration of the full Christian year; use of the common lectionary; more frequent eucharistic celebration; confession of the ancient creeds; the use of patristic forms of prayer such as collects, acts of confession, and pardon; the passing of the peace; narration of the lives of the saints; and the singing of hymn texts of patristic composition. But what is to keep a Baptist adaptation of such aspects of the catholic liturgical tradition from falling prey to the same undisciplined eclecticism evident in the services of some self-identified emergent or emerging church communities? What are the criteria for planning "catholic Baptist" liturgies, other than the preferences of the ministers and members of particular local congregations? This is merely illustrative of the larger question of how one determines which elements of catholicity Baptists can embrace without betraying their Baptist identity. Ironically, the very concept of a definable Baptist identity and the possibility that it could be betrayed point in the direction of an unacknowledged Baptist magisterium.

It is not only Baptist and evangelical academics who encounter the problem of magisterium when they turn to the Christian past for the resources they need in doing theology in the service of the church today. As more and more tradition-starved evangelicals sense that there is something in the Great Tradition—and in the ongoing Catholic and Orthodox ecclesial traditions that stand in concrete continuity with it—that their own evangelical churches lack, and begin to experiment with retrieving it, they run headlong into the problem of magisterium. Journalist Terry Mattingly recently profiled Gordon Atkinson, former pastor of Covenant Baptist Church near San Antonio, Texas, and author of the blog *Real Live Preacher*. Atkinson had completed a thirteen-week pastoral sabbatical, during which he discovered Eastern Orthodox liturgy and began to attend services at Russian, Greek, and Antiochian Orthodox churches. But now, Mattingly writes, Atkinson "is returning to his Baptist pulpit, while hearing choirs of voices arguing in his head representing many different eras of church history: 'What I don't know how to do is rank all of these voices and decide who has authority,' [Atkinson] said. 'Who is right and who is wrong? . . . And I want to know, where does Gordon Atkinson fit into this whole picture? I know that I can't go back to the old Protestant, evangelical way that I was, but I don't know where I'm supposed to go now. This is a problem.'"[22]

It is not that Baptists and other evangelicals lack magisterium—despite Martin's assertion to the contrary in his review of D. H. Williams's *Evangelicals and Tradition*. Our own Timothy George has written, "Baptists and Catholics differ on the scope and locus of the *magisterium* but not on whether it exists as a necessary component in the ongoing life of the Church."[23]

I have no illusions that I will here solve the problem of magisterium encountered whenever Baptists and other free-church evangelicals attempt to retrieve the riches of the Nicene faith and other expressions of a fuller catholicity. Instead, I will aim for the more attainable goal of entertaining a possible configuration of how teaching authority might function for evangelicals who have not typically thought that they had an authoritative teaching office. In doing so, I will focus on the particularity of my own Baptist ecclesial community of reference, but what I say about Baptists should be applicable to other free church or believers' church traditions and to evangelicals in general, *mutatis mutandis* (with the necessary adjustments).

Magisterium—Roman Catholic and Magisterial Protestant

Since many evangelicals erroneously assume that the magisterium is whatever the pope teaches, and that Protestants therefore do not have a magisterium, it is appropriate at this point to explain the respective Catholic and Protestant configurations of the teaching office.

Teaching Authority in Roman Catholicism

As the late Avery Cardinal Dulles defined it in his book *Magisterium*, "In modern Catholic teaching the term 'Magisterium' generally designates the hierarchical teachers—the pope and the bishops—who by virtue of their office have authority to teach publically in the name of Christ and to judge officially what belongs to Christian faith and what is excluded by it. This concept of the Magisterium," Dulles acknowledged, "is relatively recent."[24] Though rooted in the early patristic conviction that the bishops, as successors of the apostles, safeguarded the faith against heresy by teaching the faith handed down to them from the apostles, the more fully developed modern Catholic concept of magisterium was historically conditioned by several factors: medieval conflict between papal and imperial powers for supremacy in the ecclesiastical and civil orders; rival claims to papal jurisdiction during the "Great Schism"; the late medieval debate between those who contended that the bishops in council had authority over the pope and those who maintained that papal proclamations trumped conciliar decisions (a debate the conciliarists lost); the Tridentine responses to the challenges of the Reformation; and the ultramontanist response to the challenges of modernism at the First Vatican Council.[25]

The definitive statements of the modern Roman Catholic understanding of magisterial authority are in two key documents issued by the Second Vatican Council: the Dogmatic Constitution on the Church, *Lumen Gentium*, sections 22–26, and the Dogmatic Constitution on Divine Revelation, *Dei Verbum*, section 10. A pair of quotations from *Lumen Gentium* 25 and *Dei Verbum* 10 illustrate this Catholic pattern of magisterium:

> For in such a case [of infallible, irreformable papal teaching] the Roman Pontiff does not utter a pronouncement as a private person, but rather does he expound and defend the teaching of the Catholic faith as the supreme teacher of the universal Church, in whom the church's charism of infallibility is present in a singular way. The infallibility promised to the Church is also present in the body of bishops when, together with Peter's successor, they exercise the supreme teaching office. Now, the assent of the Church can never be lacking to such definitions on account of the same Holy Spirit's influence, through which Christ's whole flock is maintained in the unity of the faith and makes progress in it. Furthermore, when the Roman Pontiff, or the body of bishops together with him, define a doctrine, they make the definition in conformity

with revelation itself, to which all are bound to adhere and to which they are obligated to submit.[26]

By adhering to it [the sacred deposit of the Word of God] the entire holy people, united to its pastors, remains always faithful to the teaching of the apostles, to the brotherhood, to the breaking of bread and the prayers (See Acts 2:42 Greek). So, in maintaining, practicing and professing the faith that has been handed on there should be a remarkable harmony between the bishops and the faithful. But the task of giving an authentic interpretation of the Word of God, whether in its written form or in the form of Tradition, has been entrusted to the living teaching office of the Church alone. Its authority in this matter is exercised in the name of Jesus Christ. Yet this Magisterium is not superior to the Word of God, but is its servant. It teaches only what has been handed on to it. At the divine command and with the help of the Holy Spirit, it listens to this devotedly, guards it with dedication and expounds it faithfully. All that it proposes for belief as being divinely revealed is drawn from this single deposit of faith.[27]

In those texts, we encounter a decidedly hierarchical conception of teaching authority: it is ultimately defined by the papal exercise of magisterial authority—both the ordinary papal magisterium expressed in encyclicals, letters, addresses, and other forms of papal teaching, and the extraordinary papal magisterium exemplified by the two modern Mariological dogmas. Yet in this configuration of teaching authority, the pope does not exercise magisterium alone. He does so in association with the bishops. And the bishops, including the bishop of Rome, do not exercise their collective magisterium alone, for there is also a nonhierarchical magisterium in which others in the church participate and on which the bishops depend en route to the formulation of magisterial teaching. The bishops consult theologians, both lay and religious. They name scientists and others with areas of expertise beyond theology to official Vatican commissions and consultations, so that they may inform the magisterium's deliberation regarding moral issues, for example.

The Vatican II documents illustrate this participatory nature of the Roman Catholic magisterium. The documents are themselves expressions of magisterial teaching, and they underwent a long and often contentious process of formation to which many theologians who were not bishops contributed behind the scenes.[28] Even non-Catholic theologians participated in the Catholic magisterium and contributed to the formulation of its teaching during the Second Vatican Council, for they too were consulted with regard to potential difficulties for the ecumenical reception of the various decrees and constitutions. As *Dei Verbum* emphasizes, all these expressions of Roman Catholic magisterium, hierarchical and nonhierarchical, are subservient to the truth of the gospel; but when the magisterium defines dogma, it does so infallibly.

Teaching Authority in Magisterial Protestantism

That Protestants have their own version of magisterium is suggested by George Huntston Williams's use of the label *Magisterial Reformation* to distinguish the classical Protestant traditions that include the Lutheran and Reformed churches from churches of the Radical Reformation exemplified by the Anabaptists.[29] The Magisterial Reformation was accomplished with the cooperation of the civil power, the magistrates, but it was also magisterial in the sense that it was accomplished through the influence of the *magister*, the authoritative teacher, in association with the magistrate. Although this is a slightly unfair, reductionistic oversimplification, we may explain the difference between the Catholic and magisterial Protestant conceptions of magisterium in this manner: while for both Catholics and Protestants the teaching office depends upon, serves, and transmits the truth of the gospel, in the Catholic understanding of magisterium, the emphasis is on the authority of *the teaching office* that depends upon, serves, and transmits the truth of the gospel, whereas for magisterial Protestants, the emphasis is on the authority of *the truth of the gospel* that the teaching office depends upon, serves, and transmits. The Catholic version of magisterium is located in the community of bishops who teach the truth; the magisterial Protestant version of magisterium is in principle located in the truth that bishops or others in the church who fulfill their function teach.

The statements on the office of bishop in the documents of the Lutheran *Book of Concord* illustrate this magisterial Protestant approach to teaching authority. Martin Luther and the other early Lutheran doctors viewed the historical development of the office of bishop, distinguished from and overseeing the office of elder, as an ecclesial structure established by human authority but nevertheless beneficial for the unity and health of the church; they were willing to retain it and even to submit themselves to the Catholic bishops if only the bishops would teach the truth and refrain from suppressing the ministry of those who disagreed with their error. In the *Treatise on the Power and Primacy of the Pope* authored by Philipp Melanchthon in 1537, for example, he and the other theologians of the Smalcald League were able to appeal to patristic precedent for their perspective on the functional adaptability of *episkopē* (oversight) in the church:

> The gospel bestows upon those who preside over the churches the commission to proclaim the gospel, forgive sins, and administer the sacraments. . . . It is universally acknowledged, even by our opponents, that this power is shared by divine right by all who preside in the churches, whether they are called pastors, presbyters, or bishops. For that reason Jerome plainly teaches that in the apostolic letters all who preside over the churches are both bishops and presbyters. . . . Jerome goes on to say, "One person was chosen thereafter to oversee the rest as a remedy for schism, lest some individuals draw a following around themselves

and divide the church of Christ." . . . Jerome, then, teaches that the distinctions of degree between bishop and presbyter or pastor are established by human authority. That is clear from the way it works, for, as I stated above, the power is the same. One thing subsequently created a distinction between bishops and pastors, and that was ordination, for it was arranged that one bishop would ordain the ministers in a number of churches. However, since the distinction of rank between bishop and pastor is not by divine right, it is clear that an ordination performed by a pastor in his own church is valid by divine right.

As a result, when the regular bishops become enemies of the gospel or are unwilling to ordain, the churches retain their right to do so. For wherever the church exists, there also is the right to administer the gospel.

All this evidence makes clear that the church retains the right to choose and ordain ministers. Consequently, when bishops either become heretical or are unwilling to ordain, the churches are compelled by divine right to ordain pastors and ministers for themselves.[30]

Elsewhere the *Book of Concord* repeatedly mentions authoritative teaching as belonging to the office of bishop and to these other ministers in the church who exercise the ministry of oversight. When bishops teach the truth, they ought to be heeded; when they fail to teach the truth, their authority must be rejected, and their function is rightfully taken on by others.

Roman Catholic and Magisterial Protestant Teaching Authority in Free Church Perspective

From the vantage point of my own ecclesial tradition, both the Roman Catholic and the magisterial Protestant versions of magisterium have strengths and weaknesses. The Roman Catholic magisterium has the strength of collegiality in the communal formulation of authoritative teaching. The bishops, in association with the faithful, seek the mind of Christ on matters of doctrine and moral theology. Individual theological preferences must make way for communal discernment that seeks consensus under the lordship of Christ. Even when the pontiff defines doctrine *ex cathedra*, he does so not as an individual theologian but as one who self-consciously functions as supreme teacher of the church and therefore must speak with the voice of the church and not his own personal theological voice. The weakness of the Roman Catholic magisterium, however, is its assumed infallibility. In association with the distinct but not unrelated concept of the church's impeccability, this can make for an overly realized eschatology of the church, in which the church has great difficulty admitting and forsaking past errors in its pilgrim journey toward the full realization of what Christ wills his church to be.

The magisterial Protestant configuration of magisterium has the strength of adaptability. There are situations in which the embodied structures of magisterial authority may fail in their task of "teaching as [the church] must teach if she is to be the church here and now," as the late Baptist theologian James William McClendon Jr. defined the task of Christian doctrine. In such circumstances, the magisterial Protestant paradigm makes it possible to reject the authority of those who have failed to teach the truth and to point instead to other teachers whose authority derives from their faithful teaching of the gospel and to authoritative confessional documents that have definitively expressed this faithful teaching. It has the weakness, however, of becoming too tied to individual foundational teachers in all their theological idiosyncrasies. Furthermore, despite a commitment to Scripture alone as the infallible rule for faith and practice, the privileged status of foundational confessional documents in this paradigm can make for a "paper magisterium" that is difficult to reform. It is one thing to revise the Baptist Faith and Message now and then; it is quite another to revise the *Book of Concord* or the Westminster Standards. The magisterial Protestant configuration too, in its own way, can fall prey to an overly realized eschatology of the church. This susceptibility is exemplified by the most significant ecumenical agreement reached between Roman Catholics and magisterial Protestants during the sixteenth century, namely, that it was okay to kill Anabaptists. But let me hasten to point out that at a meeting of the Mennonite World Conference general council in October 2009, the Lutheran World Federation officially asked for forgiveness for Lutheran persecutions of Anabaptists. Lutheran World Federation general secretary Ishmael Noko said about the then-forthcoming apology, "We hope [this] will put us in a new relation to the anathemas in our confessional writings and will express our deep regret and repentance for the use of these writings in justification of violence that cannot be justified."[31]

A Free Church Magisterium?

Beyond the Roman Catholic and magisterial Protestant configurations of magisterium, I propose that there is yet a third major pattern according to which the church "teaches as she must teach if she is to be the church here and now." Even if unacknowledged or denied outright, there is a configuration of functional magisterial authority for Baptists and others who belong to the broader free church or believers' church tradition—by which I mean those churches that emphasize the authority of the congregation of baptized believers gathered in a covenanted community under the lordship of Christ, which include Mennonites, the Disciples of Christ and Churches of Christ, Bible churches, a great many nondenominational churches, and numerous Pentecostal and charismatic communities, as well as Baptists. In my opinion this configuration, which for the sake of convenience we will call *free church magisterium*, embodies aspects of the strengths of both the Roman Catholic

and magisterial Protestant paradigms, while in theory avoiding their suscepti-
bilities to overly realized eschatologies of the church—though the free church
tradition has its own share of those in actual practice.

The Authority of the Community Gathered under the Rule of Christ

In *Towards Baptist Catholicity*, I tried to articulate a free church vision of
teaching authority that could be labeled a magisterium of the whole. Inasmuch
as Baptists have historically granted that local churches gathered under the
lordship of Christ possess an authority that derives from Christ as Lord, I
argued that this authority can also be extended to the communion of saints,
who constitute a real community under the lordship of Christ that transcends
space and time. I drew also on Alasdair MacIntyre's definition of a living
tradition as "an historically extended, socially embodied argument, and an
argument precisely in part about the goods which constitute that tradition,"[32]
and defined the goods that constitute the tradition in terms of the Christian
narrative (the biblical story of the Triune God that is told at length and with
great particularity in the Scriptures and summarized in the ancient creeds).
Thus I portrayed the church's teaching authority as located in the communion
of saints in its ongoing argument about "what the church must teach in order
to be the church here and now."[33]

But again: who decides how the argument should be decided, however
provisionally, at various points in the historical extension of the argument?
If all members of the communion of saints are participants in this ongoing
argument, do they all participate in the same way? Do the voices of all participants carry the same weight, so that the argument is decided by majority?
This McIntyrean magisterium of the whole offers a way for Baptists and other
historic dissenters to appreciate the place their dissent has within the larger
argument that constitutes the Christian tradition, making positive contributions to the health of the living tradition through their dissent. Yet it needs to
clearly locate socially embodied ecclesial authority.

Perhaps unsurprisingly, I suggest that free church magisterial authority is
located in the gathered congregation. Though it is a clumsy English coinage,
we might call this the *magisterium-hood of all believers*—which I think is
the implication of reading the Gospels as manuals of discipleship, which
therefore means that all who become disciples of Christ are commissioned
by him in Matthew 28:18–20 to participate in the church's teaching office.[34]
But just as in the Roman Catholic configuration of magisterium, in which
the bishops exercise magisterium not only in association with the bishop of
Rome and the other bishops, but also with the faithful who participate in
various ways in the nonhierarchical dimension of the magisterium, so too in
the free church practice of teaching authority, it is not the local congregation
alone that authorizes its teaching. Nor is the membership of the congregation

undifferentiated in its participation in this practice. In the best expressions of Baptist ecclesiology, the independence of local congregations is not absolute. Local Baptist congregations are interdependent in their relations with one another, in local associations but also in various national and international associations of Baptists. When seven local Baptist congregations in London together issued the London Confession of 1644, they explained their interdependence in discerning the mind of Christ for their faith and practice in this fashion:

> Because it may be conceived, that what is here published, may be but the Judgement of some one particular Congregation, more refined than the rest; We do therefore here subscribe it, some of each body in the name, and by the appointment of seven Congregations, who though we be distinct in respect of our particular bodies, for convenience sake, being as many as can well meet together in one place, yet are all one in Communion, holding Jesus Christ to be our head and Lord; under whose government we desire alone to walk, in following the Lamb wheresoever he goeth; and we believe the Lord will daily cause truth more to appear in the hearts of his Saints . . . that so they may with one shoulder, more study to lift up the Name of the Lord Jesus, and stand for his appointments and Laws; which is the desires and prayers of the condemned Churches of Christ in London for all saints.[35]

The rule of Christ in the plurality of local congregations, therefore, has implications for the efforts of any single local congregation to discern the mind of Christ, and vice versa. Together in their mutual relations they seek to walk under the government of Christ, seeking from him a fuller grasp of the truth, as one ecclesial communion—a communion that, it is hoped, might extend beyond Baptist churches in association to include all the saints.

Within local congregations, discerning the mind of Christ is not a matter of simple majority vote of the congregation, nor is it determined by acquiescence to the will of the congregation's pastor. British Baptist theologian Paul Fiddes explains the embodied "Baptist experience" that informs Baptist theology in his book *Tracks and Traces: Baptist Identity in Church and Theology*:

> The liberty of local churches to make decisions about their own life and ministry is not based in a human view of autonomy or independence, or in selfish individualism, but in a sense of being under the direct rule of Christ who relativizes other rules. This liberating rule of Christ is what makes for the distinctive "feel" of Baptist congregational life, which allows for spiritual oversight (*episkopē*) both by the *whole* congregation gathered together in church meeting, and by the minister(s) called to lead the congregation. . . . Since the same rule of Christ can be experienced in assemblies of churches together, there is also the basis here for Baptist associational life, and indeed for participating in ecumenical clusters.[36]

Later in the same book, Fiddes fleshes out what it means for the whole congregation to seek together the mind of Christ in what British Baptists call "church meeting":

> Upon the whole people in covenant there lies the responsibility of finding a common mind, of coming to an agreement about the way of Christ for them in life, worship and mission. But they cannot do so unless they use the resources that God has given them, and among those resources are the pastor, the deacons and (if they have them) the elders. The church meeting is not "people power" in the sense of simply counting votes and canvassing a majority. . . . The aim is to search for consent about the mind of Christ, and so people should be sensitive to the voices behind the votes, listening to them according to the weight of their experience and insight. As B[arrington] White puts it, "One vote is not as good as another in church meeting," even though it has the same strictly numerical value.[37]

"In all this," Fiddes writes, "the pastor's voice is the one that carries weight"— provided that pastors have created trust in their leadership through service. In this paradigm, pastors are the ones charged with the responsibility of *episkopē*, which carries with it the catechetical task of equipping the members of the congregation with the resources they need from beyond the congregation for seeking the mind of Christ—resources including the doctrine, worship, and practice of other congregations, other Christian traditions, and indeed the whole Christian tradition. For this reason, theological educators also have a key form of participation in free church magisterium, for they have the opportunity to supply ministers with these God-given resources from beyond the local congregation and to form them in the skills they need for the discerning use of these resources.

In 1997, Curtis Freeman and Elizabeth Newman, along with James William McClendon Jr. and others, issued a statement titled "Re-envisioning Baptist Identity: A Manifesto for Baptist Communities in North America." This Baptist Manifesto, as it came to be known, functioned as a sort of Barmen Declaration for Baptists who resisted the pull toward the perilous ideological polarities of the denominational controversy then raging in the Southern Baptist Convention. The first of the manifesto's five affirmations regarding the nature of freedom, faithfulness, and community was this:

> *We affirm Bible study in reading communities* rather than relying on private interpretation or supposed "scientific" objectivity. . . . We thus affirm an open and orderly process whereby faithful communities deliberate together over the Scriptures with sisters and brothers of the faith, excluding no light from any source. When all exercise their gifts and callings, when every voice is heard and weighed, when no one is silenced or privileged, the Spirit leads communities to read wisely and to practice faithfully the direction of the gospel.[38]

Beyond an undifferentiated magisterium of the whole, the way the Baptist Manifesto frames the process—the manner in which the church discerns what it must teach on the basis of the Word of God—envisions well how this more nuanced configuration of free church magisterium might work.

The Ecumenical Extension of the Community Gathered under the Rule of Christ

What, then, are the potential sources of light that ought not be excluded? What are the voices that should be heard and weighed without being silenced in the free church practice of magisterium? I suggest that they ought to include at least the following eight types of resources. First, the ancient creeds—the Niceno-Constantinopolitan Creed and the Apostles' Creed in particular—should be recovered first and foremost as expressions of worship. The creeds are summaries of the biblical story of the Triune God, drawn from the language of the Bible itself; in their liturgical use, they form worshipers in the faith the church teaches. They declare the story to which Christians commit themselves in baptism, and they invite worshipers to locate afresh their individual stories within the larger divine story that is made present in worship. The creeds impress upon worshipers again and again the overarching meaning of the Bible and shape their capacity for hearing and heeding what specific passages of Scripture have to say. They invite worshipers into solidarity with the saints gone before, who for two millennia have confessed this story with these same words, and solidarity with sisters and brothers in Christ throughout the world who today embrace the story of the Triune God.

The second type of resource is the historic Reformation confessions and catechisms; third, the confessions of our own particular tradition; and fourth, the more recent confessions of other confessional traditions. All these belong to the whole church—including, I would argue, to the Roman Catholic and Eastern Orthodox churches. The attempts of any part of the church to teach what it must teach to be the church, here and now, are resources that the rest of the church must hear and weigh in our mutual efforts to teach the faith.

The fifth voice to which we must listen is that of Roman Catholic magisterial teaching, which includes the *Catechism of the Catholic Church*, the documents of Vatican II, papal encyclicals, and bishops' letters. Free church communities that are becoming more intentional about exercising a communal teaching authority have much to learn from Catholic processes of conciliar theological and ethical deliberation, even if we do not always agree with what these resources propose as Christian teaching. These more communal proposals have the capacity to transcend the subjectivity of the theological constructions and moral judgments of individual theologians and ethicists, and ought to be weighed accordingly—even if such weighing results in heavily qualified reception.

The sixth resource includes other types of ecclesial resolutions on ethical issues. These are often issued by Christian world communions, national denominational organizations, and regional conferences. These are various expressions of ecclesial community that are seeking to bring their churches under the rule of Christ, and therefore they must be heard and weighed by other churches—even if, again, this does not always lead to agreement with them.

Seventh are the reports and agreed-upon statements of bilateral and multilateral ecumenical dialogues at both the national and international levels. A joint commission of the delegations to a bilateral or multilateral ecumenical dialogue is not a church, but it does possess a socially embodied ecclesiality as a community of persons who represent their churches. It is not a baptizing community, but it is a community of the baptized. Like a church, these bilateral and multilateral communities of the baptized are collaboratively seeking to bring what their churches teach under the lordship of Christ. Study of these reports by local congregations from communions involved in such dialogue is an important but much-neglected resource for discerning the mind of Christ on what the church teaches as Christian faith and faithfulness.

Eighth, the contextual theologies that emerge from social locations other than our own are also resources that we can engage. These theologies too must be heard and not silenced, for they are a necessary check on the blind spots that may come from the social location of our own community when it is not intentionally engaging with the global church.

These resources are not in agreement with one another, and many of them will elicit much free church disagreement. That is why these voices must be weighed. But first they must be heard and not silenced. In much of free church Christianity most of these voices are silent, not because they have been intentionally silenced but because they have not been intentionally engaged.

As an ecumenical theologian, I tend to see openings for ecumenical convergence under every rock, so the following suggestion needs to be taken with a grain of salt. Despite the real differences between the Catholic, magisterial Protestant, and free church traditions in the way they configure teaching authority in the church, they share these rather substantial commonalities: first, magisterium is subservient to the Word of God; second, it is a communal practice that in various ways involves the whole body of Christ; and third, those who exercise *episkopē* in the church play a key role in helping the community discern the mind of Christ. Perhaps the ecumenical future will include some form of shared magisterium, or at least the mutual recognition of one another's teaching authorities as they converge toward a genuine unity in the truth in the teaching of the catholic faith.

In the meantime, each tradition must see to it that the faith it teaches is fully catholic, in continuity with Nicene catholicity. We will be helped toward that end by including the magisterial teaching of other traditions, along with the insights of the contextual readings of Scripture done in communities unlike our own, among the voices that we hear and weigh within our own church. In that way, evangelicals can retrieve the catholic tradition, not as "private historians" but as full participants in the living, teaching office of the whole church.

7

The Church Is Part of the Gospel

A Sermon on the Four Marks of the Church

Carl E. Braaten

I do not ask for these only, but also for those who will believe in me through their word, that they may all be one, just as you, Father, are in me, and I in you, that they also may be in us, so that the world may believe that you have sent me.

John 17:20–21

We have read some verses from the Gospel of John to ground the faith we confess in the familiar words of the Nicene Creed: "We believe in one holy catholic and apostolic Church." We might ask: how did these words get into the creed when they are not in the Bible? Nowhere in the New Testament is the church described as one, holy, catholic, and apostolic. The words *catholic* and *apostolic* never appear at all, and while the words *one* and *holy* are used in many contexts, there is no reference to "the one, holy church." Such observations have led some Christians and even some entire denominations to make do without the creeds of the church. "No Creed but Christ" is the slogan of one American church body. Not too far from that are several slogans that come from the Protestant Reformation: "Scripture alone" and "the Word alone." I am an heir of Luther's reform movement, but I confess that I do not like the word *alone*. How could I, when growing up I was made to memorize not only many red-letter passages of the Gospels, but every word of Luther's Small Catechism and many traditional hymns, to boot?

Years later, when I entered seminary and studied theology, we had to learn the meaning of every word in the ancient creeds—the Apostles' Creed, the Nicene Creed, and the Athanasian Creed—plus the chief confessions in the huge Lutheran *Book of Concord*. We did that because the mainstream of the classical Christian tradition maintains that the creeds are summaries of the core truths of the Bible. The creeds are like a map that helps us to make our journey through the Scriptures without getting lost. They account for the difference between a church and a cult. The cults also say they believe in the Bible—every word of it!—but they get its message wrong. And many modern biblical scholars also misinterpret the Bible, because they do not read it with the eyes of faith, as the book of the church and for the church.

Eventually, I became grateful for all the hard work it took to learn the creeds of the ancient church and the confessions of the sixteenth-century Reformation. "We believe in one holy catholic and apostolic Church": that's a piece of that great creedal and confessional tradition. But sadly, I have to admit that, inasmuch as I was raised in the context of Lutheran pietism, we did not dwell much on the church. Pietism had its strengths. It laid a strong emphasis on the way of salvation and on world missions. My father and mother were Norwegian Lutheran pietists. They went to Madagascar to preach the gospel of salvation to the Malagasy people. They planted a vibrant church, but that phrase—"one, holy, catholic, and apostolic"—was not high on the list of missionary priorities. This was, of course, before the rise of the modern ecumenical movement. Things have changed, and they have changed precisely because of the collective missionary experience. The contemporary vision of the oneness of the church was born in India. Missionaries from different denominations learned that their lack of a unified witness was an obstacle to winning people to Christ. If many churches are competing with each other and often condemning each other's teachings, how should people decide which one is true?

When I was a fledgling seminary student, I recall hearing Dr. E. Stanley Jones speak about his experience as a Methodist missionary to India. He told about the many churches witnessing to Christ in India. Each of them brings a special God-given gift to the missionary enterprise. The Anglicans bring their appreciation of liturgical worship, Presbyterians their concern for church order, Methodists their stress on holy living, Lutherans their belief in pure doctrine, Baptists their zeal for pioneer evangelism, and so forth. Then E. Stanley Jones summed it up by saying, "In conversion you are not attached to an order, nor to an institution, nor a movement, nor a set of beliefs, nor a code of actions—you are attached primarily to a Person, and secondarily to the other things."[1]

That is exactly right. It is on account of the person of Jesus Christ that we dare to believe some paradoxical things about his church. The church is one, yet most obviously divided, as anyone can see. The church is holy, yet full of sinners—each and every one of us. The church is catholic, yet every denomination tends to be centered on its own parochial interests. The church is apostolic, yet it has sometimes strayed from the teachings of the apostles, veering away from orthodoxy into heresy.

These statements about the church are paradoxical because they seem to contradict what ordinary eyes can see. That is why we say, "We believe." It's a matter of faith, not sight. Before we confess our faith in the church as one, holy, catholic, and apostolic, we have already confessed our faith in Jesus Christ, the only begotten Son of God, true God and true man. It is solely on account of Christ that we confess that the church is one. The church is one because it is the body of Christ. There are many church bodies, but Christ has only one body. There are many members in the one body of Christ, as the apostle Paul says in his letters to the Romans and the Corinthians. If you believe in Jesus as God's Messiah, and are baptized into the name of the Holy Trinity—Father, Son, and Holy Spirit—you are a member of the body of Christ.

The Four Marks

Let's examine the four marks of the body of Christ as described in the creed, with the hope that they can lead us into a deeper understanding of our identity and into closer fellowship with Christ and with each other.

One

The whole gospel of God includes both Christ and the church. The church is part of the gospel, because Christ is the head of the church and the church is the body of Christ. The head and the body belong together, forming the whole Christ. They are one, and that is why we believe in the one church. There is nothing we can do to make the church one; the church is already one in Christ. So why don't we show it more often? Churches working together in dialogue and service are all about finding better ways to show our unity in the gospel so that the world might believe. That is what Jesus prayed—unity in faith for the sake of the world's salvation.

Does it bother you, as it does me, when any given church proclaims itself to be the *one and only* true church of Jesus Christ? I find it similarly disturbing when one nation boasts of being the greatest in the world. Such statements remind me of a kid on a playground bragging that his dad could beat up everyone else's dad.

Holy

Our next confession is: the church is holy. Now, we all know it is not. There is no church without sin, none without spot or wrinkle. The holiness of the church resides in Christ and Christ alone. As members of his body we are *called* to be holy, and we believe the Holy Spirit is working to sanctify every member of the body of Christ. It is, at best, a work in progress. Every day we pray for the forgiveness of our sins. And the next day we start over and struggle to bring forth the fruits of faith pleasing to God.

I recall how shocked I was when a college classmate of mine returned from a spiritual retreat and thanked God that he was now sinless. He had received the spiritual gift of entire sanctification, of sinless perfection. This spiritual retreat was operated by a small group of charismatic Lutherans in Minnesota. Years later, I was recruited to debate the concept of sinless perfection at a theological conference with a renowned Methodist theologian. In his defense of the idea, he added many qualifications, along with the admission that sinless perfection is not to be taken literally. I have known many Mother Teresa–like, self-sacrificing, saintly servants of Christ, but none who claimed to be perfectly sinless and holy.

A Lutheran theologian does not often quote a Reformed confession, but one can hardly say it better than the Westminster Confession,[2] which states: "The purest churches under heaven are subject to mixture and error." If we have any doubt about that, all we need to do is to read the newspaper headlines, which love to publicize the heresies of Anglican bishops, the marital infidelities of evangelical televangelists, and the sexual misconduct of Catholic priests. Since churches are made up of their members, they are in and of themselves a mixed bag. A tennis friend of mine told me he doesn't go to church because it's full of hypocrites. I countered, "True, but that's why I go to church—to be part of the company of sinners who need to repent, receive forgiveness, and beg God for help to mend their ways."

To be sure, we are not free from the sin of hypocrisy and holier-than-thou demeanors. Still, we confess that the church is holy, but solely on account of Christ, who is the essence of the church in the form of his body. Does this make sense? It's a paradox. The apostle Paul says that it's a mystery. The church is holy and sinful at the same time: holy because of Christ, and sinful because we are its members.

Catholic

The most controversial attribute of the church comes next: the church is catholic. This mark of the church has been misunderstood by both Protestants and Catholics, and many Protestants won't use the term at all. They prefer to say *Christian* rather than *catholic*. They have surrendered the term *catholic* to the Church of Rome. That is understandable in a way, because many

Roman Catholics have claimed the exclusive right to the term for their own particular church. Yet the word is in the creed, our creed, so there's no good reason to give it up. The word *catholic* means *universal*. Although the word is not in the New Testament, its meaning is clearly present in Jesus's Great Commission to the apostles in Matthew 28, to go and tell the gospel to all the world, to all the nations.

St. Ignatius of Antioch was the first to apply the word *catholic* to the church at the beginning of the second century. You can find it in a letter Bishop Ignatius wrote to the Christians at Smyrna while on his journey to Rome to face martyrdom. If your church believes in spreading the gospel of the kingdom of Christ throughout the world, then your church is as catholic as any other. The nature of the church is simply to witness to Christ everywhere, always, and to everyone. That enterprise began the instant the apostles received the Holy Spirit at Pentecost. We believe in the catholic church because we are committed to the universal mission of the world-transforming gospel. I tried to teach my students two things: please don't give up the word *catholic* from your definition of the church, and please don't give in to the propaganda of any church that claims it exclusively for itself.

Apostolic

So far, so good: we believe in the one, holy, catholic church. The fourth attribute of the church is my favorite: the apostolic church. It is apostolic or it is not the church of Jesus Christ. Jesus said, "I will build my church" (Matt. 16:18). He built it on the foundation of the apostles, and he himself is its chief cornerstone. The apostolic church handed down to us six inalienable characteristics that have belonged to the church from the beginning until now.

Even if you have not studied Greek, you are probably familiar with six Greek words that have become part of every theological student's lexicon: *kerygma*, *martyria*, *didache*, *koinonia*, *diakonia*, and *leiturgia*. From the apostles we have received the *kerygma*, the message of Jesus Christ. The apostles have given us their *martyria*, their testimony and witness to Christ; they were martyrs for Christ because of the witness they bore to him. We have received the *didache*, the teaching of the apostles. We have been included in their *koinonia*, the fellowship of the apostles through prayer and the breaking of bread. And the apostles made *diakonia*, the caring ministry of the church to the poor and the oppressed, a fundamental part of the Christian life. That is the gospel in action. And finally, the apostles gathered the people of Christ together for *leiturgia*, public acts of prayer, praise, and thanksgiving. It's the worship of the people of God—their liturgy. One might ask: do you mean we have received all of these things from the apostolic tradition? Absolutely; this is what we mean when we confess that the church is apostolic.

The Importance of the Marks

Why should we care about such marks or attributes of the church? Why is it important to every one of us today? Martin Luther worried a lot about whether the church in his time was being faithful to its Christ-given apostolic nature. He asked in effect, "How can a person tell a true church from a false church?" We live in a highly mobile society. When a Christian moves to a new city, the question becomes urgent: "How do I find a church I can trust, a church that will pass on the true Christian faith to my children?" Already in the second century this had become a crucial issue. There were Christians who touted their belief in Christ and were impressively spiritual. There were gnostics. Irenaeus and Tertullian were two ancient church fathers who wrote books against the heresy of gnosticism.

The gnostics rejected the Old Testament, the God of creation, the God of Israel, the God who gave Moses the Ten Commandments. Instead, they wanted to know only the God of salvation and Christ the redeemer; they wanted only to experience their freedom in the gospel, their freedom from obedience to the law. They were what we call *antinomians*. Their message of freedom sounded very appealing. It beguiled many well-intentioned people in quest of a relevant spirituality. We are in the same boat today: New Age spirituality promises that you can know and experience God by turning inward, by dwelling on yourself. But it was then and it is now a false gospel. Some theologians today, like some members of the so-called Jesus Seminar, are trying to invent a new Christianity. They are portraying a Jesus who resembles themselves. They say they love Jesus, but it is a Jesus created in their own image.

It has been my privilege to travel around the world to meet Christians and churches on every continent except Antarctica, and to study and teach in many countries and schools around the globe. Quite naturally, the first thing I try to do is to learn the state of the church and to find a place to worship. I have always been most pleased to find congregations that are evangelical in mission and orthodox in doctrine. How can I tell one from another? I have attended churches in which the pastors preach about bunnies and springtime on Easter Sunday. That will not cut it! But here is what I am really looking for: an assembly that is centered in the Word of God, that reads the Bible and preaches its message of God's law and gospel and the whole counsel of God, that gathers around the table of the Lord to partake of the life-giving meal of bread and wine, and that participates in acts of worship by praying and singing. We are talking about the quintessential practices of proclaiming the Word of God and administering the sacraments instituted by our Lord.

Of course, these things are done differently from place to place. High church, low church, or broad church doesn't matter: just so it's real church. None of the marks or attributes of the church make sense without these practices. And when they are performed faithfully, they will generate a spirit of welcome to strangers, of sharing the staples of life with those in need, and of collaboration with fellow Christians to preach the gospel to those who do not yet believe.

Luther said, "A seven-year-old child knows what the church is, namely, holy believers and sheep who hear the voice of the Shepherd."[3] He was reacting to people who make things too complicated, by adding on this or that, perhaps a particular style of worship, organizational structure, type of piety, or code of conduct. No, the church is where Christ is really present through Word and sacrament in the power of the Holy Spirit, and that is enough to make the church of Christ one, holy, catholic, and apostolic.

I will close with some words from Martin Luther's explanation of the third article of the creed: "The Holy Spirit calls, gathers, enlightens, and makes holy the whole Christian church on earth and keeps it with Jesus Christ in the one common, true faith."[4]

Amen!

8

Confessional, Baptist, and Arminian

The General-Free Will Baptist Tradition and the Nicene Faith

❦

J. MATTHEW PINSON

Confessional, Baptist, and *Arminian*: that sounds like an oxymoron, probably because of common caricatures of Baptist and Arminian theology. After all, Baptists are supposed to be anticonfessional because of soul competency and the absolute right of private judgment, their mantra "No creed but the Bible"; supposedly this has fostered in them an antitraditional posture. Arminians are supposed to be pietistic holiness folk who define the essence of Christianity as experience, not orthodox doctrine. Further, the Arminian and Baptist movements are supposed to be modern, evangelical movements that were birthed out of the Enlightenment and imbued with the genius of romanticism, thus averse to the strong confessionalism of Protestant orthodoxy. The term *confessional* is inconsistent with all these stereotypes. Perhaps that is why some Baptist and some Arminian scholars have jettisoned confessional orthodoxy.

This chapter will argue that it is consistent for one to be orthodox, confessional, Baptist, and Arminian. It will do so by appealing to the General-Free Will Baptist tradition: the seventeenth-century English General Baptists, with emphasis on their major theologian, Thomas Grantham, and their progeny in America, the Free Will Baptists.[1]

Ecclesial

The General-Free Will Baptist tradition is an evangelical, Arminian, and Baptist communion with origins predating the Enlightenment, romanticism, pietism, and the transatlantic awakenings of the eighteenth and nineteenth centuries. This historic tradition represents a different way of being Baptist and Arminian than many modern stereotypes allow. Its spirituality was less individualistic and more ecclesial than that of many modern Protestants.[2] The General Baptist cry for religious liberty was not a prototypical version of romantic, liberal individualism. Curtis Freeman correctly argues that Baptist founder Thomas Helwys's primary concern was "the sovereignty and freedom of God, who alone is Lord of the conscience. . . . A romantic reading of Helwys fails to account for the main question of *The Mystery of Iniquity*: What must the church teach and practice to be the true and faithful church?"[3] These early Baptists were persecuted for their views on religious liberty and the priesthood of all believers, which they interpreted not primarily in terms of modern concepts of soul competency and personal autonomy but in more ecclesial terms. They did not cast their view of the priesthood of all believers merely in terms of individual rights.[4] Rather, they viewed it in terms of believers covenanting together, serving as priests to each other. They would have agreed with the following statements from "Re-Envisioning Baptist Identity: A Manifesto for Baptist Communities in North America":

> We affirm following Jesus as a call to shared discipleship rather than invoking a theory of soul competency. . . . Such discipleship requires a shared life of mutual accountability in the church. Disciples may not remain aloof from the church and its life. . . . Only as we stand together under the Lordship of Christ can we discern by the Spirit that from which we are liberated and that to which we are obligated. . . . In this life together, God has chosen us to serve as priests, not for our own selves, but to one another.[5]

Confessional

In fact, the General-Free Will Baptist tradition has historically taken these principles so seriously that it has engaged in a rather rigorous sort of confessionalism.[6] Affirming this "shared life of mutual accountability," these believers have required their churches and ministers to subscribe to corporate confessions of faith.[7] This confessionalism has been a free church confessionalism, not credalism, which Timothy George rightly says Baptists "never advocated."

Because they believe God alone is "Lord of the conscience," they do not believe that the state has "any legitimate authority to regulate or coerce" the internal lives of believers and churches. They are also noncredalists in the sense that they "deny that any humanly constructed doctrinal statement can be equal to, much less elevated above, Holy Scripture."[8] Thus, unlike some Protestant communions, the General-Free Will Baptist tradition has always held that its confessions are revisable. Yet this hearty confessionalism requires churches to unite in conferences or associations in a corporate confession of the faith once delivered to the saints, as they understand it to be taught in Holy Scripture. The presbyteries of these conferences require their ministers to assent to that confession or be disciplined by the conference.[9]

Warmhearted Orthodoxy

In addition to the autonomous individualism and lack of confessionalism that often accompanies that individualism, Arminian evangelicals are usually cast in terms of the Holiness movement and even Charles Finney. Calvinists too often equate Arminianism with the perfectionism, semi-Pelagianism, and ultra-pietism of Finney, the Holiness movement, and the Second Great Awakening. Michael Horton, for example, has questioned whether Arminians are real evangelicals.[10] Many Arminians, however, are also guilty of painting all Arminians with the same broad brush.

There is a cottage industry of defining the nature and essence of evangelicalism.[11] The debate is cast between the "Presbyterian" interpretation of scholars like George Marsden and the "Holiness" interpretation of those like Donald Dayton. Twentieth-century fundamentalism and neoevangelicalism are thought of as an amalgam of two historical streams: Protestant orthodoxy and Holiness pietism. Postconservative thinker Roger Olson states:

> On the one hand, evangelicalism has inherited from Protestant orthodoxy and Puritan Reformed theology a strongly confessional emphasis that seeks to preserve orthodoxy. Conservative evangelicals tend to work out of that side of the heritage. On the other hand, evangelicalism has inherited from Pietism and Revivalism a strong emphasis on the experience of the transforming power of God. Postconservatives tend to work out of that side of the heritage. Some might even argue that there are two evangelicalisms and that these two movements have been somewhat artificially pasted together by their common opposition to liberal defection from authentic Christianity.[12]

But is this not a false dichotomy? The General-Free Will Baptist tradition has managed to combine a warmhearted Puritan spirituality, appropriating the best of mild pietism and revivalism, with a tradition of strong theological orthodoxy and confessional subscription. The same could be said of many

Baptists who are neither strongly Calvinist nor fully Arminian (the vast majority), and who do not fit either caricature.[13] Thomas Oden is right in his analysis of Olson's false dichotomy:

> A lingering pietism surfaces in [Olson's] annoyance with "theological correctness." His polarities may also have the unintended consequence of tending to keep the evangelical theological dialogue trapped in the Protestant scholastic versus pietistic quarrel between doctrine and experience. Evangelical teaching worthy of the gospel will frame both salvific experience and sacred doctrine as derivative from revelation, from God's own merciful presence in history. Revelation is not first thought then experienced but first occurs in history, and only then thought and experienced.[14]

Mark Noll correctly maintains that the *extremes* of pietism shaped much of North American revivalism. Although they were needed correctives to dead orthodoxy, pietism and revivalism, in their extremes, encouraged religious individualism and subjectivism and de-emphasized the "objective realities of revelation," as well as the church and its tradition.[15]

The General-Free Will Baptist movement, like evangelicalism at large, has struggled with the excesses of pietism and revivalism. Yet the historic spirituality of the General-Free Will Baptist tradition is a mildly Arminian form of Puritan spirituality, different from the higher-life, perfectionist spirituality of the modern Holiness movement.[16] In its warmhearted Puritan spirituality, it made room for the best of pietism and the awakenings while remaining distinct from the excesses of pietism and revivalism as seen in Charles Finney and the Holiness movement.

Reformed Arminianism

The theology of the General-Free Will Baptist movement, even in the twentieth century, diverges from a Finneyesque model of Arminianism toward the more Reformed categories of Arminius. Some call this approach "Reformed Arminianism."[17] Unlike Wesleyan-Arminian theology as it developed in the Holiness movement, Reformed Arminianism posits a traditional Reformed notion of original sin and radical depravity that only the grace of God, via the convicting and drawing power of the Holy Spirit, can counteract. It puts forward a thoroughgoing Reformed, penal-satisfaction view of atonement, with the belief that Christ's full righteousness is imputed to the believer in justification. Thus, it demurs from the perfectionism, entire-sanctification, and crisis-experience orientation of much Arminianism, believing that one perseveres in salvation through faith alone. While believers can apostatize from salvation and be irremediably lost, this apostasy comes about through defection from faith rather than through sin.[18]

Tradition

Historically, the General-Free Will Baptist tradition has seen itself in continuity with the saints and martyrs of the Christian past—and the further back that goes, the better it is! With the individualism, consumerism, and consequent "amusing of ourselves to death" so ascendant in American evangelicalism, this mentality is most in need of revival.[19] So, with "paleo-orthodox" thinkers such as Thomas C. Oden, this chapter hopes to mine the General-Free Will Baptist tradition for resources for renewal from the church's past.[20] That Reformational tradition prized the ancient, apostolic Christian faith, both in the sense of recovering much that has been lost from the New Testament and ante-Nicene churches, and in the sense of recovering the orthodox, consensual wisdom of the ecumenical creeds, councils, and fathers of the early church. Thus, *sola Scriptura* is an essential theme in the General Baptist tradition—rooted deeply as it is in the Reformation—but not *nuda Scriptura* (Scripture and nothing else).[21]

Consequently, the individual's "communion with God," to use a phrase Thomas Grantham used so often, is balanced by a respect for the *communio sanctorum* past and present, and in this *communio* there is a *consensus fidelium* that guides the church in its orthodox confession and commitment. As Grantham and the General Baptist confessions (especially the Orthodox Creed) modeled, the church should "read the Bible with the dead."[22] Thus, the historic General-Free Will Baptist tradition eschews the individualism and antitraditionalism of modernity.[23]

This chapter commends Thomas Grantham and the orthodox General Baptists as a model for how to be confessional, Baptist, and Arminian today. They worked out an orthodox, Reformational, confessional theology together with a warmhearted Puritan piety. Yet they did this while maintaining Arminian and Baptist doctrines of salvation and the church, confessing the faith once delivered to the saints, holding ministers accountable for preaching and teaching that confession, and valuing the consensual exegesis of the church's past. This model has abiding relevance for today.

The English General Baptists and the Nicene Faith

The first Baptists, John Smyth and Thomas Helwys, were General Baptists. Smyth and Helwys were radical Puritans who separated from the Church of England, fled to Amsterdam, and came to believe that the church was a gathered community of baptized believers called out of the world and covenanted together as a countercultural kingdom community of God in the world.[24] Helwys left Smyth and went back to England with his small band of followers, because Smyth had wholeheartedly embraced Mennonite doctrine. Helwys's

ecclesiology, like Smyth's, was influenced by the Dutch Waterlander Mennonites, but Helwys rejected their Anabaptist views of the illegitimacy of the
Christian magistracy as well as baptismal succession. Anabaptist anthropology
and soteriology were more Pelagian than Helwys could tolerate.[25] Rather, like
Arminius, Helwys affirmed Reformed concepts of original sin and depravity
as well as justification by the imputation of Christ's righteousness through
faith alone.[26] Furthermore, Helwys regarded as heterodox the Hoffmanite
"heavenly-flesh" Christology that Smyth had imbibed from the Waterlander
Mennonites. While a few General Baptists in the early seventeenth century
would toy with these Mennonite doctrines, the mainstream of General Baptists
who convened the first known General Assembly in 1654 and put forth the
Standard Confession of 1660 were like Helwys in their faith and practice.[27]
Thomas Grantham of Lincolnshire was the most influential theologian among
the General Baptists, representing the mainstream General Baptist movement
to the religious community of seventeenth-century England.

Churchliness

Grantham and the early General Baptists' approach to the church and
its orthodoxy, tradition, and confession of faith was very different from the
individualistic, anticonfessional, and antitraditional views of many modern
Baptists. These early Baptists emphasized the church as a covenanted body
of believers under the lordship of Jesus Christ, as opposed to the modern
emphasis on the sole believer who answers to God alone and believes as he or
she pleases rather than submitting to the corporate confession of the church.
Philip Thompson is correct when he asserts that Grantham and the early
General Baptists viewed God's freedom over the human conscience as the
basis for their doctrine of freedom of conscience.[28]

Grantham argued that each individual retains a "judgment of science
[knowledge]" in "what he chuseth or refuseth." This judgment gives individuals the right to differ from church authority without fear of coercion by
church or state.[29] Yet this was very different from modern Baptist concepts
of people such as Francis Wayland, who championed "the *absolute right*
of private judgment in all matters of religion."[30] Rather, the church has the
right and obligation to require individuals in communion with it to maintain harmony with the corporate confession of the church. Thus, Grantham
states, the church retains "a Judgment *Authoritative*; the latter I know cannot be excercised by me, nor any other Member of the Church, because this
Power lieth in the Church as imbodied together." This corporate judgment
supersedes even that of church councils, whose conclusions must bow to the
judgment of the church "taken collectively." Individuals can dissent from the
church's leaders, helping keep the church on track and holding its leaders
accountable. Yet the emphasis of Grantham and the early General Baptists

was on the "judgment authoritative" of the gathered church, not the church's leaders or individuals.[31]

In *The Baptist against the Papist*, Grantham remarked that the primacy of Scripture in establishing doctrine did not detract from the Christian church's judgment regarding true doctrine: "You here wrong us, to say, That we will not trust the Judgment of the Church; for the Church, truly and universally taken, we do credit, as Her that is appointed of the Father to be the Pillar and Ground of the Truth; of which Church, we take the Prophets and Apostles to be the principal Members, and so in all Points of Faith, to be credited in the first place."[32] This meant that individuals must believe certain doctrines to be admitted as members of the church. Grantham held that Christians in "Communion" in "Church-Assemblies" are to hold and observe one "form of Doctrine or word of Faith." Because God has delivered only this "one Form of Doctrine to the Churches," it is "the duty of all Christians to hold and diligently observe the same, and not to be *carried about with divers and strange Doctrines*, Heb. 13. 9."[33]

Confessional Orthodoxy

These nonindividualistic, churchly sentiments led Grantham and the General Baptists to hold strong views on the centrality of orthodox doctrine. They believed in the importance of "the truly Ancient and Apostolical Faith, that was once delivered unto the Saints, by our Lord Jesus Christ."[34] This led Joseph Hooke, a Lincolnshire General Baptist whom Grantham mentored and ordained, to say, "Tho we have extensive Charity, and a tender regard to the Good of all Mankind, yet [we must] join in Communion with such Christians only, who we believe are found in the Faith: seeing we are of Opinion, That *our Fellowship is founded in our Faith*."[35]

These Christians expressed their faith in creeds and confessions. While, like many dissenters, they would not recite the creeds in public worship, they were zealous in their assent to the doctrinal content of the ancient ecumenical creeds.[36] Thus, as a preface to his reprinting and discussion of the Standard Confession in his magnum opus *Christianismus Primitivus*, Grantham reprinted the English and Latin texts of the Nicene Creed (he reprinted it again a decade later in his *St. Paul's Catechism*). He commended it and the Apostles' Creed as "of most venerable estimation, both for Antiquity, and the solidity of the matter, and for their excellent brevity," and wished to "declare to the world that we assent to the Contents thereof." He stated that the contents of these two creeds are "digested and comprehended" in the Standard Confession, and hoped that, by his public assent to these creeds, "all men may know that we are no devisers, savourers of Novelties or new Doctrines." He hoped that the Nicene Creed "might be a good means to bring to a greater degree of unity, many of the divided parties professing Christianity."[37]

Grantham's approach to the creeds was shared by the other orthodox General Baptists. This is seen no more clearly than in the Orthodox Creed of 1679, which was put forth by Thomas Monck and a number of other General Baptists from the Midlands. The Orthodox Creed, designed to demonstrate the orthodoxy of the General Baptists to the larger Protestant community in England, contained an article entitled "Of the Three Creeds." In language adapted from the Thirty-Nine Articles of the Church of England, the article confessed that the Nicene, Athanasian, and Apostles' creeds "ought thoroughly to be received, and believed. For we believe they may be proved by most undoubted Authority of holy Scripture, and are necessary to be understood of all Christians; and to be instructed in the knowledge of them, by the Ministers of Christ, according to the Analogie of Faith, recorded in sacred Scriptures (upon which these Creeds are grounded)."[38]

The General Baptists did not make much of a distinction between creeds and confessions of faith.[39] They defended written confessions of faith as vital for maintaining the orthodox belief of the church and holding people accountable for confessing that belief. Joseph Hooke, for example, self-consciously saw himself as following in Grantham's footsteps in his *Creed-Making and Creed-Imposing Considered*, which was designed to defend the confessional posture of the orthodox General Baptists from their heterodox detractors. He stated that it is "lawful to compose *Creeds*, or *Confessions of Faith*, in other than Scripture Words, while we retain the true Sense of those Oracles of God."[40] He argued against imposing creeds and confessions, however, on four categories of people: infidels, heretics, apostates, and weak believers. Infidels, heretics, and apostates have liberty of conscience and should not have creeds or confessions imposed upon them. Coercing heretics, Hooke said, is the way of Rome, not of the baptized churches.[41]

Hooke's statements on not imposing creeds and confessions on weak believers is a classic example of the distinction made in the General-Free Will Baptist tradition between ordained church leaders and laypeople. He did not wish to impose confessions of faith on laypeople, but he clarified what he was saying, stating that "professed Ignorance" and "willful Opposition" are "two far different Things." If a weak believer is ignorant of some of the terms used in describing the Trinity, Hooke said, "*We ought not to impose upon his Understanding*, but may, and ought to receive him to Communion as such a one that is *weak in the Faith*." However, "if a Man profess to understand this Mystery better than We, and *will oppose and contradict our Confessions of Faith*, and maintain a *contrary* Faith," this is "not to be allowed, this must not be tolerated; we cannot suffer this, if we must *contend earnestly for the Faith once delivered to the Saints* . . . neither can such things be permitted, and the faith be preserved."[42] Thus, for the General Baptists, there was an orthodox doctrinal center but also a circumference.

The General Baptists believed that it was the job of pastors to protect the flock of God from heresy. This involved what Grantham called "Gospel separation" from "such as pervert the Gospel by wicked Doctrine, or walk disorderly."[43] Their main concern was the well-being of the people of God. Weak believers should be nurtured and cared for, but ordained officers of the church must be held to a higher standard in protecting the corporate confession of the church's faith. Thus, Grantham says, "The Apostle was not more industrious to gain the *Galatians* who were fallen into Heretical Opinions, than sharp and severe against those that seduced them. *Gal. 5. 12. I would they were cut off which trouble you!*"[44] As Hooke said, "But if he be a *Weak Believer*, yet he is a Believer; tho he cannot understand *Our Confessions of Faith*, he owns and professes the Truth in general which is *explained in them*; he is one of Christ's Lambs that must be fed, a Babe in Christ that must be cherished; we must receive him, *Rom. 14. 1. And labour to perfect that which is lacking in his Faith* (1 Thess. 3. 10)."[45] Ministers, however, are not weak believers. Hooke recalled an ordination sermon by Grantham in which he urged, "Brethren (said he) as you are obliged to teach and maintain the Truth, beware that you be not led away with new and strange Doctrines."[46]

In these statements by Grantham and Hooke we can see, to use Thomas Oden's phrase, the "sister disciplines" of irenics and polemics. Oden maintains that, while false teaching must be met with "bold and persuasive argument," the argument "must be grounded firmly in a charitable irenic spirit that understands where the center lies."[47] The General Baptists, like most dissenters who had been in and out of prison for their beliefs, were very clear about where they stood on doctrine and with whom they would fellowship in "church communion." Yet Grantham had very strong relationships with Christians in other communions, as witnessed, for example, by his warm friendship with the Church of England priest John Connould, whom Grantham often debated and whose friendship with Grantham was so close that he had Grantham's body interred in his parish church.[48] One sees this same spirit in the Orthodox Creed's intent to "unite and confirm all true Protestants."[49] Unlike their Free Will Baptist descendants, for whom open communion was an article of faith, most General Baptists in the seventeenth century were closed communionists. Still, they desired to manifest unity with other Christians on the gospel and the consensual orthodoxy of the Christian faith.[50]

Tradition

The English General Baptists defied the antitraditionalism that would later infect many modern Baptists. Quoting of the church fathers was common among the General Baptists, especially Grantham.[51] He is very much like earlier Reformers in all wings of the Reformation in his use of the church fathers. He is atypical of those of his own time, however, because, as D. H. Williams argues, Protestant reliance on the patristic tradition declined in the seventeenth century.[52] After his reprinting of the Nicene Creed in *Christianismus Primitivus*, he reprinted the Standard Confession. After each article, Grantham provided quotations from various church fathers "to shew that though the composition of these Articles be new, yet the Doctrine contained therein, is truly ancient, being witnessed both by the Holy Scriptures, and later writers of Christianity."[53] With the exception of Augustine, from whom a fourth of Grantham's patristic citations came, he showed a preference for the ante-Nicene fathers, from which came a third of his citations of the fathers. If frequency of citation is any indication, Augustine was his favorite, followed by Tertullian, Eusebius, Jerome, and Chrysostom.

Grantham was much like Calvin in his use of the church fathers.[54] He was identical to Calvin in maintaining *sola scriptura* side by side with a high esteem for the church fathers and ecumenical councils. While enthusiastically commending and modeling the study of the church fathers, Calvin said, "We have always held them to belong to the number of those to whom such obedience is not due, and whose authority we will not so exalt, as in any way to debase the dignity of the Word of our Lord, to which alone is due complete obedience in the Church of Jesus Christ."[55] Further, like Calvin, who said that "these holy men . . . often disagreed among themselves, and sometimes even contradicted themselves," Grantham, in *The Baptist against the Papist*, stated that "the Fathers and Councils of the Church . . . could not agree to themselves; for they are opposite each to other to this day, insomuch as you are utterly unable to reconcile them."[56]

Grantham's *sola scriptura* is unmistakable. He held it both against the Roman Catholics, who he said believed the Holy Spirit speaks infallibly "in the Church" (that is, in church tradition), and the Quakers, who he said believed the Holy Spirit speaks infallibly "in the Quakers" (that is, through private revelations to them). This, he said, made the Roman Catholics and Quakers "near neighbors," because both exalted other sources of authority over the infallible Word. This, he believed, led the Roman church to erect a sort of foundationalism of infallible church tradition,[57] and it led the Quakers to a sort of relativism of private revelation that relativized Scripture, causing them to doubt its inspiration and infallibility.[58]

Grantham managed to place great value on the wisdom of the Christian tradition, relying heavily on the church fathers, creeds, and councils of the first five centuries of the Christian church, while maintaining a strong posture of *sola scriptura*.[59] Though his aim was to "restore Christianity to its primitive excellency," he was not a restorationist in the modern sense of the word. Grantham would have agreed wholeheartedly with the sentiments of J. I. Packer:

The evangelical emphasis on the uniqueness of Holy Scripture as the verbalized revelation of God and on its supreme authority over God's people is sometimes misunderstood as a commitment to the so-called restorationist method in theology. This method sets tradition in antithesis to Scripture, and places the church's heritage of thought and devotion under a blanket of permanent suspicion, thus reducing its significance to zero. . . . But the authentic evangelical way has always been to see tradition as the precipitate of the church's living with the Bible and being taught by the Holy Spirit through the Bible—the fruit, that is, of the ministry that the Holy Spirit has been fulfilling in the church since Pentecost, according to Jesus's own promise.[60]

The General Baptists were much like the Reformers, believing, as George says, in *sola scriptura*, not *nuda scriptura*. Thus, they were like Luther and the other Reformers, who argued for the "coinherence of Scripture and tradition, Holy Writ and Holy Church, while never wavering in [their] commitment to the priority of the former."[61]

The Trinitarian Controversy

Suspicions of Hoffmanite Christology began to surround the General Baptist minister Matthew Caffyn and his followers around 1670.[62] An anonymous publication entitled *A Search for Schism* criticized the General Assembly for not dealing with Hoffmanites in their midst.[63] Grantham responded in *A Sigh for Peace* (1671), indicating his surprise at these allegations. He said that most General Baptist churches had never heard of Hoffmanite doctrine until the anonymous authors informed them of it. He argued that not a single General Baptist church held that doctrine and proceeded to defend unequivocally the orthodox Christology of the General Baptists that he himself had learned. To dispense with the fully divine and human natures of Christ, he averred, would be to destroy any possibility of redemption and salvation.[64] Thomas Monck followed in 1673 with a scathing denunciation of the Caffynite "heavenly-flesh" Christology entitled *A Cure for the Cankering Error of the New Eutychians*.[65] In 1678, Grantham carefully refuted antitrinitarianism of all sorts in *Christianismus Primitivus*.[66] A year later Thomas Monck and a number of General Baptists in the Midlands published the Orthodox Creed, putting the self-conscious Nicene orthodoxy found in *Christianismus Primitivus* in confessional form.

It is hard to determine the degree of Caffyn's influence among General Baptists in the seventeenth century, although most historians of the movement have considered it very limited, both geographically and numerically.[67] Caffyn and his followers were equivocal in their views, publicly subscribing to orthodox confessions of faith while privately encouraging people to question those views. The orthodox General Baptist Christopher Cooper spoke of them as deceptive—"privily" discussing their views while publicly subscribing to orthodox confessions of faith.[68] Most of their writings that did affirm heterodox views were anonymous, and the absence of extant writings on the subject by Caffyn complicates matters.[69] The Caffyn group said one thing in public and something else in private, shrouding their antitrinitarian views under the cloak of wanting to use scriptural language. This, together with the full-blown antitrinitarianism of many eighteenth-century General Baptists, has caused some scholars to exaggerate the extent of antitrinitarianism among the General Baptists of the seventeenth century.[70]

Perhaps this perception is why Curtis Freeman has called Thomas Grantham only a moderate trinitarian, citing Daniel Allen's 1699 book *The Moderate Trinitarian*.[71] But, as Clint Bass argues in his masterful monograph, Grantham was not moderate but robust in his trinitarianism.[72] Daniel Allen was not moderate either but actually heterodox in his views of the Trinity.[73] Bass's view, and the view of this chapter, is that Grantham and the mainstream General Baptists—the vast majority—in the seventeenth century were robustly orthodox. This is the traditional view laid out in Adam Taylor's classic *History of the English General Baptists* and all the other standard histories.[74] The confusion originates from Grantham's statement that "the Trinity" is "a phrase no way offensive to Christianity . . . [yet] it is not necessary to impose words on any man which God himself has not used. Yet truly this term, the Trinity, hath very near affinity with the language of the Holy Ghost."[75] However, in this statement Grantham is making it very plain to his detractors that, while it is not necessary to impose words not found in Scripture on people, still he believes that the word *Trinity* is not offensive to Christianity in any way (his detractors believe it is) and that it has "*very near affinity*" with the Spirit's language in Scripture.[76] Grantham seems to be like Luther in this regard. As George remarks, Luther "personally disliked terms such as *homoousios* and *Trinity*," yet he still thought they were useful, contra Reformers such as Martin Bucer, "who wanted to resort to strictly biblical language."[77] Grantham's statement, especially when taken together with his wholehearted trinitarian views throughout his works, substantiates Grantham's strong trinitarian orthodoxy. Furthermore, the firebrands of the orthodox General Baptists in the early eighteenth century, such as Grantham's disciple Joseph Hooke, saw themselves as carrying on the thoroughgoing trinitarian orthodoxy of their mentor, who, said Hooke, "lived and died" with those orthodox beliefs.[78]

In the 1680s and 1690s, Caffyn and his disciples became more heretical in their views, espousing not only Hoffmanite but also subordinationist views. Joseph Wright brought charges against Caffyn before the General Assembly in the mid-1680s, but Caffyn denied being heterodox.[79] Grantham again strongly articulated Nicene orthodoxy in 1687 with the publication of his *St. Paul's Catechism*.[80] The controversy raged on until, in 1691, the General Assembly, in an attempt to quell it once and for all, revised the Standard Confession to reflect changes made by Grantham that made the christological article even more explicitly trinitarian.[81] Caffyn publicly subscribed even to this unambiguously trinitarian confession![82] Yet the controversy intensified[83] until the General Assembly of 1696, after which a large group of orthodox General Baptists withdrew from the General Assembly to form a new, orthodox assembly, the General Association. That body called on the General Assembly to "purge themselves from ye said heresye for which we made our separation from them."[84]

The irony in all this is that the General Assembly always condemned as heterodox the views ascribed to Caffyn. In the interests of unity, they did not want to engage in the sort of heresy-hunting of which they accused their brothers and sisters in the General Association. The General Association never accused the General Assembly itself of heresy, but rather of not dealing with the heresy in their midst.[85] History shows that the General Association was justified in its concerns regarding the antitrinitarian heresy of the Caffynites.[86] The ranks of the General Association increased, and it crystallized its orthodox confessionalism.[87] Despite failed attempts, the two groups did not reunite until 1734. Though they came back together on the basis of the trinitarian 1691 Standard Confession, problems of antitrinitarianism plagued the body until the beginning of the New Connexion of General Baptists in 1770.

The Confessional Heritage of the Free Will Baptists

Laker, Palmer, and the North Carolina General Baptists

By the time of the reunion of the General Association and the General Assembly in 1734, English General Baptists had been in the colonies of the American South for more than five decades, and in the North longer than that. The only major group of American descendants of these General Baptists eventually came to be dubbed "Free Willers," and the name stuck.[88] American Free Will Baptists trace themselves to the work of Paul Palmer, a North Carolina General Baptist minister and church planter who had converted to the General Baptist movement from the Quakers.[89] Palmer married the daughter of Benjamin Laker, a General Baptist layman who was a friend of Thomas Grantham and had signed the 1663 edition of the Standard Confession.[90] Laker, though not an ordained minister, had discipled a small band of General Baptist worshipers who continued after his death. In 1702, this group wrote a letter to the General Association, the orthodox group that had separated from the General Assembly. In that letter, the struggling band of General Baptist believers asked the General Association to provide them with a minister or books.[91] At its meeting with White's Alley Church, London, June 3–5, 1702, the General Association adopted the following resolution:

> Whereas our Brethren of the Baptist perswation and of the Generall Faith who haue their aboad in Caralina haue desired us to Supply them wth a Ministry

or with books, we being not able at present to doe the former haue collected ye Sum of Seuen pounds twelve Shillings whch wth wt can be farther obtain'd we haue put into the hands of our Bror S Keeling to Supply ym wth ye latter. & yt ye sd Bror Keeling doe wright a letter to them in the name of this Assembly.[92]

This is significant for Free Will Baptist historians, in view of the sparse records from this early period, because it ties the North Carolina General Baptists of the early eighteenth century to the orthodox General Association. This is strengthened by the fact that the North Carolina General Baptists came from the Midlands, a strongly orthodox area.[93]

The General Baptists of North Carolina utilized the Standard Confession as their corporate confession of faith.[94] This is natural, given Laker's public subscription to the 1663 edition of the confession. Laker's copy of Grantham's *Christianismus Primitivus* was one of his prized possessions, which he bequeathed to a daughter in his will.[95] Free Will Baptist historians would love to have a listing of the books the General Association sent their brothers and sisters in North Carolina. Given the orthodox polemical fervor of the General Association in 1702 and the spate of books that had been recently produced by General Association ministers, *Christianismus Primitivus* was no doubt joined by more recent volumes such as Joseph Taylor's *Brief Enquiry* (1698), Joseph Hooke's *The Socinian Slain with the Sword of the Spirit* (1700) and *A Necessary Apology for the Baptized Believers* (1701), and Christopher Cooper's *The Vail Turn'd Aside* (1701).

Owing to the leadership of Paul Palmer and his colleague Joseph Parker, the General Baptists moved from a small band of struggling believers in the early eighteenth century to a strong group of newly planted churches by midcentury.[96] In the 1750s, however, the strongly Calvinistic Philadelphia Baptist Association set its sights on the North Carolina General Baptists, aiming to proselytize the Arminian congregations and convert them to Calvinism. Several General Baptist churches became Calvinistic, leaving the remaining group struggling but even more entrenched in its confession of faith.[97]

The 1812 Abstract

Under leaders such as William Parker, the General Baptists (soon called Free Will Baptists) continued to grow, and by 1812, they adopted a new confession of faith and book of discipline entitled *An Abstract of the Former Articles of Faith Confessed by the Original Baptist Church Holding the Doctrine of General Provision with a Proper Code of Discipline.*[98] This document, which came to be known as the *Discipline*, tells a great deal about the nineteenth-century Free Will Baptists' confessionalism. First, it was a condensed version of the Standard Confession, "the former Confession of Faith, put forth by the former Elders and Deacons," which they had been confessing since the seventeenth century. Second, it is notable that it was a revision: "The General

Conference . . . judg[ed] it expedient to examine and re-print the former Confession of Faith." This indicated their belief that confessions of faith are revisable. Third, the document was binding on its ministers, stating that they were required to abide by the "ordinances and decrees" of the conference, that they must be "found orthodox" and "believe the Faith and Order of this Church to be altogether consonant with the Holy Scriptures" to receive ordination.[99] As the Free Will Baptists migrated from the Carolinas and other types of Baptists became Free Will Baptists, this same pattern held true. For example, many Separate Baptists in the nineteenth century became Free Will Baptists. Although as Separate Baptists they did not believe in having written confessions of faith, after they became Free Will Baptists, they drew up and published confessions of faith and required their ministers to assent to them.[100]

Confessionalism and the Disciples Controversy

This confessionalism was challenged in a protracted controversy in the 1830s and 1840s between the Disciples of Christ (the followers of Thomas and Alexander Campbell) and the Free Will Baptists. The Free Will Baptists of North Carolina are an outstanding example of the loss of members to the Disciples of Christ, a phenomenon that occurred across the Protestant spectrum in the mid-nineteenth century. The Disciples set about actively proselytizing Free Will Baptists, and a number of churches were lost. One of the major issues in this controversy was the Disciples' slogan, "No creed but the Bible." Free Will Baptists who came under the influence of the Disciples were required to renounce their traditional commitment to written confessions of faith—to "discard as utterly useless all human creeds, traditions, or commandments of uninspired men."[101] Some Free Will Baptist ministers and laymen began to teach against the use of written confessions of faith. For example, Reuben Barrow, a layman who himself had served on the 1836 revision committee for the *Discipline*, stated in 1842 that all rules of discipline "written by uninspired men, are altogether useless and unprofitable; and that they are one great cause of the divisions and contentions which pervade the Christian world at the present day."[102] Over and over again, churches were asked to vote to choose whether to "take the written discipline or the word of God, upon which [some] voted to take the word of God."[103] But those Free Will Baptists who remained committed to their received faith and practice saw this as a false dichotomy and continued to confess the *Discipline*. This controversy strengthened the confessional posture of the continuing Free Will Baptist movement.[104]

Continuing Confessionalism

The Free Will Baptists of the South continued the orthodox confessional tradition of their forebears, despite the isolation and lack of theological education that characterized most of them during the nineteenth century. A perusal of Free Will Baptist minutes and other documents throughout the nineteenth and twentieth centuries shows a solidifying of orthodox confessionalism. This intensified as the Free Will Baptists witnessed the Free Baptists of the North (with whom they were never in union) succumb to a more liberal version of Protestantism and unite with the Northern Baptist Convention in 1911. E. L. St. Claire, the foremost leader of the General Conference in the first two decades of the twentieth century, is a representative example of the continuation of the Grantham dynamic of polemics and irenics. St. Claire engaged in numerous debates over orthodox doctrine as well as distinctive Free Will Baptist doctrines. Yet despite important differences, St. Claire wished to cooperate with orthodox Christians of other communions for the proclamation of the gospel and benevolent enterprises.[105] The tradition of confessional subscription by ministers has continued, with strong conferences and associations maintaining the responsibility of the ordination and discipline of ministers, despite the intrusion in some areas of alien forms of church government such as the radical autonomy and independence of the Independent Baptist and nondenominational megachurch movements.[106]

Conclusion

The task at hand for contemporary Arminian Baptists is to reconnect with their past: their own scripturally permeated tradition, the tradition of the Reformation, and the Reformation's rooting of itself in and appropriation of the consensual orthodoxy of the creeds, councils, and fathers of the early church. The greatest temptation for modern-day Arminian Baptists, as it is for all evangelicals, is to make Christianity acceptable to its "cultured despisers." In our case, these are not so much antitrinitarians or elite liberals and modernists. Our greatest threat is not to reject our orthodoxy in favor of heterodoxy, but to water it down in our craving after the spirit of this present evil age, which is passing away with its desires. Instead, we need to tap into the powers of the age to come, which are enduring and which transcend our passing moment with its consumerism and narcissism and amusement. Engaging in the *ressourcement* of our tradition will aid us in this task.

9

Toward a Generous Orthodoxy

Curtis W. Freeman

A young boy was riding in the car with a Catholic priest. Along the way they passed by a building with a sign out front that read: "Independent-Fundamentalist, Bible-Believing, Dispensational-Premillennial, Free-Will, Feet-Washing, Missionary Baptist Church." Puzzled by the words, he asked for theological clarification. With a mixture of wit and wisdom, the priest replied, "When you belong to a church that doesn't believe in creeds, you have to fit a lot of doctrine on the sign."

Baptists, to be sure, are known to be a noncredal people, but the need for creed will have its way, even if the creed is to have no creed. Although the suspicion of creeds is widespread among evangelicals and other free churches, few denominational groups have historically been more resistant to creeds than the Baptists. But ironically, no group in the wider Christian communion is in greater need of confessing the one faith as delineated in the ancient ecumenical creeds of the church. And if the focus of this chapter seems disproportionately addressed to the Baptists, it is in the hope that if they, being the hardest to persuade, can be convinced, then perhaps other evangelicals and free churches also in need of creed might be similarly open.

At the risk of disappointing those readers who may be expecting a conversation with Brian McLaren's project by the same name, none is forthcoming.[1]

The stance outlined in this essay invokes the phrase *generous orthodoxy* as Hans Frei used it to describe the standpoint of Robert Calhoun, who helped usher in a new theological era at Yale Divinity School as it transitioned from liberalism to postliberalism. Frei characterized Calhoun's vision as a "generous liberal orthodoxy"—*generous* in its respectful and charitable openness toward an understanding of others, *liberal* inasmuch as it did not make a sharp break with modern modes of critical reflection, and *orthodox* because of its conviction that the center of Christian theology is the revelation of the Triune God in Jesus Christ. As Frei observed, Calhoun's shift was "not to neo-orthodoxy, but to a view closer to traditional orthodoxy without abandoning his liberal convictions."[2] From this perspective of a generous liberal orthodoxy, then, I will attempt to show my fellow Baptists and other noncredal churches the need for creed.

The Need for Creed

John Clifford delivered his presidential address on April 20, 1888, to a distressed assembly of the Baptist Union of Great Britain. Two unsigned pieces had appeared the previous spring in the *Sword and Trowel*, a monthly magazine published by Charles Spurgeon. The anonymous author charged that the union was on a precipitous "Down Grade." Although Spurgeon did not actually write the articles, he gave his unqualified support to the view that the union had begun to slide down the slippery slope toward "a new religion . . . which is no more Christianity than chalk is cheese." He charged, "The Atonement is scouted, the inspiration of Scripture is derided, the Holy Spirit is degraded into an influence, the punishment of sin is turned into fiction, and the resurrection into a myth, and yet these enemies of our faith expect us to call them brethren, and maintain a confederacy with them!"[3]

Spurgeon urged the need to discipline unsound ministers, asserting that "fellowship with known and vital error is participation in sin."[4] And even though he soon withdrew from the union, the controversy continued unabated.[5] Clifford's address to the assembly came in the morning, before the afternoon session that would consider the new and more evangelically inclined declaration drafted by Joseph Angus, the principal of Regent's Park College, with editorial contributions by Spurgeon's own brother, James. Clifford began by reassuring his colleagues that "even strife is a sign of vitality—uncomfortable, irritating vitality, perhaps; . . . but still it is vitality." Yet he wanted the union to move beyond this uncomfortable and irritating liberal versus conservative vitality toward a deeper confessional unity. Knowing that widespread suspicion of creeds and confessions, when used as tests of fellowship, stood in the way of approving new principles, Clifford turned their attention to primitive Christian faith during the apostolic era.

He asked, "What was the Christianity of Jesus Christ, the Christianity of the Great Forty Years?"

The heart of apostolic faith, he answered, lives in the confession of three primitive creeds. The first and "primordial germ" of all Christian creeds is the confession of the apostle Peter: "Thou art the Christ, the Son of the living God" (Matt. 16:16 KJV). As the Lord Jesus explained to Peter, this creed is not of human origin, but is a gift of divine inspiration. Thus, Clifford urged his listener to "get that creed as Peter got it." Beyond the Petrine confession is the Johannine creed, uttered from the lips of the apostle Thomas: "My Lord and my God" (John 20:28 KJV). The confession of Thomas is more concise than that of Peter. Yet, Clifford continued, the Johannine creed was "not an echo, but a voice; not a recitation, but a conviction; not an act of memory, but the articulate breath of a living soul." The third creed comes from the apostle Paul: "That if thou shalt confess with thy mouth the Lord Jesus, and shalt believe in thine heart that God hath raised him from the dead, thou shalt be saved" (Rom. 10:9 KJV). In the words of these three apostolic witnesses—Peter, John, and Paul—the substance of primitive Christian faith given once and for all was, Clifford argued, "indisputably established." And these three creeds provide the pattern for all subsequent confessions of faith.[6] It is important to note that both Spurgeon and Clifford saw a need for creed, although they conceived of it differently. For Spurgeon the need was to delineate the boundaries, whereas for Clifford the greater need was to name the center.

Clifford's statement was eloquent and ebullient, and by all accounts passionately and persuasively delivered. And after such an overwhelmingly positive reception, it was no surprise that the Declaratory Statement was adopted with only minor opposition. Following the thesis of Clifford's address, the new principles declared the union to be "an association of churches and ministers, professing not only to believe the facts and doctrines of the Gospel, but to have undergone the spiritual change expressed or implied in them." As the new declaration affirmed, genuine confession of faith presupposes a "spiritual change . . . and this change is the fundamental principle of our church life."[7] Early Baptists and other radical Puritans often thought about this change in terms of what they called "the experience of grace," and "experienced Christians" were those who offered confessions after the fashion of Peter, John, and Paul to declare their faith.[8] This experiential conviction is the reason that they firmly believed that reciting a creed is no substitute for a personal confession of faith.[9]

The experiential conviction is also the nub of the concern that Baptists, and not a few evangelicals who share a conversionist spirituality, have about the creed. It is of interest to note that the Baptist Union, in its Declaration of Principles, made no appeal to the ancient ecumenical creeds.[10] Indeed, that they had reservations about the confession of creeds became evident at the October 1889 meeting of the union, which considered a letter from the Archbishop of Canterbury inviting a Baptist response to the Lambeth Quadrilateral on steps toward reunion.[11] The second condition named acceptance of the Apostles' Creed as a baptismal symbol, and the Nicene Creed as a statement of faith.[12] The Baptists resisted, indicating the susceptibility of the creeds to a variety of interpretations. Their objection to confession of the historic creeds was a niggling criticism, especially compared with the fourth condition that specified the recognition of the historic episcopate, which the Church of England claimed but the Baptists rejected outright.

Some have held out even stronger reservations. For example, W. B. Johnson, the first president of the Southern Baptist Convention, speaking at the inaugural gathering in Augusta, Georgia, declared: "We have constructed for our basis no new creed, acting in this manner upon a Baptist aversion for all creeds but the Bible."[13] Johnson was not the first, nor was he the last, to invoke the motto "No creed but the Bible." Walter Rauschenbusch famously argued in a series of 1905–6 essays that "Baptists tolerate no creed" because they hold that "the Bible alone is sufficient authority for our faith and practice."[14] During the modernist-fundamentalist controversy, New York pastor Cornelius Woelfkin successfully persuaded the Northern Baptist Convention in 1922 not to adopt a confession of faith but instead to affirm "that the New Testament is the all-sufficient ground of . . . faith and practice."[15] In 1979, when many Southern Baptists were calling for confessional fidelity, John J. Hurt, longtime Baptist editor of the *Christian Index* and the *Baptist Standard*, declared that the "Southern Baptist Convention has no more need for a creed than it has for a pope." To which he added, "It won't get the former without the latter and either will destroy it."[16] Jimmy Allen, former president of the Southern Baptist Convention, decried a "creeping credalism" in Baptist life on the basis that "the thing that distinguishes us as Baptists is that the Bible itself is our creed."[17] Walter Shurden placed at the top of the list of most dangerous threats in contemporary Baptist life a movement "from a Christ-centered to a creed-centered faith."[18]

One of the most notable Baptists to renounce creeds was Harry Emerson Fosdick, who attributed his creed-adverse faith to his upbringing in a Baptist family of solid convictions. Fosdick boasted that he never subscribed to or repeated any creed. Reporting on a 1922 visit to Japan, he said, "I stood up . . . while the whole company shouted the creed and never opened my lips, such being my habit." Though never surrendering his Baptist convictions or ordination, Fosdick served as the pastor of the First Presbyterian Church of New York City. After his controversial sermon "Shall the Fundamentalists Win?" the Presbytery of New York called for him to submit to the doctrinal standards of the Presbyterian Church, which included adherence to the creeds. Fosdick replied that the "credal subscription to ancient confessions of faith is a practice dangerous to the welfare of the church and to the integrity of the individual conscience." He let them know that for him to subscribe to any creed "would be a violation of conscience."[19] In his 1924 Beecher Lectures, Fosdick averred: "This is the nemesis of all credalism: the creeds are promulgated to protect faith, and then, their forms of thinking being at last overpassed, insistence on them becomes the ruination of faith."[20]

Not all Baptists have thought so negatively about creeds. Hezekiah Harvey warned prospective pastors in his lectures at Hamilton Theological Seminary against reactionary anticredalism, suggesting that "the want of a definite creed, in almost all instances, results in an actual departure from the gospel."[21] Even E. Y. Mullins, who was notably cautious about the potential dangers of authoritarianism, maintained that "when used properly," creeds are "the natural and normal expression of the religious life."[22]

It seems warranted, then, that concerns about fidelity to the gospel are properly guided by regard for liberty in Christ. Both are necessary and complementary, yet each carries potential mistakes and problems. Creeds are misused when they become instruments of coercion, just as religious liberty is abused when it is invoked to legitimate deviation from the living witness of apostolic faith. How might creeds, then, be employed by Baptists and other free church Christians so as to balance the convictions of faithfulness and freedom?

One of the most striking examples of the "natural and normal" use of creeds occurred on July 12, 1905, when the Baptist World Alliance met at Exeter Hall in London for its first congress. Its president, Alexander Maclaren, addressed the session and urged that the new body declare before the world where they stand "in the continuity of the historic Church." He urged that as its very first act, the congress should make an "audible and unanimous acknowledgment of [the] Faith." Such a step, he said, would clear away misunderstanding and put an end to slander. He then invited his fellow participants to rise to their feet and confess the Apostles' Creed, "not as a piece of coercion or discipline, but as a simple acknowledgment of where we stand and what we believe." The report states that the whole gathering instantly rose and repeated, slowly and deliberately after Maclaren, the whole creed.

Reflecting on the event, editor of the *Baptist Times and Freeman* and secretary of the congress John Howard Shakespeare noted that there had never been an act of such inspiration or a moment so historic among the Baptists.[23] One hundred years later, the opening assembly of the centenary meeting of the Baptist World Congress recalled Maclaren's appeal and repeated the creed together. Such expressions of generous orthodoxy are worthy of emulation by other free and faithful Christians. Confessing the creed even more often than once every century might be a good practice to consider.[24]

The Creed as Centered Theology

John Howard Yoder famously suggested that the use of the creeds is mostly negative. He openly wondered whether they do "us much good."[25] Though with the creeds Yoder affirmed the normativity of God's revelation in Jesus, he relativized their theological importance. Summarizing his position, Yoder declaimed, "The Creeds are helpful as fences, but affirming, believing, debating for, fighting for the Creeds, is probably something which a radical Anabaptist kind of faith would not concentrate on doing."[26]

But as Mennonite theologian Thomas Finger argues, the exclusive function of the creeds that Yoder focuses on is secondary and misses the more primary, inclusive purpose of the creeds.[27] The exclusive function operates with the assumption that the creeds primarily delineate a *bounded set*, with the aim of keeping some people and their ideas out. Understood in terms of their inclusive purpose, the creeds do not offer exhaustive statements of the faith, but rather denote a *centered set* that names the nexus of the common life in Christ and seeks to draw those who confess their articles ever toward the communion envisioned therein. To suggest that the first use of the creeds is about orienting faith and practice toward the trinitarian and christological center is different from an *open set* with neither center nor circumference. But a centered approach urges that boundary making need not be the first step. This boundary-making approach, which has been called *critical orthodoxy*, imagines the line between orthodoxy and heresy as bounded by the circumference of a circle.[28]

Yet such an approach may not be the most helpful image. Another perspective views the creeds primarily as a rich resource for delineating the vectors that move toward the center, rather than as a tool for circumscribing the boundaries. This inclusive orientation is the basic standpoint of *generous orthodoxy*. How, then, might the creeds, and in particular the Nicene Creed, conceived as a centered theology, regulate faith and guide confession in the journey toward the christological and trinitarian center? Consider the following two examples.

Reorienting Toward Christ the Center

On June 19, 2008, speaking at a Baptist gathering, John Killinger dismissed traditional Christology as passé and announced: "Now we are reevaluating and we're approaching everything with a humbler perspective and seeing God's hand working in Christ, but not necessarily as the incarnate God in our midst."[29] Killinger's penchant for controversy is well known. His book *The Changing Shape of Our Salvation* tells the story of the development of soteriology in light and breezy prose. Dismissing the outcome of the church councils as the result of an unfortunate power struggle that just happened to be won by premodern fundamentalists, he attributes "the final decisions about belief and orthodoxy" in the patristic era to the exercise of sheer "power, politics, and popularity." Against the traditional account of the history of doctrine, Killinger wonders whether perhaps "the Gnostics, the Montanists, the Marcionites, and other heretics" might have been ruled out "merely because

they weren't as strong, clever, and numerous as those who voted another way."
The acceptance of the Nicene doctrine of the deity of Christ, by his account,
was simply the whim of a majority vote.[30] Killinger asserts his view with
utter confidence, almost as if he were an oracle of the zeitgeist, even though
his positions are neither grounded in solid research nor widely representative
of the scholarly guilds.[31] That he would question the incarnation without
thoughtful reflection, then, should not be surprising.

But the fact that Killinger, like many other liberals, does not acknowledge
the creed as naming the trinitarian and christological center, indicates one of
the most serious challenges that a centered approach faces. Killinger's sort of
open-set revisionism has neither center nor circumference. He consequently
offers no serious engagement with the historic stream of orthodox Christology,
which affirms of our Lord Jesus Christ—in the words of the Nicene Creed—
that he was "begotten (*gennethēnta*) from the Father before all the ages" and
is "consubstantial (*homoousion*) with the Father."[32] Baptists, to be sure, have
had their fair share of folks with an unbounded and uncentered theological
approach who chose against the way of orthodoxy—like Matthew Caffyn, a
seventeenth-century English General Baptist minister who denied the essential
divinity of Christ, or Elhanan Winchester, the eighteenth-century American
Baptist pastor and evangelist who founded the first Universalist church in
Philadelphia, or the unnamed Unitarians, warned against by Richard Furman in his 1820 *Call*, with whom he said Baptists should not collaborate on
missions and education.[33]

George Burman Foster, a Baptist theologian at the University of Chicago
Divinity School in the early twentieth century, was so wary about saying that
"Jesus is God" that he turned the phrase around, asserting instead that "God
is like Jesus."[34] According to his pragmatic-functionalist theory of religion,
Foster declared that all doctrines, including what he called the "God-idea," were
inventions of human creativity that served the needs and purposes of humanity.
He argued that because modern experience has no need for the Trinity or the
incarnation, these traditional concepts no longer served a useful purpose and
must be laid aside. What is needed, Foster reasoned, is the creation of "a new
eternal Messiah" that would be incarnate "in all human souls, born anew in
every child."[35] Yet few Baptists were interested in following the approach of
humanistic naturalism. Most of them were simply amazed that liberal theologians like Foster "could have written so much while believing so little."[36]

These examples are the exceptions that prove the rule. Whenever Baptists
have thought deeply together about faith in Christ, they have tended to echo
the language of Nicene orthodoxy. The Second London Confession (1677/1688)
of English Particular Baptists affirmed that Jesus was "the Son of God, the
second Person in the Holy Trinity, being very and eternal God."[37] Similarly,
the Orthodox Creed (1678) of the English General Baptists declared that
"the Son of God, or eternal word, is very and true God, having his personal

subsistence of the father alone, and yet for ever of himself as God."[38] Any survey of the historic Baptist confessions of faith yields the conclusion that they affirm the mystery proclaimed since the days of the apostles, that in Jesus Christ "all the fullness of God was pleased to dwell" (Col. 1:19). This conviction is the trinitarian and christological center described in the language of Nicene orthodoxy. Rather than assuming a stereotypical caricature of orthodoxy, liberal theology stands ever in need of an ongoing conversation with the theological tradition of the creed that attends to the central conviction of the incarnation—namely, that God was in Christ.

If liberals have too seldom engaged the trinitarian and christological center of the creed, so have evangelicals also failed to attend to its affirmations. In so doing, they have often embraced a diminished orthodoxy. Few matters among evangelicals are more in need of renewal than their theology of Scripture. In his book *Retrieving the Tradition and Renewing Evangelicalism*, D. H. Williams appeals to suspicious evangelicals who think that the Bible alone is sufficient grounds for their faith. He carefully shows why they have a stake in recovering the patristic tradition by unmasking the hermeneutical naïveté of readers who think that they can leapfrog from the primitive Christianity of the Bible to the contemporary situation with relative ease. Williams further explains how the basic core of apostolic doctrine was preserved and passed on in the postapostolic era through the writings of the church fathers, and how this apostolic tradition may be retrieved by carefully reading the patristic sources.

Of particular importance to evangelicals is his discussion of the patristic rule of faith, which, although like the creed, was a more elastic summary of the basic body of apostolic doctrine. Williams shows how the rule functioned as a hermeneutical guide for reading Scripture, serving as more of an intrinsic précis that disclosed the central teachings of the Bible than an extrinsic standard that was arbitrarily imposed. In so doing, Williams displays how the orthodox trinitarian and christological doctrines, to which evangelicals are committed, were not derived by the exegesis of Scripture alone but by reading the Scriptures through the lens of the rule and the creeds.[39]

An example of what Williams suggests may be seen in Article I of the Baptist Faith and Message (1963), which affirms that the Bible "is, and will remain to the end of the world, the true center of Christian union, and the supreme standard by which all human conduct, creeds, and religious opinions should be tried," but which continues by saying, "The criterion by which the Bible is to be interpreted is Jesus Christ."[40] By gesturing toward a christological hermeneutic, the confession recognized the limits of linguistic exegesis and retained a fragment of the ancient rule of faith, albeit as a very slender thread. It nevertheless preserved the conviction that the New Testament is concealed in the Old, and the Old Testament is revealed in the New, with its corresponding prospective and retrospective hermeneutical strategies.[41]

It is not a little ironic that the recent revision of the Baptist Faith and Message by conservative evangelicals replaced the statement about Christ as "the criterion by which the Bible is to be interpreted" with the line "All Scripture is a testimony to Christ, who is Himself the focus of divine revelation." Thus, they removed the last remaining vestige of the rule of faith from the confession. Given the current state of evangelical Bible study, which is still largely determined by the literal-sense meaning and grammatical-historical method, the possible hermeneutical benefits of an evangelical *ressourcement* are enormous. Steven R. Harmon recommends that serious Bible readers will find much-needed hermeneutical guidance by returning to the ancient creeds of the church. "Reciting the creeds," Harmon continues, "impresses upon us again and again the overarching meaning of the Bible and so shapes our capacity for hearing and heeding what specific passages of Scripture have to say."[42]

Retrieving an Incarnational Soteriology

But the need for the creed among evangelicals in retrieving the *sensus plenior* of the Scriptures is more acute than some may suspect or care to admit. Consider the doctrine of the atonement among evangelicals, which, drawing from the Protestant Reformers, has been understood primarily in terms of satisfaction or substitution. How might this doctrine be enriched by a sustained conversation with the affirmation about Christ the Son in the Nicene Creed that "for us humans and for our salvation he came down from the heavens and became incarnate from the Holy Spirit and the Virgin Mary"?[43] The theologians of the ancient church recognized with this article that Scriptures like Romans 8 taught that humanity, and indeed the entire cosmos, was redeemed through the incarnation. They understood that this cosmic reversal of the law of sin and death is the result of the fullness of Christ's life, not only of the sacrifice of his death. In his classic text *On the Incarnation of the Word*, Athanasius of Alexandria explained that Christ the Word became incarnate to restore the image of God in which humanity was made and from which all have fallen. He asked, "What, then, was God to do? What else could he possibly do, being God, but renew His Image in [hu]mankind, so that through it [humanity] might once more come to know Him? And how could this be done save by the coming of the very Image Himself, our Saviour Jesus Christ?"[44]

The Word, by whom humanity was created, must re-create humanity in one of Adam's heirs. In the incarnation, the immortal Son of God was united with human nature as the Second Adam, and thus all humanity was clothed in incorruption in the promise of the resurrection. To illustrate this divine drama of salvation, Athanasius suggested that just as in the ancient world, when a king entered a city and lived in one of its houses the whole city was saved from its enemies, so Christ the Son "has come into our country and dwelt in one body amid the many, and in consequence the designs of the enemy against [hu]mankind have been foiled, and the corruption of death, which formerly held them into its power, has simply ceased to be."[45]

These patristic interpreters understood the incarnation as having reversed the powers of sin and death. As Athanasius simply stated, in the Word, "[God] assumed humanity that we might become God."[46] This doctrine, which was called *theosis* in Greek, did not imply a crude divinization in which the redeemed literally become gods. Rather, it taught that as the Son was united with humanity through the incarnation, so was humanity united with the life of the Son of God through salvation.[47]

There are lingering questions about how these patristic understandings of salvation might be appropriated today. The underlying Platonism, with its notion of universal humanity in which all were thought to participate, no longer carries the persuasive power that it did in the ancient world, and Protestants have grown suspicious that the Orthodox doctrine of deification does not take seriously enough the continuing sinfulness of Christians. Still, in a sustained engagement with the patristic doctrine of the incarnation, evangelicals might find ways of retrieving the theology of ancient Christianity. More importantly, they might apprehend a fuller sense of the saving significance of the entirety of Christ's life, not only his death.[48]

Evangelicals have historically defended the soteriological theology of satisfaction and penal substitution against moral and exemplary theories put forth by liberals.[49] More recently, the evangelical theology of vicarious substitutionary atonement has been under assault by liberation theologians and those who have adapted the scapegoat theory of René Girard, both of whom object to the victimization of Jesus and the notion of divine retribution that seem to underwrite and perpetuate violence.[50]

Yet some of the harshest criticisms of penal substitution have come from within the ranks of evangelicals. Baptist minister and evangelical leader Steve Chalke went so far as to characterize penal substitution as "cosmic child abuse," which, he argued, stands in contradiction with the statement "God is love."[51] Chalke's runaway sound bite ignited a firestorm among evangelicals, with some critics dismissing his remarks as "silly" and others accusing him of "blasphemy."[52]

Baptist and evangelical theologian Stephen Holmes has offered a more constructive and nuanced defense of penal substitution for contemporary Christians.[53] Holmes appropriates a wide range of images and metaphors of atonement in the Bible. He deals responsibly with the issues of guilt transference, law and love, divine retribution, and redemptive violence. What he does not consider, however, is the biblical witness to the conviction that, in John Calvin's lovely phrase, "Christ has redeemed us . . . by the whole course of his obedience."[54] Yet Holmes is not alone in this omission. He shares this deficiency with other evangelicals for whom exclusive attention is given to the cross without considering the saving effects of the entire course of Christ's life, death, and resurrection.[55]

New Testament scholar Douglas Campbell makes a perceptive and telling observation about evangelical theology at this point when he writes:

> The justification by faith perspective on Christ's work, while placing a satisfactory emphasis on the cross, evacuates his incarnation, much of his life, his resurrection, and his ascension, of all soteriological value. According to the justification by faith model, these aspects of Christ have no real part to play in the great drama by which God saves humanity, since the justification by faith account of that drama focuses solely on the cross. Indeed, the justification by faith model struggles to justify the inclusion of these other aspects of Christ's life and ministry within a full account of salvation at all![56]

In his magisterial tome *The Deliverance of God*, Campbell discusses in great detail the divergent theories of Pauline soteriology, and offers a substantive reconstruction, not unlike that of the patristic theologians, which "understands Christ's atoning work as transformational, and . . . consequently encompasses his incarnation, life, death, resurrection, and glorification."[57] Evangelicals may well counter that there is good reason to center on "the wondrous cross." Yet, as William Placher has written, "any account of what Christ has done for us that leaves out his teaching, his preaching, his healing and the rest [of] his ministry is not faithful to the witness of the New Testament and does not meet the needs of contemporary Christians." And as Placher continues, "In short, both Jesus's life and his death matter to our salvation, and we should not rest content with one without the other."[58] By a sustained engagement with the trinitarian and christological center of the creed, evangelical theology would be enriched by retrieving the ancient and apostolic sense of the whole creation groaning for redemption and for the long-awaited adoption in Christ. As the apostle Paul attests, "for in this hope we were saved" (Rom. 8:24).[59]

A Generous Postliberal Orthodoxy

So far, two examples have been offered to indicate that both liberals and evangelicals are in need of attending more intentionally to the trinitarian and christological center named in the ancient ecumenical creeds. In both cases, however, there was only a gesture toward what a sustained engagement might look like. What follows is a brief consideration of the christological reflections of James William McClendon Jr. as an indication of what a generous orthodoxy looks like from a postliberal standpoint. The centerpiece of the second volume of McClendon's *Systematic Theology*, simply entitled *Doctrine*, is his chapter "Jesus the Risen Christ."[60] It takes as its point of reference the christological doctrine, as defined first at Nicea, that Jesus Christ "became incarnate from the Holy Spirit and the Virgin Mary [and] became human," and later at Chalcedon, which affirmed the deity and humanity of Christ: two natures existing in one person.

The two-natures doctrine, although at the center of orthodoxy, is not without problems. McClendon cites the celestial-flesh Christology of Menno Simons and the immaculate-conception Mariology of Pope Pius IX as two unfortunate examples of the limitations of the two-natures model.[61] With D. M. Baillie he agreed that modern historiography brought an end to the haunting docetism that explained away Jesus's humanity as simulation rather than reality.[62] Yet McClendon recognized that the historical purge of docetism has not been free of fallout. From the old quest of the historical Jesus to the continuing quest of the Jesus Seminar, historical-critical investigation into the human life of Jesus has continued to stretch the two-natures Christology to the limits, driving a wedge ever deeper between the Christ of faith and the Jesus of history.[63]

More pressing still for McClendon was the distillation of the life of Jesus into the philosophical category of *nature*, which abstracts the humanity of Jesus from the portrait of the humble savior found in the Gospels. McClendon's concern was grounded in what Hans Frei identified as "the eclipse of biblical narrative" in modern hermeneutics. Both held the deep conviction that doctrine should illuminate stories rather than stories illustrating doctrine. Consequently, McClendon maintained, as did Frei, that the identity of Jesus Christ was inextricable from the biblical story.[64] As an alternative to the two-natures doctrine, McClendon proposed a two-narratives Christology that called attention to two intertwined stories in the Bible: one of Israel's God and the other of God's people, Israel. One narrative is the *kenosis* (Greek, "God emptying himself" [Phil. 2:7]) story of God's self-giving; the other narrative is the *plerosis* (Greek, "fulfilling," derived from *pleros*, meaning "full" [Phil. 2:8–11]) story of divine fulfillment in human "up-reaching." Throughout the Bible, these two stories gesture toward one another; yet they remain distinct until, in the life of a faithful son of Israel, Jesus of Nazareth, they become—at last—indivisibly one.[65]

Of particular importance is McClendon's reading of the primitive Christian hymn in Philippians 2:5–11. Following a line of patristic interpretation, he took the hymn as an example of the earthly *living of Christ*, not the more common understanding of an incarnational story about the heavenly *leaving of Christ*.[66] By so rendering the hymn as a model of Christ's servant lordship, and correlatively as an example of servant discipleship for those who follow Jesus in the servant way, McClendon avoided the lingering docetism of the two-natures model that the kenotic Christology addressed by attempting to explain how deity can "empty" itself. It seems accurate, then, to describe McClendon's two-narratives Christology not so much as a corrective than as a supplement to the classical two-natures doctrine that renders it valid for contemporary theology.[67]

Anticipating the possible misunderstanding of readers who might take this two-narratives approach to regard Jesus simply as the "lucky winner" adopted by God, McClendon affirms "that there was never a time when God did not intend to raise Jesus from the dead, never a time when the whole story pointed to anything less than the ultimate exaltation of this One."[68] And indeed, it seems reasonable to extend McClendon's analogy, as does Robert Barron, to suggest that although there are two stories, human and divine, "there is one storyteller, God, who acknowledges both stories as his own, who tells himself in both." Thus, "the fully and richly human story of Jesus is enhypostatically grounded in the intentionality of the divine storyteller."[69] Careful readers need look no further for McClendon's orthodoxy, but careless ones may miss the seriousness with which he takes the challenge of historicism.[70] As the two-natures model provided previous generations of Christians with a useful account of the faith, McClendon hopes that a two-narratives Christology might enable contemporary Christians to faithfully teach what entitles Jesus to be their Lord, or why the confession of Christ's lordship is consistent with the conviction that God is one, and finally how Christlike the lives of disciples are to be. Whatever one makes of McClendon's proposal, there is no question that it represents a sustained reflection on the center from the standpoint of a generous postliberal orthodoxy.

In the early 1980s the Faith and Order Commission of the World Council of Churches began working toward the common expression of apostolic faith today. It resulted in the publication of the book *Confessing the One Faith*. They took as their text for reflection the Nicene Creed. The commission recognized the historic concern from noncredal churches that credal formulas can easily degenerate into formalism and, consequently, they did not want to be perceived as requiring the acceptance of the creed by noncredal churches. Nevertheless, the commission expressed hope that since the noncredal churches shared the apostolic faith expressed in the creed, they might, at least on special occasions and perhaps more often, join in the confession of the Nicene Creed "as a witness to their communion in the faith of the one, holy, catholic and apostolic Church."[71] Meetings and consultations were held beginning in 1981, and as the process continued, it began to appear to the members of the Apostolic Faith Steering Committee that there would be little prospect of getting a document approved. The tide turned surprisingly and decisively in favor of the statement when Horace Russell, a Baptist theologian and minister from Jamaica, expressed his support for confessing the creed. Russell acknowledged that though Baptists are not a creedal people, the accounts of the faith with which he, as a Baptist, found the most striking resonance and were most faithful to the biblical witness as he understood it were those that were solidly grounded in the creed. His support encouraged approval of the document.

The examples of Horace Russell and Alexander Maclaren commend Baptists, along with other free and faithful Christians, to join in confessing the creed as a simple acknowledgment of where they stand and what they believe. Doing so demonstrates continuity with the historic church and the apostolic faith on which it was built. More importantly, by a sustained engagement with the trinitarian and christological center expressed in the creed, those who confess it, study it, pray it, reflect on it, and practice it are drawn into a deeper knowledge of and union with the One whom it names. My hope is that such a practice might be carried out with generosity toward others who are also seeking to confess the one faith, liberality in a desire to interpret the old faith anew in changing contexts, and orthodoxy in the conviction that the center of apostolic faith is the revelation of the Triune God in Jesus Christ our Lord. This is the generous orthodoxy to which I am committed and the practice of which I commend.

Part 3

Practice

10

Practicing the Nicene Faith

E L I Z A B E T H   N E W M A N

What language shall I borrow to thank Thee, dearest friend,
For this Thy dying sorrow, Thy pity without end?

What language shall we borrow? These words from the familiar hymn "O
Sacred Head, Now Wounded"[1] suggest that human speech can never fully
grasp our gratitude for God. The hymnist writes, in a later verse, "The joy can
never be spoken . . . When in Thy body broken I thus with safety hide." Such
words echo those of the psalmist: "You have multiplied, O LORD my God,
your wondrous deeds and your thoughts toward us; none can compare with
you! I will proclaim and tell of them, yet they are more than can be told" (Ps.
40:5–6). If words cannot capture human gratitude, how much less can they
convey fully the nature of God. As the Fourth Lateran Council (1215) claimed:
"Between the Creator and the creature no similarity can be expressed without
including a greater dissimilarity."[2] God is greater than we can possibly imagine:
God is more than we can fully say. This apophatic or negative theology, as it
came to be known, protects the deep Mystery that is God.

Yet if this were all we could say, we might well be left in silence. Karl Barth
reminds us that God is incomprehensible not in God's remoteness but in

God's nearness in Jesus Christ.[3] What is most profoundly mysterious about God is that the Word has become flesh. This divine mystery, then, is not a door slammed shut, but a depth so great that we can never fully exhaust it.

The Nicene Creed is the church's acknowledgment that it lives on borrowed language. In fact, the shaping of the creed embodies an argument about language. What words ought the church use to worship and speak of God faithfully? Is the one Lord Jesus Christ "begotten, not made, being of one substance with the Father"? Or, as Arius famously argued, is Jesus a perfect creature, created by God before the beginning of time? What language shall we borrow?

The philosopher Ludwig Wittgenstein uses the phrase *language game* to describe how language gives rise to a form of life. The word *game* in this sense is not trivial (as if one is just playing around) but serious (as in how one lives). As Stanley Hauerwas puts it, "You can only live in the world you can see, and you can only see the world you have learned to say."[4] Our words can open up or shut down how we see and therefore live in the world. In this sense, "our words are deeds." The familiar Hebrew word *dabar*, which can mean both word and deed, reflects this reality. God's *dabar* "makes a world appear."[5] As the psalmist writes, "By the word [deed] of the LORD were the heavens made, and all their host by the breath of his mouth" (Ps. 33:6 RSV). In human speech, our covenantal words are also deeds, as witnessed in the performance of marriage vows or the declaration at baptism. To ask, then, "What language shall we borrow?" is also to ask, "What life shall we live?"

In our context today, we face serious challenges in "borrowing" the language of the Nicene Creed. How does saying the creed square with personal freedom? Isn't the creed better understood as a historical document, certainly an interesting one but not necessarily crucial in the church's worship? Finally, do not arguments over the exact wording of credal statements easily obscure the simple call to Christian discipleship? In what follows, I want to engage three challenges to borrowing the language of the creed in order to say more fully what it means to practice the Nicene faith in worship and in the life of the church today.

"Freedom" versus Creedalism

Years ago, when I began teaching Christian ethics to undergraduates, a familiar question—"Who am I to judge?"—often hovered in the air. No doubt this question often seeks to avoid judgmentalism: "Why do you see the speck in your neighbor's eye, but do not notice the log in your own eye?" (Matt. 7:3 NRSV). But on one particularly disturbing occasion, a student followed this question to its logical conclusion: "Who's to say whether Hitler was right or wrong?" The implication: all judgments are private, personal choices. She had absorbed (like most of us have, to greater or lesser degrees) a dominant language of our American culture, one in which words like *values* and *religion* have become commodified. Alasdair MacIntyre describes this conviction as *emotivism*: "the doctrine that all evaluative judgments are nothing but expressions of preference, expressions of attitude or feeling, insofar as they are moral or evaluative in character."[6] My "personal values," my "personal spirituality," and, as some of my students now say, my own "personal theology" all reflect emotivism. As theologian Steve Long notes in his essay "God Is Not Nice," the language of "personal Savior" is now used to portray Jesus as a nice guy who is there to meet my needs, sort of like a personal tailor.[7]

Our dominant culture is a culture of choice. One might well argue that choice is good: we have freedom to be who we want to be. Any child can be president of the United States, we are told in grade school. Choice determines identity.[8] From this perspective, "We are what our choices have made us." To live in a culture of choice is to define freedom itself in terms of our ability to choose. We are free to the extent that we can choose our own values, our own way of life, and our own creeds. From this perspective, the Nicene Creed seems like an imposition.

And, one might well ask, why shouldn't we be free to choose? Is it right to impose our beliefs or values on others? This use of *freedom* and *belief* forms the background for those today—Christians and others—who equate the saying of creeds with the loss of individual freedom. The creed contradicts what one theologian calls "the voluntary principle in religion."[9] This voluntary principle refers to an emphasis on the individual will and the Holy Spirit acting upon that will. This stands in contrast, he notes, to corporatism and the Holy Spirit effecting obedience through the corporate will.

Some of us might well resonate with this language of the Holy Spirit speaking to the individual and with the desire not to "impose" or "coerce" belief. Institutions of higher education, for example, typically say, "We are not here to indoctrinate students." Certainly at the heart of the gospel is a Savior who does not use force or violence to make others follow him. In the familiar parable of the rich young ruler, for example, Jesus allows the young man to walk away—although as Mark's Gospel poignantly states, "Jesus, looking at him, loved him" (Mark 10:21).

The word *impose*, however, begs for closer examination. For example, when we tell ourselves we are not indoctrinating students but allowing them to choose or make up their own minds, are we not in fact indoctrinating them into a way of life? As one critic notes, students and others easily come to believe that "choosing between 'ideas' (or 'values') is like choosing between" an iPod or a cell phone. "It never occurs . . . that the very idea [one] should 'choose' is [itself] imposed."[10] Such language is not neutral but borrowed from the prevailing ethos of a market society, and from a politics focused on the individual and his or her rights. The belief that identity is self-generated is itself a creed, albeit an invisible one that seductively initiates its adherents into a way of life subject to dominant economic and political forces. In this creed, *choice* is taken to be revelatory of identity but not of character, which is defined by a common story.[11] By contrast, the Nicene Creed habituates its speakers not into the language of autonomous choice but into the language of God choosing us in and through Christ.

Of course, this way of speaking about the creed will not allay the anxiety of some. As one theologian and historian has recently said about his own denomination, "They forget the very principles that birthed and nurtured them. They move from freedom to fear . . . then . . . they get dangerous because they move from a Christ-centered to a creed-centered faith. They get dangerous because they move from freedom for the individual to fear of the individual."[12] In this view, freedom is the opposite of fear, and Christ-centered opposes creed-centered. Creeds are thus viewed as instruments used by those who fear the freedom of others.

I think there is no question that creeds—the ancient ones, as well as the more modern and postmodern ones—can be used in manipulative ways. "No creed but the Bible," for example, is a creed that can be used (manipulatively, in my opinion) to undercut the task of theology and the gift of dogma. But in thinking through the concept of freedom, Isaiah Berlin's famous distinction between negative and positive freedom is illuminative.[13] Negative freedom is the absence of restraint. For example, I am free *from* having to work long hours. Positive freedom is the ability to achieve some good purpose. An example of this would be, "The father is free to go to the park with his children." Positive freedom is tied to a purpose. Theologian Philip Thompson describes divine freedom as analogous to this twofold pattern: "First, God is free *from* any sort of control by creation in God's work of redemption. Second, God is also free *for* using creation in the same work of redemption."[14]

If we follow this twofold pattern, human freedom, from a Christian perspective, relates ultimately to fulfilling a purpose, a purpose we do not choose. (As I learned from a childhood Presbyterian friend, the response to the first question of the Westminster Catechism, "What is the chief end of man?" is, "To glorify God and Enjoy Him forever.") The Nicene Creed describes this end more fully: communion with the Triune God. The opposite of freedom, understood in this light, is not being "creed-centered" but failing to be faithful to the gifts of God's calling and purpose.

Creeds as "Baggage"

Some have borrowed the language of *baggage* to describe the ancient creeds. From this perspective, the creeds are historical "accretions" or "layers" that have been placed over Scripture, obscuring the purity of the Word of God. An analogy would be a great piece of art discovered under a modern church:

the original must be recovered by careful cleansing and labor in order to see its true beauty and meaning.

I came across the word *baggage* in the title of a lecture given by William Louis Poteat, president of Wake Forest University from 1905 to 1927. Poteat was a charming man by all accounts, a committed Christian and someone who cared deeply about both the church and the university. Poteat got into trouble with North Carolina Baptists, however, because he was an evolutionist. In response to his critics, Poteat delivered the McNair Lectures at Chapel Hill, under the topic, "Can a Man Be a Christian Today?" In his first lecture, he described the essence of religion as "the soul's apprehension of the spirit world." In Christianity, this is a world "mediated by Christ." Poteat's focus on the "soul's apprehension" of a spiritual realm prepared the ground for his second lecture, entitled simply "Baggage." In this lecture, he counseled his audience to look beyond the theorizing of theology (which would include dogma and creed) and find inspiration in the direct teachings of Jesus. "Baggage" referred to all that got in the way of the inward experience of Christ's call to "man's soul," and to the teachings of Christ. Poteat (with evolution obviously in his mind) worried about the requirement that one had to believe certain propositions or biblical interpretations to be considered a Christian.[15] Poteat would have agreed with his later successor as president of Wake Forest, Thomas Hearn (served from 1982 to 2005), who said that "each person is spiritually competent from God without the guidance of any ecclesiastical organization or creed."[16]

While we might sympathize with Poteat's struggle to reconcile science and theology in his day, we can also hear in his language echoes of Enlightenment speech. The word *enlighten* itself marked a shift in the way one thought about the past. Thus, words like *dogma* and *creed* took on negative connotations. Kant famously summarized the meaning of *enlightenment* when he wrote (in 1784): "Enlightenment is man's release from his self-incurred tutelage. Tutelage is man's inability to make use of his understanding without direction from another. 'Have courage to use your own reason!'—that is the motto of enlightenment."[17] From this perspective, dogma stifles thinking, and creeds become a way of avoiding true thought.

In light of this, one would think that even Scripture itself would fall in the category of "unenlightened" dogma or myth. And to some extent, this in fact happened. Poteat, for example, saw Scripture as a moral guidebook and an inspiration for the spiritual self, but not as a description for how things are. Within Enlightenment language, Scripture easily becomes either "an inspired supernatural guide for individual conduct or a piece of detached historical record—the typical exaggerations of Biblicist and liberal approaches respectively."[18] Both of these are present in Poteat's thinking—Scripture as supernatural guide in the spiritual realm, and in the natural realm as an "objective" historical document.

As committed and faithful as President Poteat no doubt was, the kind of vision that he held forth for Wake Forest (that separated the spiritual realm from the material realm) was simply unable to sustain the Baptist identity of the institution in any sort of vibrant intellectual way. Once faith becomes reduced to the realm of the individual subject before Scripture, it becomes difficult, if not impossible, to give a coherent account of why or how faith pertains to all of reality. In its own "realm," faith can have at best only an indirect relation to politics, economics, or the material world.[19]

We might ask, finally, in terms of the word *baggage*: isn't the individual reading the biblical text for himself or herself what the Reformers sought to initiate (or reclaim) with *sola scriptura*? D. H. Williams argues that in the polemical context of post-Reformation thought, *sola scriptura* became distorted, "more a principle of negation: all else was unnecessary or disallowed in the construction of saving faith." For the earlier Reformers, however, *sola scriptura* was "an affirmation of scriptural authority within the church."[20] From this perspective, the ancient creeds enhanced Scripture because they provided a faithful and coherent lens through which to receive and be formed by the Word of God.

Borrowing the Language of "Deeds, Not Creeds"

Creeds can be divisive. The Nicene Creed was born out of heated and drawn-out debates. The word *debate* is even too mild. So much was at stake; how could this not be much more—a contest, a battle, a division, a drawing of lines? "Deeds, not creeds" has become a familiar way to recommend uniting around action rather than arguing over beliefs. One stream of the ecumenical movement shared this popular sentiment in the 1930s when it claimed, "Doctrine divides, service unites."

Jaroslav Pelikan cites Henry Wadsworth Longfellow (1807–82) setting this perspective to verse. Longfellow writes about a Cambridge theologian who simply preaches, "The Gospel of the Golden Rule, The New Commandment given to men, *Thinking the deed, and not the creed*, would help us in our utmost need. . . ."[21] If we just all followed the golden rule (our personal beliefs aside), the world would be a better place.

There is some truth to this position. If the gospel becomes reduced to belief alone, then it contradicts one of the gospel's own claims. As we read in James: "So also faith by itself, if it does not have works, is dead" (James 2:17). Even more to the point, James states, "You believe that God is one; you do well. Even the demons believe—and shudder!" (James 2:19). Passages like these seem to indicate that "faith alone," or the creed alone, is insufficient for our life in Christ. Deeds are necessary.

And yet, in the final analysis, deeds and creeds cannot be separated. The question left unaddressed in the "deeds, not creeds" formula is, "Which deeds?"

Jesus's parable of the talents is instructive on this point. The servants receiving five and two talents use theirs to make more, while the servant with one talent buries it in the ground. When asked why, he responds, "I knew you to be a hard man . . . so I was afraid" (Matt. 25:24–25). He has obviously performed a deed, but the point of the parable is that it is not a good one. In this case, it is not simply that the servant needs to do more deeds. It's rather that, deeper down, his very understanding of the master is in disrepair. The language, or creed, he uses to describe the master has diminished his own life. Fear of the master, rather than gratitude for the master's generosity, shapes his deed. The repair is not to do away with creed, but rather for him to acquire a richer, more truthful account of Christian faith.

Such an account will always be, in a sense, divisive. Unity is not simply the absence of conflict, as assumed in Rodney King's famous question after the LA riots, "People, I just want to say, you know, can we all get along? Can we get along?"[22] Such a question in a Christian context easily masks how our dominant politics (right versus left) and economics (upper versus lower class) are often more decisive for unity among Christians than the unity of the church. Practicing the Nicene Creed, however, witnesses to a unity more universal than nation, race, or class.

Practicing the Nicene Creed in Worship

Jaroslav Pelikan states that the creed is "not in the first instance the business of the professional and learned theological elite; it is meant to be prayed, right alongside the Lord's Prayer, as an act of adoration and worship."[23] Neither is saying the Nicene Creed like reading an "instruction manual, simply following a set of instructions in order to construct a product."[24] Rather, the ancient creeds are more like ways of speaking and seeing doxologically. What must the church say and do, and therefore see, to worship God faithfully?

As has been frequently observed, in this day of "church shopping," it is difficult to know what to make of worship. We want people to come to our church, so should we not make worship appealing, meet their spiritual needs, and generally give them an authentic worship experience? My husband pastors a small rural church, and recently we had a visitor give us training in how to be welcoming and hospitable. In addition to giving our guests something (a mug or loaf of bread), he emphasized that we should greet visitors at the door with a friendly face and then offer to sit with them. Such welcome can be a good thing, but our guest showed little awareness of what exactly we were welcoming people into other than a friendly place with a friendly God where we try to be nice to one another.

According to James B. Torrance, the most common view of worship today is that it is something "we, religious people, do—mainly in church on Sunday.

We go to church, we sing our psalms and hymns to God, we intercede for the world, we listen to the sermon . . . we offer our money, time and talents to God. [And I would add: If we follow the hospitality trainer, we try to be nice to people.] No doubt we need God's grace to help us do it. We do it because Jesus taught us to do it and left us an example of how to do it." Torrance, however, describes this understanding of worship as unitarian, because worship is about "what *we* do before God."[25] The agent of worship—the one who makes worship happen—is the self. The worshiper has to generate certain feelings, experiences, thoughts, and so forth.

To practice trinitarian and Nicene worship, however, is to see that we do not make worship happen. This does not mean that Christians worship "the Trinity in the sense that they stand, as it were, off from it and gawk reverently from a safe distance."[26] Rather, it is to acknowledge that there is a communion, a worship already going on in the life of God. From this perspective, the Spirit enables those gathered to share in the Son's communion with the Father. As Geoffrey Wainwright summarizes, "The classical movement of Christian worship has always meant a participatory entrance into Christ's self-offering to the Father and correlatively being filled with divine life."[27] Christ holds his priesthood permanently, as Hebrews states, and therefore "is able to save to the uttermost those who draw near to God through him, since he *always lives* to make intercession for them" (Heb. 7:25, italics mine). That Christ is always interceding before the Father means that we do not "make" worship happen. Rather we share, through the gift of the Spirit, in the communion of the Holy Trinity. "The movement from the human creature up to God is no independent human movement," as Eugene Rogers states, "but belongs within the movement from God to God by which the Spirit adds a new song to the love between the Father and the Son."[28]

To illustrate the difference between unitarian and trinitarian worship, Torrance tells about an elderly gentleman he once met. Upon hearing that Torrance was a Presbyterian minister, the man told Torrance that his wife of forty-five years was dying of cancer and that he didn't know how to face the future without her. Though his father was a Presbyterian minister, he had drifted away from church. He went on to say that he had been trying to pray but could not. Torrance writes:

> Did I tell him how to pray—throw him back on himself? No, I did not. I said, "May I say to you what I am sure your father would have said to you? In Jesus Christ we have someone who knows all about this. He has been through it all—through suffering and death and separation—and he will carry you both through it into resurrection life. . . . You have been walking up and down this beach, wanting to pray, trying to pray, but not knowing how to pray. In Jesus Christ we have someone who is praying for you. He has heard your groans and is interceding for you and with you and in you."[29]

Torrance directs the man away from the notion of prayer or worship as primarily something he does (or fails to do, in this instance). To pray is "to recognize that none of us knows how to pray as we ought to. But as we bring our desires to God, we find that we have someone who is praying for us, with us, and in us."[30] Jesus takes our prayers—feeble and inarticulate though they are—and makes them his prayers, and "presents us to the Father as his [adopted] children crying: 'Abba Father.'"[31]

Unitarian worship can easily engender a kind of weariness. I can think of no heavier baggage (to use that word again) when it comes to worship than having to have certain feelings, experiences, or even thoughts in order for worship to really "happen." When one sits beside young children, for example, distraction is almost inevitable (as are unpleasant thoughts). There are folks who come to worship who cannot hear well or who have a mental disability. For all of us, our thoughts and experiences will fluctuate depending upon personal circumstances. To *try* to worship, from this perspective, is ironically to make worship more about us than about God.

By contrast, trinitarian worship draws worshipers into a world of gift. When we say, in the context of worship, "We believe in one God, the Father, the Almighty . . . one Lord, Jesus Christ, the only son of God . . . in the Holy Spirit, the Lord, the giver of Life . . . [and] in one holy catholic and apostolic Church," we are doing so not as individuals but as the body of Christ. A familiar prayer found across Christian traditions states, "Lord Jesus Christ . . . regard not our sins but the faith of your church." The implication is that we are bound up with a people, a communion, much larger than ourselves whose faith is greater than our personal inadequacies, struggles, and doubts. To confess this faith is to join the grand communion of saints as when we sing, "Holy, holy, holy! All the saints adore Thee, casting down their golden crowns around the glassy sea." This means that even if a person is distracted or feeling depressed, worship is still taking place in the universal body of Christ. And Christ through the Spirit still unites our offering, humble though it may be, to his own. As Teresa of Avila tells her fellow Carmelite sisters, the Son takes whatever we can offer and unites it with his offering to the Father, "so it may have the value won for it by our will, even though our actions in themselves may be trivial."[32] The dynamism of trinitarian worship comes from our learning to receive God's grace (through Word and sacrament) and learning to participate in God's own dynamic love for the world. In this cosmic liturgical context, the creed is not mere words or blind ritual but a *deed* whereby we acknowledge and join in the unity of the body of Christ.

This is not to deny that faith is personal in the sense of self-involving. Christian faith includes both "the faith *which* one believes" and "the faith *with which* one believes" (that is, faith as knowledge and faith as trust).[33] Both aspects of faith call for training and practice. Faith is always a gift, but it is one that we learn, over time, how to receive and live into—often through blood, sweat, and tears. I have always loved Mother Teresa's words on this point: "Teach your children to pray. . . . If they don't, it will be difficult for the children to become holy."[34] When we say the Apostles' Creed, my nine-year-old son thinks that the word *quick* in "he shall come to judge the quick and the dead" refers to those who can run fast. Learning the words, even if you don't understand them, is part of the process. Learning to pray and confess also involves learning certain postures: bowing the head, or closing the eyes, or standing with those with whom we might not necessarily choose to be. As Mother Teresa embodied, such liturgical training ultimately becomes a way of life in which one is able to receive Christ even in the lowliest of society.

Practicing the Nicene Faith as an Ecclesial Way of Life

In writing on the Nicene Creed, Susan K. Wood states that "the church is not simply the place of our baptism. We are baptized not simply *in* the church, but *into* the church. . . . This is much more than church membership or a matter of confessional identity; it is an ecclesial way of being in the world."[35] Confessing the Nicene Creed is part of an ecclesial way of life.

Yet in our context today, practicing the Nicene faith across the landscape of our lives can be difficult. What does the creed have to do with our jobs, the daily grind of various routines, our families, the way we make or spend money, and the political and economic challenges facing our country? MacIntyre states that compartmentalization has so fragmented our lives today that *adaptability* is now the new virtue, and *inflexibility* the new vice. To adapt is to compete in the global market. McDonald's has served the same Chicken McNuggets to my children for years, but at the same time, McDonald's must engage "in a never-ending process of trying to produce novelty, [reconfiguring] the sizes and sauces of its products to give at least the appearance of something new to attract the consumer."[36] My husband and I once saw a church marquee announcing, "Worship just got better!"— much better, the message suggests, than anything that has come before. In a context in which the dominant virtue is not faith or hope or love but adaptability, practicing the Nicene faith will be subversive activity.

It seems poor stewardship, however, to ignore the reality of economics: we *must* compete to survive. Ray Kroc, the man who made McDonald's a worldwide sensation, summed up economic logic when asked about his business philosophy. Kroc dismissed any sophisticated analysis and responded, "This is rat eat rat, dog eat dog. I'll kill 'em, and I'm going to kill 'em before they kill me. You're talking about the American way of survival of the fittest."[37] Though bluntly stated, something like this economics seems necessary for the American way of life.

Wittgenstein describes a limited way of seeing from which we are unable to extricate ourselves as "the *hardness* of the logical must." The imagination gets so locked into a particular logic that it becomes unable to see other possibilities. As Michael Budde states, "so many of us come from churches deeply accommodated to secular power (the so-called Constantinian compromise) that we seem to have lost a sense of how substantial Christian identities and convictions could be formed *without* the support of the dominant culture."[38] The failure to imagine things differently will make it almost inevitable that the dominant politics and economics will determine our lives.

The Nicene Creed, however, describes a different economic logic. The word *economics*, like the words *ecology* and *ecumenical*, is rooted in the Greek word *oikos*, meaning "dwelling" or "household," and signifies the management of the household—arranging what is necessary for well-being.[39] The dwelling that the creed describes is not the competitive market, but the noncompetitive triune communion of God. The Son is "eternally begotten of the Father," and the Holy Spirit "proceeds from the Father and the Son." God is not three competitive parts, nor does divine giving diminish the being of God. Rather, Father, Son, and Holy Spirit name an extravagant, noncompetitive relation of life in which the Father is eternally one with the Son, united by the Holy Spirit. This triune economy freely creates the world, Israel, and the church as pure gift.

To be adopted into this divine economics, we do not have to compete. God graciously and abundantly gives each of us uniquely and the church abundantly what we need to be faithful. According to Athanasius, Christ came "to put himself at the disposal of those who needed Him and to be manifested according *as they could bear it, not vitiating the value of the Divine appearing by exceeding their capacity to receive it.*"[40] God's abundance manifests itself by coming to all of us, in Christ, in a way that we can receive him.

The divine economics seems difficult to square, however, with the church today. The fact that churches exist in close proximity (even side by side) no longer registers as a concern on most radars. Ecclesial division (competition) is accepted as normal. We are trained to compete at a very young age. Schools of all ages now routinely describe the goal of education as making students competitive for the global market.

In this context, practicing the Nicene faith calls for attending more closely to the practices that constitute the life of the church. This is slow and patient work, like nurturing a tiny green shoot in our overgrown garden. One waters and feeds the plants, but one also waits and watches. Sabbath keeping is one way that the church both waters and waits. There is a Jewish saying: "More than the Jews keep the Sabbath, the Sabbath keeps the Jews." Abraham Heschel describes the Sabbath as a "palace in time," because "Judaism is a *religion of time* aiming at the *sanctification of time*."[41] By contrast, the global market depends upon every day being just like every other; all days are interchangeable. Nicholas Boyle describes this market timelessness: "In the unsleeping fluorescent glow of round-the-clock commerce, consumption is as instantaneous as the signature on the contract of sale, the electronic transfer of funds from account to account, the emptying of the supermarket shelf."[42] Individual consumption defines market time.

Sabbath time involves consumption as well, but a different kind of consuming. Alexander Schmemann, quoting the philosopher Feuerbach, states that "we are what we eat."[43] While Feuerbach meant that the material world is all there is (a conviction that easily generates competition for scarce goods), Schmemann applies this phrase to the Eucharist. We are what we eat in partaking the body and blood of Christ. Augustine describes how the Lord's Supper reverses the normal pattern of consumption. "Other food is digested by Christian believers, but the Eucharist as a heavenly food digests its own communicants, making them immortal and giving them a share in resurrection life."[44] This is not simply an otherworldly or purely spiritual reality. Jesus's sacrifice at the altar is not only his death, but his resurrected life—"a bodily presence that is no longer bound by the limitations of time and space."[45] Because of this, Jesus can be fully present in the Eucharist: he is never exhausted in our consumption. Eucharistic consumption, therefore, does not need to be competitive, because God can never be used up.

Of course, we still live in a limited world. But the limits can now be negotiated through an economics of love. In the Eucharist, we are "simultaneously fed and become food (body of Christ) for others."[46] An economics of love might sound simple or idealistic. But, as Michael Bowling, pastor of Englewood Christian Church in Indianapolis, describes it, the economics his church seeks to embody is based not on getting rich people to give money but on how you envision the kingdom of God in the concrete place where you are.[47] For Englewood Christian, this has meant remaining in its "declining" neighborhood (after many moved away), befriending its neighbors, helping them become homeowners, and creating local businesses in which they could share. All of these things flow out of the congregation's liturgical (eucharistic) life together.

If the Nicene Creed describes an alternative economics, it also involves a unique politics. Historical sources often note that the creed developed in a politicized context: Constantine wanted to shore up his imperial power through a common statement that would unite all Christians. Yet the creed itself relies upon a very different politics than the politics of empire. Nor is this the politics of statecraft, in which to be political is to involve oneself in the politics of the nation through voting, lobbying, or running for office. The politics of the body of Christ is not about guaranteeing security while maximizing individual liberty, which is the political good of modern liberal democracies, a politics that was advocated early on by John Locke (1632–1704). According to Locke, the church is a voluntary association of individuals. "The church's distinct realm concerns divine salvation, and is characterized as private, otherworldly and inward. . . . The state [by contrast] deals with civil interests: 'Life, Liberty, Health, and Indolency of Body; and the Possession of outward things, such as Money, Lands, Houses, Furniture and the like.'"[48] Locke's politics places the church in a private, spiritual realm, thus compromising the visibility of the body of Christ. For Locke, toleration becomes the "chief characteristic mark of the true Church,"[49] rather than the church as one visible body, holy, catholic, and apostolic. It is not coincidental that today the politics of the nation is more determinative in the lives of believers than that of the body of Christ. Divisions within denominations typically replicate the divisions between Democrats and Republicans.

The politics produced by the Nicene faith, however, is not "interest" politics that involves a "cacophonous conflict of wills." Politics is the art of ordering our lives around a common good. Understood theologically, "politics entails the ordering of human relationships according to their ultimate end: God." The true polis for Christians, then, "is constituted by the practices of assembled Christians called 'the church,' the 'pilgrim City of God.'"[50]

The politics of this pilgrim people makes the church more rather than less vulnerable to the world.[51] This past summer my family and I had the opportunity to go to Rome, where we visited the Church of Santa Cecelia. St. Cecelia was a third-century martyr known as the patron saint of musicians, because she apparently sang even while dying. A sixteenth-century statue of St. Cecelia shows her lying on the ground, draped in a robe. Her head is turned away from the viewer, though you can see a cut across her neck. She appears almost to be sleeping, but the artist vividly illustrates the reason for her martyrdom: three outstretched fingers, visually displaying her belief in the Trinity even to her dying breath. Cecelia's story might sound morbid, or, in any case, far removed from our time and place. But the triune faith of the church enabled her to witness to a politics that surpasses that of any empire or nation.

Confessing the creed makes possible this kind of faithful politics. For most of us, such faithfulness will probably not involve a martyrdom like Cecelia's, although we cannot know for sure where daily acts of faithfulness will lead. At the end of *Interior Castle*, Teresa imagines her sisters saying, "[We are] unable to teach and preach like the Apostles." A modern version of this might be, "We are not saints," or "We cannot change society." Teresa replies: "Instead of setting our hand to the work which lies nearest to us, and thus serving Our Lord in ways within our power, we may rest content with having desired the impossible."[52] This kind of politics is not a system, a party, or something other people do. It is rather a community living in friendship with God, willing to live a cruciform life in response to God's love.[53] In this politics of the kingdom of God, it does not matter if one does "great" things. This politics does not require heroes, much less warriors. Rather, it requires a willingness to do the small thing that lies in front of us with great love. Such a politics is grounded finally not in human effort, but in the divine King who heals not through violence but through the cross.

From this perspective, the Nicene Creed is a political statement, a pledge. We are called to have the courage to participate more fully in God's triune communion, for the sake of the church and the world.

11

The Nicene Faith and Evangelical Worship

DAVID P. NELSON

When the church fails to appreciate and to enact the interrelation between doctrine and doxology, she falls conspicuously short of her call to worship God authentically. When the church, however, properly appreciates and lives in accord with the interrelation between doctrine and doxology, she attains the capacity for authentic worship.

The relationship of doctrine and worship, of creed and liturgy, of *credemus* and *laudamus*—however one may construe our various notions of what we Christians believe and how we respond in faith to our Creator—is not often enough recognized or given the importance it deserves among evangelicals. This is unfortunate, to say the least. To be completely honest, I think it is devastating for any Christian community to divorce what it believes from how it worships. Jaroslav Pelikan, in his *Credo*, writes of the "Creedal and Confessional Imperative," which includes the correlatives "believing and confessing."[1]

Pelikan is correct about this imperative for the church. I wish to make a further correlation between believing and confessing and the church's imperative to worship. By doing so, I hope to counter what is in deed (if not always in word) a "credal indifference," to borrow Pelikan's words, regarding the relationship of doctrine and worship among evangelicals.[2]

One ancient writer insisted upon the significance of this relationship by pen-ning the phrase *legem credendi lex statuat supplicandi*—"let the law of prayer establish the law of belief."[3] The phrase has become an adage, perhaps even an axiom in its variant coinage—*lex orandi, lex credendi*. Evangelicals have rarely paid attention to the adage, written by the fifth-century papal secretary Prosper of Aquitaine, or to the tradition that surrounds the phrase. In the minds of many evangelicals, it is, I suppose, simply one of those old Roman Catholic ideas and, as such, not of much use to the heirs of the Reformation. This is, as I said before, unfortunate. It is also ironic, because Prosper was defending the necessity of grace for salvation against the semi-Pelagians when he coined the phrase in his *Capitula*. That we, heirs of the Reformers who boast of maintaining the purity of the gospel of grace, would be inattentive to the tradition that was itself fighting to preserve that same gospel is, yes, ironic—and likely even worse.

But my task is not to provide a history lesson or to chide evangelicals for their attitudes about ancient tradition. Rather, I want to lay out a proposal for retrieving the significance of the relationship of doctrine and worship for evangelical congregational worshipers. I will present an argument, and then trace some of the implications of the position I advocate for the worship of the Triune God in those congregations described by the term *evangelical*.

My goal is to do something entirely unoriginal, that is, resourcing a little-known ancient writer, Prosper of Aquitaine, in order to remind us that wor-ship cannot be divorced from *credemus*.[4] The *credemus* of our creeds and confessions is, if truly an expression of faith, wedded to our *laudamus*. Right worship and right belief belong together. This is the real stuff of Christian orthodoxy. First, I pose the question this way: is there a need for creed in a liturgical sense? Then, I answer in the affirmative and make my case while offering some compelling suggestions at the pastoral level.

The Wedding of Doctrine and Worship

At least two words of explanation are in order. First, when I use the term *doctrine*, I mean simply what Pelikan describes as "what the church of Jesus Christ believes, teaches, and confesses on the basis of the Word of God."[5] The biblical *didache* or *didaskalia* (teaching or doctrine) is what we confess as the Nicene faith. Second, I should say a word about how I employ the terms *wor-ship* and *liturgy*, as well as what in the world I mean by *evangelical* worship. While I could say more, suffice it to say that by *worship* I mean "the human response to the self-revelation of the Triune God." That response may be individual or corporate, it may be formal or informal, it may be part of one's everyday way of life, or it may be in the gathered assembly of believers. By *liturgy* I mean, in a more technical sense, the worship of the gathered assembly of believers. I do not mean, as some do, to use the term only of gatherings by those in the liturgical tradition. This assumes, wrongly, that those in the free church tradition do not have liturgies. But of course, everyone who gathers to worship forms a liturgy of some sort, even if they do not do so self-consciously and reflectively.

Since my task is to discuss the Nicene faith and evangelical worship, I should say a word about what constitutes *evangelical* in my mind. In one sense, in what Richard Lints calls a "conceptual definition,"[6] we can clarify what we mean by *evangelical* as George Marsden or Carl F. H. Henry do, by noting what evangelicals believe and confess. Marsden, in summary fashion, identifies *evangelical* with the Reformation tradition of *sola scriptura* (Scripture alone) and *sola fide* (faith alone).[7] Henry includes beliefs like the incarnation, virgin birth, substitutionary death, bodily resurrection, salvation of penitent sinners, and Christ's return to vindicate good and evil.[8] Interestingly, this sounds much like the Nicene faith, although for some reason we have no explicit mention of the Trinity, and it doesn't sound strictly like those we know in America as evangelical. That is because *evangelical* is used not only in the conceptual sense but also in the social sense, as Lints describes. To be evangelical suggests certain sensibilities.

I will not even attempt to describe evangelical sensibilities; the social description of *evangelical* has become so broad today that it is, perhaps, meaningless. But, more narrowly, to be truly evangelical is to have a love for Christ and his gospel, and to believe, confess, and enact the gospel for the sake of God's name among the nations (Rom. 1). When I speak of evangelical worship, I speak of this.

To return to our question: is it possible to worship authentically without creed? John 4:22 indicates the necessity of belief for authentic worship, the kind the Father seeks (John 4:21). Jesus reveals the significance of ignorance about matters central to the faith when he tells the woman, "You worship what you do not know" (John 4:22). Apparently, ignorance about the salvation that comes through the Messiah prohibits the kind of worship that the Father seeks, the kind of worship that is described as "in spirit and truth" (John 4:24). In this most basic sense, then, right doctrine is necessary for right worship; there is indeed a need for creed in a liturgical sense.

This liturgical need for creed is underscored in significant ways in the Scriptures. And since I am speaking of evangelical worship, I will start there, although we must not ignore the important sense in which the credal imperative relies on Christian tradition, and how our unfortunate creedal indifference is too often an indifference to tradition. I begin by noting how doctrine and worship, when wedded as they should be, provide a means to guide both the reading and practice of Scripture, and to guide the formation of a Christian way of life among the worshiping faithful that we call "church." Reading the Bible is simply too dangerous to do without the liturgical community and the guidance of the *regula fidei* (rule of faith) that is maintained when doctrine and doxology are rightly interrelated.

We observe such a wedding of doctrine and worship, including the significance of the relationship of liturgy and our reading and practice of Scripture, in various ways. Think, for example, of baptism. When Paul wishes to encourage a particular way of life for those in the church, for those who struggle with sin, he calls them back to what they professed in the public liturgy when they were baptized (Rom. 6). Baptism serves as a way of interpreting life and doctrine for Paul. We are reminded about both how we must live and what we must believe by our recollection of baptism. The Lord's Supper functions similarly in the Christian life. In this case, believers are sorting out their way of life in the context of a eucharistic community. This is an eschatological community—a little proleptic gathering—that lives today but not only for today, and not only in light of today, but in light of the dawning of the kingdom of Christ in all its fullness. So the Last Supper reminds us to live in light of the gospel, including the cross and grace and the age to come, and to do so now and in an ongoing fashion, as long as we live between the times of the first and second advents of Christ, until he comes (1 Cor. 11:26). Since baptism and Eucharist are primary means of worshiping in the Christian community, they should become guides for other elements of worship in the sense that the relationship of worship and doctrine is observed throughout any and all liturgical practices.

Prosper's Adage and Its Various Interpretations

Prosper's *Capitula Coelestini* was probably written sometime between 435 and 442, and is directed against the semi-Pelagians.[9] Prosper "intended to prove the necessity of grace for the *initium fidei*."[10] After an appeal to the "inviolable sanctions of the blessed and apostolic See,"[11] Prosper introduces the adage in the context of an appeal to universal liturgical practices: "Also, let us look at the sacred testimony of priestly supplications that have been delivered from the apostles and that are uniformly celebrated throughout the world and in every catholic church, so that the law of prayer may establish the law of belief."[12] Prosper's argument is that the prayers of the church indicate the reality that unbelievers must be saved by God's grace, a refutation of the semi-Pelagian view: "His point is that the apostolic injunction to *pray* for the whole human race—which the Church obeys in its intercessions—proves the obligation to *believe*, with the Holy See, that all faith, even the beginnings of good will as well as growth and perseverance, is from start to finish a work of grace."[13] This much is clear.

Less clear is the authority behind the argument. Is it simple conformity with apostolic faith? And, if so, does this refer to Scripture alone, or Scripture and tradition?[14] Does the See or the magisterium hold authority?[15] Or does the liturgy itself wield authority?[16] One discovers a certain lack of clarity when examining the employment of the adage in liturgical theology. Irwin states, "As we will see, this relationship [*lex orandi, lex credendi*] can mean giving priority to liturgy over theology, giving priority to theology over liturgy and to the mutual relation of liturgy and theology."[17] Hohenstein suggests that the adage "acquired a life of its own as a statement of general principles which Prosper himself had not contemplated."[18] As well, De Clerck observes that the adage does not "shine with the clarity which it supposedly expresses. It serves as a blanket over documents as diverse as the books of the modernist Tyrrell and the pontifical bulls defining the dogmas of the Immaculate Conception and of the Assumption. . . . But if it is a blanket, one must recognize that each pulls at it from his own side!"[19]

Prosper's adage is commonly employed in Roman Catholic and Orthodox liturgical studies.[20] The adage does not figure so prominently in Protestant theology. It is noteworthy, however, that the adage is used in the work of Protestant theologians such as Geoffrey Wainwright, Frank Senn, and Don Saliers.[21] Robert Jenson suggests that recognition of the *lex orandi, lex credendi* "rule" may be useful to Protestant systematic theology.[22]

The varied use of Prosper's adage raises a question concerning the original meaning of the text. Teresa Berger states "that this axiom is often reduced to the oscillating phrase *lex orandi–lex credendi*, which, when taken out of its context, can be drawn into a variety of constructs rarely having anything in common with the phrase's origin." She notes "the very limited original meaning of the phrase," which is often ignored.[23] So what is the original meaning of the adage?

Aidan Kavanagh argues that the adage means that the law of prayer founds the law of belief. Wainwright sees a material interplay between the two. Irwin maintains that it is papal authority, not the *lex supplicandi*, that is the underlying authority in Prosper's statements: "The argument . . . about justification deriving from God's grace is based principally on a summary of decrees of the Holy See about this doctrine."[24] Robert Taft, who believes that liturgy does establish belief, notes that the adage, "taken out of context, has become an aphorism to express the notion—true if properly understood—that liturgy is the norm of faith."[25] While Taft agrees with Kavanagh that liturgy is primary theology, that liturgy forms our doctrine, he does not believe that Prosper's adage means that worship establishes belief. Instead, Prosper "summarizes the relationship between a community's worship and its beliefs. As you pray, so do you believe. If you want to know what Christians are all about, observe what they do and say when they gather in church to express before God and one another what they think about him, themselves, and their relation to one another and him."[26] Liturgy, then, is an observable means by which to ascertain the beliefs of the worshiping community.

The considerable ambiguity and disagreement, even within Catholic theology, over the meaning and purpose of Prosper's adage is further demonstrated in the writings of Pius XII. Pius XII argues in the encyclical *Mediator Dei* that the adage actually works both ways. While it is true that liturgy has influenced doctrine, it is also true that doctrine has authority over the liturgy: "But if we wish these things, to distinguish and delimit the relations that exist between sacred faith and liturgy in an absolute and general way, it is justly and rightly able to be said, 'Let the law of belief establish the law of prayer.'"[27] In 1956, in an address before the first International Congress on Pastoral Liturgy, he reaffirmed the views expounded in *Mediator Dei*, stating that the Catholic hierarchy controls "the *depositum fidei* . . . the truth of Christ as contained in the Scriptures and Tradition," and that "the Church in the liturgy abundantly dispenses the treasures of the 'deposit of faith,' the truth of Christ."[28] This is contrary to the view of Kavanagh. Liturgy is not primary theology, per Kavanagh; it is, in a real sense, doxological envoy under the authority of the magisterium.

At this point, the diversity of interpretations of Prosper's adage is clear. One may ask, with such ambiguity about its meaning, whether the adage is of any use at all for the present discussion. De Clerck seeks to bring clarity as to the meaning of the adage. In order to understand the adage, one must determine Prosper's use of the term *lex*.[29] Both De Clerck and Wainwright turn at this point to a parallel passage in Prosper's *De vocatione omnium gentium*.[30]

De vocatione is also written against the semi-Pelagians. It similarly argues for the necessity of grace in order for one to believe. Chapter 12 of *De vocatione* also mentions a law of prayer: "Thus all priests and all the faithful harmoniously hold to this law of prayer in their devotions, so that there is no part of the world in which the Christian people do not celebrate these kinds of prayers."[31] One should note the common appeal to the *quod semper, quod ubique, quod ab omnibus* principle in both passages. In the *Capitula* the prayers are "uniformly celebrated throughout the world and in every catholic church" and "joined by the groans of the whole church."[32] In *De vocatione* the practice of the *Ecclesia universalis* is central to Prosper's argument. What is essential to understanding Prosper here is the basis for such a universal practice. Prosper forms his argument in *De vocatione* with reference to 1 Timothy 2:1–6a. This he refers to as *doctrinae apostilicae regula*, or the "rule of apostolic doctrine."[33] The *lex supplicandi* is not, therefore, the foundation of doctrine. It is, rather, the action taken by the church in light of the biblical truth that humanity stands in the need of grace and that God, "who desires all people to be saved and to come to the knowledge of the truth,"[34] commands the faithful to pray for the salvation of the lost. Karl Federer insists that the meaning of Prosper's adage is that "*the necessity of prayer for grace is a proof of the necessity of grace.*"[35] The necessity of grace, therefore, is founded on the apostolic *regula* found in 1 Timothy 2:1–6.[36]

Ambrose, commenting on 1 Timothy 2:1–4 about fifty years prior to Prosper, states, "This is an ecclesiastical rule, handed down by the teacher of Gentiles, which our priests use so that they might pray for all."[37] In his comparison of the writings of Prosper and Ambrose, De Clerck determines that "above all it is the use of the word *regula* by the two authors which is striking, and which confirms the exegesis of the Prosperian texts: the *regula* in question, as also the *lex supplicandi*, is clearly the recommendation of 1 Tim. 2:1–2."[38] Therefore, the *lex* of Prosper's adage is founded upon the *regula* of the apostles contained in Scripture.[39] De Clerck concludes that, for Prosper of Aquitaine, "the liturgical formulas have value as a theological argument only insofar as they are founded on scripture and attested by tradition."[40] Maurice Wiles draws a similar conclusion about the adage: "When first used, those words had a specific reference. They were an appeal to the implications of the particular injunctions about prayer set out in 1 Timothy ii.I with reference to the Pelagian controversy. In the course of history, they have often been quoted with a very much wider reference."[41] Berger states, "Above all, it became clear that Prosper's method did not necessarily (as had been assumed) represent a theological argument based on tradition, but rather on Holy Scriptures."[42]

Prosper's adage establishes that liturgy, in its faithfulness to Scripture, may apply as a corrective to aberrant doctrine. While the adage does not say that the *lex orandi* establishes the *lex credendi*, it does demonstrate that Prosper saw a genuine and important relationship between the church's worship and doctrine. And this impulse is, as Prosper understood, to be read throughout the pages of Scripture and to be maintained within the Christian tradition.

A Liturgical Way of Life

The sheer number of biblical texts that evidence the interrelationship of doctrine and worship is staggering.[43] It will suffice to note a couple of examples of the interrelationship that are so common in both testaments. These examples begin to shape for us the notion of a liturgical way of life, in which the church's enactment of faith is rooted in its doctrine and worship.

The Psalter is a primary locale for texts that elucidate the interrelationship of doctrine and doxology and that point us to a liturgical way of life. For example, Psalm 96 weds the praise of God with the encouragement to proclaim God's glory and mighty works among the nations. Psalm 136 serves as a song of praise as the people recall Yahweh's deliverance, with the intention of encouraging the faith of the people and edifying the people of God. These texts ascribe praise to God while simultaneously providing doctrinal instruction and encouraging faith. Paul weds these themes similarly in the Epistle to the Romans.

After an exposition of the gospel that runs for several chapters, in Romans 10 Paul speaks of the gospel believed and confessed. Here he demonstrates that Christ, in his gospel work, occasions a liturgical way of life for those who follow him. This is nowhere more clearly seen than in the doxology that concludes chapter 11. In view of God's mercies in Christ (Rom. 1–11), Paul finds himself quite out of words to express his praise: "Oh, the depth of the riches and wisdom and knowledge of God! How unsearchable are his judgments and how inscrutable his ways! . . . For from him and through him and to him are all things. To him be glory forever. Amen" (Rom. 11:33, 36). What follows this ascription of praise is a description not of a worship service but of a way of life. It is at this point that Paul reminds us that in view of God's mercies, it is simply the reasonable thing to do (*logikēn latreian*) to worship God with one's life. More simply put, in view of what God has done for us in Christ, it makes sense to worship God with our whole beings for our whole lives. This notion of worship as a way of life is reflected in the idea of Sabbath and in the Jewish and Christian calendars, which indicate a rhythm of life lived before God. In this way, we see that the Scriptures themselves pattern a liturgical way of thinking and living.

The liturgical life is not confined to public assemblies but extends to all of life. This liturgical way of life is multidimensional in that it accounts for various settings in life, whether the congregation, the workplace, or the home. But liturgy is multidimensional in another important respect as well; that is, the liturgical way of life is manifested in a variety of interpersonal relationships in addition to a variety of settings and contexts. While these relationships may be described in different ways, I prefer to refer to them as the *doxological*, the *hortatory*, and the *kerygmatic*.[44]

The doxological dimension receives the most attention of the three, as it is the primary focus of worship in the Scriptures, centered on the glory of God and his praise by the people of God. So prominent is the call to praise God in the Scriptures that I need not make an argument for this dimension of worship. We will stipulate that it is the primary liturgical dimension.

The hortatory dimension is that which has to do with the exhortation and edification of the body that occur while the doxological dimension is being practiced. In 1 Corinthians 11–14, we see Paul prioritize the edification of the saints even in the assembly of believers gathered to worship God. Repeatedly, he insists that if what one does in the assembly does not build up the body, then it is not to be done in the assembly. In Ephesians 5:18 and Colossians 3:16, this involves mutual edification through teaching and admonition that occurs as the congregation enacts the doxological dimensions. These interpersonal relationships—between God and human worshipers and between the worshipers themselves—are all affected in the acts of praise offered by the assembled believers.

The third dimension, the kerygmatic, involves the act of proclaiming the gospel as the church reminds itself of the gospel (for example, in the Lord's

Supper), as well as speaking the truth of the gospel to unbelievers who are gathered in the midst of the worshiping assembly. Paul assumes that unbelievers will be present in the assembly (1 Cor. 14:13–25), and this is consistent with the instructions in the Hebrew Scriptures to proclaim the glory and saving power of God to the nations (also see Ps. 96).

In Christian tradition, as in the Scriptures, the movement among these dimensions is not linear; it does not move neatly from one dimension to the next. Rather, the multidimensionality of the liturgy is perichoretic. There is an interpenetration of the dimensions at every turn. For example, the Roman Mass begins with a greeting and a rite of the blessing of God, along with corporate confession and the recitation of the Gloria. In this way the hortatory and the kerygmatic are woven into the doxological. The church is, for example, enacting the hortatory dimension as it says, "I confess to you, my brothers and sisters," which is spoken in a confession ultimately addressed to God. Similarly, the church prays, "Lord, have mercy, Grant us peace." The people address God (doxology) while speaking together. Similarly, the introduction to the eucharistic rite includes the Sanctus and the Acclamation that rehearses the gospel before the whole congregation—Christ has died, Christ is risen, Christ will come again—again with a doxology. Here we have all three dimensions intertwined with one another. This same phenomenon is observed in the Protestant rites, seen, for example, in the text of the Te Deum, which includes the lines *Te Deum laudamus* (We praise) and *Te Dominum confitemur* (We confess). The liturgy in these instances is seen to be truly multidimensional, involving not only varied contexts but interpenetrating relationships between God, his people, and the unbelievers who are drawn into the midst of the assembly. This impulse, observed throughout the church's history, has scriptural foundations. Like Prosper's adage, it is rooted in a fundamentally biblical way of thinking and enacting that I take to be truly evangelical.

Many implications can be drawn from my proposal, and at this point I will make some pastoral proposals. To this point, I hope I have helped us *appreciate* the interrelationship of doctrine and doxology, of creed and liturgy. Now I wish to point out some ways to *enact* this interrelationship as good shepherds to God's flock, and I will do so by following the shape of the Nicene Creed.

The Triunity and Majesty of God

First, I propose that we renew a love for God by retrieving the fundamental nature of Christian worship of the Triune God. The doctrine of the Trinity and the creeds associated with the statements and construals of the doctrine are remarkable in that they do not lose sight of the personal God about whom they were written. The doctrine is not an abstraction; it is the way the Scriptures and the church understand and call upon the one, true, living God. We see in the triunity of God the very nature of personal relationships that is imaged in our own relationships with God and people. But many evangelicals have no concept of trinitarian doctrine, largely because pastors have failed to appreciate the doctrine for what it is and have failed to teach the people who the Triune God is. This doctrine is a means of confessing that God in his oneness exists in personal relations, and that God's being is not an abstraction but a personal reality. Therefore, the great commandment to love God and the second to love others are not abstractions but a personal reality. A congregation with little doctrine of God is a congregation that will have little doxology, no matter how loud and long the music may be. This is a way of retrieving the gospel for our people. And evangelicals, if they are evangelicals, must be marked by the gospel.

One further reason that worship in evangelicalism is perhaps anemic or why certain evangelicals leave their churches for other traditions is that evangelicals have lost some sense of the majesty of God in their assemblies. This may be because evangelicals simply do not know much of God these days. Like the woman at the well, we worship what we do not know.

Baptism and the Table

Second, I propose we recover the significance of baptism and the Last Supper, the central enactments of Christian worship commanded by our Lord, which remind us of the verities of the second article of the Nicene Creed, which is the gospel. I would hope that reflection on the significance of baptism and the table would renew a fuller, richer, and more biblical appreciation of all the elements of worship. We have tended to minimize certain elements or enactments—certainly baptism and the table, but also corporate prayer, the public reading of Scripture, and confession both of sins and of faith—to the detriment of our worship. These elements and enactments do happen in evangelical Presbyterian or Anglican churches, I am aware, but they are all too often the exception in evangelical congregations. Such a recovery would, I hope, rescue us from our obsession with music as the *sine qua non* (essential action) of worship, which confuses the matter of worship with its means too often.

Further, I would hope that such a recovery would lead us to move beyond the merely notional to the more fully credal and confessional liturgical expression. By *notional*, I refer to our habit of speaking in ill-formed terms about God, humanity, life, and the gospel—for example, when we pray carelessly in public (thanking the Father for dying on the cross for us or praying rote prayers that rival any written prayer for vanity). Put another way, I hope that we who speak so loudly and frequently about biblical authority would retrieve some sense of truly expositing the Scriptures in our public liturgies, and I do not mean simply in a sermon, though we certainly should do that. I mean, however, that our liturgies would be shaped by, drawn from, and reflective of the grand narrative of Scripture and the story of creation, fall, redemption, and restoration that is embedded in the Bible's grand narrative and its smaller narratives that make up the whole.[45] We evangelicals talk a lot about being biblical, but many times our worship is anything but.

A Vital Pneumatology

Third, I propose we renew a vital pneumatology, one that rightly recognizes the church as a community of the Spirit, which is the very nature of the kingdom community, the little proleptic gathering that we are. I am not proposing another charismatic movement as we saw globally in the twentieth century and that continues today. That movement has its strengths and weaknesses, and I am grateful for its contribution to the vitality of the church. But I am suggesting different emphases when I call for pneumatological renewal. Such a renewal would make much of Christ, since this is the mission of the Holy Spirit (John 16:14), and we would witness such a renewal in both doxology and evangelism. Likewise, such a renewal would be grounded in truth and would make truth known, since the Spirit is the Spirit of truth. And finally, a pneumatological renewal would promote the unity of the church (Eph. 4:3–6). This challenges the notion that those who are truly Christians have as their general trajectory separation from other believers. To the contrary, those who appreciate the ministry of the Spirit will always be longing for and working toward unity with other believers, even those with whom they may disagree. We will find ourselves more and more worshiping together, celebrating the Eucharist together, and proclaiming Christ together.

Renewal of Love for the Church

Finally, I propose a renewal of love for the church as God's people. We say yes to personal faith, which moves us from enmity with God to reconciliation, and moves us from "not his people" to "his people." The sinner who repents and confesses faith in Jesus is no longer God's enemy and is no longer estranged from God's people. To worship, therefore, is to worship as one among God's people, to be part of the temple of the Holy Spirit, to be a part of God's house, part of the "living stones" being built as a spiritual dwelling for God. We are not, as William James said, "individual men in our solitude" when we come to worship. Even if alone in a given instant, we worship with the company of saints and angels throughout the ages who cry out *Laudamus te* (You, God, we praise). It is all too common for us to forge divisions in Christianity. And these days, it is all too common for us to fashion those divisions along the lines of worship. It is as if we have said that the gospel reconciles us to God but not to one another. Yet our Lord taught us that the world would know that we are his disciples if we love one another. Genuine renewal of the kind I call for would help us to enact the reality that such enmity between people is obliterated by the gospel, and it will lead us to be one, as Jesus prayed, and to worship our God in the unity of the Spirit.

Conclusion

I began this essay by proposing that the church's appreciation for and enactment of the interrelationship of doctrine and doxology directly affects the authenticity of the church's worship. This is so for corporate liturgy as well as for the formation of a liturgical way of life among the people of God. The observance of this interrelationship, in all its dimensions, is at the core of the church's ability to maintain the gospel of Christ in the unity of the Spirit. Where the church loses liturgy, the church loses the gospel. The loss of unity is then inevitable, because there is nothing of substance to bind the church together. When, however, the church recognizes this crucial interrelationship as it should, there is a context in which the gospel may flourish, and the beauty of the church's unity will then be on display for the world to see. Yes, there is a need for creed in the liturgical sense. In fact, the church's liturgy cannot survive without it.

12

Taking In His Coming Down

KATHLEEN B. NIELSON

This chapter focuses on one phrase from the Nicene Creed: "Who for us and for our salvation came down from heaven." [1]

The Scripture reading:

> Have this mind among yourselves, which is yours in Christ Jesus, who, though he was in the form of God, did not count equality with God a thing to be grasped, but made himself nothing, taking the form of a servant, being born in the likeness of men. And being found in human form, he humbled himself by becoming obedient to the point of death, even death on a cross. Therefore God has highly exalted him and bestowed on him the name that is above every name, so that at the name of Jesus every knee should bow, in heaven and on earth and under the earth, and every tongue confess that Jesus Christ is Lord, to the glory of God the Father. (Phil. 2:5–11)

The truth is that you have an English teacher, rather than a preacher, speaking to you. The truth is also that this English teacher has often thought it would be lovely to address a seminary audience. I've always enjoyed speaking to college students, and to graduate students, and to various conference participants—but I've secretly thought that seminary students, more than many other groups, need to be inspired with a love of literary texts. One friend of mine who is a pastor recently told me that he didn't like reading poetry but that he was coming to

terms with the fact that a huge portion of the Scriptures is given to us in poetry.
As he was realizing that God must love poetry to inspire so much of it, he was
being convicted that he needed to learn to read and love poetry in general and
Scripture's poetry in particular. Paying attention to the poetic elements is not
a luxurious extra; it is one of the most basic parts of our reading and understanding—and communicating—the Word. Well, this pastor-friend bought a
Norton Anthology of Poetry and now reads a few poems every evening before
going to bed; how wonderful is that! Such a habit will affect his understanding and his love and his preaching of Isaiah, and the Psalms, and on and on.

English teachers, you know, tend to be a little compulsive about words. In
the interest of full disclosure, I'll share with you a silly little poem I wrote
for my pastors a number of years ago. The only contextual note you need in
order to understand this poem is that my husband's name is Niel. The poem
is called "To My Pastors."

> To my pastors, whom I love and much esteem,
> you who preach, from whom amazing sermons stream:
> Would you entertain a small, respectful mention
> of a matter that has come to my attention
> not just once, but on quite numerous occasions
> as I've sat and worshiped with the congregations
> listening every Sunday to your wise orations?
>
> As I give my full attention to your words
> (Please don't tell me you think grammar's for the birds!),
> there often comes a phrase or two, I must affirm,
> that makes me wiggle, squiggle, flinch, or sometimes squirm.
> And that phrase sounds something like, as it goes by:
> "God's given many gracious gifts to you and I."
> Since "you" and "I" are objects of a preposition,
> may I suggest, in this objective situation,
> that you use the objective "me" instead of "I":
> "To you and I" will not grammatically fly.
> So, as *subject*, "I" and "he" and "they" and "we"
> do the job and fit the bill quite accurately.
> But, as *objects*, "me" and "him" and "them" and "us"
> hit the spot, and quiet an English teacher's fuss.
>
> Thank you humbly for your kind consideration;
> you deserve the very highest commendation.
> For so many pastors in this world there be,
> but you're the best, according to Niel and . . . me.

The point is that words are important. Having acknowledged that point,
let's devote our attention to every word in the credal phrase given to us for
our consideration today. Certainly those who composed this creed discussed

and debated carefully every word of the original Latin. If you've served on a committee charged with creating a mission statement or a public statement of some sort, you know the heated debates over words that take place in such contexts. It is clear that the fourth-century debates in that Council of Nicea were fiery, as the very foundations of Christian doctrine were being solidified. We pay respect to the work carried out centuries ago by looking carefully into every word. But even more, by taking in every word of this phrase, "Who for us and for our salvation came down from heaven," we will be taking in once again the huge, universe-transforming truth of the coming down of God to us in Christ Jesus. Taking in this truth, or even beginning to, we take into our very lives a bit deeper grasp not just of God's coming down, but also of the rhythm of that coming down as it is lived out in us who believe.

From Heaven

It is helpful to start at the end of the credal phrase, with the words "from heaven"—partly because those words unleash the meaning of the others, and partly because starting there reflects the shape of today's Scripture passage from Philippians 2. That passage begins high, high up in the heavens with God, in the very form of God, and then takes the dive down to the depths of earth, even to the deepest depths of death on a cross, before rising up again to exaltation and glory. Philippians 2:5–11 draws right before our eyes the shape of a V—moving from high, down to the lowest low, and then back up to the highest high. The credal phrase we are considering is all about the left side of that V, the coming down. It isn't even so much about the bottom of that V—that is, the incarnation itself; that will come in the subsequent phrase, which is all about the wonder of the Word made flesh.

We understand this coming down most profoundly when we see the point from which God came down: he came down from heaven. "Well, of course he did!" you say. We know that's true. But we sometimes know it rather abstractly. I've been spending time in the Gospel of John these past months and have noticed more than ever before how often Jesus talks about heaven and his Father in heaven; heaven is a vivid, concrete reality to him. "I have not come of my own accord," Jesus says; "He who sent me is true, and him you do not know. I know him, for I come from him, and he sent me" (John 7:28–29). Jesus talks about his Father who sent him and his Father's house from which he was sent (recall John 14:2), just like a person in love talks about the visit he had last weekend to the home of the person he's in love with; he's full of it! Jesus is full of heaven. He has just come from there. He knows that it's right there and that it's real, in a way we don't usually know because it's invisible to us. We know heaven is there, somewhere. We say we believe in heaven. But because we can't see it, it is often not real to us—sort of like the interior of the womb was, for years, before we began to be able to see into it by means of modern technology, before we began to glimpse the actual forms of babies swimming around in there.

Sometimes Scripture gives us glimpses into heaven. You remember that scene from Genesis 28 in which Jacob in his dream is allowed to see heaven opened up, that ladder stretched out between earth and heaven, the angels of God ascending and descending on the ladder, and the Lord himself standing at the top speaking to him. Jacob got to glimpse it. He awoke, you recall, and "was afraid and said, 'How awesome is this place! This is none other than the house of God, and this is the gate of heaven'" (Gen. 28:17).

The glimpses are there, and they are indeed "awesome." We recall Stephen right before he was stoned, "full of the Holy Spirit" and gazing into heaven where he "saw the glory of God, and Jesus standing at the right hand of God." Stephen looked deep—"gazed"—and put it into words: "Behold, I see the heavens opened, and the Son of Man standing at the right hand of God" (Acts 7:55–56). The moment just before, at the close of his fiery speech, he had been talking about heaven, quoting Isaiah 66 in which God says heaven is his throne and earth his footstool (Isa. 66:1). Stephen believed it, talked about it, saw it, and testified to it—right before he got to enter it. The apostle John saw it from the island called Patmos—saw and entered that "door standing open in heaven" (Rev. 4:1). He saw it in full color and wrote it down, as he was told, so that we could see it with him, through his words, until we ourselves get to see the heavens open.

Most of us, most of the time, don't get to see it yet. We're asked to believe, to take the Word into our hearts and turn it into belief: faith that these words about things we can't see are words about things that are real and true even though they are invisible. C. S. Lewis, in his *Reflections on the Psalms*, talks about words—poetry, in particular—as "a little incarnation, giving body to what had been before invisible and inaudible."[2] Lewis might have quarreled with that Athenian duke named Theseus, who disparages the poet in those most remarkable lines of poetry:

> The poet's eye, in a fine frenzy rolling,
> Doth glance from heaven to earth, from earth to heaven,
> And as imagination bodies forth
> The forms of things unknown, the poet's pen
> Turns them to shapes, and gives to airy nothing
> A local habitation and a name.[3]

How wonderful that God, the original word-speaker, should allow us, his creatures who are made in his image, to experience the power of words to make, to name, to reach out to a reality greater than we can see—in effect, to glimpse the meaning of the Word made flesh and the one who ultimately connects us to that reality. Scripture leads us to this connection in a uniquely powerful way, with its living, active, God-breathed words.

When Scripture's words reach out to heaven, they always reach *up*. Heaven, as it is fleshed out for us in the Word, always pulls our gaze above ourselves. Jacob saw a ladder whose top "reached to heaven," with the Lord standing above it (Gen. 28:12–13). Stephen gazed up and saw the heavens open. John heard a voice calling, "Come up here" (Rev. 4:1). Jesus ascended up into the clouds, into heaven. Paul writes about being "caught up to the third heaven" (2 Cor. 12:2). Scripture's pictures of heaven make us look up, to the most high God—because heaven is, above all, the place where God dwells and the place from which he rules over all. It is not a place apart from him; it is his place. When we sing the doxology, we should in effect realize our lowness when we sing the words, "Praise him, all creatures here below." We should then almost literally look up to the reality of heaven and the very presence of God when we sing those words, "Praise him above, ye heavenly host." Heaven is really there, and it changes our whole consciousness to be aware of and to look up to that invisible reality.

Came Down

Looking up in this way also changes our conception of what it means that God came down. To look up to the reality of heaven is to begin to imagine what it meant for Jesus to stand on the edge of it, being there with God, being God—being the "Who" at the very beginning of our phrase, the "Who" previously considered in light of that prior phrase: "God of God, light of light, very God of very God; begotten, not made, being of one substance with the Father, by whom all things were made." *That* one, the one way up there, high and exalted, was the one who made that dive down from those heights. Standing at the edge of the Grand Canyon gives only the tiniest hint. Pictures of the earth from a spaceship give only the tiniest hint. The words *from heaven* should dizzy us, if we truly begin to take them in.

And so we come to these words: *came down*. That *down*, of course, is most fully explained by the words *from heaven*. We don't have a clue what it means to come down. Jesus does. The apostle Paul, in our reading from Philippians, gets at it in this famous kenosis passage, this talk of emptying in which Christ Jesus made himself nothing. I will not venture to join in the theological controversy surrounding this word, but I would suggest that looking up to the heights where Jesus began helps point to the meaning of the emptying—not, of course, that Jesus emptied himself of any of his divinity, but rather that he emptied *himself* (all that he was) by taking that leap down into the very flesh and earth made by his own hand. Far down. The creed says it so beautifully when it says he *came down*.

Recently, in a Bible study group, I was studying Joshua 5:13–15, in which Joshua, right before the battle of Jericho, lifts up his eyes "and behold, a man was standing before him with his drawn sword in his hand." Joshua immediately asks this clearly divine visitor, "Are you for us, or for our adversaries?"—which is an understandable question. We want God on our side, right? Whether we're Republican or Democrat, we're interested in having God on our side. I want God on my side when I'm having an argument with my husband. But you know the response that came to Joshua: first, "No"—which probably meant something like, "Wrong question." This man says to Joshua, "No; but I am the commander of the army of the LORD. Now I have come." What amazing words! These words show the very dive down we're talking about. First, "I am the commander of the army of the LORD": that's how high up this man is. In military thinking, position and rank are crucial. This man is the top, as high as you can get—not just on earth (like Joshua, who commands God's people), but in heaven. But then these ringing words follow: "Now I have come." Oh, the mercy of this dive down! The commander of the Lord's army came all the way down to Joshua, in person. What mercy in this pre-incarnate figure—a *man*, the text calls him, standing there before Joshua and talking to him. The point is not which side he's on; the point is for Joshua to see who this man is and to see that he has come to his people. The ultimate point is for Joshua to take off his shoes and bow down.

The words *came down* are indeed merciful words—beautifully merciful, beyond our understanding as we live our little lives down here on this earth. These words make me think of nights in the house where I grew up, which was a split-level home. For our family it was truly split between the adult and guest quarters on the upper level and the kids' quarters on the lower level. When my sister and I were teens and staying up at night much later than our parents, often with groups of friends, sometimes we'd hear a call from above. It would be my father's voice saying, "Keep it down down there!" But sometimes, if it got really late, and if we were especially loud, or if it was just absolutely time to break it up and go to bed, my father would come down. My father—who was a quite gentlemanly and reserved seminary professor by day—would come down the stairs in his bathrobe and tousled hair into the territory of his teenage daughters and ask us to be quiet. And when we were sick, he would also come down and check on us, in that same rumpled robe and tousled hair. He wouldn't just call; he would get out of bed and come down.

Came down is active, isn't it? Jesus wasn't just sent; he embraced his coming, and he *came*. He *made himself* nothing and *took on* the form of a servant. A former pastor of mine, Kent Hughes, does the best job of anyone I know at making vivid that picture, that moment of divine dialogue in which Jesus stood on the high edge of heaven, looked out over the universe, and spoke those words to his Father which appear in Hebrews 10 but which include a paraphrased quotation from Psalm 40: "Sacrifices and offerings you have not desired, / but a body have you prepared for me" (Heb. 10:5). We cannot miss Christ's active offering of himself at the moment of the incarnation, as he presents himself and says, "Behold, I have come to do your will, O God, / as it is written of me in the scroll of the book" (Heb. 10:7). Hughes has published the words that his congregation first heard him speak as part of a riveting Christmas message: "It was a leap down—as if the Son of God rose from his splendor, stood poised at the rim of the universe, and dove headlong, speeding through the stars over the Milky Way to earth's galaxy, finally past Arcturus, where he plunged into a huddle of animals. Nothing could be lower."[4]

Jesus, from the heights of heaven and on the brink of the incarnation, with his Father looks out and embraces full obedience to the word his Father has declared concerning his coming down. "Here I am," he says—and then he takes the dive down. And the Word was made flesh.

But it's the next phrase of the creed that gets to that part. We're looking at the dive, the coming down from heaven, and at how amazing and beautiful it is. Pictures and imaginings cannot capture it, but pictures can help, can't they? The poet Gerard Manley Hopkins pictured it through a bird, in a poem he called "The Windhover," in which he describes seeing a glorious falcon one morning sweeping and swooping high in the sky. The sight pulls his heart up to yearn for the heights of heaven and God himself—but then listen as the poem captures the dive down with the crucial word "buckle"—and listen for the beauty that comes out of the dive.

The Windhover

To Christ our Lord

I caught this morning morning's minion, king-
    dom of daylight's dauphin, dapple-dawn-drawn Falcon, in his riding
    Of the rolling level underneath him steady air, and striding
High there, how he rung upon the rein of a wimpling wing
In his ecstasy! Then off, off forth on swing,
    As a skate's heel sweeps smooth on a bow-bend: the hurl and gliding
    Rebuffed the big wind. My heart in hiding
Stirred for a bird,—the achieve of, the mastery of the thing!

Brute beauty and valour and act, oh, air, pride, plume, here
    Buckle! And the fire that breaks from thee then, a billion
Times told lovelier, more dangerous, O my chevalier!

    No wonder of it; sheer plod makes plough down sillion
Shine, and blue-bleak embers, ah my dear,
    Fall, gall themselves, and gash gold-vermilion.[5]

The sonnet's octave (the first eight lines) pulls our hearts high up, along with the narrator's bursting heart, as we follow the masterful flight of the falcon. The sestet (the last six lines) not only swoops down for a landing, but its images gradually change to those of fire—fire shining out of the depths of the dive, fire in the end like the shining that comes from clods of earth under the plough, or like the golden-hot heat that pulses out from hot embers that fall and break open. Hopkins's images get at the beauty and the precious value of one from glorious heights coming down to the stuff of earth and even to the gall of death. Hopkins gets the coming down. His "Windhover" offers a powerful picture.

Who for Us and for Our Salvation

Finally, let's consider the words *for us and for our salvation*. This amazing reality of Jesus's coming down from heaven had a purpose, and the creed states that purpose in two ways: *propter nos homines et propter nostrum salutem*. I've always thought this phrase had a beautiful rhythm in the speaking of it, even just in the English: *Who for us and for our salvation*. But why put it in two parts? Why not just say "for our salvation"—which obviously implies "for us"? But the church fathers separated out the theological part from the personal part, didn't they? "For our salvation" is the theological way to say it: Jesus came down to accomplish as the perfect sacrifice on the cross the salvation which we, being sinful, could not accomplish for ourselves, so that God could be at the same time both just and justifier. That's why he came: to accomplish this salvation, through his death on the cross and his resurrection from the dead. He *was* the ladder that came down from heaven, in order that he might himself be our way there. Jesus came to save!

But how beautiful that the creed also states the purpose personally: he came down for us. He didn't come for an abstract theological reason; he came because he loved us. He knows his sheep, and he came to rescue them. Here is the truth to marvel at: not just that God himself came down to accomplish salvation, but that he came to do it for us. When we speak this creed and believe these words, these are not abstract truths to which we assent; we're speaking of and being heard by the Lord God we have come to know personally, through his Son who came. If we dare to speak these words falsely, without belief, I imagine that the universe is jarred and that the one with whom these words should by faith connect is personally offended. Jesus didn't come like a king who parades royally through the streets waving lovingly but generally at the crowds. Jesus came all the way down and lived in the flesh with us. He knows his sheep by name. And we his people can know him, this incarnate Son of God who brought down God's glory personally to all who put their faith in him. This is the wonder: that we can and must take this creed and take our Savior utterly personally.

Taking In His Coming Down

To take these words personally involves not only a true believing in the person of Jesus Christ our Lord, but also an internalization of this rhythm of coming down. We grow to see and love this dive, and it starts to happen in us. We truly take in his coming down. We start to live the theme of the whole Philippians 2 passage, which is that we believers should have the very mind of Christ, who offers the ultimate example of lowering himself for the sake of others. We start to experience the left half of the V for ourselves, in a little way, in Christ and through Christ. We pray for this kind of coming down in our own hearts, the kind of humility that counts others as more significant than ourselves. The missionary and poet Amy Carmichael wrote a poem called "Like Low Green Moss," in which she prayed:

> We are too high; Lord Jesus, we implore Thee,
> Make of us something like the low green moss
> That vaunteth not, a quiet thing before Thee,
> Cool for Thy feet sore wounded on the Cross.[6]

We ourselves live the coming down in a whole variety of ways, don't we? Recently, I listened to a web link sent by a friend from Boston's Park Street Church, in which Harvard law professor Bill Stuntz was telling that congregation the story of God's gifts to him during his battle with cancer.[7] At the time of the telling, Professor Stuntz was fifty-one years of age and had been given six to eighteen months to live. In an amazingly strong voice, Professor Stuntz not only vividly communicated the ugliness, the smell, the taste, and the indignities of cancer and cancer treatment. He also gave powerful testimony to the fact that the Lord Jesus, who came all the way down to the worst suffering of the worst death, redeems every single awful moment of our suffering, having gone the way before us and for us. This man was calling from deep in the depths of a pit, up to his brothers and sisters gathered around the edge, and telling them what he was finding down there—namely, Jesus himself.

Many of us here have perhaps called out with such a voice—or perhaps will. Many of us need to listen to such voices from the depths. If we lean down to listen, we in the church can hear and must hear each other's voices from the depths—voices of suffering, voices of the persecuted church around the world, voices that are singing the way of the cross. This is a way that comes down and serves and suffers on the way to glory.

Some depths we would not choose, but God grants them in his unfathomable mercy. Other depths we can choose: the putting aside of my own pressing schedule to talk with a brother or sister in need; the foregoing of a chance to insert vaunting or defensive words into a conversation; the choice to go or to live where I can minister; the willingness to perform enthusiastically some bothersome task. We can do all these things with the spirit that would pray, "We are too high; Lord Jesus, we implore Thee, / Make of us something like the low green moss / That vaunteth not, a quiet thing before Thee. . . ."

The good news of the gospel is that the V shape has not just the left side plummeting to the bottom point, which Jesus plumbed for us, but also the right side—the side of high exaltation, of rising toward the heavens, the side Jesus has already ascended and along which we follow him to resurrected glory. That captain of the Lord's army who said to Joshua, "I have come," prefigured not only the man of sorrows who would come down in the flesh, but also the glorious risen Christ who will come again, the one pictured in Revelation 19 with all the armies of heaven following him, and that sharp sword coming out of his mouth, with which, it says, he will strike down nations. He has come, and he will come again, to complete the shape of the gospel story for all God's people forever.

But today, even as we know and affirm the whole shape of our salvation, which gives us such context and comfort and hope, for today let us take in deeply this first coming down of the Lord Jesus from heaven, for us and for our salvation. Because he took the form of a servant, we can follow him in that coming down low, in service and in suffering, even today. What a coming down of God this was—what a plunge, from the heights and fellowship of heaven. How marvelous that the Son of God came down. How we benefit from inviting these words deep into our souls, as we believe in and bow down before the one who for us and for our salvation came down from heaven.

Prayer

Our most high God, we look up to heaven and wonder at your glory, Lord, as you are over all the universe that you created and that you sovereignly rule. We humbly praise you for your coming down into this broken world of sinful people. Thank you that our Lord Jesus came down in the flesh to save us—to save even us—because you love us. Let us, we pray, take into our hearts your coming down. Until we see your face, we pray that you would help us follow the way of coming down, the way of the cross, the way to glory and exaltation found only in you and through you. We praise you in the name of our risen and glorious Lord and Savior Jesus Christ. Amen.

13

The Will to Believe and the Need for Creeds

John Rucyahana

The Christian faith, as lived and expressed not only in words but also in conduct, evidences God's grace to the church. The divine plan for our salvation (redemption) was wrought by God without human contribution. The human groan for salvation, however, meets the embrace of the divine love in Jesus. The Holy Spirit counsels with us, and our role is to surrender in obedience. Our decision is to trust God and obey.

The creeds developed as a process, beginning with Jesus who confessed and taught that he was the Son of Man sent by the Father. The Father sent the Son, and Jesus promised his disciples to send the Holy Spirit to represent him. The transfiguration bore witness to Jesus's claim of sonship. For the early church, this became the beginning of the tenets of faith.[1]

The beginning of 2 Peter reads:

> Grace and peace be multiplied to you in the knowledge of God and of Jesus our Lord; seeing that His divine power has granted to us everything pertaining to life and godliness, through the true knowledge of Him who called us by His own glory and excellence. For by these He has granted to us His precious and magnificent promises, so that by them you might become partakers of the divine nature, having escaped the corruption that is in the world by lust. Now for this very reason also, applying all diligence, in your faith supply moral excellence;

and in your moral excellence, knowledge; and in your knowledge, self-control; and in your self-control, perseverance; and in your perseverance, godliness; and in your godliness, brotherly kindness; and in your brotherly kindness, love. For if these qualities are yours and are increasing, they render you neither useless nor unfruitful in the true knowledge of our Lord Jesus Christ. For he who lacks these qualities is blind or short-sighted, having forgotten his purification from his former sins. Therefore, brethren, be all the more diligent to make certain about His calling and choosing you; for as long as you practice these things, you will never stumble; for in this way the entrance into the eternal kingdom of our Lord and Savior Jesus Christ will be abundantly supplied to you. (2 Pet. 1:2–11 NASB)[2]

The human will to believe in God through Jesus connects with what Paul expresses in Ephesians 1:3–12 as the will of God. This is for our redemption from sin so that we can praise and worship God.

Not only does the church need to have the will to believe; it needs to have the tenets of Christian faith as principles of faith. The church also needs to commit and relate to Jesus Christ, its Redeemer. This relationship will involve prayer, walking in light, and being transparent and accountable to God with the help of the Holy Spirit. The early church and the church fathers bear witness to this reality.

In 2 Peter 1:16–17, Peter says: "For we did not follow cleverly devised tales when we made known to you the power and coming of our Lord Jesus Christ, but we were eyewitnesses of His majesty. For when He received honor and glory from God the Father, such an utterance as this was made to Him by the Majestic Glory: 'This is my beloved Son with whom I am well-pleased.'" The Christian's relationship with Christ requires trusting in him and his promises as expressed in the Scriptures. These promises prompt our decision to trust and obey. The danger to the church today, as it was in the early church experiences, is that people want to twist the faith requirements and avoid the divine plan in order to make it acceptable to the demands of life and cultural pressures. This always becomes an issue for the community of faith.

As the Bible talks about broad and narrow ways, individuals choose their way: either to have faith in Christ by trusting and serving him, or to deny him! According to the Scriptures and principles of faith as expressed by the creeds, the church is protected. Adjusting and twisting scriptural teaching to fit it into the demands of the society results in heresy and apostasy. Thus, the creeds were developed from baptismal instructions to what we have today (the standards of faith).

It is amazing that those who trust in Jesus relate to him in prayer, service, and worship, and sometimes even die for him. Believers who were forced to deny their faith or persuaded to live otherwise became martyrs instead.[3] This steadfastness resounds in the words of Patrick Henry in 1775, which inspired the American Revolution against colonialism: "Is life so dear or peace so sweet, as to be purchased at the price of chains and slavery? Forbid it, Almighty God! I know not what course others may take, but as for me, give me liberty, or give me death!"[4] It also resounds in the words of Malcolm X: "If you are not ready to die for it, put the word freedom out of your vocabulary."[5]

The early church, therefore, did not only labor to set the fundamental tenets of Christian faith, creeds, and dogmas in place, but also suffered persecution and died for the same faith, and for the Lord Jesus. The church flourished and spread during these hard times, and the church diminished and became confused when it compromised and relaxed its commitment and obedience to Christ Jesus.

It is written in 1 Corinthians 1:18: "For the word of the cross is foolishness to those who are perishing, but to us who are being saved it is the power of God." The educated Greeks of the time viewed the cross as foolishness—indeed, even as a curse. These philosophical realities apply in our times as well. The powers and authorities of nations have tried to eradicate Christianity, which has resulted in persecution and martyrdom. The Protestant churches in commonwealth countries were more affected by the shift from Christendom to pluralism. The membership of Protestant churches in England, Wales, and Scotland dropped from 13 percent of the population in 1920 to 8 percent in 1970, which represented a loss of almost 40 percent of their members in only fifty years.[6] This loss covered mainline churches and denominations in the United Kingdom, including Methodists, Baptists, Lutherans, and Anglicans.

The church of Christ declined in membership for various reasons, including three main ones:

1. The church lost its call for mission, as stated in the Great Commission in Matthew 28:18–19, as well as the witness and livelihood of believers in Christ Jesus the Redeemer.
2. The church changed its approach from persuasion to being living witnesses to the world. The Roman church started persecuting and killing its own fellow Christians because these Christians had new ideas or different opinions. New Protestant denominations mushroomed because of the Roman church's use of force (e.g., Martin Luther and the deaths of many, like Archbishop Cranmer).
3. The church lost its influence in society. I recall reading somewhere that Indira Gandhi, the former prime minister of India, once said: "I love Jesus and his teaching, but I will become a Christian when I see one."

When the church surrenders to pluralism, it loses the ability to accept challenges such as those posed by Charles Colson in his book *Kingdoms in Conflict*. John Stott summaraizes Colson when he writes that "the radical values of the Kingdom of God, which was inaugurated by Jesus Christ, confront, challenge and change the kingdoms of men, especially through the agency of what Edmund Burke in the eighteenth century called 'little platoons.'"[7]

Colson had in mind small, voluntary associations of people who love God and their neighbor, exhibit transcendence in the midst of secularism, refuse to acquiesce to evil, oppose injustice, and spread mercy and reconciliation in the world. The combined witness of history and Scripture is that faithful Christian people have had an enormous influence on society.

Since we believe in a living God and since our creative Christ, the master of our history and destiny, is on the throne, the victory should be ours under his banner. Colson is right to challenge today's church. In Romans 12:1–3, we read:

> Therefore I urge you, brethren, by the mercies of God, to present your bodies a living and holy sacrifice, acceptable to God, which is your spiritual service of worship. And do not be conformed to this world, but be transformed by the renewing of your mind, so that you may prove what the will of God is, that which is good and acceptable and perfect. For through the grace given to me I say to everyone among you not to think more highly of himself than he ought to think; but to think so as to have sound judgment, as God has allotted to each a measure of faith.

We need to engage the modern world humbly and prayerfully with the true, undiluted, and uncompromised gospel of Jesus Christ. It is true that there are real pressures from our societies and in the world today. The educated and uneducated, rich and poor, developed and developing all have their own unique pressures and frustrations, but their remedy is the gospel of Jesus, the Redeemer. We cannot, therefore, afford to remain passive and let our societies decay and degenerate when we have been entrusted with the redemptive message of Jesus. He promises us in Matthew 28:20: "I am with you always, even to the end of the age."

The Formation of Creeds

In the early church, the apostles required their converts to repent, believe, and be baptized. There are authentic expressions and formulas of the Christian faith found in 1 Peter 3:21–22: "Baptism now saves you—not the removal of dirt from the flesh, but an appeal to God for a good conscience—through the resurrection of Jesus Christ, who is at the right hand of God, having gone into heaven, after angels and authorities and powers had been subjected to Him." Instruction about the Trinity to baptismal candidates was imperative. Paul also shared the same requirements in 1 Corinthians 12:3: "Therefore I make known to you that no one speaking by the Spirit of God says, 'Jesus is accursed'; and no one can say, 'Jesus is Lord' except by the Holy Spirit." This emphasizes the need to confess the lordship of Jesus and the faith in God the Father, the Son, and the Holy Spirit.

These instructions for baptismal candidates grew into baptismal services as early as Tertullian of Africa (AD 160–220), who also required thrice immersion in the name of the Father, Son, and Holy Ghost. St. Cyril of Jerusalem describes the divine baptism: "And each one was asked whether he believed in the Name of the Father and of the Son and the Holy Ghost and ye confessed the saving confession."[8]

The creeds were developed over time as the church instructed her converts and as baptismal services were established. It was a process employed to share faith. Of course, the creeds were dominated by the New Testament expression of the historical facts of Jesus Christ, the Son of God, who spoke of his Father, whom he obeyed, and the Holy Spirit of God, whom he would send. Thus, the terms *Father*, *Son*, and *Holy Spirit* refer to the manifestation of God (the divine) through the life of Jesus Christ. The Son is begotten of the Father, and the Spirit proceeds from the Father.

It would be wise to mention the fact that the church remained alert because of rising heresies (e.g., Ebionism, docetism, and modalism, also known as Sabellianism). The Christian church today desperately needs the creeds for their relevance and their truths, more than ever before. The snag may be that the church may not see the relevance of creeds or, if the church sees it, may choose to ignore it.

The Arian heretical concepts may be as present today as they were in the days of Arius (AD 250–336). The denial of Christ's deity and his redemptive mission is not strange to our ears. To refute the principal truth that Christ is the only way, truth, and life, however, destroys the basis of Christ's mission to the world. We read in Mark 14:61–62: "Again the high priest was questioning Him, and saying to Him, 'Are you the Christ, the Son of the Blessed One?' And Jesus said, 'I am; and you shall see the Son of Man sitting at the right hand of power, and coming with the clouds of heaven.'"

The creeds to this day remain relevant and are needed to challenge and correct errors. Some churches in modern times, although confessing to have sound preaching, have adopted a lax, monastic attitude. They think it is good enough to be in a good church and to have good loving experience of worship and praise, but to keep it in the walls of the church. Sometimes these churches do not even influence families and neighborhoods. These types of churches, big or small, lack deliberate mission strategies and do not exercise the purpose for which the church is created: to be witnesses of Jesus to the ends of the earth!

Acts 1:8 reads: "But you will receive power when the Holy Spirit has come upon you; and you shall be My witnesses both in Jerusalem, and in all Judea and Samaria, and even to the remotest part of the earth." The kingdom's growth was entrusted to the disciples of Jesus, within Christian communities known as churches. So it is sad that merely maintaining an institution has become the goal of many churches. Most of the time, their leaders and the congregations themselves become preoccupied by developing skills into specialized membership and resources for self-maintenance and self-service, rather than outreach to the groaning world in need of salvation. The true gospel challenges the pessimistic view of history, which unfortunately repeats itself. There is hope in Jesus Christ who redeems humanity by the sovereign God.

In addition, Christian churches are challenged and muted by reports such as the Global 2000 Report to the President on world population and environmental degradation, which suggested threats to people and animal species. These reports do not mention the continuous moral decay of values and dignity, and they forget that as the human condition gets worse, humans will continue to destroy the world. But if the reverse becomes true, the salvation of humanity can redeem the environment in the sense that the saved person who loves and has faith in God recognizes that the earth belongs to God. Humankind just manages the earth as stewards, and we are answerable to God and accountable to our fellow human beings. This reality applies to communities and families that are overrun by selfishness and individualism. There continues to be no serious consideration for family values and community values.

The church must be regarded as a community of hope that carries a message of restoration and trust in the Almighty, who changes history and circumstances and blesses those who await him. In Jeremiah 29:11–14, we read:

> "For I know the plans that I have for you," declares the LORD, "plans for welfare and not for calamity, to give you a future and a hope. Then you will call upon Me and come and pray to Me, and I will listen to you. You will seek Me and find Me, when you search for Me with all your heart. I will be found by you," declares the LORD, "and I will restore your fortunes and will gather you from all the nations and from all the places where I have driven you," declares the LORD, "and I will bring you back to the place from where I sent you into exile."

God has a plan for us, but the call to the church is to engage societies for spiritual transformation and change of attitude, from idolatry to faith and from doubt to trust in God through Jesus Christ. Thus, the creeds are extremely relevant and crucial today. Language can change, but the truth expressed in creeds is imperative for our transformation.

The fact that the church gives up in the face of the challenges and pressures of societies renders it powerless, reduces its impact, and erases its influence on society. Generations therefore grow up with no knowledge of, interest in, or respect for the Christian church. Thanks be to God that the church remains by the divine hand, but the church can do better.

If the early church spread far despite persecution, martyrdom, and the hardest conditions of the first centuries, why can't the church in modern times do even better, especially considering all the tools at its disposal for communication and education? What it lacks are the truths expressed in the creeds and the early church's open preaching, accompanied by the witnessing for Christ. It lacks truths about the Savior who saved us and with whom we relate—the Lord we pray to, love, worship, praise, trust, and serve.

The creeds speak of the Holy Spirit. Jesus instructed his disciples to remain in Jerusalem until they were empowered by the Holy Spirit, the promised comforter, counselor, and power from above. The early church depended on the Holy Spirit and divine empowerment. In Acts 1:4, we read: "Gathering them together, He commanded them not to leave Jerusalem, but to wait for what the Father had promised, 'Which,' He said, 'you heard of from Me.'" Also, Luke 24:49 reads: "And behold, I am sending forth the promise of My Father upon you; but you are to stay in the city until you are clothed with power from on high."

This was true of the early church—prayers were offered for its converts to be empowered by the Holy Spirit. This dependence, trust, and faith in the Holy Ghost were requirements. We find in Acts 9:17 these words: "So Ananias departed and entered the house, and after laying his hands on him said, 'Brother Saul, the Lord Jesus, who appeared to you on the road by which you were coming, has sent me so that you may regain your sight and be filled with the Holy Spirit.'"

Divine Business

In business, it is logical for a worker in a company to depend on the CEO's plans. The same is true for divine business. Believers cannot engage in the divine mission of Christ to redeem the world without consultations with Christ and without the help from the Holy Spirit.

In practice, however, the reverse is true. Many of the modern churches today do not believe that they need the empowerment of the promised Holy Spirit. They have developed principles of managing a church and strategies for retaining their membership and do not seriously desire to serve Jesus Christ. The simple reason is that not many pastors today want to lose control. They develop and implement the right church programs to command the needed financial resources, so they think they can do without the Holy Spirit. But many such churches have lost the power to preach for transformation to a Christian life, the repentance of sins, and surrender to Christ. People can be members as long as Christ is adjusting to *their* ways of life, instead of the membership being transformed to be like Christ. This is done under the pretext that Christ loves them. Some do not even mention that Christ died for them, out of fear that they may be then required to believe in redemption and atonement of sins.

We desperately need the credal faith and credal teaching today for our salvation and to have the church once again influence our societies.

The Catholic Church and the Communion of Saints

The "holy catholic church," as written in the Nicene Creed (not the Roman Catholic Church), means the universal body of believers in *Jesus Christ*: the holy Son of God, born of the Virgin Mary, and crucified for the atonement of our sins, whom we receive by believing that he died to set us free from the bonds of sin. The Christian church universally shares its communion in Christ by his Spirit and through the sacraments. Faith, trust, service, worship, and praises distinguish us from other religions. For Christ is our identity, and our lives bear fruit in witness to him. Without the above, our different cultures and backgrounds would not command communion. It would be difficult, if not impossible, to share this universality and communion. But Christ, who is our Redeemer and our hope, allows all of us to find a place in him; hence, our common identity. The church has suffered fragmentation by cultural influences, attitudes, geographical differences, and racial tensions. The church may prefer to retain racial clubs or limit itself to cocoons in which to serve, but Christ sent us to the ends of the earth on a mission together.

The early church, drawing from the creeds' tenets, lovingly and sacrificially preached the good news for results. Early followers believed that preaching the good news was their duty, for the sake of those who heard them and to whom the Holy Spirit had sent them. Like their Lord Jesus, they poured out their lives in love, and some even lost their lives for the sake of preaching the gospel. It is written in Philippians 2:6–7 that Christ, "who, although He existed in the form of God, did not regard equality with God a thing to be grasped, but emptied Himself, taking the form of a bond-servant, and being made in the likeness of men."

After meeting Christ, receiving faith, and being empowered by the Holy Spirit, Paul—a Pharisee, a member of the Sanhedrin, and a Roman citizen— totally surrendered to Christ and his gospel. He chose to surrender to Christ and serve with him for the salvation of Gentiles to whom he was sent. Philippians 3:7–9 states:

> But whatever things were gain to me, those things I have counted as loss for the sake of Christ. More than that, I count all things to be loss in view of the surpassing value of knowing Christ Jesus my Lord, for whom I have suffered the loss of all things, and count them but rubbish so that I may gain Christ, and may be found in Him, not having a righteousness of my own derived from the Law, but that which is through faith in Christ, the righteousness which comes from God on the basis of faith.

The church today needs to get back to the foundations of Christian faith. We have to realize that without Jesus and the Holy Spirit, our institutions will continue to have no transforming power and little influence in society.

Mark 16:17–18 reads: "These signs will accompany those who have believed: in My name they will cast out demons, they will speak with new tongues; they will pick up serpents, and if they drink any deadly poison, it will not hurt them; they will lay hands on the sick, and they will recover." Members of the credal church loved, obeyed, and trusted dearly in Christ who saved them. Jesus fulfills what he promised his own. As seen in Acts 12:7: "And behold, an angel of the Lord suddenly appeared and a light shone in the cell; and he struck Peter's side and woke him up, saying, 'Get up quickly.' And his chains fell off his hands."

Churches whose faith and trust are put in the living Jesus are growing. Repentance is being preached, and people are experiencing release from their guilt. God is at work in the lives of those who believe that Jesus is the Son of God. So the real question for the church today may be this: how can Jesus empower those who do not trust him and who deny his deity? How can a church that holds Jesus as just a historical figure who made a political mistake and got himself killed make an impact? Some may not even have the grace to believe in his resurrection or salvation from our sins, since they do not believe in the atonement.

The authority of Christ has to be understood as dispensed to individual believers in the church for witnessing and service to the community. In the same way, the powers of the Holy Spirit are given to those with faith and to those who seek him. There is no monopoly on divine empowerment by the church hierarchy or any other group in the church. In 2 Peter 1:1, we read: "Simon Peter, a bond-servant and apostle of Jesus Christ, To those who have received a faith of the same kind as ours by the righteousness of our God and Savior, Jesus Christ."

The challenge is real. The church of Christ needs to seek faith and trust in him who called it with humility. Groan for a deeper knowledge of him who called us to serve in the vineyard. Finally, realize the truth that the living church depends on him who called it and empowers it to remain on mission and to continue to be a living witness in the world.

Conclusion

Jesus Christ was born Jewish, and his disciples were Jews. They worshiped one God known to their fathers, and Jesus taught from the Scriptures as experienced by their forefathers. The Trinity was taught after being revealed by Jesus himself. He taught and spoke about the Father who sent him, spoke of himself as the Son of Man, and performed miracles. Peter confessed him as the Messiah in the presence of the Eleven. Jesus approved Peter's confession, affirming that it was by the Holy Spirit that Peter had said it. The transfiguration witnessed to the fact that Jesus was the Son in whom God is well pleased, and who listens to him. Jesus instructed his disciples to remain in the city (Jerusalem) until he sent them the Holy Spirit after he left. This constituted the revelation of the Holy Trinity. Christ is the revelation of God to humankind. Over time, these truths became the baptismal instructions and the creeds. These truths are crucial for the church today if we are to make an impact and command influence.

14

Can the Church Emerge without or with Only the Nicene Creed?

MARK DeVINE

One particular emerging community of faith in midtown Kansas City launched itself in 1998 with no confessional statement whatsoever. Even five years later, after their formal adoption of the Apostles' Creed, elders felt compelled to append to those ancient, historic words these words of their own:

> We do not think the best way to know what we believe is to read it off a page. We believe the best way to determine what someone, or some group of people, believe is to watch them—or better yet, join them and discover it from the inside. When we are handed a sheet of paper or click on a link with a list of statements, we believe that something vital is short-circuited. More than that, we become a brand: "Oh, you're *that* kind of Christian/church." We are a brand culture. We don't want to be a brand church. We are a community of people seeking to follow Jesus in faith and freedom.[1]

At one level, such a statement belongs to the history of the church's long struggle to comprehend the relationship between doctrine and life. Compulsion to attenuate the power and circumscribe the pretensions of doctrine surely overlaps with historic pietist protests against all head-heavy, Spirit-deprived pretenders to true Christianity. The scholastic periods that seem to follow inevitably upon the heels of great historic theological watersheds seek to preserve the gains achieved once the prophets of those exhilarating days of theological and ecclesial renewal pass from the scene. And surely much-needed preservation is thereby achieved.

Yet often one can detect a certain lapsing from the spirit that gives life into the letter that kills. At such moments, the threats seemingly posed by doctrine to the church loom so large that a reflexive throwing of the creedal baby out with the bathwater of overly intellectualized faith may be suggested. From time to time the church must, with both deliberation and gusto, reject the false faith that, in Calvin's terms, merely "flits in the brain" and saves no one. Doctrine can easily become an intended or unintended casualty in the midst of these periodic efforts to reclaim the holistic claims of God upon the lives of his children. For this particular Kansas City community of faith, that meant the way of Jesus would have to be followed without the supposed spiritually stultifying dangers posed by doctrine.

The governing documents and websites of many so-called emerging churches are replete with expressions ranging from a palpable doctrinal and confessional squeamishness to outright hostility toward anything creedal. As Eddie Gibbs and Ryan Bolger have noted, "standing up for truth . . . has no appeal to emerging church leaders."[2] Those congregations that do adopt some modicum of confessional language typically settle for the Apostles' Creed and/or the Nicene Creed. These two paths—aversion to doctrine and wariness toward doctrine—shed light on the question I wish to explore: Can the church emerge without or with only the Nicene Creed?

Doctrine Behaving Badly

We should admit right at the outset that the fearful premise that animates the emerging church's wariness toward creeds is not without foundation. The dangers posed to the Christian faith by creeds, including the Nicene Creed, are real and formidable. Revered doctrinal formulas, hallowed as they are by both demonstrable antiquity and impressive universality, may suggest that everything needful for God's people to hear and obey Holy Scripture has been captured nicely in a few beautiful lines of authoritative creedal text. But this is just not so. The meaning of Holy Scripture, divinely inspired as it is and presently wielded as a tool by the living God, has not been exhausted by the church and cannot be tamed, domesticated, harnessed, or silenced by any means. Attempts to do so are both ill advised and ultimately abortive. God the Holy Spirit sees to it that the written Word remains the living Word. John Robinson, the pastor of the pilgrims, knew and we should also know that "the Lord hath still more truth and light to break forth out of His Holy Word."[3] Praise be to God!

When God addresses his church through his Holy Word and the church hears, does it not know itself to have been addressed anew by the living voice of the only God? Does it not know itself, in the wake of such an encounter with the revelation of God, to be in living confrontation with the living God? God speaks old words with new and living power. In the wake of such new "breakings out" of God's living voice, the church has seen fit again and again to confess that the Bible is not just another means by which God speaks to his children and reveals himself. Instead, the church has felt compelled to confess that it has pleased God here to speak with a clarity and a sufficiency and an authority as nowhere else. The church learns the prudence of testing all other speech, including its own speech—whether preached, sung, confessed, or taught—by this divine speech. When the church knows itself aright, it knows that it can never attempt to achieve a superior standpoint over against Holy Scripture. It can never judge that Scripture or sift wheat from chaff from among the contents of that divinely inspired text. Should the church attempt to do so, Karl Barth has warned, the threat of a lapse into idolatry looms, and the perhaps unintended and unwitting construction of a "god" may well ensue. This threat arises whenever some secondary word or even a faithfully intended responsive word of doctrine usurps the rightful place of the divine Word of Holy Scripture.

Perhaps most of the dangers posed by the employment of creed and confession can be effectively headed off if only the church keeps before it this distinction between the Word of God written and responses to that Word. However ancient and edifying and necessary certain responses to the Word of God have proven to be (and this is especially true of the Nicene Creed), such statements still constitute *response* to the divine speech, not divine speech itself. In the Nicene Creed we are confronted with human speech—very impressive human speech—that has been repeatedly found effective as a protection of and at least a partial confession of what the church has heard from God in Holy Scripture. Yet it is human speech nonetheless, and, as such, it is provisional and revisable speech in the face of God's own Holy Word. Proper respect for and subscription to the Nicene Creed or any creed should arise from confidence and gratitude that these words serve the written Word of God. The legitimacy of the Nicene Creed as a fit word for the church depends—as does any other word, whether preached, taught, or sung—upon not only its compatibility with the Bible but its faithful defense of, proclamation of, and application of that Word.

Loyalty to and protectiveness of the Bible's true character are sometimes advanced by emerging church leaders as major justifications for their antipathy toward doctrine. Doctrine, they insist, tends to reduce, distort, and obscure the narrative power of the story of God's activity recounted in the pages of Holy Writ even as it also undercuts the divinely intended mystery of that revelation. As Debbie Blue of House of Mercy in St. Paul has stated, "We are comfortable with having a lot of unanswered questions. We think maybe that's what it's like being in relationship with a living Being. We think it's more honest than providing a lot of answers, abstract notions of truth."[4]

Emerging church attraction to narrative, along with its effort to reclaim the arts and the language of mystery, reflects an underlying acknowledgment of and appreciation for the ineffable dimensions of God's revealed truth and, in the language of Michael Polanyi, that "we know more than we can tell."[5] Truth, emerging church leaders insist, more effectively achieves its ends in life than in formal, dogmatic speech. Pressed for a statement of his community's beliefs, Brad Cecil of Axxess in Arlington, Texas, responds, "Community is our apologetic. The only answer to others we have is our community."[6] Fixation upon propositional truth, employment of doctrinal instruments as tests of faith, and zeal for the boundaries of fellowship among followers of Jesus smack of an unseemly pharisaism, a dogmatism incompatible with the considered modesty appropriate to would-be worshipers of the God of Abraham, Isaac, and Jacob.

Postmodern truth-seekers, they insist, reflexively draw back from the imposition of creedal demands, insisting instead upon truth encountered, enjoyed, and embodied in community, a truth springing up organically and developing more holistically among those whose stories merge with God's own ongoing creative and redemptive story. For the doctrine-averse and doctrine-wary streams of the emerging church, compulsion to craft and impose doctrinal constraints upon what the church of Jesus Christ believes, teaches, and confesses involves a distortive intrusion of the modern world upon followers of the way of Jesus.

Varieties of Humility

For doctrine-wary emergents, doctrine employed as a confession of what the church believes but, even more so, doctrine employed as an instrument circumscribing tolerable limits of diversity for the church, smacks of a high-handed and illegitimate confidence in the face of truth and its elusive mysteries. From the very beginning, partly justified by such convictions touching mystery and the modesty compatible with such mystery, influencers within the emerging church have advocated for a new kind of conversation among believers. They sought, for reasons similar to some seventeenth-century pietists in the face of a theologically nitpicky scholasticism, a conversation "between friends," a conversation devoid of the illegitimate and counterproductive polemics they observed among evangelicals seemingly trapped within endless cycles of orthodoxy-fixated one-upmanship.[7] Where the only true God is concerned, emergents insist, a considered humility that displays itself in modesty should govern conversation between fellow truth-seekers who know and feel keenly that they and everybody else yet "see through a glass darkly."

But it will be helpful to recognize that not all humility is the same. The humility and modesty advocated by the left wing of the emerging movement is of a particular sort. It certainly values tolerance of a wide diversity of views in theological conversation, patience with contrary opinions, and even a kind of strategic and provisional agnosticism—or at least the bracketing of one's own convictions for the sake of genuine listening to those with whom one may ultimately have to, theologically speaking, part company. Yet the doctrine-wary and doctrine-averse streams of the emerging church seem at least deficient in, if not oblivious to, another sort of humility. This humility displays itself not so much in expansive tolerance for a wide and widening array of views, but in a considered docility or teachableness that yields to superior wisdom, a humility that thinks better of Bible and tradition than of any newish insights it might happen to fancy. I am speaking of that humility that lets its own mouth be stopped, lets itself be told and taught something on the basis of authority. This expression of humility, in a more profound sense, also proceeds from encounter with the living God, who is mystery but who also acts and speaks and, in so doing, makes himself known. Left-wing emergent humility may facilitate clearheaded and respectful theological conversation, but does it not fall short of the humility of confession born of having been addressed and commanded by the living voice of almighty God? Resistance to confession in the face of revelation may be more the child of insubordination and pride than of true humility.

Doctrine and the Enlightenment Boogeyman

Alongside an acute contemporaneity, emerging church leaders also exhibit a marked openness to the past. The late Robert Webber anticipated, affirmed, and then helped to shape this dually directed vision most obviously through publication of his Ancient-Future series of books, the maintenance of his Ancient-Future website, and the founding of the Institute for Worship Studies. Emerging church planters, committed as they are to the building of communities of faith that are relevant to a postmodern mindset, also intend a recovery of the past neglected and even despised by Enlightenment sensibilities. For the emerging church, rejection of modernity means, among other things, openness to miracles, to the ongoing work of God the Holy Spirit, and to the Christian past. Yet doctrine, along with the articulation of propositional truth in general, is viewed as the pernicious offspring of modernity and remains unwelcome. Enlightenment-shaped modernity, understood primarily in ideological terms, functions as something of an all-purpose boogeyman for many within what I call the left wing of the emerging church phenomenon. The tagging and censuring of any idea or practice as *modern* routinely provokes convulsions of consensual and self-congratulatory agreement within the community of emerging church influencers.

Viewed against the backdrop of church history, it is here that emerging churches display a profound historical blind spot, together with the potentially rescuing seeds of recovery from that same blind spot—namely, the ancient and universal will to believe and the need for creed among the people of God reaching back three millennia to the Israelites themselves. Confronted with so many and varied creedlike expressions —ranging from the Old Testament Shema to Peter's confession at Caesarea Philippi, from the plethora of Pauline credal formulations in the Pastorals, to his "I delivered to you . . . what I also received" of 1 Corinthians 15:3, to the kenotic hymn of Philippians 2, together with the repeated convulsions of doctrinal construction across history and geography—quests to finally be done with doctrine once and for all appear not only naïve but wrongheaded and doomed. Especially offensive to emerging church concerns is the historic deployment of doctrine, confession, and dogma not only as a means to declare what the church believes, but also as a tool of discipline through which tolerable limits of doctrinal diversity within the church are set. Luther's response to Erasmian latitudinarianism remains as relevant today as it was in the sixteenth century. By its very nature as a revealed religion, Christianity is about assertions.

As it turns out, emerging church attempts to subsume credal seriousness within what they see as a discredited, bankrupt, and increasingly irrelevant modernity are grounded in a profoundly erroneous understanding of both modernity and premodernity. The ancient Christianity that emerging churches wish to recover—a tradition supposedly devoid of the nastiness of confession-fixated religion—turns out to be a mirage. Instead, review of the history of the church exposes the antiquity, universality, and inevitability of doctrinal formulation among the people of God. Doctrine and Christianity go hand in hand. Followers of the way of Jesus believe, and so they confess.

However pernicious the acids of the Enlightenment and the modern world that arose in its wake may have been, and however regrettable certain aspects of doctrinal construction and the use of doctrine on the soil of modernity turned out to be, that the will to believe and the need for creed proves endemic to the nature of Christianity itself seems beyond doubt. To the extent that emerging churches fail to come to grips with the intrinsically believing and confessing character of Christianity, their drift away from anything recognizably Christian seems inevitable. One hopes that their stated rejection of what Thomas Oden has called "modern chauvinism," combined with concrete and friendly engagement with the Christian past, will reveal how characteristic of modernism their wariness and aversion to doctrine actually is.[8]

On the left wing of the emerging movement, we can discern an unintended lapse into patterns of theologizing reminiscent of Protestant liberalism. Here the Bible, along with every other theological resource, may be exploited in search of support for the advance of values and often unacknowledged "doctrines" that shape and animate core convictions and goals, but the community of faith remains answerable to nothing outside itself.

Friedrich Schleiermacher was happy to ransack the Bible (though he found little in the Old Testament suited to his purpose) in search of whatever might advance the exposing and nurturing of the religious self-consciousness as he defined it. Now piety would judge both Bible and doctrine, not the reverse.[9] Likewise, Paul Tillich, having identified the quest for meaning as the ultimate concern of modern men and women, made eclectic selection from the Bible and sometimes history serve his method of correlation.[10] Doctrine-averse emergents are happy to exploit not only the Bible but also tradition to advance conviction-laden goals without really acknowledging the doctrinelike content and function of those goals.

Protestant liberals sought to salvage and thus rescue Christianity in the face of an Enlightenment onslaught against its foundational epistemological moorings. The strategy involved, at its heart, a genuflection before the epistemological dictates of the Enlightenment. Authoritative appeal to Holy Scripture gave way, in both Schleiermacher and Tillich, to a more existential and pragmatic appeal to the facts of human experience. Some within the emerging church envision a similar mission of salvage and rescue for the sake of felt relevance. Only this time the strategy calls not for accommodation to Enlightenment sensibility but rejection of the Enlightenment, with both its identification of the mind as the omnicompetent organ of shareable knowing and the corollary proposition that metaphysical objects of inquiry such as God cannot be known directly by the mind. Both envision a mission of salvage and rescue for the sake of achieving felt relevance. The only difference is that, for the emerging church, the audience targeted is not the modern but the postmodern world.

Yet what can be found relevant most readily and widely here and now may tell us next to nothing of what may be found relevant most profoundly and enduringly. Here the distinction between *felt* and *true* relevance comes to the fore and brings in its train the questions of truth and authority. And just here, modesty, joined with passion for evangelism and church planting, finds itself grateful for doctrine and dogma. That the left wing of the emerging church shares significant strategic and methodological instincts with Protestant liberalism becomes more apparent when we recall what lay at the very heart of liberalism's aim, especially as it grew on American soil. The ideal of liberal theology, as Gary Dorrien has succinctly put it, "is the idea that Christian theology can be genuinely Christian without being based upon external authority."[11] John Henry Newman understood his life's work as a protracted battle against liberalism, by which he meant "the anti-dogmatic principle and its development."[12] Doctrine-averse emerging churches recoil at authoritative dogmatic speech. In its place, they want more modesty, mystery, and conversation. Yet cannot the history and development of doctrine and of dogma to which the Nicene Creed belongs be rightly comprehended as the church's conversation with itself? It is a conversation *coram Deo* (before almighty God) about what it believes it has heard from God in the face of what strikes it as discordant voices. But that *coram Deo* makes all the difference, does it not? To the extent that the church is confident it has heard aright God's voice in Holy Scripture and that a discordant voice parades as truth, love, and loyalty to the living God as well as prudent self-preservation, the church is compelled to acknowledge and submit to the authority of the divine voice. The church across the ages knows itself to be answerable to the God before whom it engages in holy conversation. Emerging communities of faith that eschew doctrine and dogma need to ask themselves whether they have a word from God, and if so, in what way are they answerable to that voice.

At some level, antidogmatisms of many stripes, including what we observe in doctrine-averse emerging churches, for all their admirable and sincere resistance to arrogance and their quest for modesty, do nevertheless exhibit, albeit unwittingly, an unmistakable immodesty. This immodesty is the refusal to be told something, the refusal to admit to having heard something, and the refusal to be commanded and constrained. Might not the aversion to doctrine and so also to dogma mask a deeper aversion to authority as such? Thus, the rejection of dogma carries with it an incapacity for docility, a docility inherent within all genuine hearing and obeying of God's Word. So long as they remain answerable to nothing outside themselves, do they not fall prey to the idol making against which Calvin warned and that Feuerbach later described? What is the antidote to such reflexive idol making? Is it not the self-revelation of almighty God? And if so, how is such divine revelation accessed, comprehended, and applied? Will not modesty answer that this accessing, comprehending, and applying take place *within*—not without—the history of the church's listening together to the Word of God? Will it not occur within that consensual exegesis extended in time and space?

Doctrine and dogma deal with this revelation. The emerging church thinks itself open to all voices except modern ones, and indeed these ostensibly doctrineless emerging communities welcome and make use of many voices yet remain answerable to none. And one voice seems to be missing or least greatly muted among them—the voice of God.

Up to Their Necks in Doctrine

I have just designated these doctrine-averse emerging voices as ostensibly doctrineless, and I now want to explore my use of that word *ostensibly*. Of course from one standpoint, these communities of faith are indeed without doctrine. No formal adoption of or subscription to actual articulated doctrines prevails among them. Yet does this fact alone justify their perception of themselves as doctrine-free?

Two anecdotes will help to illuminate my interest in this matter. In 1979, a protracted battle among Southern Baptists over the nature and authority of the Bible ensued in earnest. The consequences of that struggle continue to reverberate among Baptists today. During the mid-1980s the two sides locked in dispute came to be characterized in various ways, most commonly as the fundamentalist/conservatives on the right and the moderate/liberals on the left. But another characterization also gained significant acceptance, especially among moderates who thought of themselves as the freedom party in dispute with fundamentalists who loved doctrine at the expense of the Baptist birthright: freedom of the conscience before God. But then, in the midst of the titanic struggle among Southern Baptists, liberal Baptist and scholar Nancy Ammerman published a major examination of the controversy in which she acknowledged that liberal and moderate Baptists also held to strong beliefs. Moderates and liberals too held to convictions and, as matters of conviction, would not knowingly hire Baptists who could not affirm a hefty chunk of those convictions to serve in the institutions over which they, the moderates and liberals, held sway.[13]

Such an acknowledgment amounted to a sea change in perception of what was happening within the Southern Baptist Convention. If Ammerman was correct, then perhaps moderates and liberals did not occupy a pristine doctrine-less perch from which to observe and chastise the fundamentalists, who were ostensibly confined within narrow and narrowing ideological ghettoes where indoctrination reigns and where neither thinking nor freedom can flourish. Instead, if Ammerman was to be believed, the liberals and moderates were motivated by conviction too. The liberals were actually slogging around in the nastiness of the doctrinal muck with the conservatives. Conversations between those who know themselves to be ideological, convictional, shaped, and motivated by doctrine take on quite a different, more realistic, and more honest tone than conversations in which one side only acknowledges this reality.

Anecdote number two: Many emerging churches employ a dialogical form of worship, which provides time for congregants to ask questions and to receive and discuss answers provided during the sermon. I asked a respected, effective pastor of one of these churches what would happen if, on successive weeks, someone openly and strongly challenged or contradicted him during one of these dialogical episodes. "Give me an example," he said. "Okay," I replied. "Let's say on the first week, your notion of community was contradicted from the floor. Week two, the use of narrative approaches to Scripture and your use of the word 'story' were questioned. Week three, the contradiction was about the way in which you highlight mystery and the arts. Week four, it was your convictions about culture and postmodernism and so on." "Oh," he responded. "That would not be welcome. That would be disruptive." "So are not these your doctrines?" I asked. "Do not these nonnegotiable convictions, which shape your preaching and which you intend to shape this community of faith, function like doctrines among you? Would it not be helpful and more honest to acknowledge this? Then we could face and clearly explore what is already true: that our conversation at some level, as well as our goals for the communities of faith we plant and nature, is about doctrine."

Is it not the case that anything recognizable as Christian community is shaped by convictions that cry out for open doctrinal articulation? An enormous burst of light can be shed on conversations between Christians who hold different views once the imagined possibility of a doctrineless Christianity is exposed as a fantasy. A bracing, clarifying, and potentially quite comforting effect can follow the stark realization that we are all necessarily and inescapably up to our necks in doctrine. If that is so, how quickly or strongly or confidently should we wish to dissociate ourselves from (and much less flee from) a creed such as the Nicene Creed that has been affirmed repeatedly across time and geography? And what would such a course have to do with modesty? Then the next question can come to the fore: by what authority do we hold those convictions that already function as doctrines among us and perhaps even as settled dogma among us? And if that authority does not reside outside of us, how do we hope to escape the specter of Feuerbachian idol making?

But if the left wing of the emerging church recognizes itself as already inextricably up to its neck in doctrine, much could be said in an attempt to rehabilitate doctrine in its eyes. Doctrine and dogma have been viewed as the enemies of several of the doctrinelike convictions or values that characterize emerging church aspiration related to culture, authenticity, mystery, modesty, and community. Doctrine and dogma have been the protectors, nurturers, and purveyors of the values and convictions underlying these terms, and they could be put to use by a historically humbled and informed emerging church.

Community and Conviction

This seems especially so when we consider how important authentic community is to the emerging church. While interest in culture dominates much of the conversation within the emerging church, seriousness about culture matters to them because they believe culture profoundly affects their efforts to plant churches where they want to experience what they call variously *community*, *authentic community*, and *organic community*. But whether we or they like it or not, or recognize it or not, the depth of fellowship, of relationship—indeed, the depth of the quality of what we tend to mean by *community*—is, at a constitutive level, dependent upon shared conviction, especially conviction about the things that matter most to us.

It is true that the quality of community characterized by healthy and authentic relationships is not reducible to shared conviction or shared doctrine. In fact, one mark of authentic Christian community is the ability to tolerate diverse opinions about matters of secondary and tertiary importance within the body of Christ. The same apostle Paul who could invite the disturbers of the Galatians to castrate themselves (Gal. 5:12) and then declare these same folk "anathema" (Gal. 1:9 ASV) could also "go soft," if you will, in Romans 14. Do you recall that passage? You have at least two feuds up and running: one between the carnivores and the herbivores, and one between the sabbatarians and the nonsabbatarians. Is it not fascinating that Paul does not advise a period of study and prayer, at the end of which the church would discern which side God is on in the two disputes? Rather, each person is to do what his own conscience dictates and then—and here's the more difficult part—not look down on the one with whom they differ.

In light of Romans and Galatians, a profound and fearful burden falls to leaders of God's flocks on earth: discerning which matters belong in the Galatian hopper and which belong in the Roman hopper. What an awesome responsibility. But what a help it is to know that from the beginning, God intended that this ferreting out of primary, secondary, and tertiary matters would be the common and ongoing responsibility of the church. It is hard to imagine a more ready-to-hand set of tools and guides for this task than the tradition of the church, especially the history of doctrine, and, even more especially, the history of creeds and confessions, and—even *more* especially— the Niceno-Constantinopolitan Creed itself. In each of these we have to deal with, among other things, the church's long struggle to accomplish just this task. And the urgency of this task attaches to perhaps the core value of the left wing of the emerging church: the yearning for authentic community within the body of Christ, in which differences on some doctrines should and will over time divide us but in which other doctrines must not.

But the left wing of the emerging church wants to do without that primary doctrine hopper altogether, and that is just not possible where anything historically recognizable as Christianity can flourish. This ill-fated attempt to opt out of doctrinal Christianity is also impossible where any deep, enduring community is flourishing, because, at some constitutive relational level, the depth of sustainable fellowship between human beings is proportionate to shared conviction.

You may ask me how things stand between my next-door neighbors and my family. And I may answer honestly that things are just peachy keen. We have no problem with our neighbors whatsoever. In fact, we have borrowed from one another everything from cups of sugar to lawn mowers and snow shovels. But as soon as we find out that the next-door neighbors like to crucify cats over a pyre on Saturday nights, we order our children to stay clear of that property, and we might just approach the neighbors on the other side the next time we run low on any condiment. "Familiarity breeds contempt" did not achieve cliché status for nothing. And the same kind of community-destroying convictions and practices exist wherever the pursuit of authentic relationship is attempted, especially within the church. Prudent development and employment of doctrine proves to be a necessary tool where successful negotiation of this treacherous relational terrain is achieved.

With Only Nicea

For a variety of reasons, some emerging churches, while wary of doctrine, have subscribed to either the Apostles' Creed or the Nicene Creed or both. Such subscription may not indicate a sudden burst of attraction to doctrine or even a strong felt need related to the community's identity or purpose. One growing community of faith embraced both of these ancient creeds five years after its founding. But like many other such communities, the motivation for doing so was not so much a new love for doctrine as it was an attempt to pacify those who demand to know what they believe.

For some of these congregations, however, the step into confessional Christianity does reflect an acknowledgment (often the fruit of engagement with the Christian tradition) that followers of the way of Jesus have always and must now concern themselves not only with doing but also with believing. Once this new and unexpected acknowledgment takes root, it usually leads to formal subscription to some doctrinal formulation, typically the Apostles' Creed, the Nicene Creed, or both. And where this occurs, conflict with communities of faith with comparatively more doctrinal awareness sometimes arises because, as David Wells has described it, many evangelicals, while not dispensing with their fully orbed confessions of faith, have marginalized and neglected those doctrinal instruments.[14] Less and less does the formal confessional stance of these congregations inform and shape their mission, their preaching, and their life together.

Nevertheless, alertness to the dangers posed by doctrine continues to inform the emerging church ethos. The intention and expectation of the leaders of these congregations is that no expansion of the new formal confessional stance should occur. "Enough is enough" fairly expresses the sentiment of those who have made the transition from doctrine-averse and doctrineless postures to merely doctrine-wary communities of faith.

So how should we assess such attempts by the church to emerge with *only* the Nicene Creed? First of all, we can welcome the taking on of the Apostles' or the Nicene Creed by some of these congregations. Such wary embrace of a measure of doctrinal identity into the ecclesial psyche could prove to be the proverbial "camel's head under the tent" kind of thing—almost as dangerous, in a fortuitous way, as handing a sinner a Bible. Even such a wary embrace can function like a time bomb that may eventually explode into a dazzling and spectacular confrontation with and embrace of doctrinal Christianity.

But is the Nicene Creed really enough? Over time, especially where lay believers have read and are encouraged to read their own Bibles as the holy, authoritative Word of almighty God, as the *norma normans* of faith and practice for the body of Christ, can the Nicene Creed provide a sufficient basis for enduring fellowship, especially when it comes to the broad question of the redeeming work of God in Jesus Christ and the narrower question of the atonement?

Given the prominence and the amount of ink spilled in Holy Scripture with regard to the question, "What did God achieve in Jesus Christ by means of the incarnation and, especially, what was accomplished on the cross of Calvary?," does the Nicene Creed say enough? Does not the history of the church in the West suggest that the answer is no?

We should, however, give credit where credit is due. Nicea is not silent here. "For us and for our salvation he came down from heaven." "For our sake he was crucified under Pontius Pilate." This is *not* nothing! Indeed, it is far from nothing! But if more had been articulated or subsequently added, could Nicea have achieved such enduring and universal subscription across these sixteen some centuries? Almost certainly not. But I suspect that this tells us little regarding the clarity achievable by the church on these questions or the status a clearer comprehension of these matters deserves. As Protestants at least, do we not confront here the article by which the church stands or falls?

What about expiation, propitiation, and substitution? What about a whole cluster of terms meant to comprehend the so-called *Christus Victor* dimension of the work of Jesus Christ who takes on and defeats sin, death, hell, and the devil in a dramatic rescue of sinners?[15] Does the language of Nicea do enough to prevent that unbiblical, pernicious instinct by heretics across the millennia to reduce the atoning work of Jesus Christ to moral influence notions or other varieties of subjective or exemplarist construal of the redeeming work of God in Jesus Christ? Does it do enough to insist upon comprehension of the atonement in objective terms, in which God in Jesus Christ, through the incarnation and especially on the cross, saves us sinners, without our help, in the face of our opposition? While we were his enemies, while we were sinners, Christ died. I think the answer has to be no.

Once again, doctrine-wary emerging church voices tend to harmonize with the voices of Protestant liberals in significant ways. Steve Chalke notoriously characterized the doctrine of the vicarious substitutionary atonement as a case of cosmic child abuse.[16] Such an assessment corresponds nicely with the more elaborate reinterpretation of the atonement by the father of American liberal theology, Horace Bushnell, who also judged substitutionary atonement to be a morally repugnant doctrine.[17] Like Bushnell and Protestant liberalism, generally, the left wing of the emerging church has increasingly construed the atonement largely in terms of moral influence and rejected objective views of the atonement. More to the point is the fact that doctrine-wary emerging

churches prefer to avoid formal doctrinal articulation on the atonement altogether. Even where radical statements, such as Chalke's, are avoided, zeal
for the doctrine of the atonement proves difficult to find in the left wing of
the emerging church.

The emerging church's wariness of doctrine and of objective understanding of the atonement displays significant affinities and continuities with the
earliest and most spectacular source of Protestant liberalism. Skittishness
with regard to the atonement belongs to the original impulse of Protestant
liberalism. Let us be reminded that the religious shaping of Friederich Daniel
Ernst Schleiermacher occurred in the cradle of an impressive pietistic Moravian community of faith.[18] There among the Moravians, strong exemplars
of doctrinal latitudinarianism, Schleiermacher became convinced that he
achieved what was essential to Moravian identity within the church, not only
without embracing their minimalist doctrinal demands but while positively
doubting these demands. It would be difficult to exaggerate the importance
of that conviction of Schleiermacher in any attempt to understand the history
of the church in the West, stretching from Schleiermacher's death in 1834 to
this very day.

And what were the minimalist nonnegotiables of the Moravian community
of faith that Schleiermacher, try as he might, could not affirm? They included
a heartfelt confession of "Jesus in my heart" and the vicarious substitutionary
atonement of Jesus Christ on the cross.

But might not caution and hesitance where atonement issues are concerned
reflect a kind of studied wisdom born of careful historical reflection? Is it
not, after all, around the controverted issues of "things soteriological" that
the theological knives tend to come out? Where might studied caution and
strategic modesty prove more prudent where the quest for Christian unity is
concerned than here, in the doctrinal thicket that has characterized the doctrine
of salvation? As Jaroslav Pelikan observed, "The most surprising historical
instance of the distinction between what became Dogma and what did not is
the contrast between the doctrine of the incarnation and the doctrine of the
atonement or redemption through the work of Christ."[19] After all, the failure of
the doctrine of the atonement to achieve the status of dogma lies at the heart
of the division of Western Christianity. Yet I would suggest that attempts to
purchase a more robust and more global Christian group hug at the price of
an ambiguous or more muted articulation of the doctrine of the atonement
must push up against a formidable foe—the content of Holy Scripture.

Does the havoc wreaked in the body of Christ over soteriological issues
reflect clear-eyed recognition of the prominence given to the doctrine of
salvation in the Bible, or does it represent the intrusion of a marginal issue
into the center of Christian reflection? That the doctrines of the incarnation,
the person of Christ, and the Trinity could achieve the status of dogma provides cause for rejoicing indeed, but I doubt that it tells us much about the

comparative legitimacy of the claim the doctrine of the atonement makes to such status.

Does not the church typically achieve increased clarity and confidence regarding particular doctrines when it is compelled to, usually by influential teachers later identified as heretics? The long train of false teaching associated with the names Arius, Appolinarius, Nestorius, and Eutychus reminds us that the development of doctrine and the need for creed has been spurred along not so much by an abstract or ahistorical assessment of which doctrines are most important, but rather by which doctrines come under assault. Out of the crucible of clashes between orthodox and heterodox teaching, the church often gains clarity and confidence in relation to the controverted doctrines. Thus, controversy serves the church by clarifying and also deepening its confession.

Yet engagement with the plethora of issues attaching to the redemption wrought in the work of Jesus Christ, far from yielding a doctrinal formulation to bind believers in global and historic consensus, has seemingly had the opposite effect. Where Nicea articulates ancient and deep consensus, Trent and Westminster represent entrenched, long-standing opposition and stalemate.

In such a circumstance, the promise and appeal of a "mere Christianity" that either sidesteps, mutes, or stays silent with respect to the heart of the doctrine of salvation seem obvious. But can the church really emerge with only the Nicene Creed? Why cannot the same considered modesty of Christian confession, which should mute the voices and relax protruding neck veins about the intricacies of eschatology or the most obscure dimensions of the relationship between human responsibility and divine sovereignty, also extend to this question: just what was the Triune God in Jesus Christ up to at Golgotha? And just how do sinners come to benefit from what was done there? Are we less confronted with mystery here than in the doctrines of the Trinity or the person of Christ? No. Not at all. Both in the incarnation and at Calvary, we not only confront mystery as profound and inexhaustible as that met with in the doctrines of God and Christ; we also confront divine activity and revelation no less central and no less essential to believing and confessing than we do in the doctrines confessed in the Nicene Creed.

For good reason then, the church has felt no less compelled to formal doctrinal articulation of the soteriological mysteries than of the mysteries attaching to Christology and theology proper. That historic and global consensus where the atonement is concerned continues to elude the church, at least compared to that achieved on the doctrines of God and Christ, may well commend a certain modesty or encourage an ongoing teachableness regarding the doctrine of the atonement. But this same elusiveness, however regrettable or inconvenient, ought not to justify a shirking of confessional responsibility where the saving work of God in Jesus Christ is concerned. What might parade and congratulate itself as unity-seeking modesty or mystery-acknowledging ecumenism too often turns out be irresponsible failure of theological nerve. The same compulsion to confess formally and doctrinally what the church knows where God and the person of Jesus Christ were concerned also accounts for the central place given in the confessional history of the church to the question, What happened on the cross? Surely the source of that compulsion cannot be in doubt: it is the revelation of God in Holy Scripture. The Bible is the whistleblower on those who would relegate the doctrine of salvation generally or the doctrine of the atonement specifically to a confessional status below that rightly commanded by the doctrines of the Trinity and of the person of Jesus Christ. The church across the ages may have failed to reach consensus, but make no mistake, this must be acknowledged as a real failure, not as the inevitable confessional limitations endemic to matters taught but left largely unexplicated in Holy Scripture, as might be justly claimed for other teachings which are then given secondary or nonessential status within the believing community.

Whoever wishes to inoculate the Christian community against intense concern and potential upset over soteriological matters, including the atonement, would do well to play down reverent, trusting study of and meditation on the Holy Scriptures by lay Christians. Wherever a robust doctrine of the authority of the Bible takes hold, the question "What happened on the cross?" and its corollary "What is the gospel?" will animate the community of believers. Not only will these questions engage believers every bit as much as questions about who God is and who Jesus is, they will rightly take their place beside them and even, in some sense, above or at least beyond them. That Western Christianity on the Roman Catholic and Protestant sides could not and do not restrain their compulsion to believe and confess on these matters has been appropriate to the essential nature of the atonement and the larger question of redemption achieved in and by Jesus Christ. In short, where the Bible is acknowledged as the authoritative and sufficient Word of God, doctrinal articulation on the atonement and redemption will arise out of the same ancient will to believe and the need for creed that resulted in the Niceno-Constantinopolitan Creed.

A reminder of the proper and peculiar function of the term *Christian mysteries* can help us here. The apostle Paul spoke of mysteries not as that about which we can say nothing, but precisely as that about which we once could say nothing but that now, confronted with God's self-revelation, we may and must speak. *Mystery* for Paul was "open secret." The acknowledgment and confession of Christian mysteries is provoked by the gaining of knowledge, not by the admission of either ambiguities or doubts. Confession of the mystery of the Trinity and of the relation between divinity and humanity in Jesus Christ involves first of all the identification of the mystery, of the occurrence and reception of revelation—both that God *is* three and one and that Jesus Christ *is* both divine and human. The confession is that we are not in ignorance and thus we are capable of confession as the grateful receptors of knowledge: inexhaustible knowledge that is too high for us and that consists not only of effable but also ineffable dimensions. But even here—perhaps especially here—we are receptors of knowledge nonetheless.

A constitutive dimension of the church's task, and the task of every minister of the Word who dares to answer God's call to preach the gospel, is the attempt, especially where nonnegotiable articles of faith are concerned, not to go beyond what is written but also not to fall short of what the Bible makes clear. Here, and wherever the Nicene Creed is pressed to provide a sufficient summary of orthodox evangelical doctrine, the doctrine-wary stream of the emerging church is placing a burden on that creed beyond what it can bear.

15

Life after Life after Death

A Sermon on the Final Phrase of the Nicene Creed

❦

Ralph C. Wood

And in the life of the world to come.
Revelation 21:1–8

Hell as False Life in the City of the Dead

Death everlasting is nowhere mentioned in any of the ecumenical Christian creeds, nor has the church ever declared anyone to be definitively damned: not even Judas, Stalin, Hitler, Mao, or Pol Pot, nor those who incinerated Hiroshima and Nagasaki and Dresden. Hell and damnation are not articles of Christian belief. In the strict sense, we do not even *believe* in the devil. While we indeed affirm *Credo in Deum*, we do not declare *Credo in diabolum*. To believe in Satan would credit him with real existence, when in fact he is a great nothing, a zero, a nullity, the utter absence of being. Yet exactly because he is nothing, he can assume myriad false forms, thereby doing his demonic work by deceptive appearances.

The Christian refusal to make definitive claims about death in the world to come is not a sign of cowardice, much less of false comfort. The authors of

196

the Nicene Creed were as certain about the devil and hell as was the Scottish preacher who was once asked a question intended to trap him. It concerned the biblical claim that "there shall be weeping and wailing and gnashing of teeth." How would such punishment apply, the preacher was asked, to those many hellish souls who die without teeth? "Teeth will be provided," the Scotsman answered. So did the Alabama Baptist rightly reply to the Unitarian who declared that there ain't no hell. "The hell there ain't," replied the Baptist.

Yet even the teeth-providing Scot and the hell-certain Alabamian must have known not to grant hell either primacy or ultimacy in making our Christian witness. The gospel is first and last God's great yes. God's thunderous no must surely be spoken, but only on behalf of his infinitely greater yes as it is uttered in Israel and Christ and the church. The good news would not be "tidings of comfort and joy" if it were concentrated on the bad news of death in the world to come.

Yet we Christians have not been immune from centering our work on hell, as if the main reason for being a follower of Christ were to flee the wrath to come. I once saw a slogan on the signboard of a church in Bessemer, Alabama, that stated this perversion with cold candor. "We sell fire insurance," this Baptist congregation unapologetically declared. The "Turn or burn" slogan does similar damage. However well intended, such catchphrases enable many people to dismiss the doctrine of life everlasting. These clever caveats about hell transfer our attention from living faithfully in this world to living fearfully about the next world. Our pagan friends and enemies want empirical evidence for such otherworldly fears and hopes, and we Christians are often unable to give them any satisfactory answer except to roll our eyes to the skies and utter pious predictions about the afterlife.

Thus, the presence of ever more defiantly pagan mottoes should not surprise us. Consider this one: "Living well is the best revenge." The best way to strike back at the hardships of life is to live luxuriantly. The ancient Roman motto *Carpe diem* (Seize the day) also has a new currency. "This is not a dress rehearsal" is a similar slogan. Earthly life and its hedonic pleasures are quite sufficient for many self-satisfied souls: they are preparing for no life in the world to come. For them, the only drama concerns *this* world. "We work hard all week," these brazen new pagans declare, "in order to party hard all weekend. We do not want to be burdened with wives or husbands and children and grandchildren. We do not want to live sacrificially in order to end up as just a bunch of grumpy old folks. We want to enjoy life while we can." Our new pagans are right without knowing it. We are not participating in a dress rehearsal. We are enacting our roles—whether ill or well—in God's cosmic drama. It began with the creation and will end in the consummation. Not to play our part in the divine theatricals is to become mere creatures of play, as we turn into lonely old men and women, cut off from family and friends and the church, dwelling in the solitude of our own little hell.

This is the perilous state of living death that we must discern in ourselves no less than our pagan neighbors. Walker Percy depicts such death in his apocalyptic novel of 1971, *Love in the Ruins*. In one of the book's most frightening scenes, Rinaldo Smith, the parish priest of a small band of faithful Catholics living near the end of the world, rises to the pulpit for his weekly homily. Suddenly, Father Smith falls silent. The prolonged hush discomfits his parishioners, as they cough and shift in their pews. "Excuse me," he says at last, "but the channels are jammed and the message is not getting through." Father Smith is remanded, of course, to a psychiatric hospital where he is attended by Dr. Max Gottlieb, a Jewish physician who is completely oblivious to the significance of his splendid name (God-love). When Gottlieb asks Smith what went wrong, the priest explains: "They've won and we've lost." The psychiatrist is still befuddled by the priest's answer. "Death is winning," repeats Father Smith; "life is losing."

It is evident that the priest's verbal blockage was not caused by a short circuit in the church's PA system or by a nervous collapse. This faithful man of God was telling the terrible truth. He was referring to the principalities and powers of the air, to wickedness in high places, to the demons that have clogged and stifled our spiritual atmosphere. They are thwarting the gospel of life everlasting, replacing it with the culture of death unending. "I am surrounded by the corpses of souls," Father Smith concludes, in perhaps the novel's darkest pronouncement. "We live in a city of the dead." He is referring not to New Orleans or Birmingham but to the moribund condition of our entire culture. Already in the fourth century, St. Athanasius warned against such an extinction of people's souls. We can destroy the divine image in which we are made, he taught, returning to the nothingness from which we came. We can become what C. S. Lewis calls "trousered apes." Worse still, we can become devils.

Heaven as True Life after Life after Death

More than any other contemporary theologian known to me, N. T. Wright has called us to a right doctrine of heaven. The Anglican bishop of Durham claims that we misunderstand the final phrase of the Nicene Creed if we view it as a strictly post-earthly affair—as if the life of the world to come were a paradisal existence that begins only beyond the grave. Wright is being thoroughly biblical when he claims that we are *already* living "the life after death." Once we were dead in sins and trespasses, declares St. Paul, but in Christ we have been made a new creation. In our baptism, we have already died to sin, been buried with Christ, and thus have risen with him to newness of life. Hence, Wright's insistence that we adopt a new and more accurate phrase to define the life of the world to come: we should call it *life after life after death*.

The most fundamental Christian claim is that we already inhabit the New Aeon. "The kingdom is in your midst," declares our Lord. We are awaiting its consummation, not its beginning. "The battle is o'er, the victory won," we sing in the splendid Easter hymn.[1] Satan is already checkmated, declares Karl Barth. The prince of this world is making his last desperate moves, and they are terrible maneuvers indeed—more people having been killed by violent means in the twentieth century than in all previous centuries combined. Even so, these futile, final tactics to bar the gates of hell shall not prevail against the coming of Christ's kingdom to set the captives free. It is as if the clock of time had finally wound down, as if its last tick had been struck, though its pendulum continues to swing a few bootless strokes before coming to its final halt. We are the bearers of this unbearably good news, and thus privileged to live and move and have our being in this life everlasting that has already begun on earth. A Methodist friend explains John Wesley's passion for evangelism exactly in these terms: Wesley was afire with the desire to get people into heaven, but only if he could first get heaven into them—and, I would add, to get the hell out. Hence, Wesley's stress on what the Eastern church calls *theosis*: our ever-increasing participation in God's own life, as we grow more fully human and more fully divine.

C. S. Lewis probes this hard truth in *The Great Divorce*. There he envisions everyone as having already embarked on one of two paths, either the hellish or the heavenly. Our every thought, word, and deed advances us along one of these tracks. Yet note well that Lewis is no dualist. He does not place these two destinies over against each other as if they were equal. On the contrary, this is the false teaching I once heard articulated by a radio preacher: "God has cast a vote for you," said the well-intentioned Bible-banger, "and the devil has cast a vote against you. Now it's up to you to break the tie." There are at least a dozen heresies lurking unwittingly in these two sentences. Lewis avoids them all by observing that everyone whose life pilgrimage is cast toward paradise is becoming ever more real, ever more dense and solid, ever more fully conformed to the likeness of God. Our already experienced "life after death" will thus be magnified on an unimaginable scale at the final judgment, when we shall hear the words, "Well done, my good and faithful servants. Enter your true country."

Lewis also tells the truth about those who are venturing down the path toward perdition. The enormous sadness of their fate is not that they face horrific physical pain so much as they face a far more appalling spiritual torment. They are becoming ever thinner and gossamer-like, ever more distanced from their neighbors, ever more isolated and alone, ever less real, ever more unreal. What they await, therefore, is what they are already experiencing: the utter absence of life, the pain of absolute loss. To adapt N. T. Wright: they are headed for death after death after life.

This is not to say that there can be no turning back, of course. To reverse course once we have embarked on the route to redemption is to revert to the former things, to return to the fleshpots of American bondage, like a hog to its husks and a dog to its vomit. It is to join Milton's fallen angels and to "find no end" but to "wander in mazes lost."[2] It is to declare unto the Lord God himself: "Leave me alone." And so, alas, God may heed our hellish wish. To do an about-face on the road to doom, by contrast, is to be converted, much like Paul on the road to Damascus, and thus to enter life after death.

This radical reversal is the real interest of the opening lines of Revelation 21. The heart of these first eight verses lies in the shout uttered by the Lamb who rules from his throne: "Behold, I am making all things new. . . . It is done!" (Rev. 21:5–6). Why does Christ repeat his final cry from the cross: "It is finished!"? Because he has finally conquered the final enemy, death. We must understand that, biblically speaking, death is not merely our mortality—the fact that we will all die—but something infinitely worse: it is the dreaded penalty for sin, the anguished tears of guilt, the emblem of sin and shame. The fear of death, not the fear of hell, is what makes people commit the most egregious evils. All of our substitutes for trust in God are attempts to fend off death. Whether in seeking greater power or status or possessions, whether among nations or in persons, death is the great enemy because it makes us do wicked things. Christ cries out, therefore, "It is done!" He has robbed the grave of its power to make us do desperate things. By death, Jesus has "done down death," as the liturgy of the Eastern Orthodox churches so finely proclaims.

The contemporary jingle admonishing us to "Turn or burn" gets things exactly backward. It should read, "Turn *and* burn." Christ calls us to a *lifelong* conversion that burns us clean of sin. Only then do we dare speak of our deliverance from the inferno and thus dare to hope for life everlasting. The third-century Roman saint named Lawrence had been purified by fire, and it gave him a witty approach to his martyrdom. Legend has it that after lying for several minutes on the burning gridiron, he declared, "This side's done; turn me over and have a bite."[3] No wonder that he is the patron saint of comedians.

On the morning of April 9, 1945, less than a month before World War II ended, the resident physician at the Flossenburg concentration camp witnessed Dietrich Bonhoeffer kneeling in fervent prayer just before his execution. Earlier, Bonhoeffer had written that to whomever God is "real and ever close," death is a "station on the road to freedom." It can even be called "the highest feast." Hence Bonhoeffer's final words to his fellow prisoners: "This is the end—for me the beginning of life."[4] The saintly German martyr was not disdaining his earthly life but announcing his entry into the life of the world to come. Having made his courageous Christian witness via the life after death, Bonhoeffer longed for the face of God, there to find his own faith finished and made perfect in the life after life after death.

Our humble ancestors of the Bible Belt, both black and white, often hymned heaven better than they preached it. Their great gospel song about *already* "dwelling in Beulah Land"[5] is not an instance of sentimental escapism. That "the way of the cross leads home" is not the hope of cowardly Christians refusing to deal with the horrors of this world in exchange for a "payday someday." "I am a poor wayfaring stranger" is a poignant confession of what it costs to pass through "this world of woe." "Deep River" hauntingly invites us to cross over Jordan and to enter "campground." "We're Marching to Zion" summons us to stride confidently through Emmanuel's ground because it is Christ's *already* conquered territory. Everlasting life has *already* begun.

Let us too march into the New Jerusalem, embracing Christ's call in this present life after death, so that we shall enter the eternal life after life after death. Amen.

16

Delighted by Doctrine

A Tribute to Jaroslav Pelikan

TIMOTHY GEORGE

Historian Jaroslav Pelikan (1923–2006) thought theology was too important to be left to the theologians.[1] When Pelikan died at age eighty-two on May 13, 2006, the world of Christian scholarship lost its greatest living advocate and the best church historian America has ever produced. Words like *greatest* and *best* are frequently used in a loose manner simply to say something nice about someone—but in the case of Jary, as his friends called him, they are really true.

The achievements of his life are remarkable: he wrote nearly forty books and over a dozen reference works on numerous aspects of Christian history. He taught several generations of students at Valparaiso University, Concordia Theological Seminary, the University of Chicago, and, since 1962, Yale University. He served as dean of the Graduate School at Yale and was also president of the American Academy of Arts and Sciences. He received the Jefferson Award of the National Endowment for the Humanities in 1983 and the John Kluge Prize for Lifetime Achievements in the Human Sciences in 2004. He presented the Gifford Lectures at the University of Aberdeen, and the Gilson Lectures at the University of Toronto, and was awarded honorary degrees from forty-two universities around the world.

Many other accomplishments could be listed, but accomplishments alone do not reveal the deepest passion of his soul: to tell the story of the Christian tradition in all of its fullness, drama, coherence, romance, and rigor, thereby exposing the deepest textures of meaning inherent in the Christian message itself.

A Slavic Heritage

Pelikan loved to quote this line from Goethe, his favorite poet: "What you have received as heritage, take now as task and thus you will make it your own." Pelikan's remarkable scholarly career was rooted in his Slavic family background. Both of his parents were born in Europe. Both his father and grandfather were Lutheran pastors. His mother was a schoolteacher who learned English by reading the essays of Emerson. They bequeathed to young Jary both a love for learning and a desire for God.

When he was a little boy and could not quite reach the dinner table, his parents had him sit on stacked-up volumes of Migne's *Patrologia*, a collection of patristic writings in the original languages. He later quipped, "I thus absorbed the church fathers *a posteriori*!" His facility with languages was astounding—not only the classical tongues of Greek, Latin, and Hebrew, but also German, Slovak, Czech, Dutch, Russian, Serbian, all the romance languages, and many more. On occasion he would stay up late at night listening to a shortwave radio to keep fresh his language skills—including Albanian, which he once found useful in a conversation with a taxi driver. Pelikan's deep religious faith was nurtured on Luther's Small Catechism, the great chorales of J. S. Bach, and, above all, the Bible. Each of these—Luther, Bach, and the Bible—would play a major role in his scholarly work. Though he became an ordained Lutheran minister, Pelikan spent most of his life in the environs of the secular academy. But he never lost the rich faith he received as a small child. As he once confessed, "I was quite out of step with many in my generation, especially among theological scholars at universities, in never having had fundamental doubts about the essential rightness of the Christian faith, but having retained a continuing, if often quite unsophisticated, Slavic piety."[2]

The Grand Scope of Tradition

A precocious young Pelikan received both his seminary degree and a PhD from the University of Chicago in 1946 at age twenty-two. His first book, *From Luther to Kierkegaard*, came out a few years later (1950). Soon Pelikan established himself as one of the most prolific Luther scholars of his generation. He was general editor for the fifty-five-volume American Edition of *Luther's Works*, and he wrote a separate volume on Luther's biblical exposition. Pelikan always had a great interest in ecumenical affairs. His book *The Riddle of Roman Catholicism* (1959), written on the eve of the Second Vatican Council, offered an irenic introduction to the world's largest Christian community.

It is said that Karl Barth drew up a plan for his "collected works" at age ten. Similarly, Pelikan had a clear, detailed plan of what he called his "big book" early in his career. He would write a comprehensive history of Christian doctrine, an account of what "the church of Jesus Christ has believed, taught, and confessed on the basis of the word of God."

Only Adolf Harnack, the great scion of German liberal Protestantism, had attempted such a massive project, with his three-volume *History of Dogma*. Harnack, however, for all his erudition, had little sympathy with the doctrinal content of his subject and presented a version of Christianity freed from the dogmatic shackles of the past. Pelikan, working with the same historical rigor, approached his subject with much more sympathy. As he put it, "I found, not in theological liberalism and historical relativism (as so many of my predecessors, teachers, contemporaries did) but in tradition and orthodoxy, the presupposition from which to interpret any portion or period."

Pelikan's magnum opus eventually became five volumes that he called simply *The Christian Tradition*. Though Pelikan fully recognized the great diversity and varied expressions of Christian teaching across the ages, he also stressed the underlying unity and continuity of what the New Testament calls "the faith that was once for all delivered to the saints" (Jude 3).

Jesus on Safari

As a capstone to his lifelong interest in the central texts of the Christian faith, Pelikan edited (with Valerie Hotchkiss) what could only be called a second magnum opus—*Creeds and Confessions of Faith in the Christian Tradition*, a four-volume critical edition with a one-volume historical and theological guide called simply *Credo*.

Judaism has its Shema, and Islam its Shahadah, but Christians, responding to Jesus's question "Who do you say that I am?" (Mark 8:29) have produced literally thousands of statements of faith across the centuries. Pelikan's collection includes several hundred of these, among them the Masai Creed from East Africa. This creed Africanizes Christianity by declaring that Jesus "was always on safari doing good."[3] It also declares that after Jesus had been "tortured and nailed hands and feet to a cross, and died, he lay buried in the grave, but the hyenas did not touch him, and on the third day, he rose from the grave. He ascended unto the skies. He is the Lord."[4]

This creed was brought to Pelikan's attention by one of his students, a woman who had been a member of a religious order working in a hospital in East Africa. Pelikan commented on his reaction to this text: "And so she brought it to me, and I just got shivers, just the thought, you know, the hyenas did not touch him and the act of defiance—God lives even in spite of the hyenas."[5]

Living Faith

Pelikan dealt with many deep and difficult subjects in his scholarly work, but he wrote in a simple, elegant style and with a clarity that is compelling. He had a way of capturing profound truths in short, unforgettable statements. Among his most memorable are these: "Jesus Christ is too important to be left to the theologians"; "Everybody else is an expert on the present. I wish to file a minority report on behalf of the past"; and "Tradition is the living faith of the dead; traditionalism is the dead faith of the living."[6] Though he never quite matched the popular appeal of his Yale predecessor, Roland H. Bainton, some of Pelikan's books did reach a wider audience, including his *Jesus through the Centuries: His Place in the History of Culture* and *Whose Bible Is It? A Short History of the Scriptures*.

On March 25, 1998, the Feast Day of the Annunciation to the Blessed Virgin Mary, Pelikan and his wife, Sylvia, were received into the fellowship of the Orthodox Church in America. Pelikan remarked that while some might have been shocked by his act, few who knew him well could have been surprised. As he put it, "Any airplane that circled the airport for that long before landing would have run out of gas!" Indeed, Pelikan's tilt toward the East can be traced back to his Slavic roots, his love for the Eastern liturgy, his close friendship with the Orthodox theologian Georges Florovsky, and the sheer joy that permeates the pages of *The Spirit of Eastern Christendom*, the second volume of his history of doctrine. He spent the last years of his life serving on the board of trustees of St. Vladimir's Orthodox Theological Seminary.

I never had Jaroslav Pelikan as a classroom teacher, but I was one of his students, as everyone seriously interested in Christian history has to be. As a young student of historical theology, I once determined to read everything Pelikan had written. It is a daunting task, let me assure you: a 1995 bibliography of his works, which does not include his last prolific decade, runs to some fifty printed pages. He was a generous colleague and friend and a great encourager.

Pelikan thrived in the world of the arts and sciences and wrote learnedly about art, politics, law, poetry, educational theory, and public ethics, as well as history and theology. But he did all of this as a scholar who was also a Christian. Jary Pelikan had a love for all things human and humane, and his work will enrich every person who looks at the world with intellectual curiosity and moral imagination. But his legacy will shine especially brightly among those who follow Jesus Christ, belong to his church, and see the world through the eyes of the Savior's love.

Pelikan's *Bach among the Theologians* concludes with a chapter titled "Johann Sebastian Bach—Between Secular and Sacred." Pelikan points out that Bach began his compositions by writing *Jesu Juva* (Jesus, Help) and closed them by writing *Soli Deo Gloria* (To God Alone Be the Glory). These are also good grace notes for one of the most diligent and faithful of the "Lord's remembrancers," as Cotton Mather called church historians.

Abbreviations

1 Apol.	*First Apology* (Justin Martyr)
2 Apol.	*Second Apology* (Justin Martyr)
ACCS	T. C. Oden, ed. Ancient Christian Commentary on Scripture. Downers Grove, IL: InterVarsity Press, 1998–2009
Adv. Haer.	Irenaeus. *Against Heresies.* From *St. Irenaeus of Lyons Against the Heresies.* Translated and annotated by Dominic J. Unger. New York: Paulist Press, 1992
ANF	Alexander Roberts, James Donaldson, and A. Cleveland Coxe, eds. *Ante-Nicene Fathers.* Buffalo: Christian Literature Publishing, 1885
Augsburg	Augsburg Confession
Bapt.	*Baptism* (Tertullian)
BOC	Robert Kolb and Timothy J. Wengert, eds. *The Book of Concord: The Confessions of the Evangelical Lutheran Church.* Translated by Charles Arand and others. Minnneapolis, MN: Augsburg Fortress, 2000
Brief Explanation	*A Brief Explanation of the Ten Commandments, the Creed, and the Lord's Prayer* (Martin Luther)
BSLK	*Die Bekenntnis-Schriften der evangelisch-lutherischen Kirche.* Göttingen: Vandenhoeck & Ruprecht, 1998
CC	John H. Leith, ed. *Creeds of the Churches.* 3rd ed. Louisville: Westminster John Knox, 1982
CH	*Church History* (Socrates of Constantinople)
C. litt. Petil.	*Against the letters of Petilian, the Donatist* (Augustine)
COC	Schaff, Philip. *The Creeds of Christendom.* 6th ed. Grand Rapids: Baker, 1990
Comm.	*Commonitory* (Vincent of Lérins)
Comm. Gal.	*Commentary of Galatians* (John Chrysostom)
CR	*Corpus Reformatorum: Huldreich Zwinglis sämmtliche Werke; Johannis Calvini Opera; Philippi Melanchthonis Opera.* Edited by C. G. Bretschneider and H. E. Bindseil. Halle: Halis Saxonium, 1834–60

Credo	Jaroslav Pelikan. *Credo: Historical & Theological Guide to Creeds and Confessions of Faith in the Christian Tradition.* New Haven: Yale University Press, 2003
Dial.	*Dialogue with Trypho* (Justin)
Dom. or.	*The Lord's Prayer* (*De dominica oratione*) (Cyprian)
Eph.	*To the Ephesians* (Ignatius)
ET	English Translation
Hist. eccl.	*Ecclesiastical History* (Eusebius)
Holmes	Michael W. Holmes, trans. and ed. *The Apostolic Fathers in English.* 3rd ed. Grand Rapids: Baker Academic, 2007
Hom. 2 Tim.	*Homilies on 2 Timothy* (John Chrysostom)
Inc.	*On the Incarnation* (Athanasius)
Jov.	*Against Jovinianus* (Jerome)
Loci Communes	*Common Places in Theology or Fundamental Doctrinal Themes* (*Loci communes rerum theologicarum seu hypotyposes theologicale*) (Philipp Melanchthon)
LTCF	Christopher Hall. *Learning Theology with the Church Fathers.* Downers Grove, IL: InterVarsity, 2002
LW	Jaroslav Pelikan and Helmut T. Lehmann, eds. *Luther's Works.* 55 vols. St. Louis: Concordia Publishing House; Minneapolis: Fortress, 1957–86
Magn.	*To the Magnesians* (Ignatius)
$NPNF^2$	Philip Schaff and Henry Wace, eds. *Nicene and Post-Nicene Fathers.* Series 2. 14 vols. Buffalo: Christian Literature Publishing, 1885
OFP	Origen. *On First Principles.* Translated by G. W. Butterworth. London: SPCK, 1936. Reprint, Gloucester, MA: Peter Smith, 1973
Pan.	*Panarion* (*Adversus haereses*) (*Refutation of All Heresies*) (Epiphanius)
PCW	Dorothea Frede, trans. *Plato: Complete Works.* Edited by John M. Cooper. Indianapolis: Hackett Publishing, 1997
PG	*Patrologia graeca* [= *Patrologiae cursus completus: Series graeca*]. Edited by J.-P. Migne. 162 vols. Paris, 1857–86
Phileb.	*Philebus* (Plato)
Phld.	*To the Philadelphians* (Ignatius)
PL	*Patrologia latina* [= *Patrologiae cursus completus: Series latina*]. Edited by J.-P. Migne. 217 vols. Paris, 1844–64
Praescr.	*Prescription against Heretics* (Tertullian)
SCD	Henry Denzinger, ed. *Sources of Catholic Dogma.* Translated by Roy Deferrari. New York: Herder, 1954
Smyrn.	*To the Smyrnaeans* (Ignatius)
Strom.	*Stromata* (Clement of Alexandria)
Symb.	*Commentarius in symbolum apostolorum* (Commentary on the Apostles' Creed)
Tim.	*Timaeus* (Plato)
Trall.	*To the Trallians* (Ignatius)
WML	*Works of Martin Luther with Introductions and Notes.* 6 vols. Philadelphia: A. J. Holman & Castle, 1915–32

Notes

Preface

1. Valerie Hotchkiss and Patrick Henry, eds., *Orthodoxy and Western Culture: A Collection of Essays Honoring Jaroslav Pelikan on His Eightieth Birthday* (Crestwood, NY: St. Vladimir's Seminary Press, 2005), 165–84.

2. Jaroslav Pelikan, *The Christian Tradition: A History of the Development of Doctrine*, vol. 1, *The Emergence of the Catholic Tradition (100–600)* (Chicago: University of Chicago Press, 1971), 1.

3. Quote of Jaroslav Pelikan by Warren W. Wiersbe, in "Esther," *Bible Exposition Commentary: Old Testament Wisdom and Poetry* (Colorado Springs, CO: Victor, 2004), 749.

Introduction The Faith We Confess

1. William James, *The Varieties of Religious Experience* (New York: Simon & Schuster, 1997), 326.

2. W. G. Land, *Harvard University Handbook* (Cambridge, MA: Harvard University Press, 1936), 44. Land notes that G. H. Palmer had suggested Protagoras's statement "Man is the measure of all things" for Emerson Hall's inscription. For reasons that Land does not make clear, however, President Charles W. Eliot chose the psalm text instead (Ps. 8:4 KJV). Also, see D. Shand-Tucci, *Harvard University: An Architectural Tour* (New York: Princeton Architectural Press, 2001), 163.

3. James, *Varieties of Religious Experience*, 42.

4. See Timothy George, "The Nature of God: Being, Attributes and Acts," in *A Theology for the Church*, ed. Daniel L. Atkin (Nashville: B&H Publishing, 2007), 213.

5. See James Turner, *Without God, without Creed: The Origins of Unbelief in America* (Baltimore: Johns Hopkins University Press, 1985).

6. T. F. Lull, ed., *Martin Luther's Basic Theological Writings* (Philadelphia: Fortress, 2005), Article 97.

7. Jaroslav Pelikan, *The Christian Tradition: A History of the Development of Doctrine*, vol. 1, *The Emergence of the Catholic Tradition (100–600)* (Chicago: University of Chicago Press, 1971), 1.

8. John Webster, "Confession and Confessions," in *Nicene Christianity: The Future for a New Ecumenism*, ed. Christopher R. Seitz (Grand Rapids: Brazos, 2001), 119.

9. James C. Livingston, *Modern Christian Thought*, vol. 1, *The Enlightenment and the Nineteenth Century* (Upper Saddle River, NJ: Prentice Hall, 1997), 94.

Chapter 1 The Faith Once Delivered

1. Cyril, *Catechetical Lectures* 5.12.

2. See Rufinus, *A Commentary on the Apostles' Creed*, trans. and anno. J. N. D. Kelly (London: Longmans, Green & Co., 1955).

3. See Philip Schaff, *The Creeds of Christendom: With a History and Critical Notes*, vols. 1–3 (New York: Harper, 2009), www.ccel.org/print/schaff/creeds1/ix.ii.v. For more reading, see Owen Jones, *The Church of the Living God* (London: Caryl Book Society, 1865); see also the Swiss and Belgian confessions and expositions of the faith, printed in Latin during the time of the Reformation in 1566 and in 1582 and translated into English in 1862 (London: Caryl Book Society, 1865).

4. Origen, *Origen on First Principles* (Gloucester, MA: Peter Smith, 1973).

5. Documents of Vatican Council I and II may be found at www.vatican.va.

6. J. I. Packer and Thomas C. Oden, *One Faith: The Evangelical Consensus* (Downers Grove, IL: InterVarsity, 2004).

7. See W. H. Fremantle, *Against Jovinianus 2.27*, NPNF², vol. 6 (New York, 1893), 346–416.

Chapter 2 The Gospel Promised by the Prophets

1. John Behr, *The Way to Nicea*, vol. 1, *Formation of Christian Theology* (Crestwood, NY: St. Vladimir's Seminary Press, 2001), 17.

2. For a fuller description of Marcion's gnostic dualism, see Irenaeus, *Adv. Haer.* 27.48.

3. Ibid.

4. A. H. J. Gunneweg, *Understanding the Old Testament*, trans. J. Bowden (London: SCM Press, 1978), 2.

5. Hans von Campenhausen, *The Formation of the Christian Bible*, trans. J. A. Baker (Mifflintown, PA: Sigler Press, 1997), 64.

6. Much of the debate here—regarding the Old Testament's "canonical" role in the apostolic era and problems attendant to such a claim because of the complexity of the Tanak's writings—has to do with an overplayed and overly formalized distinction between canon and Scripture. See Christopher R. Seitz, *The Goodly Fellowship of the Prophets: The Achievement of Association in Canon Formation* (Grand Rapids: Baker Academic, 2009).

7. See Bernd Janowski, "The One God of the Two Testaments: Basic Questions of a Biblical Theology," *Theology Today* 57, no. 3 (2000): 303.

8. See Heinrich Heppe, *Reformed Dogmatics: Set Out and Illustrated from the Sources*, trans. G. T. Thomson (Grand Rapids: Baker Books, 1950), 452. See also Eberhard Jüngel, *God's Being Is in Becoming: The Trinitarian Being of God in the Theology of Karl Barth*, trans. John Webster (Edinburgh: T&T Clark, 2001).

9. On the role ontology plays for the church fathers' exegesis of Scripture, see Gerald Bray, "The Church Fathers and Biblical Theology," in *Out of Egypt: Biblical Theology and Biblical Interpretation*, vol. 5, Scripture and Hermeneutics Series, ed. C. Bartholomew, M. Healy, K. Möller, and R. Perry (Grand Rapids: Zondervan, 2004), 23–40.

10. Frances Young relates Athanasius's retort against the Arian reading of Prov. 8:22 as a reading that does not do justice to the overarching διάνοια (mind) of Scripture. Particular texts needed to be fitted within the overarching mind of the Scripture. Frances Young, "The 'Mind' of Scripture: Theological Readings of the Bible in the Fathers," *International Journal of Systematic Theology* 7, no. 2 (2005): 127.

11. In *Adv. Haer.* 1.8.1, Irenaeus actually uses the image of a king reconfigured to look like a dog. See Behr, *Way to Nicea*, 31.

12. Ibid., 32–33.

13. Quoted in David S. Yeago, "The Bible," in *Knowing the Triune God: The Work of the Spirit in the Practice of the Church*, ed. J. F. Buckley and D. S. Yeago (Grand Rapids: Eerdmans,

2001), 49. Yeago states, "Faithful interpreters must therefore resist those hermeneutical regimes, despite their continuing authority in contemporary high culture, that tell them that 'real science' begins with the suppression of such distinctively ecclesial knowledge" (65).

14. Irenaeus affirms the unity of Christian faith throughout the whole world provided in the gospel and witnessed to by the Law and the Prophets. The apostolic deliverance of the faith is the deliverance of something unalterable in time and space. See *Adv. Haer.* 1.10.1 for Irenaeus's description of what this trinitarian and salvific account of the canon of truth is, i.e., the gospel.

15. On the cohesion between the content of Scripture and the rule of faith for Irenaeus, see Eric Osborn, *Irenaeus of Lyons* (Cambridge: Cambridge University Press, 2001), 145.

16. David Yeago, "The New Testament and the Nicene Dogma," *Pro Ecclesia* 3, no. 2 (1994): 152–78.

17. Quoted in Behr, *Way to Nicea*, 45.

18. Young, "The 'Mind' of Scripture," 127.

19. Karl Barth, *Church Dogmatics*, 1.1, ed. G. W. Bromiley and T. F. Torrance, trans. G. W. Bromiley (London: T&T Clark, 1975), 16.

20. Gerhard Sauter, *Protestant Theology at the Crossroads: How to Face the Crucial Tasks for Theology in the Twenty-First Century* (Grand Rapids: Eerdmans, 2007), 38.

21. For example, Irenaeus can say of the Old Testament fathers that they "receive the Revelation when the Son revealed himself." *Adv. Haer.* 4.7.2.

22. Brevard S. Childs, *Biblical Theology of the Old and New Testaments: Theological Reflection on the Christian Bible* (Minneapolis: Fortress, 1992), 376. Childs borrows his phraseology from Barth, *Church Dogmatics*, 1.1, 319.

23. Similarly, an essential connection is observed between YHWH as a good shepherd in Psalm 23 and Jesus's claim in John 10 to be the good shepherd himself.

24. For a very helpful engagement with the role Christology plays for our understanding of the ontology of Scripture, see John Webster, "Resurrection and Scripture," in *Christology and Scripture: Interdisciplinary Perspectives*, ed. A. T. Lincoln and A. Paddison (London: T&T Clark, 2008), 138–55.

25. Especially helpful here is Murray Rae, "Texts in Context: Scripture in the Divine Economy," *Journal of Theological Interpretation* 1 (2001): 23–46.

26. MacDonald makes the distinction between *historicity* (the facticity of the event) and *historicality* (the substance of the event). Furthermore, he claims that the Scriptures assume the former while emphasizing the latter. Neil B. MacDonald, *Karl Barth and the Strange New World within the Bible: Barth, Wittgenstein, and the Metadilemmas of the Enlightenment*, Paternoster Biblical and Theological Monographs (Carlisle, UK: Paternoster Press, 2000).

27. Readers should, of course, take into account issues of genre or literary type.

28. For example, one may be able to prove historically that Jesus of Nazareth died on a Roman cross in the early first century. This is to focus on the event. To claim that Jesus of Nazareth died on a Roman cross in the early first century for the sins of humankind, thus inaugurating the promised kingdom of God, is quite another sort of claim. Here the substance of the event is the focus, with the necessity of revelation presupposed.

29. On these figures in the history of ideas, see Richard Popkin, *The History of Scepticism: From Savonarola to Bayle* (Oxford: Oxford University Press, 2003).

30. For more on Benjamin Jowett, see Evelyn Abbott and Lewis Campbell, *The Life and Letters of Benjamin Jowett*, vols. 1 & 2 (London: J. Murray, 1897); and Ieuan Ellis, *Seven Against Christ: A Study of "Essays and Reviews,"* Studies in the History of Christian Thought, vol. 23 (Leiden: E. J. Brill, 1980), 477, 504, 505.

31. In relation to patristic exegesis, Torrance shows how their approach to exegesis was governed by the goal and orientation of their pursuit, namely, the Logos. Therefore, language such as *homoousios* analogically flows from the interior logic of the apostolic witness itself. Torrance states, "The *homoousion* is thus an articulation of what the Fathers of Nicea had to

think and say when they set themselves to a disciplined and objective inquiry into the biblical witness to Christ, for its basic formulation had already been given by the Apostles themselves. Hence true theological thinking is basically and inescapably apostolic, for it is determined by the form in which the Apostles handed on the Word which they themselves received." Thomas F. Torrance, *Divine Meaning: Studies in Patristic Hermeneutics* (Edinburgh: T&T Clark, 1995), 386.

32. *Shema* means "hear" in Hebrew. The Hebrew Shema is the first prayer that Jewish children learn. Religious Jews say the Shema three times each day as part of their regular prayers and in synagogue services. It comes from Deut. 6:4–9.

33. For example, see the appendix in Benjamin D. Sommer, *The Bodies of God and the World of Ancient Israel* (Cambridge: Cambridge University Press, 2009), 145–73.

34. In interlocution with Moberly, Seitz argues against standard source-critical investigation of Exod. 6:2, where Moses is told that he is made to know the divine name YHWH for the first time. Abraham et al. knew him only as *El Shaddai*. Seitz recognizes the complexity of the issue, but he argues that within the narrative construal of Genesis, the divine name was already known (compare Gen. 4:26). What God is making clear to Moses is the fullness of the divine name in association with his redemptive act to rescue his people from Egypt. They may have known the name of God, "but they have yet to know who God wishes to reveal himself as." The fullness of the divine name is not the knowledge of the name itself, but the knowledge of YHWH's redemptive identity associated with his name. Christopher R. Seitz, "The Call of Moses and the 'Revelation' of the Divine Name," in *Theological Exegesis: Essays in Honor of Brevard S. Childs*, ed. Christopher Seitz and Kathryn Greene-McCreight (Grand Rapids: Eerdmans, 1999), 158–59.

35. Neil B. MacDonald, *Metaphysics and the God of Israel: Systematic Theology of the Old and New Testaments* (Grand Rapids: Baker Academic, 2006), 71.

36. Ibid.

37. Gerhard von Rad, *Old Testament Theology*, vol. 1, trans. D. M. G. Stalker (San Francisco: HarperSanFrancisco, 1962), 286–87.

38. Ibid., 287.

39. Brevard S. Childs, *Isaiah*, The Old Testament Library (Louisville: Westminster John Knox, 2001), 523.

40. Von Rad, *Old Testament Theology*, 1:287. Von Rad makes the interesting observation that in these stories if God is spoken of apart from the people concerned in the story, the proper name YHWH is used. When, however, God is spoken of in a way that makes him perceptible to the human hearers, then the angel of YHWH is used. The voice of God is mediated through the messenger. Later trinitarian formulations provide a substantial theological framework for understanding such claims within the Old Testament's revelation of the identity of YHWH. There is but one mediator between humans and God: the man Christ Jesus (1 Tim. 2:5).

41. Herman Bavinck, *The Doctrine of God*, trans. William Hendriksen (Edinburgh: Banner of Truth, 1977), 257.

42. Robert Jenson, *Ezekiel*, Brazos Theological Commentary on the Bible (Grand Rapids: Brazos, 2009), 42–43.

43. Brevard S. Childs, *The Church's Guide for Reading Paul: The Canonical Shaping of the Pauline Corpus* (Grand Rapids: Eerdmans, 2008), 193.

44. This language has been intentionally borrowed from Robert Jenson's *Systematic Theology*.

45. Barth formulates the nature of the situation in the following: "Inaccurate explanations of the Bible, made in the speech of a later period, had to be countered in the speech of the same period. There thus arose in every age the task of dogma and dogmatics. This is what gives dogma and dogmatics their own special character as distinct from the Bible. But they are not necessarily on this account unbiblical or contrary to the Bible. As we must admit at once, they find themselves in the same dangerous sphere as the errors which they must repel. But this is no other sphere than that of the *ecclesia militans* which seeks to listen to the prophets and apostles

but seeks to understand their word in the language of the later periods, to understand it aright even at the risk of misunderstanding." Barth, *Church Dogmatics,* 1.1, 309.

46. Ibid., 1.2, 693.

Chapter 3 The Road to Nicea

1. Rowan Williams, *Arius: Heresy and Tradition*, rev. ed. (Grand Rapids: Eerdmans, 2001), 110–11.

2. Adam Drozdek, *Greek Philosophers as Theologians: The Divine* Arche (Aldershot, UK: Ashgate, 2007), 157.

3. Translations of Plato come from *Plato: Complete Works*, ed. John M. Cooper (Indianapolis: Hackett, 1997).

4. Richard Bauckham, *Jesus and the God of Israel* (Grand Rapids: Eerdmans, 2009), 6–7.

5. Williams, *Arius,* 100–101, 270. See also R. P. C. Hanson, *The Search for the Christian Doctrine of God: The Arian Controversy, 318–381* (Grand Rapids: Baker Academic, 2005), 560; and Maurice Wiles, *Archetypal Heresy: Arianism through the Centuries* (Oxford: Clarendon, 1996), 10.

6. Jack Dean Kingsbury, *The Christology of Mark's Gospel* (Philadelphia: Fortress, 1983), 129–33.

7. Bauckham, *Jesus*, 9.

8. Ibid., 17.

9. Translations in the rest of this paragraph are the author's.

10. On the worship of Jesus as God by early Christian monotheists, see especially Bauckham, *Jesus*, 127–51.

11. This summary of the passage reflects a few critical exegetical decisions that this is not the place to justify, but they are not eccentric judgments. For a full discussion of this text, with all the critical options clearly explained, see Peter T. O'Brien, *The Epistle to the Philippians: A Commentary on the Greek Text*, New International Greek Testament Commentary (Grand Rapids: Eerdmans, 1991), 186–271; and Gordon D. Fee, *Paul's Letter to the Philippians*, New International Commentary on the New Testament (Grand Rapids: Eerdmans, 1995), 191–229.

12. David S. Yeago, "The New Testament and the Nicene Dogma: A Contribution to the Recovery of Theological Exegesis," in *The Theological Interpretation of Scripture: Classic and Contemporary Readings*, ed. Stephen E. Fowl (Cambridge, MA: Blackwell, 1997), 89–90; Bauckham, *Jesus*, 42.

13. C. F. D. Moule, "Further Reflections on Philippians 2:5–11," in *Apostolic History and the Gospel*, ed. W. Ward Gasque and Ralph P. Martin (Grand Rapids: Eerdmans, 1970), 264–76.

14. On what follows, cf. Bauckham, *Jesus*, 141–42.

15. See David E. Aune, *Revelation 1–5*, Word Biblical Commentary (Nashville: Thomas Nelson, 1997), 352.

16. Quotations of Celsus come from *Celsus: On the True Doctrine, a Discourse against the Christians*, ed. and trans. R. Joseph Hoffmann (Oxford: Oxford University Press, 1987), 103–4, 107.

17. On Cerinthus and the possible connection between Cerinthianism and the false teaching resisted in 1 John, see Raymond E. Brown, *The Epistles of John*, Anchor Bible 30 (Garden City, NY: Doubleday, 1982), 766–71.

18. Translations of Ignatius are from Michael W. Holmes, *The Apostolic Fathers: Greek Texts and English Translations*, 3rd ed. (Grand Rapids: Baker Academic, 2007).

19. Hoffmann, *Celsus*, 90.

20. Ibid., 77–78. Cf. Plato, *Resp.* 2.380c–383c.

21. Hoffmann, *Celsus*, 110.

22. Hanson, *Search*, 112.

23. On this, see Wiles, *Archetypal Heresy*, 15.

24. Bauckham, *Jesus*, 1–59.

25. Quoted from Hanson, *Search*, 8.

26. See, in this regard, Bauckham's treatment of Origen's Christology in *Jesus*, 148–50.

Chapter 4 Whosoever Will Be Saved

1. J. N. D. Kelly, *The Athanasian Creed* (London: Adam and Charles Black, 1964), vi.

2. The Nestorians emigrated to Persia in 484, where they were given asylum, and the vacuum created by their departure was filled by preachers from Egypt, creating a united front against the Chalcedonians.

Chapter 5 The Reformers and the Nicene Faith

1. Hermann Sasse, "I Believe in the Apostolic Church," in *We Confess Anthology*, trans. Norman Nagel (St. Louis: Concordia Publishing House, 1999), 1:95.

2. Augsburg Confession, 7.1; *The Book of Concord*, ed. Theodore Tappert (Philadelphia: Fortress, 1959), 32; *Die Bekenntnis-Schriften der evangelisch-lutherischen Kirche* (Göttingen: Vandenhoeck & Ruprecht, 1998), 61. Hereafter, references to the Lutheran confessions are listed as Tappert (English) and *BSLK* (German and Latin).

3. Martin Luther, *Luther's Works* (St. Louis: Concordia Publishing House; Minneapolis: Fortress, 1957–86), vol. 26, *Lectures on Galatians (1535)*, ed. Jaroslav Pelikan (St. Louis: Concordia Publishing House, 1963), 24–25. Hereafter, all references to Luther's Works are cited as *LW*.

4. Luther writes the following about the Leipzig debate: "On the basis of a number of quotations from the holy church fathers, [Johann] Eck accuses me of being an enemy of the church." *LW*, vol. 31, *Career of the Reformer 1*, ed. Harold J. Grimm and Helmut T. Lehmann (Minneapolis: Fortress, 1957), 313.

5. John C. Olin, ed., *A Reformation Debate: John Calvin and Jacopo Sadoleto* (Grand Rapids: Baker Academic, 2004), 40–41.

6. Cf. Philipp Melanchthon, who in March 1537 writes, "We embrace and defend with our whole hearts the concord of the universal church of Christ, but the name 'church' must not be ascribed to the pontifical errors and tyranny." See *CR* 3:322, no. 1543b; quoted in *LW*, vol. 34, *Career of the Reformer 4*, ed. Helmut T. Lehmann and Lewis W. Spitz (Minneapolis: Fortress, 1960), 199.

7. *Preface to the Complete Edition of Luther's Latin Writings*, LW 34:337.

8. Cf. Olin, *A Reformation Debate*, 37.

9. See Article 8, "On the Three Creeds," in the Thirty-Nine Articles. The 1563 version mentions only the Apostles' and Nicene creeds. The authorized English text of 1571, however, adds the Athanasian Creed to the list. See *Creeds of the Churches*, ed. John H. Leith, 3rd ed. (Louisville: Westminster John Knox, 1982), 269.

10. *Decrees of the Ecumenical Councils*, ed. Norman P. Tanner (Washington, DC: Georgetown University Press, 1990), 2:663.

11. For a similar argument, see Edmund Schlink, *Theology of the Lutheran Confessions* (Minneapolis: Augsburg Fortress, 1961), xvii.

12. Augsburg Confession, conclusion, 5; Tappert, 95. This is actually the second time in the Augsburg Confession that this claim is made. At the beginning of the second part of the confession on matters in dispute, the Lutherans assert that "nothing is taught in our churches concerning articles of faith that is contrary to the Holy scriptures or what is common to the Christian church." Tappert, 48; *BSLK*, 84.

13. Apology of the Augsburg Confession, 4.389; Tappert, 166; *BSLK*, 232.

14. Augsburg Confession, conclusion to first part, Tappert, 47; *BSLK*, 83c–83d.

15. Smalcald Articles, 2, 2.15; Tappert, 295; *BSLK*, 421.

16. Apology of the Augsburg Confession, 24.95; Tappert, 267; *BSLK*, 375.

17. Apology of the Augsburg Confession, 8.21; Tappert, 172; *BSLK*, 238.

18. Epitome of the Formula of Concord, Part 1, preface, 1–2; Tappert, 464–65; *BSLK*, 767–68.

19. For further discussion of Calvin and the fathers, see the following and their respective bibliographies: Johannes van Oort, "John Calvin and the Church Fathers," in *The Reception of the Church Fathers in the West*, ed. Irena Backus (Leiden: Brill, 2001), 2:661–700; and Anthony N. S. Lane, *John Calvin: Student of the Church Fathers* (Grand Rapids: Baker Academic, 1999).

20. John Calvin, *Institutes of the Christian Religion*, trans. Ford Lewis Battles, ed. John T. McNeill (Philadelphia: Westminster Press, 1960), 1:13.

21. Ibid., 1:14–15.

22. Ibid., 1:16.

23. Ibid., 1:18.

24. Ibid.

25. Ibid., 1:19.

26. Ibid., 1:19–22.

27. Ibid., 1:25; Hilary of Poitiers, *Contra Auxentium*, xii (*PL* 10:616).

28. Calvin, *Institutes*, 1:24; Augsburg Confession, 7.1; Tappert, 32; *BSLK*, 61.

29. Large Catechism, 2.42; Tappert, 416; *BSLK*, 655.

Chapter 6 The Nicene Faith and the Catholicity of the Church

1. D. H. Williams, *Retrieving the Tradition and Renewing Evangelicalism: A Primer for Suspicious Protestants* (Grand Rapids: Eerdmans, 1999).

2. D. H. Williams, "The Patristic Tradition as Canon," *Perspectives in Religious Studies* 32, no. 4 (Winter 2005): 357–79. See also D. H. Williams, *Evangelicals and Tradition: The Formative Influence of the Early Church*, Evangelical *Ressourcement*: Ancient Sources for the Church's Future (Grand Rapids: Baker Academic, 2005); and D. H. Williams, ed., *The Free Church and the Early Church: Bridging the Historical and Theological Divide* (Grand Rapids: Eerdmans, 2002).

3. Dennis D. Martin, review of *Evangelicals and Tradition: The Formative Influence of the Early Church*, D. H. Williams, *Pro Ecclesia* 18, no. 2 (Spring 2009): 216–19.

4. Steven R. Harmon, *Towards Baptist Catholicity: Essays on Tradition and the Baptist Vision*, ed. Anthony R. Cross, Studies in Baptist History and Thought, vol. 27 (Milton Keynes, UK: Paternoster, 2006).

5. According to the Particular Baptist Second London Confession (1677/89), chap. 26.1, "The Catholick or universal Church, which (with respect to internal work of the Spirit, and truth of grace) may be called invisible, consists of the whole number of the Elect, that have been, are, or shall be gathered into one, under Christ the head thereof." William L. Lumpkin, ed., *Baptist Confessions of Faith*, rev. ed. (Valley Forge, PA: Judson Press, 1969), 285. Likewise, the General Baptist Orthodox Creed (1678/79) appropriated three of the four Niceno-Constantinopolitan *notae ecclesiae* in confessing in Article 29, "There is one holy catholick church, consisting of, or made up of the whole number of the elect, that have been, are, or shall be gathered, in one body under Christ, the only head thereof," and in Article 30, "We believe the visible church of Christ on earth, is made up of several distinct congregations, which make up that one catholick church, or mystical body of Christ." Lumpkin, *Baptist Confessions of Faith*, 318–19.

6. Harmon, *Towards Baptist Catholicity*, 204.

7. Some material in this and the next three paragraphs is adapted from Steven R. Harmon, "Qualitative Catholicity in Ignatius of Antioch—and the New Testament: The Fallacies of a Restorationist Hermeneutic," *Perspectives in Religious Studies* 38, no.1 (forthcoming 2011).

8. See the *Catechism of the Catholic Church* (Liguori, MO: Liguori Publications, 1994), section 834 (221): "Particular Churches are fully catholic through their communion with one of them, the Church of Rome 'which presides in charity' [quotation from Ignatius of Antioch

Romans 1.1]. 'For with this church, by reason of its pre-eminence, the whole Church, that is the faithful everywhere, must necessarily be in accord' [quotation from Irenaeus, *Adv. Haer.* 3.3.2]. Indeed, 'from the incarnate Word's descent to us, all Christian churches everywhere have held and hold the great Church that is here [at Rome] to be their only basis and foundation since, according to the Savior's promise, the gates of hell have never prevailed against her'" [quotation from Maximus the Confessor, *Opuscula theologica et polemica*]. While the *Catechism* reserves the fullest sense of catholicity for churches in communion with Rome, in section 838 (222), it also grants that there are other senses in which non–Roman Catholic churches and Christians participate in the catholicity of the church, though to a lesser extent: "'The Church knows that she is joined in many ways to the baptized who are honored by the name of Christian, but do not profess the Catholic faith in its entirety or have not preserved unity or communion under the successor of Peter' [quotation from *Lumen gentium* 15]. Those 'who believe in Christ and have been properly baptized are put in a certain, though imperfect, communion with the Catholic Church' [quotation from *Unitatis redintegratio*]. With the Orthodox Churches, this communion is so profound 'that it lacks little to attain the fullness that would permit a common celebration of the Lord's Eucharist'" [quotation from Paul VI, Discourse, December 14, 1975].

9. G. W. H. Lampe, ed., *A Patristic Greek Lexicon* (Oxford: Clarendon Press, 1961), s.v. "καθολικός," A.2.b–c and A.3; Charlton T. Lewis and Charles Short, *A Latin Dictionary* (Oxford: Clarendon Press, 1879), s.v. "catholicus," 2. For particular examples, see notes 29 and 30 below.

10. Ignatius of Antioch, *Smyrneans* 7.1–2, in Ehrman, *Apostolic Fathers* (Cambridge, MA: Loeb Classical Library, 2003), 1:302–3.

11. Ibid., 6.2, 303 (modifications in brackets).

12. I grant that in suggesting this, I am guilty of a most tendentious theological reading of a specific episode of ecclesiastical history. Yet I wonder if it is not merely coincidental that these connections also manifested themselves in the nineteenth-century Oxford Movement in the Church of England: the recovery of an incarnational sacramentalism went hand in hand with the commitment of Anglo-Catholic priests to doing social ministry in the slums of inner-city England. See C. Brad Faught, *The Oxford Movement: A Thematic History of the Tractarians and Their Times* (University Park: Pennsylvania State University Press, 2003): 151–52.

13. Ehrman, *Apostolic Fathers*, vol. 1, 305 (modifications in brackets).

14. Eusebius of Caesarea, *Hist. eccl.* 7.30.16 (*PG* 20:716), in contrast to heterodoxy, and 10.6.1 (*PG* 20:892), in contrast to schism; Athanasius, *Adversus Arianos* 1.4 (*PG* 26:20); Epiphanius, *Pan.* 73.21 (*PG* 42:414).

15. Cyril of Jerusalem, *Catecheses* 18.23 (*PG* 33:1047; ET, *The Works of Saint Cyril of Jerusalem*, trans. Leo P. McCauley and Anthony A. Stephenson, vol. 64, *Fathers of the Church* [Washington, DC: Catholic University of America Press, 1970], 2:132). In the Latin West, the same fuller sense of catholicity is reflected in the hymn on the passion of Hippolytus of Rome by the poet Prudentius (d. after 405) in the *Peristephanon* 11.23–32: "Nor is it strange that the aged man who once was an apostate / Should be endowed with the rich boon of the Catholic faith. / When, triumphant and joyful in spirit, he was being conducted / By the unmerciful foe onward to death of the flesh, / He was attended by loving throngs of his faithful adherents. / Thus he replied when they asked whether his doctrine was sound: / 'Leave, O unhappy souls, the infernal schism of Novatus; / Rally again to the true fold of the Catholic Church. / Let the one faith of ancient times in our temples now flourish, / Doctrines by Paul and the high chair of Peter maintained'" (*PL* 60:534–36; *Corpus Christianorum: Series Latina*, vol. 126, *Aurelii Prudentii Clementis Carmina*, ed. Maurice P. Cunningham [Turnhout, Belgium: Brepols, 1966], 370–71; ET, *The Poems of Prudentius*, trans. M. Clement Eagan, vol. 43, *Fathers of the Church* [Washington, DC: Catholic University of America Press, 1962], 242–43).

16. Philipp Melanchthon, "De appellatione Ecclesiae Catholicae," in *Postilla Melanthoniana*, *CR*, vol. 24, cols. 397–99; quoted in Avery Cardinal Dulles, *Magisterium: Teacher and Guardian of the Faith* (Naples, FL: Sapientia Press of Ave Maria University, 2007), 182.

17. See Carl E. Braaten and Robert W. Jenson, eds., *The Catholicity of the Reformation* (Grand Rapids: Eerdmans, 1996).

18. Committee of the Oxford Society of Historical Theology, *The New Testament in the Apostolic Fathers* (Oxford: Clarendon Press, 1905), 67, 69, 71–72, 79, 83; Walter J. Burghardt, "Did Saint Ignatius of Antioch Know the Fourth Gospel?" *Theological Studies* 1 (1940): 7–15; Christian Maurer, *Ignatius von Antiochien und das Johannesevangelium,* Abhandlungen zur Theologie des Alten und Neuen Testaments, no. 18 (Zürich: Zwingli-Verlag, 1949), 25–43, 92–93; Édouard Massaux, *Influence de l'Évangile de saint Matthieu sur la littérature chrétienne avant saint Irénée* (Leuven: University Press, 1950) [ET, *The Influence of the Gospel of Saint Matthew on Christian Literature before Saint Irenaeus,* bk. 1, *The First Ecclesiastical Writers,* trans. Norman J. Belval and Suzanne Hecht, ed. Arthur J. Bellinzoni, New Gospel Studies, no. 5 (Macon, GA: Mercer University Press, 1990), 86–96]; Helmut Köster, *Synoptische Überlieferung bei den apostolischen Vätern,* Texte und Untersuchungen zur Geschichte der alt-christlichen Literatur, no. 17 (Berlin: Akademie-Verlag, 1957), 24–61; Heinrich Rathke, *Ignatius von Antiochien und die Paulusbriefe,* Texte und Untersuchungen zur Geschichte der alt-christlichen Literatur, no. 99 (Berlin: Akademie-Verlag, 1967), 39, 41–47, 64–66, 98–99; J. Smit Sibinga, "Ignatius and Matthew," *Novum Testamentum* 8 (1966): 263–83; Richard Bauckham, "The Study of Gospel Traditions outside the Canonical Gospels: Problems and Prospects," in *Gospel Perspectives,* vol. 5, *The Jesus Tradition outside the Gospels,* ed. David Wenham (Sheffield: JSOT Press, 1984), 398.

19. Paul Avis, "Foreword," in Harmon, *Towards Baptist Catholicity,* xviii.

20. "Selective catholicity" is language employed by Elizabeth Newman in raising a similar question in a review of *Towards Baptist Catholicity,* published as part of a book symposium in the journal *Pro Ecclesia*: Elizabeth Newman, "Remembering How to Remember: Harmon's Subversive Orthodoxy," *Pro Ecclesia* 18, no. 4 (Fall 2009): 375–80.

21. E.g., Barry Harvey, *Can These Bones Live? A Catholic Baptist Engagement with Ecclesiology, Hermeneutics, and Social Theory* (Grand Rapids: Brazos, 2008). A recent doctoral dissertation offers a critical and constructive analysis of this development in Baptist theology: Cameron H. Jorgenson, "Bapto-Catholicism: Recovering Tradition and Reconsidering the Baptist Identity" (PhD diss., Baylor University, 2008).

22. Terry Mattingly, "A Baptist Minister's Eye-Opening Sabbatical," *San Angelo Standard-Times,* August 10, 2009, www.gosanangelo.com/news/2009/aug/10/terry-mattingly -baptist-ministers-eye-opening-sabb/.

23. Timothy George, "Scripture and Tradition: An Evangelical Baptist Perspective" (paper presented to the first session of the 2006–10 bilateral conversations between the Baptist World Alliance Doctrine and Interchurch Cooperation Commission and the Vatican Council for Promoting Christian Unity, Beeson Divinity School, Samford University, Birmingham, AL, December 10–15, 2006). Also, Timothy George, "An Evangelical Reflection on Scripture and Tradition," *Pro Ecclesia* 9, no. 2 (Spring 2000): 206.

24. Avery Cardinal Dulles, *Magisterium: Teacher and Guardian of the Faith* (Naples, FL: Sapientia Press of Ave Maria University, 2007), 35.

25. Johannes Brosseder, "Teaching Office: 1. Roman Catholic," in *Encyclopedia of Christianity,* vol. 5, ed. Erwin Fahlbusch et al., trans. Geoffrey W. Bromiley (Grand Rapids: Eerdmans, 2008), 316–19; Dulles, *Magisterium,* 21–34.

26. Vatican II, *Dogmatic Constitution on the Church (Lumen Gentium),* November 21, 1964, in *Vatican Council II: The Conciliar and Post Conciliar Documents,* ed. Austin Flannery, rev. ed. (Northport, NY: Costello Publishing, 1992), 380.

27. Vatican II, *Dogmatic Constitution on Divine Revelation (Dei Verbum),* November 18, 1965, in Flannery, *Vatican Council II,* 755–56.

28. A process evidenced by the conciliar history of Giuseppe Alberigo, *History of Vatican II,* trans. Joseph A. Komonchak, 5 vols. (Maryknoll, NY: Orbis Books, 1995–2006).

29. George Huntston Williams, *The Radical Reformation*, 3rd ed., Sixteenth Century Essays and Studies, vol. 15 (Kirksville, MO: Sixteenth Century Journal Publishers, 1992).

30. Philipp Melanchthon, "Treatise on the Power and Primacy of the Pope," 60–72, in *The Book of Concord: The Confessions of the Evangelical Lutheran Church*, ed. Robert Kolb and Timothy J. Wengert, trans. Charles Arand et al. (Minneapolis: Fortress, 2000), 340–41.

31. Lutheran World Information, "Lutherans' Reconciliation with Mennonites Would Be an Occasion for Healing: Mennonite World Body Hears Study Commission Results and Proposed Lutheran Action," August 14, 2009, www.lutheranworld.org/News/LWI/EN/2406.EN.html.

32. Alasdair MacIntyre, *After Virtue: A Study in Moral Theory*, 2nd ed. (Notre Dame, IN: University of Notre Dame Press, 1984), 222.

33. James Wm. McClendon Jr., *Systematic Theology*, vol. 2, *Doctrine* (Nashville: Abingdon Press, 1994), 28.

34. This reading of the role of the disciples in Matthew's Gospel is influenced by Andrew T. Lincoln, "Matthew—A Story for Teachers?" in *The Bible in Three Dimensions: Essays in Celebration of Forty Years of Biblical Studies in the University of Sheffield*, ed. David J. A. Clines et al., JSOT Supplements, no. 87 (Sheffield: JSOT Press, 1990), 103–25.

35. London Confession (1644), preface; Lumpkin, *Baptist Confessions of Faith*, 155–56.

36. Paul S. Fiddes, *Tracks and Traces: Baptist Identity in Church and Theology*, vol. 13, *Studies in Baptist History and Thought* (Milton Keynes, UK: Paternoster, 2003), 6. A similar point about the possibilities of free church ecclesiology for envisioning an ecumenical gathering as a gathered community under the lordship of Christ that gathers for the purpose of seeking his rule in the community was made by John Howard Yoder, *The Royal Priesthood: Essays Ecclesiological and Ecumenical*, ed. Michael G. Cartwright (Grand Rapids: Eerdmans, 1994), 236: "This view gives more, not less, weight to ecumenical gatherings. The 'high' views of ordered churchdom can legitimate the worship of a General Assembly or a study conference only by stretching the rules, for its rules do not foresee ad hoc 'churches'; only thoroughgoing congregationalism fulfills its hopes and definities whenever and wherever it sees 'church' happen."

37. Fiddes, *Tracks and Traces*, 86.

38. Mikael Broadway et al., "Re-envisioning Baptist Identity: A Manifesto for Baptist Communities in North America," section 1; published in *Baptists Today* (June 1997): 8–10; *Perspectives in Religious Studies* 24, no. 3 (Fall 1997): 303–10; reprinted as appendix 1 in *Towards Baptist Catholicity*, 215–23; available online at www.divinity.duke.edu/sites/default/files/documents/faculty-freeman/reenvisioning-baptist-identity.pdf.

Chapter 7 The Church Is Part of the Gospel

1. E. Stanley Jones quotes from BrainyQuote.com, www.brainyquote.com/quotes/authors/e/e_stanley_jones.html.

2. Orthodox Presbyterian Church, *The Westminster Confession of Faith and Catechisms: As Adopted by the Orthodox Presbyterian Church* (Lawrenceville, GA: Christian Education & Publications Committee of the Presbyterian Church in America, 2007).

3. Smalcald Articles, 3, 12.2. For further reading, see www.bookofconcord.org/smalcald.php.

4. *The Ministry of Children's Education: Foundations, Contexts, and Practices* (Minneapolis: Augsburg Fortress, 2004), 77. For further information, the Small Catechism may be found online at www.bookofconcord.org/smallcatechism.php.

Chapter 8 Confessional, Baptist, and Arminian

1. For lack of space and other considerations, this essay will not consider the Randall movement of Free Baptists in the North, which merged with the Northern Baptist Convention in 1911. In 1935, a small remnant of that movement united with the larger Free Will Baptist General

Conference of the South to form the National Association of Free Will Baptists. Probably about 15 percent of present-day Free Will Baptists originated with the Randall movement.

2. A poignant symbol of this ecclesial, communal orientation is the ritual of the washing of the saints' feet, which was widespread among English General Baptists and was prescribed in the American Free Will Baptist confession of faith, the *1812 Abstract*, as one of nine gospel ordinances that must be practiced by churches in fellowship with the conference. See A. C. Underwood, *A History of the English Baptists* (London: Kingsgate, 1947), 123; J. Matthew Pinson, *A Free Will Baptist Handbook: Heritage, Beliefs, and Ministries* (Nashville: Randall House, 1998), 147; J. Matthew Pinson, *The Washing of the Saints' Feet* (Nashville: Randall House, 2006).

3. Curtis W. Freeman, "A New Perspective on Baptist Identity," *Perspectives in Religious Studies* 26 (1999): 59–65. Both Freeman and Philip E. Thompson trace a shift in Baptist life to romantic, liberal individualism as early as John Leland. See Thompson, "Re-envisioning Baptist Identity: Historical, Theological, and Liturgical Analysis," *Perspectives in Religious Studies* 27 (2000): 287–302. The most masterful treatment of this theme is Gregory A. Wills, *Democratic Religion: Freedom, Authority, and Church Discipline in the Baptist South, 1785–1900* (New York: Oxford University Press, 1997).

4. Timothy George, "The Priesthood of All Believers," in *The People of God: Essays on the Believers' Church,* ed. Paul Basden and David S. Dockery (Nashville: Broadman, 1991), 85–98.

5. Mikael Broadway et al., "Re-envisioning Baptist Identity: A Manifesto for Baptist Communities in North America," published in *Baptists Today* (June 1997): 8–10; *Perspectives in Religious Studies* 24, no. 3 (Fall 1997): 303–10; available online at http://baptiststudiesonline .com/wp-content/uploads/2007/02/reenvisioningbaptistidentity2.pdf.

6. A revival of confessionalism, a sort of *ad fontes*, especially among young adults, is discussed in Thomas C. Oden, *The Rebirth of Orthodoxy: Signs of New Life in Christianity* (San Francisco: HarperSanFrancisco, 2002); and Colleen Carroll, *The New Faithful: Why Young Adults Are Embracing Christian Orthodoxy* (Chicago: Loyola University Press, 2002). On confessionalism and Baptists, see Timothy George, "Southern Baptist Ghosts," *First Things* 93 (1999), 18–24.

7. J. Matthew Pinson, *Free Will Baptists and Church Government* (Nashville: Historical Commission, National Association of Free Will Baptists, 2008), 6, 10. According to Gregory Wills, even (non–Free Will) Baptists in the American South had similar sentiments: "Populist religious leaders touted private judgment, personal autonomy, and individual conscience over creedal systems. But when John Leland, the most famous Baptist exponent of individual autonomy, exercised his right of private judgment in scripture interpretation, his association disfellowshiped him. Baptists opposed this kind of individualism. Conscience was not supreme" (Wills, *Democratic Religion*, 33). Conference minutes from the General-Free Will Baptist tradition are replete with such cases of ministerial discipline for the lack of sound doctrine. Wills convincingly contends that this mentality eroded in the late nineteenth century among Southern Baptists and was gradually replaced with views of individual autonomy and private judgment.

8. Timothy George, "Southern Baptist Ghosts," 21. He goes on to say: "But this principle, sacred to Baptists through the ages, is fully compatible with voluntary, conscientious adherence to an explicit doctrinal standard. . . . All confessional traditions are liable to lapse into legalism. . . . But confessionless Christianity poses an even greater danger. Forsaking the distilled wisdom of the past makes every man's hat his own church."

9. It is interesting that the postconservative, Arminian, and Baptist Roger E. Olson signed "Re-envisioning Baptist Identity," given his recent comments on confessionalism that sound much like the sort of autonomous individualism the above paragraph of the document is meant to avoid: "In the current lively discussion about these matters conservatives have arrogated to themselves the label 'confessional evangelicals.' I wish to affirm that I, too, am a 'confessional evangelical' because I also confess the gospel. A difference lies in the fact that I, like many postconservatives, prefer to confess my own faith for myself rather than affirm or swear allegiance to a historic creed or written confessional statement. My own statement of faith is no less a confession of

faith, however, than is another evangelical's signing of the Westminster Confession or the Baptist Faith and Message" (Roger E. Olson, *Reformed and Always Reforming: The Postconservative Approach to Evangelical Theology* [Grand Rapids: Baker Academic, 2007], 75, n. 15).

10. Michael S. Horton, "Evangelical Arminians," *Modern Reformation* 1 (1992): 15–19.

11. Two of the more interesting debates about the definition of evangelicalism are those between Donald W. Dayton and George M. Marsden (*Christian Scholar's Review* 23 [1993]: 12–40) and Michael S. Horton and Roger E. Olson (*Christian Scholar's Review* 31 [2001]: 131–68).

12. Olson, *Reformed and Always Reforming*; see also Stanley J. Grenz, *Renewing the Center: Evangelical Theology in a Post-Evangelical Era* (Grand Rapids: Baker Academic, 2000). A number of scholars cogently argue for continuity between the early pietism and the theological content of Protestant orthodoxy. See William G. Travis, "Pietism and the History of American Evangelicalism," in *Reclaiming the Center*, ed. Millard J. Erickson, Paul Kjoss Helseth, and Justin Taylor (Wheaton: Crossway, 2004), 251–79.

13. Admittedly, many (non–Free Will) Baptists in the nineteenth century, such as the Separate Baptists, eschewed confessional subscription, probably owing to the emphasis of the Disciples of Christ (the Stone-Campbell movement).

14. Thomas C. Oden, "The Real Reformers Are Traditionalists," *Christianity Today*, February 9, 1998, 46.

15. Mark Noll, *The Scandal of the Evangelical Mind* (Grand Rapids: Eerdmans, 1994), 48–49, 60–64. The Free Will Baptists of the South were slower to be influenced by the revivalism and social reform characteristic of northern evangelicalism in the nineteenth century. The Free Will Baptists of the late eighteenth and most of the nineteenth century were leery of "new light" revivalism. See Rufus K. Hearn, "Origins of the Free Will Baptist Church of North Carolina" (1860s), reprinted in the *Historical Review* (Summer 1994): 37.

16. The use of the word *Holiness* here does not exclude the Keswick movement, which George Marsden shows was a milder version of the popular Holiness theology of Charles Finney and others in nineteenth-century America. For one of the best discussions of the Holiness movement in print, see George M. Marsden, *Fundamentalism and American Culture* (Oxford: Oxford University Press, 1980), esp. chapters 8 and 11.

17. Stephen M. Ashby, "Reformed Arminianism," in *Four Views on Eternal Security*, ed. J. Matthew Pinson (Grand Rapids: Zondervan, 2002).

18. See the following recent Free Will Baptist works along these lines: F. Leroy Forlines, *The Quest for Truth: Theology for Postmodern Times* (Nashville: Randall House, 2000); Robert E. Picirilli, *Grace, Faith, Free Will: Contrasting Views: Calvinism and Arminianism* (Nashville: Randall House, 2002); Ashby, "Reformed Arminianism," and J. Matthew Pinson, "Introduction," in Pinson, *Four Views on Eternal Security*; Stephen M. Ashby, "Introduction," in *The Works of James Arminius*, 3 vols. (Nashville: Randall House, 2007); Pinson, *Free Will Baptist Handbook*; J. Matthew Pinson, "Will the Real Arminius Please Stand Up? The Theology of Arminius in Light of His Interpreters," *Integrity: A Journal of Christian Thought* 2 (2003): 121–39; J. Matthew Pinson, "Atonement, Justification, and Apostasy in the Thought of John Wesley," *Integrity: A Journal of Christian Thought* 4 (2008): 73–92.

19. Neil Postman, *Amusing Ourselves to Death: Public Discourse in an Age of Show Business* (New York: Penguin, 1985).

20. Oden, *Rebirth of Orthodoxy*; Thomas C. Oden, *After Modernity . . . What?* (Grand Rapids: Zondervan, 1990); Thomas C. Oden, "Toward a Theologically Informed Renewal of American Protestantism: Propositions for Debate Attested by Classical Arguments," in *The Believable Futures of American Protestantism*, ed. Richard John Neuhaus (Grand Rapids: Eerdmans, 1988), 72–102.

21. Timothy George, "The Reformation Roots of the Baptist Tradition," *Review and Expositor* 86 (1989): 9–22; Anthony N. S. Lane, "*Sola Scriptura?* Making Sense of a Post-Reformation Slogan," in *A Pathway into the Holy Scripture*, ed. Philip E. Satterthwaite and David F. Wright

(Grand Rapids: Eerdmans, 1994), 297–328; Timothy George, *Theology of the Reformers* (Nashville: Broadman, 1988), 79–86, 314–17.

22. John Lee Thompson, *Reading the Bible with the Dead: What You Can Learn from the History of Exegesis That You Can't Learn from Exegesis Alone* (Grand Rapids: Eerdmans, 2007).

23. Nineteenth- and twentieth-century Southern Baptist concepts of soul competency, individualism, and antitraditionalism are being rethought by moderate and conservative Southern Baptists alike. See, e.g., Curtis W. Freeman, "A New Perspective on Baptist Identity"; Curtis W. Freeman, "Can Baptist Theology Be Revisioned?" *Perspectives in Religious Studies* 24 (1997): 273–310; George, "Southern Baptist Ghosts"; George, "Priesthood of All Believers"; Steven R. Harmon, "The Authority of the Community (of All the Saints): Toward a Postmodern Baptist Hermeneutic of Tradition," *Review and Expositor* 100 (2003): 587–621. For treatments from the perspective of Baptist individualism, see Jeff B. Pool, *Against Returning to Egypt: Exposing and Resisting Credalism in the Southern Baptist Convention* (Macon, GA: Mercer University Press, 1998); and Walter B. Shurden, *Not an Easy Journey: Some Transitions in Baptist Life* (Macon, GA: Mercer University Press, 2005).

For a contemporary Baptist perspective that values tradition with an emphasis on the value of patristic Christianity for the free church tradition, see D. H. Williams, ed. *The Free Church and the Early Church: Bridging the Historical and Theological Divide* (Grand Rapids: Eerdmans, 2002), esp. Williams's preface and his chapter "Scripture, Tradition, and the Church: Reformation and Post-Reformation," 101–28. Cf. D. H. Williams, *Retrieving the Tradition and Renewing Evangelicalism: A Primer for Suspicious Protestants* (Grand Rapids: Eerdmans, 1999). For a renewed emphasis on the wider Christian tradition and its import for Baptists, see Steven R. Harmon, *Towards Baptist Catholicity: Essays on Tradition and the Baptist Vision*, ed. Anthony R. Cross, vol. 27, *Studies in Baptist History and Thought* (Milton Keynes, UK: Paternoster, 2006). For a Reformed Baptist approach, see Michael A. G. Haykin, "Why Study the Fathers?" *Eusebia* 8 (2007): 3–7.

24. See B. R. White, *The English Separatist Tradition: From the Marian Martyrs to the Pilgrim Fathers* (London: Oxford University Press, 1971), for an account of Smyth and Helwys. See also B. R. White, *The English Baptists of the Seventeenth Century* (Didcot, UK: Baptist Historical Society, 1996).

25. J. Matthew Pinson, "Sin and Redemption in the Theology of John Smyth and Thomas Helwys" (paper presented at the Theological Symposium of the Commission for Theological Integrity, National Association of Free Will Baptists, 2004), 13–29. See Alvin J. Beachy, *The Concept of Grace in the Radical Reformation* (Nieuwkoop, Neth.: B. De Graaf, 1977).

26. Pinson, "Sin and Redemption," 22–26.

27. The expression "General Baptist" was in flux during the English Civil War and Interregnum, the period between the unseating of Charles I as king of England and the assumption of the restoration of the monarchy under Charles II in 1660. For example, general-atonement Baptists and political radicals such as Henry Denne and Thomas Lambe were antinomian and more predestinarian and did not accept the laying on of hands after baptism, as affirmed by the General Assembly and the Standard Confession of 1660. Furthermore, General Baptists such as Jeremiah Ives were more politically radical, rejected the imposition of hands, and were more semi-Pelagian in their soteriology than the mainstream General Baptists.

28. Philip E. Thompson, "A New Question in Baptist History: Seeking a Catholic Spirit among Early Baptists," *Pro Ecclesia* 8 (1999): 61.

29. Thomas Grantham, *Christianismus Primitivus* (London: Francis Smith, 1678), Book 4, 1.

30. Freeman, "Can Baptist Theology Be Revisioned?," 283.

31. Grantham, *Christianismus Primitivus*, Book 4, 11–12.

32. Ibid., Book 4, 15. *The Baptist against the Papist* (originally written in prison in 1663) is reprinted in *Christianismus Primitivus*, Book 4, 1–42.

33. Ibid., Book 2, 5.

34. "An Orthodox Creed," *Southwestern Journal of Theology* 48 (2006): 132.

35. Joseph Hooke, *Creed-Making and Creed-Imposing Considered* . . . 2nd ed. (London: J. Darby and T. Browne, 1729), 9–10. First published in 1719.

36. A. G. Matthews, "The Puritans," in *Christian Worship: Studies in Its History and Meaning*, ed. Nathaniel Micklem (Oxford: Clarendon, 1936), 172–88. See also Davies, *The Worship of the English Puritans* (1948; repr., Morgan, PA: Soli Deo Gloria, 1997), 46–48, 81–83, 98–114, 273–77.

37. Grantham, *Christianismus Primitivus*, Book 2, 59–61.

38. William Lumpkin, *Baptist Confessions of Faith* (Valley Forge, PA: Judson Press, 1969), 326.

39. This is also true of the American Free Will Baptists of the nineteenth century. See, e.g., Hearn, "Origins of the Free Will Baptist Church," 35.

40. Hooke, *Creed-Making and Creed-Imposing Considered*, 6.

41. "After the first and second admonition, [a heretic] is to be rejected; but we must not suffer him to abide in the Church: but we should suffer him to abide in the World, Math. 13. 30, 38, 39. Not driving him out of it with Fire and Faggot; that is Popish Discipline, but no Discipline of the Church of Christ" (ibid.).

42. Ibid., 8.

43. Grantham, *Christianismus Primitivus*, Book 2, 53. "That place of the Apostle, *Tit*. 3. 10, 11. *A man that is an Heretick after the first and second Admonition reject, knowing that he that is such, is subverted and sinneth, having damnation of himself*; Made some think, that Hereticks being so admonished, can never be received into the Communion of the Faithful. But then it must be only such an obstinate Heretick as these words do set forth: otherwise, the consequence would be dreadful, if all that are led astray by Heretical Doctrine, should be exposed to such a severe Censure. This opinon, with respect to *contumacious Hereticks* seems to be strengthened by 1 Cor. 16. 22. *If any man love not our Lord Jesus Christ, let him be Anathema Maranatha*" (Ibid., Book 2, 154).

44. Ibid., Book 2, 53.

45. Hooke, *Creed-Making and Creed-Imposing Considered*, 8.

46. Ibid., 39.

47. Oden, *Rebirth of Orthodoxy*, 128.

48. Clint C. Bass, *Thomas Grantham and General Baptist Theology* (Milton Keynes, UK: Paternoster, 2010), 38.

49. Lumpkin, *Baptist Confessions of Faith*, 297.

50. The Free Will Baptists in America differed from the earlier General Baptists in their open communion posture. Free Will Baptists admitted all believing Christians to the Lord's Table regardless of their baptism but required immersion for full church membership.

51. An ironic example of this is the Orthodox Creed, which quotes Chrysostom on its title page as a proof text for *sola scriptura*: "I beseech you, regard not what this, or that man saith but inquire all things of the Scripture." A. C. Underwood was right when he remarked that Thomas Monck was a "remarkable farmer," because, in the preface of the Orthodox Creed, he quotes Ambrose, Augustine, Chrysostom, Gregory the Great, and Bernard of Clairvaux in Latin (Underwood, *History of the English Baptists*, 107). See also the works of Thomas Monck and Joseph Hooke.

52. Williams, "Scripture, Tradition, and the Church," 102. Grantham's views were much like sixteenth-century Reformers in both the Magisterial and Radical wings of the Reformation, such as Martin Luther, John Calvin, and Balthasar Hubmaier. See Wolfgang A. Bienert, "The Patristic Background of Luther's Theology," *Lutheran Quarterly* 9 (1995): 263–79; Anthony N. S. Lane, *John Calvin: Student of the Church Fathers* (Edinburgh: T&T Clark, 1999); Andrew P. Klager, "Balthasar Hubmaier and the Authority of the Church Fathers," in *Historical Papers 2008: Canadian Society of Church History, Annual Conference, University of British Columbia, 1–3 June 2008*, 18 (2008), 133–52; Phyllis Rodgerson Pleasants, "Sola Scriptura in Zurich?" in Williams, *Free Church and the Early Church*, 77–99.

53. Grantham, *Christianismus Primitivus*, Book 2, 61.

54. Lane, *John Calvin*, 28–29. For example, like Calvin, Grantham tended to cite the fathers when he was arguing with those who give more weight to them. Calvin used much patristic material when arguing with Roman Catholics but little when arguing with Anabaptists. Similarly, Grantham extensively used the fathers against the church of Rome in *The Baptist against the Papist* but rarely quoted them in *The Baptist against the Quaker*. However, when arguing against his fellow Baptists for the validity of laying on of hands after baptism for the promised Spirit, Grantham cited patristic sources abundantly.

55. Lane, *John Calvin*, 26–27.

56. Grantham, *Christianismus Primitivus*, Book 4, 6–7. Ironically, Grantham, again like Calvin, cited fathers like Augustine to prove his *sola scriptura*.

57. Grantham chided the papists for saying, "The Tradition of our Fore-Fathers . . . [is] *the only thing that is unquestionable, and needs no other ground to stand upon, but it self*. And against the Scripture's being received, upon its own Evidence or Authority, they usually do thus object, *That before we can receive what it teacheth, we must be assured of its truth*. . . . And by these, and other-like Objections, they usually in all their Writings, invalidate the Scripture's Certainty, Authority, and Sufficiency, that so they may advance the Authority of their Traditions" (Grantham, *Christianismus Primitivus*, Book 4, 24).

58. "But now it would be known . . . how much of the Scripture the *Quaker* will own, for a true Declaration, *&c*. What Books by name, what Chapters, and what Verses in these Books will abide his Censure. . . . [The Scriptures are] written by Inspiration of God's Spirit, or the Motion thereof. . . . Otherwise this passage would be doubtful, and all the Historical part of the Scripture also, which declares matter of Fact: For either these things were written in the Book of God, by the Motion and Direction of his Spirit, or else they only rest on Humane Authority, and Conjecture . . . but when God speaketh, we must submit our Reason; by Faith receive, what by Science we cannot understand. . . . for shame never doubt but that he [God] speaketh in the *holy Scriptures*. Now we are sure that the Holy Spirit speaketh in the Scripture; but we are not sure that he speaks in thee. . . . The Spirit speaking in the Scriptures, ought to be heard, rather than you, O *Quakers!* When you speak without, or against the Authority and Truth of them" (Grantham, *Christianismus Primitivus*, Book 4, 46–51. *The Baptist against the Quaker*, originally written in 1673, was reprinted in *Christianismus Primitivus*, Book 4, 43–74).

59. Grantham rarely quoted the medieval scholastics.

60. J. I. Packer, "A Stunted Ecclesiology?" in *Ancient and Postmodern Christianity: Paleo-Orthodoxy in the 21st Century: Essays in Honor of Thomas C. Oden*, ed. Kenneth Tanner and Christopher A. Hall (Downers Grove, IL: InterVarsity, 2002), 122.

61. George, *Theology of the Reformers*, 82. The intent of this essay is to deal with the theme "The Will to Believe and the Need for Creed: Evangelicals and the Nicene Faith." Thus, its narrow aim is neither to outline a General-Free Will Baptist theological method nor to probe the question of the sufficiency of Scripture and its relation to tradition, but rather to focus on the value that the General-Free Will Baptist tradition placed on the Christian tradition while always upholding the sufficiency of Holy Scripture for Christian faith and practice.

62. Bass, *Thomas Grantham*, 180n19; 203n127.

63. Ibid., 180.

64. Thomas Grantham, *A Sigh for Peace* (London, 1671), 104–5.

65. Thomas Monck, *A Cure for the Cankering Error of the New Eutychians* (London, 1673). Richard Haines followed in 1674 with *New Lords, New Laws* (London, 1674), another strongly trinitarian work.

66. Grantham was responding to heterodox General Baptists as well as to the wave of anti-trinitarianism in the Church of England and among the Presbyterians during that time.

67. Bass, *Thomas Grantham*, 182; Adam Taylor, *History of the English General Baptists* (London: T. Bore, 1818), 1:364–76, 463–80. Taylor, W. T. Whitley, and others have traditionally

argued that antitrinitarian sentiments among the General Baptists were limited to Kent and Sussex, where even there they were strongly opposed. See W. T. Whitley, *A History of the British Baptists* (London: Charles Griffin, 1923), 172–74. See also Underwood, *History of English Baptists*, and Thomas Crosby, *The History of the English Baptists* (London: John Robinson, 1740).

68. Christopher Cooper, *The Vail Turn'd Aside: Or, Heresie Unmask'd, Being a Reply to a Book Entituled The Moderate Trinitarian* (London: J. Marshal, 1701), 116–20. By law, Parliament required all Baptist and other dissenting ministers to subscribe to the Thirty-Nine Articles of the Church of England (with the exception of the articles that dealt with distinctive Baptist doctrines). Cooper said that the Caffynites were deceivers, because they publicly subscribed to this confession under oath in court, and publicly subscribed to the 1691 edition of the Standard Confession in the General Assembly, but still propagated antitrinitarian heresy privately.

69. Cooper also accused Caffyn and his group of dishonesty because they forged a copy of the 1691 Standard Confession, making changes to its third article on the person of Christ, yet keeping the orthodox Joseph Wright's name at the top of it. Furthermore, Cooper stated, the "pretended Tryal" of Caffyn in London in 1700 was "just like the rest," with Caffyn denying that he was heretical and his group drawing up "a paper in *Ambiguous* words, which looked like Orthodox" (ibid., 120–21). There was always confusion and misperception about what exactly Caffyn believed. For example, the orthodox group alleged at one point that Caffyn had told an antitrinitarian that his truths were "precious," but Caffyn's followers said that he had said they were "pernicious truths" (but this attempt at a defense is dubious—how can a truth be said to be pernicious?).

70. Bass, *Thomas Grantham*, 11.

71. Curtis W. Freeman, "God in Three Persons: Baptist Unitarianism and the Trinity," *Perspectives in Religious Studies* 33 (2006): 326. Freeman mistakenly conflates Grantham with Allen. Freeman avers that Allen is representative of "the moderate position" in his work, which was a response to Joseph Taylor. Yet Grantham's views align with Taylor's, not with Allen's unorthodox views. Cf. Bass, *Thomas Grantham*, 201.

72. Bass, *Thomas Grantham*, 185–91, 195–97.

73. Ibid., 201.

74. Taylor, *History of the English General Baptists*, 1:364–76, 463–80. See Taylor for a careful, point-by-point defense of the orthodoxy of the mainstream of the General Baptists of the seventeenth century.

75. Grantham, *Christianismus Primitivus*, Book 2, 40.

76. Ibid. (emphasis added).

77. George, *Theology of the Reformers*, 182.

78. There is no better defense of Grantham's robust trinitarianism than that of Clint Bass in his monograph on Grantham's theology. While Bass misunderstands some of the nuances of Grantham's soteriology, his study is otherwise stellar.

79. Bass, *Thomas Grantham*, 195.

80. Thomas Grantham, *St. Paul's Catechism, Or a Brief Explication of the Six Principles of the Christian Religion . . .* (London, 1687).

81. W. T. Whitley, ed., *Minutes of the General Assembly of the General Baptists* (London: Kingsgate, 1909), General Assembly, 1691.

82. Ibid.

83. Other charges were brought against Caffyn in 1692 (Whitley, *Minutes*, General Assembly, 1692). The General Assembly apparently adjourned for three years, reconvening in 1696.

84. Whitley, *Minutes*, General Association, 1697.

85. See, e.g., Whitley, *Minutes*, General Assembly, 1686, 1693, 1700, 1702, 1704, 1705. Taylor, *History of the English General Baptists*, 477–78. The early Baptist historian Thomas Crosby

even believed that Caffyn himself was orthodox and simply "var[ied] a little in some abstruse *unrevealed* speculations" (Crosby, *History of the English Baptists*, 280–83).

86. Underwood, *History of the English Baptists*, 126–28.

87. As is seen in works by Joseph Hooke, Christopher Cooper, Joseph Taylor, and William Russell.

88. The General Association of General Baptists is an Arminian Baptist movement that arose spontaneously in the Midwest in the middle nineteenth century but had no organic ties to the English General Baptists.

89. Michael R. Pelt surmises that Palmer might have been a General Baptist "messenger," the third, itinerant office of the English General Baptists (in addition to elder [i.e., pastor, bishop] and deacon) for planting churches and helping settle church disputes and ordain ministers, whose counsel could be disregarded by local congregations. See Pelt, *A History of Original Free Will Baptists* (Mount Olive, NC: Mount Olive College Press, 1998).

90. George Stevenson, "Benjamin Laker," in *Dictionary of North Carolina Biography*, ed. William S. Powell (Chapel Hill: University of North Carolina Press, 1991), 4:3–4.

91. William F. Davidson shows that this was the church in the Perquimans Precinct of North Carolina where Laker had exerted his influence (Davidson, *The Free Will Baptists in History* [Nashville: Randall House, 2001], 34–35). Pelt (*History*, 24) concurs, as does George Stevenson ("Benjamin Laker," 3–4). The only other scholar to discuss this was W. T. Whitley, who mistakenly assumed that the plea could have come from either the Perquimans group or the Charleston, South Carolina, church. But the Charleston church already had a pastor, William Screven (since 1696), and was Calvinistic in doctrine. See W. T. Whitley, "General Baptists in Carolina and Virginia," *Free Will Baptist* 75/29 (1960): 12–14.

92. Whitley, *Minutes*, General Association, 1702.

93. Whitley, "General Baptists in Carolina and Virginia," 13.

94. Elizabeth Smith, "The Former Articles of Faith of the North Carolina Free Will Baptists," *Free Will Baptist* 75/29 (1960): 9–11; Davidson, *Free Will Baptists*, 92–99; Pelt, *History*, 109–13.

95. Stevenson, "Benjamin Laker," 3–4.

96. Davidson, *Free Will Baptists*, 25–47; Pelt, *History*, 33–67.

97. Hearn, "Origins of the Free Will Baptist Church," 37.

98. *An Abstract of the Former Articles of Faith Confessed by the Original Baptist Church Holding the Doctrine of General Provision with a Proper Code of Discipline*, 2nd ed. (New Bern, NC: Salmon Hall, 1814).

99. *Abstract* (1855), 12, 16, 17.

100. Davidson, *Free Will Baptists*, 175. See, e.g., *Minutes of the Thirty-Third Annual Convention of Free Will Baptists* (n.p.: Cumberland Association, Middle Tennessee, 1876), 14.

101. Pelt, *History*, 140; Charles C. Ware, *Tar Heel Disciples* (New Bern, NC: Owen G. Dunn, 1942), 36.

102. Pelt, *History*, 135; Ware, *Tar Heel Disciples*, 22–24.

103. Pelt, *History*, 137.

104. See Pelt, *History*, 128–43, for the best documentation and analysis of this controversy.

105. J. Matthew Pinson, "E. L. St. Claire and the Free Will Baptist Experience, 1893–1916," *Viewpoints: The Journal of the Georgia Baptist Historical Society* 17 (2000): 28–29.

106. See, e.g., minutes, issues of the weekly magazine the *Free Will Baptist*, which began to be published in 1873; books such as Thad F. Harrison and J. M. Barfield, *History of the Free Will Baptists of North Carolina* (1897; repr., Ayden, NC: Free Will Baptist Press, 1959); and the many works by E. L. St. Claire.

Chapter 9 Toward a Generous Orthodoxy

1. Brian D. McLaren, *A Generous Orthodoxy* (Grand Rapids: Zondervan, 2004). While I am a sympathetic and appreciative reader of McLaren's book, in the end it seems to be more about generosity than orthodoxy. Although the former is crucial, it is the latter that is my concern.

2. Robert L. Calhoun, "A Liberal Bandaged but Unbowed," in the series "How My Mind Has Changed in This Decade," *Christian Century*, May 31, 1939, 701–4; Calhoun, *Lectures on the History of Christian Doctrine*, 3 vols. (New Haven: Yale Divinity School, 1948), 1:14; Hans Frei, "In Memory of Robert L. Calhoun 1896–1983, *Reflection* 82 (1984): 8–9; George A. Lindbeck, *Robert Lowry Calhoun as Historian of Doctrine*, Yale Divinity School Library Occasional Publication No. 12 (New Haven: Yale Divinity School Library, 1998).

3. C. H. Spurgeon, "Another Word concerning the Down-Grade," *Sword and Trowel*, August 1887.

4. C. H. Spurgeon, "A Fragment upon the Down Grade Controversy," *Sword and Trowel*, November 1887. The anonymous articles were written by Robert Shindler, a close associate of Spurgeon. Shindler produced a pamphlet entitled "Creed or No Creed?" that was distributed at the time of the March meeting of the union. See C. H. Spurgeon, *The Down Grade Controversy*, ed. Bob Ross (Pasadena, TX: Pilgrim Publications, 1978).

5. Ernest A. Payne, *The Baptist Union: A Short History* (London: Carey Kingsgate Press, 1959), 127–43. John Briggs identifies three liberal Baptist ministers who were most immediately in Spurgeon's thoughts about the Down Grade: W. E. Blomfield, J. G. Greenhough, and James Thew, in *The English Baptists of the Nineteenth Century* (Didcot, UK: Baptist Historical Society, 1994), 181–88.

6. John Clifford, "The Great Forty Years," in *A Baptist Treasury,* ed. Sydnor L. Stealey (New York: Thomas Y. Crowell, 1958), 98–113.

7. "Declaratory Statement, Adopted by the Baptist Union Assembly, 23rd April 1888," Appendix VI, in Payne, *Baptist Union*, 271.

8. In Puritan theology, *experience* was a technical term that denoted a constellation of convictions and affections between the awakening to sin and the conversion of the sinner through effective grace. See the Westminster Confession of Faith, 10, in *Creeds of the Churches*, ed. John H. Leith (New York: Anchor Books, 1963), 206. Christian experience so understood is *theocentric* and *theological* and should not be mistaken for or confused with *anthropocentric* and *psychological* notions of experience associated with evangelical revivalism, Protestant liberalism, or psychological theories. Two classic examples of early Baptist conversion narratives that describe conversion in terms of experience are Jane Turner, *Choice Experiences of the Kind Dealings of God before, in, and after Conversion* (London: H. Hils, 1653); and Katherine Sutton, *A Christian Womans Experiences of the Glorious Working of Gods Free Grace* (Rotterdam: Henry Goddaeus, 1663).

9. Walter Rauschenbusch appealed to this early Baptist conviction—although recasting it in later evangelical and psychological language—when he wrote: "The Christian faith, as Baptists hold it, sets spiritual experience boldly to the front as the one great thing in religion. It aims at experimental religion. . . . We ask a man: 'Have you put your faith in Christ? Have you submitted your will to His will? Have you received the inward assurance that your sins are forgiven and that you are at peace with God? Have you made experience of God?' If anyone desires to enter our churches we ask for evidence of such experience and we ask for nothing else. We do not ask him to recite a creed or catechism. . . . When we insist on experience, and not on ritual or creed, we place religion where it is necessarily free, and then, if it is freely given, it has value in God's sight." Walter Rauschenbusch, "Why I Am a Baptist," *Rochester Baptist Monthly*, 1905–6; reprinted in *Colgate Rochester Divinity School Bulletin*, December 20, 1938.

10. "Declaratory Statement," Payne, *Baptist Union*, 271.

11. The text of the Lambeth Quadrilateral reads: "A. The Holy Scriptures of the Old and New Testaments, as 'containing all things necessary for salvation,' and as being the rule and

ultimate standard of faith. B. The Apostles' Creed, as the Baptismal Symbol; and the Nicene Creed, as the sufficient statements of the Christian Faith. C. The two Sacraments ordained by Christ Himself—Baptism and the Supper of the Lord—ministered with unfailing use of Christ's Words of Institution, and of the elements ordained by Him. D. The Historic Episcopate, locally adapted in the methods of its administration to the varying needs of the nations and peoples called of God into the Unity of His Church." In *The Oxford Dictionary of the Christian Church*, ed. E. A. Livingstone, 3rd ed., s.v. "Lambeth Quadrilateral" (Oxford: Oxford University Press, 1997), 946.

12. The liturgical context of the Apostles' Creed as a baptismal confession may be traced to the second century as is indicated by the baptismal creed of Hippolytus, in *The Apostolic Tradition of St Hippolytus*, ed. Gregory Dix and Henry Chadwick, 2nd ed (London: Alban Press, 1992), 21.12–18, 36–37. See also J. N. D. Kelly, *Early Christian Creeds*, 3rd ed. (New York: Longman, 1972), 113–19. Kelly describes how, from the sixth century on, the Nicene Creed came to be almost universally used in both East and West as a eucharistic confession of faith (Kelly, *Early Christian Creeds*, 348–57).

13. *Proceedings of the Southern Baptist Convention* (Richmond: H. K. Ellyson, 1845), 19. When the SBC in 1925 adopted the Memphis Articles on the Baptist Faith and Message, the committee added the caveat "That the sole authority for faith and practice among Baptists is the Scriptures of the Old and New Testaments. Confessions are only guides in interpretation, having no authority over the conscience."

14. Rauschenbusch, "Why I Am a Baptist," Fourth Reason.

15. *Annual of the Northern Baptist Convention* (Philadelphia: American Baptist Publication Society, 1922), 133.

16. John J. Hurt, "Should Southern Baptists Have a Creed/Confession?—No!" *Review and Expositor* 76, no. 1 (Winter 1979): 85. Joe T. Odle, in a companion article, answered "Yes!" to the same question. Joe T. Odle, "Should Southern Baptists Have a Creed/Confession?—Yes!" *Review and Expositor* 76, no. 1 (Winter 1979): 89–94. In the same issue, Walter Shurden invoked Johnson's "No creed but the Bible!" against what he argued was the reversal of Johnson's anticreedalism, in "Southern Baptist Responses to Their Confessional Statements," *Review and Expositor* 76, no. 1 (Winter 1979): 69–84.

17. Jimmy R. Allen, "The Takeover Resurgence Is Creedalism," *Texas Baptists Committed*, August 2004, 14.

18. Walter B. Shurden, "The Coalition for Baptist Principles," *Baptist Studies Bulletin* 6, no. 6 (June 2007), www.centerforbaptiststudies.org/bulletin /2007/june.htm.

19. Harry Emerson Fosdick, *Modern Uses of the Bible* (New York: Macmillan, 1924), 262; Robert Moats Miller, *Harry Emerson Fosdick: Preacher, Pastor, Prophet* (New York: Oxford University Press, 1985), 107–18; and Harry Emerson Fosdick, *The Living of These Days: An Autobiography* (New York: Harper & Brothers, 1956), 172.

20. Fosdick, *Modern Uses of the Bible*, 262. Fosdick conceded that noncreedal churches unfortunately do not "have a better understanding of what [the creeds] really meant to say." And he added that when he hears "some fresh and flippant modern mind condescending to them, treating the fathers who wrote them as quibblers and fools, I am strongly tempted to bear a hand in their defense." Yet for Fosdick, "what they really meant to say" came down to abiding experience in changing categories (ibid., 97–130).

21. Hezekiah Harvey, *The Church: Its Polity and Ordinances* (Philadelphia: American Baptist Publication Society, 1879), 37.

22. E. Y. Mullins, *Baptist Beliefs* (Philadelphia: Judson Press, 1925), 6.

23. *The Baptist World Congress*, London, July 11–19, 1905 (London: Baptist Union Publications Department, 1905), vii, 19–20.

24. Curtis Freeman, Steven Harmon, Elizabeth Newman, and Philip Thompson, "Confessing the Faith," *Biblical Recorder*, July 8, 2004. Several news stories were published on the statement,

including Steve DeVane, "Educators Support BWA Recitation of Creed," *Biblical Recorder*, July 17, 2004; Russell Moore, "The Moderates Were Right," *Baptist Press News*, July 7, 2004; and Bob Allen, "Proposal Sparks Debate over Baptists and Creeds," *Ethics Daily*, July 16, 2004.

25. John Howard Yoder, *Preface to Theology: Christology and Theological Method* (Grand Rapids: Brazos, 2002), 204.

26. Ibid., 223. J. Denny Weaver extends Yoder's argument by further emphasizing the politics of creedal formation, which he argues served to undergird the stability of the empire; see Weaver, "Nicea, Womanist Theology, and Anabaptist Particularity," in *Anabaptists and Postmodernity*, ed. Susan Biesecker-Mast and Gerald Biesecker-Mast (Telford: Pandora Press, 2000), 251–59. A. James Reimer argues against Yoder and Weaver that theological orthodoxy and Constantinianism are not intrinsically linked, and that in particular the notion of a Constantinian "fall" is historically and theologically problematic; see Reimer, "Theological Orthodoxy, Constantinianism, and Theology from a Radical Protestant Perspective," in *Faith to Creed: Ecumenical Perspectives on the Affirmation of the Apostolic Faith in the Fourth Century*, ed. S. Mark Heim (Grand Rapids: Eerdmans, 1991), 129–61. Alain Epp Weaver problematizes the argument by suggesting that Yoder developed a two-pronged strategy that, on the one hand, appealed to the creeds in ecumenical conversations but, on the other, relativized their importance for theology; see Epp Weaver, "Missionary Christology: John Howard Yoder and the Creeds," *Mennonite Quarterly Review* 74, no. 3 (July 2000): 423–39.

27. Thomas N. Finger, "The Way to Nicaea: Some Reflections from a Mennonite Perspective," *Journal of Ecumenical Studies* 24, no. 2 (Spring 1987): 229.

28. The phrase *a critical orthodoxy*, depicted as a circle with a center and a circumference, is proposed by Thomas C. Oden, *The Rebirth of Orthodoxy: Signs of New Life in Christianity* (San Francisco: HarperSanFrancisco, 2003), 130–33.

29. John Killinger, "The Changing Shape of Our Salvation" (breakout session at the General Assembly of the Cooperative Baptist Fellowship, Memphis, Tennessee, June 19, 2008). Press reports: David Roach, "CBF Presenter Questions Christ's Deity," *Baptist Press*, June 19, 2008, www.baptistpress.org/bpnews.asp?id=28326; James A. Smith, "Is CBF Baptist? Christian?" *Florida Baptist Witness*, June 23, 2008, www.floridabaptistwitness.com/9027.article; "Dan Vestal Corrects Claim That CBF Is 'Unchristian,'" *Religious Herald*, July 10, 2008, www.religiousherald .org/index.php?option=com_content&task=view&id=2433&Itemid=113.

30. John Killinger, *The Changing Shape of Our Salvation* (New York: Crossroad Publishing, 2007), 71–73.

31. Killinger offers no theoretical framework for his account of doctrinal development. He does not follow the familiar liberal Protestant historicism of Adolf von Harnack, who proposed that "dogma in its conception and development is a work of the Greek spirit on the soil of the Gospel," and who encouraged the retrieval of the gospel kernel from the Hellenistic husk. Harnack, *History of Dogma*, 7 vols., trans. Neil Buchanan (New York: Dover Publications, 1961), 1:17; and Harnack, *What Is Christianity?* trans. Thomas Bailey Saunders (New York: Harper & Row), 12–18. Nor does he accept the nuanced Catholic thesis of John Henry Cardinal Newman, which conceived of catholic orthodoxy as "the legitimate growth and complement, that is, the natural and necessary development, of the doctrine of the early church." Newman, *An Essay on the Development of Christian Doctrine*, 6th ed. (Notre Dame, IN: University of Notre Dame Press, 1989), 169. Instead, Killinger assumes a political theory of doctrine in which orthodoxy and heresy are arbitrary conventions based on the result of winners and losers in theological conflict. His thin description could have been strengthened by a more nuanced reading of the history, such as R. P. C. Hanson's revisionist account of Arianism in his massive study *The Search for the Christian Doctrine of God* (Edinburgh: T&T Clark, 1988), or even the shorter version, "The Achievement of Orthodoxy in the Fourth Century AD," in *The Making of Orthodoxy*, ed. Rowan Williams (Cambridge: Cambridge University Press, 1989), 142–56. Through a dazzling treatment of the primary sources, Hanson shows the conventional account

of an established orthodoxy challenged by a coherent Arian party to be inaccurate and misleading. His revisionist account displays the development of orthodoxy mixed with the misuse of power. This more complex reading of doctrinal development could have provided Killinger with facts for thoughtful refection instead of stereotypes, caricatures, and unexamined assumptions.

32. The Niceno-Constantinopolitan Creed, in *Creeds and Confessions of Faith in the Christian Tradition*, ed. Jaroslav Pelikan and Valerie Hotchkiss, 4 vols. (New Haven: Yale University Press, 2004), 1:162–63.

33. A. C. Underwood, *A History of the English Baptists* (London: Baptist Union, 1847), 127; Elhanan Winchester, *The Universal Restoration: Exhibited in Four Dialogues between a Minister and His Friend* (London: printed for the author by T. Gillet, 1792; repr., Bellows Falls, VT: Bill Blake, 1819), commonly called *Dialogues on the Universal Restoration*; and Richard Furman, John M. Roberts, and Joseph B. Cook, "Call for a State Convention in South Carolina," November 8, 1820, in H. Leon McBeth, *A Sourcebook for Baptist Heritage* (Nashville: Broadman Press, 1990), 246–51.

34. George Burman Foster, *The Finality of the Christian Religion* (Chicago: University of Chicago Press, 1906), 495.

35. George Burman Foster, *The Function of Religion in Man's Struggle for Existence* (Chicago: University of Chicago Press, 1909), 57, 86–88, 142–43.

36. I have adapted this wonderful phrase, so apt of Foster's modernist theology, from Stephen Webb, review of *Heaven: The Logic of Eternal Joy*, by Jerry L. Walls, in *Christian Century*, December 4–7, 2002, 42. Grant Wacker charitably attributes some of the problem to Foster's "richly allusive . . . prose style," in *Augustus H. Strong and the Dilemma of Historical Consciousness* (Macon, GA: Mercer University Press, 1985), 169. But as Gary Dorrien documents, Foster's theology was a "humanistic naturalism." Dorrien, *The Making of American Liberal Theology*, 3 vols. (Louisville: Westminster John Knox, 2001), 2:178.

37. The Second London Confession, 8.2, in William L. Lumpkin, *Baptist Confessions of Faith*, rev. ed. (Valley Forge, PA: Judson Press, 1969), 260.

38. The Orthodox Creed, 4, in Lumpkin, *Baptist Confessions of Faith*, 299.

39. D. H. Williams, *Retrieving the Tradition and Renewing Evangelicalism: A Primer for Suspicious Protestants* (Grand Rapids: Eerdmans, 1999), 95–99.

40. Baptist Faith and Message (1963), in Lumpkin, *Baptist Confessions of Faith*, 393. It is important to note that the 2000 revision of the Baptist Faith and Message deleted the sentence "The criterion by which the Bible is to be interpreted is Jesus Christ." It was replaced by the statement "All Scripture is a testimony to Christ, who is Himself the focus of divine revelation." The revision significantly altered the hermeneutical force of the christological reference, which functions prospectively (reading forward from the Old Testament to the New Testament) but not retrospectively (reading backward from the New Testament to the Old Testament).

41. Augustine, *On the Spirit and the Letter* 27.15, in the *Nicene and Post-Nicene Fathers*, ed. Philip Schaff (Grand Rapids: Eerdmans, 1971), 5:95. See also my "Figure and History: A Contemporary Reassessment of Augustine's Hermeneutic," in *Collectanea Augustiniana. Augustine: Presbyter Factus Sum*, ed. J. T. Lienhard, E. C. Muller, and R. J. Teske (New York: Peter Lang, 1993), 319–29.

42. Steven R. Harmon, "Do Real Baptists Recite Creeds?" *Baptists Today*, September 2004, 27.

43. The Niceno-Constantinopolitan Creed, in *Creeds and Confessions of Faith in the Christian Tradition*, 1:162–63.

44. Athanasius, *On the Incarnation of the Word: The Treatise De Incarnatione Verbi Dei*, trans. and ed. by a religious of CSMV, with an introduction by C. S. Lewis (Crestwood, NY: St. Vladimir's Seminary Press, 1953), 41. This was a consistent theme for Athanasius, who elsewhere argued, "Why did the Word come among us, and become flesh?" To which he answered, "That He might redeem [hu]mankind, the Word did come among us; and that he might hallow and

deify them, the Word became flesh." Athanasius, *Four Discourses against the Arians* 3.39, in *Nicene and Post-Nicene Fathers* (Grand Rapids: Eerdmans, 1978), 4:415.

45. Athanasius, *On the Incarnation* 9, 35.

46. Ibid., 54, 93.

47. Christopher A. Beeley argues that Gregory of Nazianzus was the first patristic theologian to advance a developed theory of *theosis*, in *Gregory of Nazianzus on the Trinity and the Knowledge of God: In Your Light We See Light* (New York: Oxford University Press, 2008).

48. It may be of interest to note that in his introduction to Athanasius, *On the Incarnation*, C. S. Lewis describes it as "a masterpiece" (9). Lewis drew extensively from the dramatic *Christus Victor* theology of Athanasius and the other patristic writers when he wrote his allegory *The Lion, the Witch and the Wardrobe*.

49. Augustus H. Strong, *Systematic Theology*, 8th ed., 3 vols. (Valley Forge, PA: Judson Press, 1907–9), 3:713–75.

50. Among Baptist (and baptistic) theologians who have offered thoughtful reflections on the atonement from the standpoints of liberation theology, scapegoat theory, and nonviolence are James H. Evans, *We Shall All Be Changed: Social Problems and Theological Renewal* (Minneapolis: Fortress, 1997), 45–66; S. Mark Heim, *Saved from Sacrifice: A Theology of the Cross* (Grand Rapids: Eerdmans, 2006); and J. Denny Weaver, *The Nonviolent Atonement* (Grand Rapids: Eerdmans, 2001).

51. Steve Chalke and Alan Mann, *The Lost Message of Jesus* (Grand Rapids: Zondervan, 2003), 182.

52. Among the harshest critics are Steve Jeffery, Michael Ovey, and Andrew Sach, in *Pierced for Our Transgressions* (Wheaton: Crossway, 2007).

53. Stephen R. Holmes, *The Wondrous Cross: Atonement and Penal Substitution in the Bible and History* (London: Paternoster, 2007). Holmes makes it clear that unlike other critics, he does not regard penal substitution to be the sine qua non of evangelicalism, when he writes: "I will say as clearly as possible now that I do not for a moment suppose that penal substitutionary atonement is the article by which the church stands or falls; nor do I accept that there is any reason to call for those who object to penal substitution to be expelled, on account of that rejection per se, from Evangelical bodies, let alone from the church." Holmes, "Of Babies and Bathwater? Recent Evangelical Criticisms of Penal Substitution in the Light of Early Modern Debates concerning Justification," *European Journal of Theology* 16, no. 2 (2007): 93–105. See also Holmes, "Cur Deus Po-mo? What St. Anselm Can Teach Us about Preaching the Atonement Today," *Epworth Review* 36, no. 1 (January 2009): 6–17; Holmes, "Death in the Afternoon: Hebrews, Sacrifice and Soteriology," in *Hebrews and Christian Theology*, ed. Richard Bauckham, Daniel R. Driver, Trevor A. Hart, and Nathan MacDonald (Grand Rapids: Eerdmans, 2009), 229–52.

54. John Calvin, *Institutes of the Christian Religion*, 2.16.5 (Philadelphia: Westminster Press, 1960), 1:507.

55. Baptist theologian Fisher Humphreys acknowledges the incarnational dimension of what he calls "cruciform forgiveness." Though his focus is on Christ's death, Humphreys states: "Cruciform forgiveness is incarnate forgiveness at its highest pitch. From this it follows that the death and dying of Jesus are one piece with the rest of his historical life." Humphreys, *The Death of Christ* (Nashville: Broadman Press, 1978), 124.

56. Douglas A. Campbell, *The Quest for Paul's Gospel* (London: T&T Clark, 2005), 168. Campbell indicates a variety of texts in which Paul attributes saving significance to the resurrection (including 1 Cor. 15:17; Rom. 4:25) and the incarnation (Rom. 8:1–4; 2 Cor. 5:21; Phil. 2:5–11).

57. Douglas A. Campbell, *The Deliverance of God: An Apocalyptic Rereading of Justification in Paul* (Grand Rapids: Eerdmans, 2009), 76. See also 210–12.

58. William C. Placher, "How Does Jesus Save?" *Christian Century*, June 2, 2009, 23–27. See also Placher, "Christ Takes Our Place: Rethinking Atonement," *Interpretation* 53, no.1 (January 1999): 5–20. Placher notes at this point that both the Apostles' and Nicene creeds move

immediately from Christ's birth to his death without attesting to the fullness of his life. Calvin observed that the "Apostles' Creed passes at once in the best order from the birth of Christ to his death and resurrection, wherein the whole of perfect salvation consists. Yet the remainder of the obedience that he manifested in his life is not excluded." Calvin, *Institutes of the Christian Religion*, 2.16.5, 1:508. It is this great omission which gave John Howard Yoder, Denny Weaver, and other Anabaptists cause for concern about the creeds. Willard M. Swartley consequently has proposed the following additions to the Apostles' Creed to address the omission of Christ's life: "Lived obediently to his Abba. Lived and taught love, peace, and forgiveness. Healed the sick, cast out demons, forgave sins, raised the dead, confounded the powers." Swartley, *Covenant of Peace: The Missing Peace in New Testament Theology and Ethics* (Grand Rapids: Eerdmans, 2006), 425.

59. A recent collection of essays on the atonement by Orthodox, Catholic, liberal and evangelical Protestants, and Anabaptists is one example of such a conversation: Brad Jersak and Michael Hardin, eds., *Stricken By God? Nonviolent Identification and the Victory of Christ* (Grand Rapids: Eerdmans, 2007).

60. James Wm. McClendon Jr., *Systematic Theology*, vol. 2, *Doctrine* (Nashville: Abingdon Press, 1994), 238–79.

61. Ibid., 256–57.

62. Ibid., 262–63. D. M. Baillie, *God Was in Christ* (New York: Scribner's, 1948), 11.

63. McClendon, *Doctrine*, 257–63.

64. Hans W. Frei, *The Eclipse of Biblical Narrative: A Study in Eighteenth and Nineteenth Century Hermeneutics* (New Haven: Yale University Press, 1974), 1–16; and Frei, *The Identity of Jesus Christ: The Hermeneutical Bases of Dogmatic Theology* (Philadelphia: Fortress, 1975; repr., Eugene, OR: Wipf & Stock, 1997), 59–64.

65. McClendon, *Doctrine*, 274–79.

66. Ibid., 266–69. In taking the Christ hymn of Philippians to refer to Christ's earthly life, McClendon follows the minority view of Cyprian in the history of interpretation. The leading contemporary proponent of the nonincarnational reading is James D. G. Dunn, who has argued that "Phil. 2:6–8 is probably intended to affirm that Christ's earthly life was an embodiment of grace from beginning to end, of giving away in contrast to the selfish grasping of Adam's sin." Dunn, *Christology in the Making* (Philadelphia: Westminster Press, 1980), 121. N. T. Wright is one of the leading proponents of the incarnational reading of the Pauline Christ hymn, in Wright, *The Climax of the Covenant: Christ and the Law in Pauline Theology* (Minneapolis: Fortress, 1992), 90–97. McClendon does not take a position in the debate between the "low and slow" developmental Christology of Dunn and the "early high" Christology of Wright. He does, however, find that Cyprian's view of imitating Jesus in his earthly life coalesces nicely with the Christology of John Howard Yoder and its corollary of servant discipleship. One might reasonably argue for a two-narratives Christology based on the sort of incarnational reading supplied by Wright, although McClendon found the appeal to imitate the preexistent Christ to be less compelling than the imitation of Christ in his earthly life.

67. Robert Barron, *The Priority of Christ: Toward a Postliberal Catholicism* (Grand Rapids: Brazos, 2007), 65.

68. McClendon, *Doctrine*, 272.

69. Barron, *The Priority of Christ*, 66. David H. Kelsey suggests that a kind of two-narratives approach is at work in the Christology of Karl Barth's treatment of "The Royal Man" in *Church Dogmatics*, 4.2, Section 64.3 (Edinburgh: T&T Clark, 1958), 154–264. For Barth, the biblical narrative renders the identity of Jesus Christ as God with us: (1) as the revelation of Israel's Messiah (namely, the disciples' perspective), and (2) by narrating Jesus's death as an act in which he achieved his intention to live in unbroken response to God's will. Kelsey, *Proving Doctrine: The Uses of Scripture in Modern Theology* (Harrisburg, PA: Trinity Press, 1999), 39–50.

70. Finger, for example, maintains that McClendon unwisely critiques the proclivity of the Chalcedonian definition for minimizing Jesus's humanity. He suggests that, in fact,

McClendon's two-narratives revision of the liberal-historical Christology makes a more problematic move similar to that of Faustus Socinus, in "McClendon's Theology Reaches Comple-
tion," 125–26. See also Thomas Finger, *A Contemporary Anabaptist Theology* (Downers Grove,
IL: InterVarsity, 2004), 398–99. This criticism misses the point of McClendon's qualification
and further his postliberal use the historical-critical critique. To answer McClendon, Finger
takes refuge in a metaphysical essentialism that seems to lead back to the sort of Melchiorism
invoked by Baptists that McClendon was criticizing. (Melchiorism denotes the celestial-flesh
Christology popularized by Melchior Hoffman, a German Anabaptist preacher of the 1530s
who taught that Jesus did not receive his humanity from Mary but moved through her like
water through a pipe.) Additionally, Finger fails to acknowledge in his exegesis of Phil. 2:1–11
that the phrase "the form of God" is by no means settled in the scholarship as a reference
to preexistence. (See the above discussion of Dunn vs. Wright.) McClendon acknowledged
the stream of historical scholarship Finger cites that reads the Pauline hymn as ascribing
preexistence to Christ, in McClendon, "Philippians 2:5–11," *Review and Expositor* 88, no.
4 (Fall 1991): 439–44. McClendon followed another line of interpretation, however, that he
traced to patristic sources.

71. *Confessing the One Faith: An Ecumenical Explication of the Apostolic Faith as it is Confessed in the Nicene-Constantinopolitan Creed (381)*, Faith and Order Paper No. 153 (Geneva:
WCC Publications, 1991), 4.

Chapter 10 Practicing the Nicene Faith

1. "O Sacred Head, Now Wounded," *Worship and Rejoice* (Carol Stream, IL: Hope Publishing, 2001), 284.

2. For further reading see the Fourth Council of the Lateran convoked by Pope Innocent III
on April 19, 1213, and held November 1214 at Rome's Lateran Palace. www.dailycatholic.org
/history/12ecume1.htm.

3. Paraphrased by Stanley Hauerwas, *With the Grain of the Universe: The Church's Witness
and Natural Theology* (Grand Rapids: Brazos, 2001), 199.

4. Hauerwas makes this claim throughout his writings. See, for example, *The Peaceable
Kingdom: A Primer in Christian Ethics* (Notre Dame, IN: University of Notre Dame Press,
1991).

5. For a theological and philosophical analysis of *dabar*, see especially William H. Poteat,
Polanyian Meditations: In Search of a Post-Critical Logic (Durham, NC: Duke University Press,
1985), 104–32.

6. Alasdair MacIntyre, *After Virtue: A Study in Moral Theory* (Notre Dame, IN: University
of Notre Dame Press, 1984), 11–12.

7. D. Stephen Long, "God Is Not Nice," in *God Is Not . . .* , ed. D. Brent Laytham (Grand
Rapids: Brazos, 2004), 49.

8. As MacIntyre observes, the individual has no alternative other than now choosing what is
to become good or bad for him or her. To criticize another's choices is to take a negative view of
the individual making the choices, and more often than not his or her response is a retreat into
solidarity with those with whom he or she agrees. Alasdair MacIntyre, "A Culture of Choices
and Compartmentalization" (lecture, "Culture of Death" Conference, University of Notre
Dame, Notre Dame, IN, October 13, 2000). A video of this lecture is available from the Notre
Dame Center for Ethics and Culture.

9. E. Glenn Hinson states, "The heart of our [Baptist] tradition is the voluntary principle in
religion." Hinson, "Forming Baptist Identity(ies) in American Higher Education," *Perspectives
in Religious Studies* 34, no. 4 (Winter 2007): 366.

10. Stanley Hauerwas, *Dispatches from the Front: Theological Engagements with the Secular*
(Durham, NC: Duke University Press, 1994), 13. The original quotation used the example of
choosing between a Sony and a Panasonic.

11. MacIntyre, "Culture of Choices and Compartmentalization."

12. Walter B. Shurden, "The Coalition for Baptist Principles," *Baptist Studies Bulletin* 6, no. 6 (June 2007), www.centerforbaptiststudies.org/bulletin /2007/june.htm.

13. See Isaiah Berlin, *Four Essays on Liberty* (Oxford: Oxford University Press, 2002).

14. Philip Thompson, "Re-envisioning Baptist Identity: Historical, Theological and Liturgical Analysis," *Perspectives in Religious Studies* 27, no. 3 (Fall 2000): 300. Thompson is describing particularly the early Baptists' theological rationale for affirming the sacraments.

15. Poteat's lectures are described in Suzanne C. Linder, *William Louis Poteat: Prophet of Progress* (Chapel Hill: University of North Carolina Press, 1966), 139. See also Randal L. Hall, *William Louis Poteat: A Leader of the Progressive-Era South* (Lexington: University Press of Kentucky, 2000).

16. Thomas K. Hearn Jr., *To Dream with One Eye Open: A Ten-Year Report to the University: 1983–1993* (Winston-Salem, NC: Wake Forest University, 1993), 15.

17. Immanuel Kant, "What Is Enlightenment?," in *Foundations of the Metaphysics of Morals and What Is Enlightenment?* (Indianapolis: Bobbs-Merrill Educational Publishing, 1959), 85.

18. Archbishop Rowan Williams, "Church Needs to Listen Properly to the Bible," www .archbishopofcanterbury.org/532.

19. I think James Burtchaell is basically right to discuss the story of Wake Forest University in terms of the "dying of the light," although his thesis has been controversial. See Burtchaell, *The Dying of the Light: The Disengagement of Colleges and Universities from Their Christian Churches* (Grand Rapids: Eerdmans, 1998).

20. D. H. Williams, "Scripture, Tradition and Church: Reformation and Post-Reformation," in *The Free Church and the Early Church: Bridging the Historical and Theological Divide,* ed. D. H. Williams (Grand Rapids: Eerdmans, 2002), 105.

21. Henry Wadsworth Longfellow, *Tales of a Wayside Inn,* as cited by Jaroslav Pelikan, *Credo: Historical and Theological Guide to Creeds and Confessions of Faith in the Christian Tradition* (New Haven: Yale University Press, 2003), 278.

22. Words of Rodney King, May 1, 1992, as stated in "Rodney King: 17 Years after the Riots," *LAist,* http://laist.com/2009/04/29/meet_rodney _king.php.

23. Jaroslav Pelikan, "The Will to Believe and the Need for Creed," in *Orthodoxy and Western Culture: A Collection of Essays Honoring Jaroslav Pelikan on His Eightieth Birthday,* ed. Valerie Hotchkiss and Patrick Henry (Crestwood, NY: St. Vladimir's Seminary Press, 2005), 179.

24. Michael Gorman, ed., *Scripture: An Ecumenical Introduction to the Bible and Its Interpretation* (Peabody, MA: Hendrickson, 2005), 169.

25. James B. Torrance, *Worship, Community and the Triune God of Grace* (Downers Grove, IL: InterVarsity, 1996), 20. Torrance adds that this is Unitarian because there is no understanding of Christ as mediator and no doctrine of the Holy Spirit, and because it is nonsacramental.

26. Richard Norris, cited by Eugene F. Rogers Jr., *After the Spirit: A Constructive Pneumatology from Resources outside the Modern West* (Grand Rapids: Eerdmans, 2005), 15.

27. Geoffrey Wainwright, *Doxology: The Praise of God in Worship, Doctrine, and Life* (New York: Oxford University Press, 1980), 23.

28. Rogers, *After the Spirit,* 193.

29. Torrance, *Worship, Community and the Triune God of Grace,* 44.

30. Ibid., 46.

31. Ibid. As stated in Romans, "the Spirit helps us in our weakness. For we do not know what to pray for as we ought, but the Spirit himself intercedes for us with groanings too deep for words" (Rom. 8:26).

32. Teresa of Avila, *Interior Castle,* trans. E. Ellison Peers (New York: Image, 2004), 238.

33. Pelikan, *Credo,* 49.

34. Mother Teresa, *A Simple Path* (New York: Random House, 1995), 35.

35. Susan K. Wood, "I Acknowledge One Baptism for the Forgiveness of Sins," in *Nicene Christianity: The Future for a New Ecumenism*, ed. Christopher R. Seitz (Grand Rapids: Brazos, 2001), 199.

36. William T. Cavanaugh, *Being Consumed: Economics and Christian Desire* (Grand Rapids: Eerdmans, 2008), 66.

37. As quoted by Eric Schlosser, *Fast Food Nation: The Dark Side of the All-American Meal* (Boston: Houghton Mifflin, 2001), 37.

38. Michael L. Budde, "Global Culture Industries," in *The Blackwell Companion to Christian Ethics*, ed. Stanley Hauerwas and Samuel Wells (Malden, MA: Blackwell Publishing, 2004), 129.

39. Sharon Parks, "Household Economics," in *Practicing Our Faith*, ed. Dorothy Bass (San Francisco: Jossey-Bass, 1997), 44.

40. Athanasius, *Inc.* 39 (emphasis mine). In the fuller context Athanasius states that some may ask "why [God did] not manifest Himself by means of other and nobler parts of creation, and use some nobler instrument, such as sun or moon or stars or fire or air, instead of mere man." He responds: "The Lord did not come to make a display."

41. Abraham Heschel, *The Sabbath: Its Meaning for Modern Man* (New York: Farrar, Straus & Giroux, 1951), 21, 8.

42. Nicholas Boyle, *Who Are We Now?: Christian Humanism and the Global Market from Hegel to Heaney* (Notre Dame, IN: University of Notre Dame Press, 1998), 154.

43. M. Craig Barnes, *The Pastor as Minor Poet: Texts and Subtexts in the Ministerial Life* (Grand Rapids: Eerdmans, 2009), 32.

44. David Steinmetz, *Memory and Mission* (Nashville: Abingdon, 1988), 136. Similarly, William Cavanaugh writes, "The individual consumer of the Eucharist does not simply take Christ into herself, but is taken up into Christ" (*Being Consumed*, 54).

45. D. Stephen Long and Nancy Ruth Fox, with Tripp York, *Calculated Futures: Theology, Ethics and Economics* (Waco: Baylor University Press, 2007), 200.

46. Cavanaugh, *Being Consumed*, 97.

47. Even a partial list of the community projects supported by Englewood is remarkable: a lawn-care business, bookkeeping and PC repair services, and a bookstore with online ordering capability. All of these benefit their neighbors in the streets around the church. Their largest area of outreach has been in the housing sector, where they have helped over twenty-five householders become homeowners in their neighborhood. Even more impressive is Englewood's story (loss of membership through "white flight") and how the congregation came to discern how to be faithful in the place where they are.

48. As cited in Mikeal Broadway, "The Ways of Zion Mourned: A Historicist Critique of the Discourses of Church-State Relations" (PhD diss., Duke University, 1993), 186.

49. Locke's full statement is: "I esteem that toleration to be the chief characteristic mark of the true Church." John Locke, "A Letter Concerning Toleration," in Mortimer J. Adler, ed., *Great Books of the Western World* (Chicago: Encyclopedia Britannica, 1996), 1.

50. Michael Baxter, cited by Scott Moore, *The Limits of Liberal Democracy: Politics and Religion at the End of Modernity* (Downers Grove, IL: InterVarsity, 2008), 218–19. Baxter adds that "Christianity does not 'work with politics,' nor 'apply to politics' nor have 'political implications.' Christianity is *always already* political."

51. As von Balthasar states, "The less Church is identical with the world and the more it is itself, the more open and vulnerable it is to the world and the less it can be marked off from it," as quoted by David Schindler, *Heart of the World, Center of the Church: Communio Ecclesiology, Liberalism, and Liberation* (Grand Rapids: Eerdmans, 1996), 1.

52. Teresa, *Interior Castle*, 237.

53. Ibid. Teresa writes, "Do you know when people really become spiritual? It is when they become the slaves of God and are branded with His sign, which is the sign of the Cross, in token that they have given Him their freedom" (234).

Chapter 11 The Nicene Faith and Evangelical Worship

1. Jaroslav Pelikan, *Credo: Historical and Theological Guide to Creeds and Confessions of Faith in the Christian Tradition* (New Haven: Yale University Press, 2003), 37.

2. The phrase *creedal indifference* is employed by Pelikan in his lecture. Of course, it is true that even "noncreedal" people are typically creedal. Those who ignore the Nicene Creed with respect to worship may well have other creedal formulas that control their liturgy. Forms of dress, musical style, and approaches to the sermon can be every bit as "creedally" held as one of the creeds.

3. Prosper of Aquitaine, *Capitula Coelestini* 8 (*PL* 51:209c). "Let the law of prayer establish the law of belief." The phrase is often shortened to the "tag" *lex orandi, lex credendi* (law of prayer/worship, law of belief), in which *orandi* is substituted for *supplicandi*. The phrase is often referred to as an axiom and sometimes as a maxim. One might argue whether the phrase is technically an axiom, in the sense that it is a universally recognized law or rule. In fact, the diversity of opinion about the meaning of the phrase indicates that it is not, in the fullest sense, an axiom. It is more properly an adage. See Paul De Clerck, "'Lex orandi, lex credendi': The Original Sense and Historical Avatars of an Equivocal Adage," *Studia Liturgica* 24 (1994): 178–200, originally published as "'Lex orandi, lex credendi': Sens originel et avatars historiques d'un adage équivoque," *Questions Liturgiques* 59 (1978): 193–212.

4. Pelikan, *Credo*, 35.

5. Jaroslav Pelikan, *The Christian Tradition: A History of the Development of Doctrine*, vol. 1, *Emergence of the Catholic Tradition (100–600)* (Chicago: University of Chicago Press, 1971), 1.

6. Richard Lints, *The Fabric of Theology: A Prolegomenon to Evangelical Theology* (Grand Rapids: Eerdmans, 1993), 30.

7. George Marsden, ed., *Evangelicalism and Modern America* (Grand Rapids: Eerdmans, 1984), x.

8. Carl F. H. Henry and Kenneth Kantzer, eds., foreword to *Evangelical Affirmations* (Grand Rapids: Academie Books, 1990), 17.

9. Geoffrey Wainwright, *Doxology: The Praise of God in Worship, Doctrine, and Life* (New York: Oxford University Press, 1984), 225.

10. De Clerck, "Lex Orandi," 180.

11. Prosper, *Capitula* 8 (*PL* 51:209c): "beatissimae et apostolicae sedis inviolabiles sanctiones."

12. Ibid. "Obsecrationum quoque sacerdotalium sacramenta respiciamus, quae ab apostolis tradita, in toto mundo atque in omni catholica Ecclesia uniformiter celebrantur, ut legem credendi lex statuat suplicandi."

13. Wainwright, *Doxology*, 225 (emphasis in original).

14. Mary M. Schaefer, "Lex orandi, lex credendi: Faith, Doctrine and Theology in Dialogue," *Religious Studies* 26, no. 4 (1997): 471: "For Prosper the Church's practice, founded on Scripture and attested by tradition, proves against the semi-Pelagians everyone's need of grace."

15. Kevin W. Irwin, *Context and Text: Method in Liturgical Theology* (Collegeville, MN: Liturgical Press, 1994), 4–5.

16. David W. Fagerberg, *What Is Liturgical Theology? A Study in Methodology* (Collegeville, MN: Liturgical Press, 1992), 17: "Because encounter with God precedes reflection upon that encounter, liturgy is the ontological condition for theology. This is what tradition means when it says that the law of prayer (*lex orandi*) establishes (*statuat*) the law of belief (*lex credendi*), and not vice-versa."

17. Irwin, *Context and Text*, 3.

18. Charles R. Hohenstein, "'Lex Orandi, Lex Credendi': Cautionary Notes," *Wesleyan Theological Journal* 32 (Fall 1997): 140.

19. De Clerck, "Lex Orandi," 178.

20. For the importance of the adage in Roman Catholic studies, see the survey in Irwin, *Context and Text*. From the Orthodox perspective, see Alexander Schmemann, *Introduction to*

Liturgical Theology, trans. Asheleigh E. Moorhouse (Bangor, ME: American Orthodox Press, 1966). Daniel Clendenin notes, "In Eastern Christianity theology and doctrine originate and find their ultimate expression in the aesthetic images of liturgy and worship, in intuition and contemplation rather than in rational discourse. The rule of prayer (*lex orandi*) is the basis, origin, and fullest expression of the rule of faith or belief (*lex credendi*)"; Daniel B. Clendenin, *Eastern Orthodox Christianity: A Western Perspective* (Grand Rapids: Baker Academic, 1994), 79. He also says that "many see the sum and substance of Orthodoxy as encapsulated in the dictum that "'the rule of prayer and worship is the rule of faith and doctrine' (*lex orandi est lex credendi*)" (ibid., 149).

21. See Wainwright, *Doxology*; Frank Senn, *Christian Liturgy: Catholic and Evangelical* (Philadelphia: Fortress, 1979); Don E. Saliers, *Worship as Theology: Foretaste of Glory Divine* (Nashville: Abingdon Press, 1994).

22. Robert W. Jenson, *Systematic Theology*, vol. 1, *The Triune God* (New York: Oxford University Press, 1997), 13–14. Jenson's chief concern is that "to attend to the gospel in its character as witness to a determinate reality is to worship in trinitarian specificity: in petition and praise to the Father with the Son in the Spirit. It is by failure intentionally to cast its theology in the space determined by these coordinates that much Protestant theology slips its object." At this point he appeals to "an ancient catholic rule: *lex orandi lex credendi*" (14).

23. Teresa Berger, *Theology in Hymns? A Study of the Relationship of Doxology and Theology according to a Collection of Hymns for the Use of the People Called Methodists (1780)*, trans. Timothy E. Kimbrough (Nashville: Kingswood Books, 1995), 32.

24. Irwin, *Context and Text*, 4.

25. Robert F. Taft, "The Epiclesis Question in the Light of the Orthodox and Catholic *Lex Orandi* Traditions," in *New Perspectives on Historical Theology: Essays in Memory of John Meyendorff*, ed. Bradley Nassif (Grand Rapids: Eerdmans, 1996), 316.

26. Ibid., 210–11. See also Irwin, who says that the adage indicates "that the liturgy manifests the Church's faith" (Irwin, *Context and Text*, 6).

27. Pius XII, *Mediator Dei*, in *Acta Apostolicae Sedis* 39 (1947), 541: "Quodsi volumes eas, quae inter fidem sacramque Liturgiam intercedunt, rationes absoluto generalique modo internoscere ac determinare, iure meritoque dici potest: Lex credendi legem statuat supplicandi." Also compare Wainwright, *Doxology*, 222–24; De Clerck, "Lex Orandi," 195–99.

28. Vincent A. Yzermans, ed., *The Major Addresses of Pope Pius XII*, vol. 1 (St. Paul: North Central Publishing, 1961), 375.

29. De Clerck, "Lex Orandi," 182.

30. Ibid., 182–85; Wainwright, *Doxology*, 225–26.

31. Prosper, *De vocatione omnium gentium* 1:12 (PL 51: 664c): "Quam legem supplicationis ita omnium sacerdotum, et omnium fidelium devotio concorditer tenet, ut nulla pars mundi sit in qua hujusmodi orationes non celebrentur a populis Christiantis."

32. Prosper, *Capitula* 8 (PL 51:209c): "in toto mundo atque in omni catholica Ecclesia uniformiter celebrentur" and "et tota secum Ecclesia congemiscente."

33. Prosper, *De vocatione* 1:12 (PL 51:664c). Cf. De Clerck, "Lex Orandi," 186.

34. 1 Tim. 2:4.

35. Karl Federer, *Liturgie und Glaube* (Fribourg, Switzerland: Paulusverlag, 1950), 15–16, quoted in De Clerck, "Lex Orandi," 186 (emphasis in German original).

36. De Clerck, "Lex Orandi," 186.

37. Ambrose, *Commentarius in epistolam B. Pauli ad Timotheum primam* 2 (PL 17:492c): "Haec regula ecclesiastica est, tradita a magistro gentium, qua utuntur sacerdotes nostri, ut pro omnibus supplicent." See De Clerck, "Lex Orandi," 187.

38. De Clerck, "Lex Orandi," 187.

39. In this case, the *ecclesiasticis regulis* (ecclesiastical rule) of Prosper's *Capitula* 9 is read in the context of Prosper's previous appeal to Scripture. Here, he argues that the exorcisms and

exsufflations performed at the baptismal rite demonstrate various truths of Scripture (John 12:31; Matt. 12:39, par.; Ps. 68:18/Eph. 4:8) (*Capitula 9 [PL 51:210c]*).

40. De Clerck, "Lex Orandi," 192.

41. Maurice Wiles, *The Making of Christian Doctrine: A Study in the Principles of Early Doctrinal Development* (Cambridge: Cambridge University Press, 1967), 93. Wiles says, "Undoubtedly the practice of prayer has had its effect on doctrine; undoubtedly the practice of prayer *should* have its effect on doctrine. But that is not to say that the effect which prayer has actually had is at every point precisely the effect which it should have had" (emphasis in original).

42. Berger, *Theology in Hymns?* 35.

43. Among those books that treat the interrelation of doctrine and doxology, I should mention David Peterson, *Engaging with God: A Biblical Theology of Worship* (Grand Rapids: Eerdmans, 1993); and Allen P. Ross, *Recalling the Hope of Glory: Biblical Worship from the Garden to New Creation* (Grand Rapids: Kregel Publications, 2006). The third chapter of my own dissertation, "In Spirit and Truth: The Holy Spirit and the Interrelation of Doctrine and Doxology," is devoted entirely to demonstrating this interrelation through a set of New Testament passages.

44. I have discussed this previously, in "The Use of Music in Worship," in *Authentic Worship*, ed. Herb Bateman (Grand Rapids: Kregel Academic, 2002): 150–55. This idea is also treated in David Pass, *Music in the Church* (Nashville: Broadman, 1989); and in A. M. Triacca, "Le sens théologique de la liturgie et/ou liturgique de la théologie: Esquisse initiale pour une synthèse," in *La Liturgie, son senses, son ésprit, sa method: Liturgie et théologie*, ed. A. Pistoria and A. M. Triacca (Rome: CLV Edizioni liturgiche, 1982): 321–37.

45. Steve Harmon, "Praying and Believing: Retrieving the Patristic Interdependency of Worship and Theology," in *Towards Baptist Catholicity: Essays on Tradition and the Baptist Vision*, ed. Anthony R. Cross, vol. 27, *Studies in Baptist History and Thought* (Milton Keynes, UK: Paternoster, 2006), 153–77.

Chapter 12 Taking In His Coming Down

1. This chapter was originally delivered as a chapel address on October 20, 2009, in Hodges Chapel at Beeson Divinity School as part of the 2009 chapel series "The Faith We Confess." The *Traditional* wording of the Nicene Creed used in this chapter is from *Common Worship: Services for the Church of England* (London: Church House Publishing, 2000), 213. We find it appropriate and helpful to retain the personal tone and content of the original address.

2. C. S. Lewis, *Reflections on the Psalms* (New York: Harcourt, Brace, 1958), 5.

3. William Shakespeare, *A Midsummer Night's Dream* (Oxford: Oxford University Press, 1994), 5.1.12–17.

4. Kent Hughes, *The Gift: Seven Meditations on the Events Surrounding Jesus's Birth* (Wheaton: Crossway, 1994), 38.

5. Gerard Manley Hopkins, *Poems and Prose of Gerard Manley Hopkins*, ed. W. H. Gardner (Harmondsworth, UK: Penguin Books, 1975), 30.

6. Amy Carmichael, *Mountain Breezes: The Collected Poems of Amy Carmichael* (Fort Washington, PA: Christian Literature Crusade, 1999), 200.

7. Dr. Stuntz's testimony was originally available and may still be requested through the website of Park Street Church (www.parkstreet.org/sermon_audio).

Chapter 13 The Will to Believe and the Need for Creeds

1. E. J. Bicknell, "The Creeds," in *A Theological Introduction to the Thirty-Nine Articles of the Church of England* (London: Longmans, 1925), 149.

2. Unless noted otherwise, all Scripture citations in this chapter are from *New American Standard Bible*, text edition concordance (Anaheim, CA: Foundation Publications, 1997).

3. Eusebius, "The Success of Bishops, Their Writings and Martyrdoms," in *The History of the Church from Christ to Constantine*, trans. G. A. Williamson (London: Penguin Books, 1989), 154–92.

4. Quote from Patrick Henry's "Liberty or Death" speech delivered in St. John's Church in Richmond, Virginia, March 23, 1775, to the colony's delegates before the vote for Virginia to join the American Revolution. Speech available at The History Place, www.historyplace.com /speeches/henry.htm.

5. James H. Cone, *Risks of Faith: The Emergence of a Black Theology of Liberation, 1968– 1998* (Boston: Beacon Press, 1999), 104.

6. For more information on this trend, see John H. Y. Briggs, *The English Baptists of the Nineteenth Century* (Didcot, UK: Baptist Historical Society, 1994).

7. John R. W. Stott, *Issues Facing Christians Today*, 4th ed., fully revised and updated by Roy McCloughry, with an additional chapter by John Wyatt (Grand Rapids: Zondervan, 2006), 82. For more on this discussion, see Charles W. Colson, *God & Government: An Insider's View on the Boundaries Between Faith & Politics*, formerly titled *Kingdoms in Conflict* (Grand Rapids: Zondervan, 2007), 267–275, esp. 271.

8. For more on baptism, see Daniel A. Keating, *The Appropriation of Divine Life in Cyril of Alexandria* (Oxford: Oxford University Press, 2004), esp. 20–39; and Keating, "The Baptism of Jesus in Cyril of Alexandria: The Re-creation of the Human Race," *Pro Ecclesia* (1999): 201–22. For further reading on divine baptism, see Cyril of Jerusalem's *Jerusalem Catecheses*. Suggested further reading includes: John R. W. Stott, "Alienation: Have We Any Influence?" in *Decisive Issues Facing Christians Today* (Old Tappan, NJ: F. H. Revell, 1990); L. Berkhof, *The History of Christian Doctrine* (Carlisle, PA: Banner of Truth, 1975); Kenneth Scott Latourette, *A History of Christianity* (New York: Harper, 1953); M. L. Brown, "The Driving Force of Revolution," in *Revolution! The Call to Holy War* (Ventura, CA: Regal Books, 2000); and Bradley P. Nystrom and David P. Nystrom, "The History of Christianity: An Introduction," in *The History of Christianity* (New York: McGraw-Hill, 2004).

Chapter 14 Can the Church Emerge without or with Only the Nicene

1. Jacob's Well, Our Beliefs, www.jacobswellchurch.org/our_beliefs.

2. Eddie Gibbs and Ryan Bolger, *Emerging Churches: Creating Christian Community in Postmodern Cultures* (Grand Rapids: Baker Academic, 2005), 124.

3. Quote is from Timothy George, *John Robinson and the English Separatist Tradition* (Macon, GA: Mercer University Press, 1982), xii.

4. Ibid.

5. See Michael Polanyi, *The Tacit Dimension* (Chicago: University of Chicago Press, 1966), 4.

6. Gibbs and Bolger, *Emerging Churches*, 125.

7. See, e.g., Philip Jacob Spener, *Pia Desideria*, trans. Theodore G. Tappert (Eugene, OR: Wipf & Stock, 2002), 5–7, 87–102.

8. See especially Thomas Oden, *Agenda for Theology* (New York: HarperCollins, 1979); *Two Worlds: Notes on the Death of Modernity in America & Russia* (Downers Grove, IL: InterVarsity, 1992); *Requiem: A Lament in Three Movements* (Nashville: Abingdon, 1995); and *After Modernity . . . What?* (Grand Rapids: Zondervan, 1990).

9. Friedrich D. E. Schleiermacher, *The Christian Faith*, trans. H. R. Mackintosh (Edinburgh: T&T Clark, 1830).

10. Paul Tillich, *Systematic Theology*, 3 vols. (Chicago: University of Chicago Press, 1951–63).

11. Gary Dorrien, *The Making of American Liberal Theology: Imagining Progressive Religion, 1805–1900* (Louisville: Westminster John Knox, 2001), xiii.

12. John Henry Cardinal Newman, *Apologia Pro Vita Sua* (New York: Doubleday, 1956), 205–12.

13. Nancy Tatom Ammerman, *Baptist Battles: Social Change and Religious Conflict in the Southern Baptist Convention* (New Brunswick, NJ: Rutgers University Press, 1990).

14. David F. Wells, *No Place for Truth: Or, Whatever Happened to Evangelical Theology?* (Grand Rapids: Eerdmans, 1993).

15. See, e.g., Gustav Aulén, *Christus Victor* (New York: Macmillan, 1958); and John R. W. Stott, *The Cross of Christ* (Downers Grove, IL: InterVarsity, 1986).

16. Steve Chalke, *The Lost Message of Jesus* (Grand Rapids: Zondervan, 2003), 182–83.

17. See Horace Bushnell, *Christ and His Salvation: In Sermons Variously Related Thereto* (New York: Charles Scribner, 1864); and *The Vicarious Sacrifice, Grounded in Principles of Universal Obligation* (New York: Charles Scribner, 1866). Though Bushnell passed through at least four "conversions" of his thought on the matter, he remained essentially opposed to classic Reformation objectivism and embraced various subjectivist construals of the atonement. See the fine treatment in Dorrien, *Making of American Liberal Theology*, 165–73.

18. See my "Friendship and the Cradle of Liberalism: Revisiting the Moravian Roots of Schleiermacher's Theology," *Churchman* 112, no. 4 (1998): 339–56.

19. Jaroslav Pelikan, *The Melody of Theology: A Philosophical Dictionary* (Cambridge, MA: Harvard University Press, 1988), 12.

Chapter 15 Life after Life after Death

1. "The Strife Is O'er," in *Baptist Hymnal* (Nashville: Convention Press, 1991), 172.

2. For further reading see John Milton, *John Milton's Paradise Lost*, ed. Harold Bloom, Chelsea House Publishers' Modern Critical Intepretations (New York: Chelsea House, 1987). An electronic version of *Paradise Lost* is available at Dartmouth's Milton Reading Room, www.dartmouth.edu/~milton/reading_room/pl/book_1/index.shtml.

3. For further reading on Lawrence, deacon and martyr, see http://guardianoftheredeemer.wordpress.com/2009/08/10/st-lawrence-deacon-and-martyr.

4. Michael Balfour, *Withstanding Hitler in Germany, 1933–45* (New York: Routledge, 1988), 224.

5. For further information and lyrics for "Dwelling in Beulah Land" by Charles Austin Miles, based on the verse "Thou shalt be called Hephzibah, and thy land Beulah" (Isa. 62:4 KJV), see www.practicalbible.com/?q=dwellinginbeulah.

Chapter 16 Delighted by Doctrine

1. This tribute was previously published in *Christian History & Biography* 91 (Summer 2006), 43–45, and is republished with permission.

2. Jaroslav Pelikan, "A Personal Memoir: Fragments of a Scholar's Autobiography," in *Orthodoxy and Western Culture: A Collection of Essays Honoring Jaroslav Pelikan on his Eightieth Birthday*, ed. Valerie Hotchkiss and Patrick Henry (Crestwood, NY: St. Vladimir's Seminary Press, 2005), 32.

3. See *Creeds and Confessions of Faith in the Christian Tradition*, vol. 3, *Modern Christianity*, ed. Jaroslav Pelikan and Valerie Hotchkiss (New Haven: Yale University Press, 2003), 23, 568, 569. Masai was the spelling used in 1960 and the mission fields were East Africa. Also see *Orthodoxy and Western Culture*, 176.

4. Ibid., 569.

5. Ibid. For more discussion on the Masai (Maasai) people and their location, East Africa, see William C. Placher, review of *Creeds and Confessions of Faith in the Christian Tradition*, ed. Jaroslav Pelikan and Valerie Hotchkiss, *The Christian Century*, September 20, 2003, 20–24, www.religion-online.org/showarticle.asp?title=2942. The Masai people are from Kenya and Tanzania. However, Pelikan and Hotchkiss note in their book that the mission fields were East Africa in 1960.

6. Pelikan, "The Will to Believe and the Need for Creed," 176.

Index